Exploring the APPALACHIAN TRAIL™

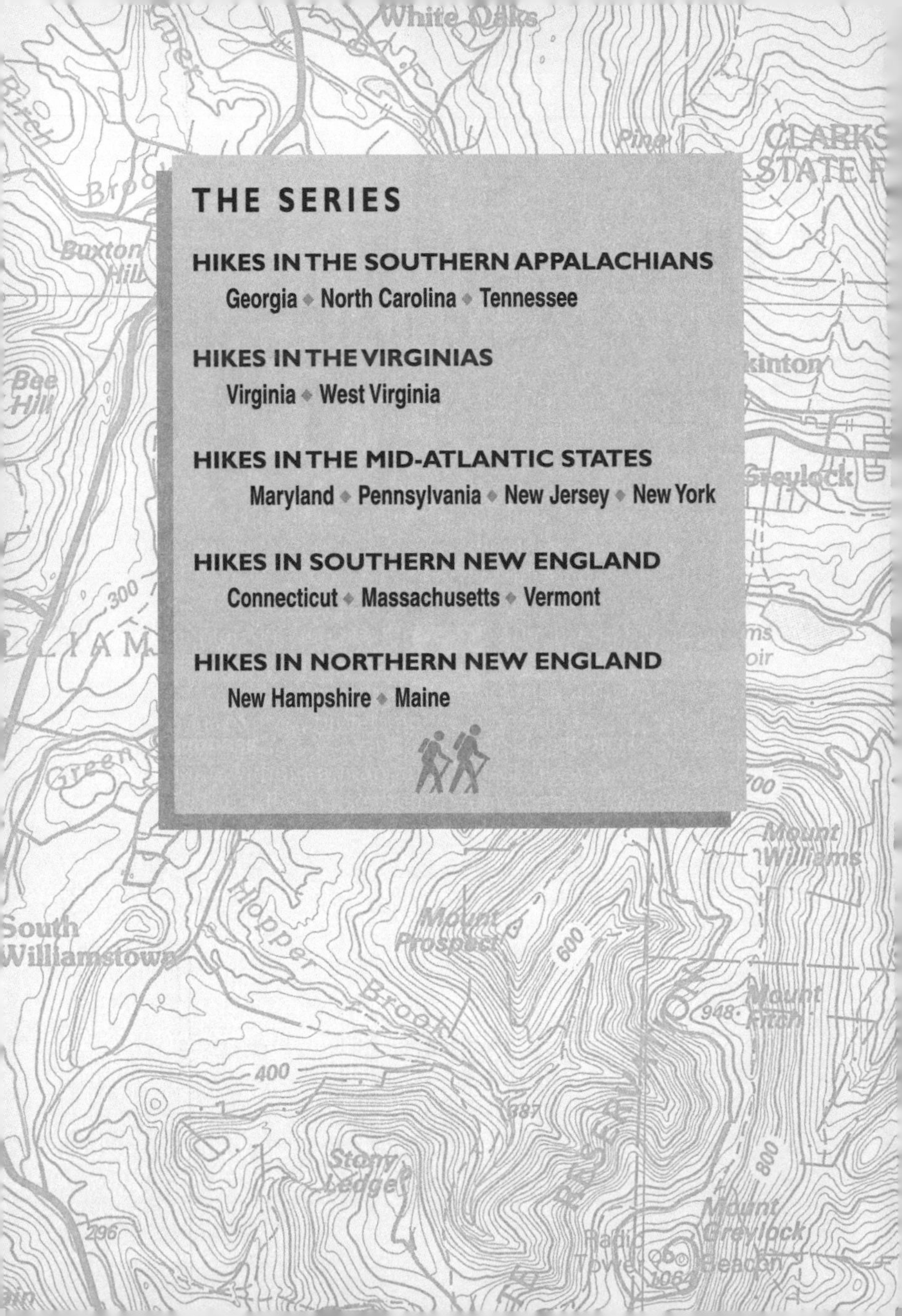

THE SERIES

HIKES IN THE SOUTHERN APPALACHIANS
Georgia ◆ North Carolina ◆ Tennessee

HIKES IN THE VIRGINIAS
Virginia ◆ West Virginia

HIKES IN THE MID-ATLANTIC STATES
Maryland ◆ Pennsylvania ◆ New Jersey ◆ New York

HIKES IN SOUTHERN NEW ENGLAND
Connecticut ◆ Massachusetts ◆ Vermont

HIKES IN NORTHERN NEW ENGLAND
New Hampshire ◆ Maine

Exploring the
APPALACHIAN TRAIL

HIKES in SOUTHERN NEW ENGLAND

Connecticut Massachusetts Vermont

DAVID EMBLIDGE

STACKPOLE BOOKS

Mechanicsburg, Pennsylvania

A Word of Caution

Readers are advised that trail conditions and locations change frequently due to both natural factors (e.g., erosion) and legal factors (e.g., National Park Service real estate acquisitions). Information in this volume was as accurate as the authors could make it at the time of printing. However, readers should check with their local Appalachian Trail hiking clubs (see "Useful Information") for updated information. Readers are also advised that hiking involves some risk of accident and exposure to potentially harmful weather, animals, or impure water. Precautions are advised here under "Hiking: The Basics," and the reader uses this guide at his or her own risk. The publisher assumes no liability.

Exploring the Appalachian Trail™ Series Concept: David Emblidge
Series Editor: David Emblidge
Researcher and Editorial Assistant: Marcy Ross
Copy Editor: Katherine Ness
Book design and cover design: Walter Schwarz, of Figaro, Inc.
Page make-up: Figaro, Inc.
Cartography: Jean Saliter and Lisa Story, of Figaro, Inc. (topo maps); Peter Jensen, of OpenSpace (trail drawing); Kevin Woolley, of WoolleySoft, Ltd. (trail profiles)
Cover photograph: (The Hopper, Mt. Greylock) by Nancy Hecker
Page xii: photograph of Springer Mt. AT plaque (southern terminus) by Doris Gove
Page 26: photograph by David Emblidge
Interior photographs: See credits with each image.
Proofreader: Rodelinde Albrecht
Indexer: Letitia Mutter

Library of Congress Cataloging-in-Publication Data
Emblidge, David.
Hikes in southern New England / David Emblidge.— 1st ed.
p. cm.—(Exploring the Appalachian Trail)
ISBN 0-8117-2669-X
1. Hiking—Connecticut—Guidebooks. 2. Hiking—Massachusetts—Guidebooks. 3. Hiking—Vermont—Guidebooks. 4. Hiking—Appalachian Trail—Guidebooks. 5. Connecticut—Guidebooks. 6. Massachusetts—Guidebooks. 7. Vermont—Guidebooks. 8. Appalachian Trail—Guidebooks. I. Title. II. Series.
GV199.42.C IN PROCESS
917.404'43—dc21 97-50085
CIP

ISBN 978-0-8117-2669-6

Printed in the United States
10 9 8 7 6 5 4 3 2

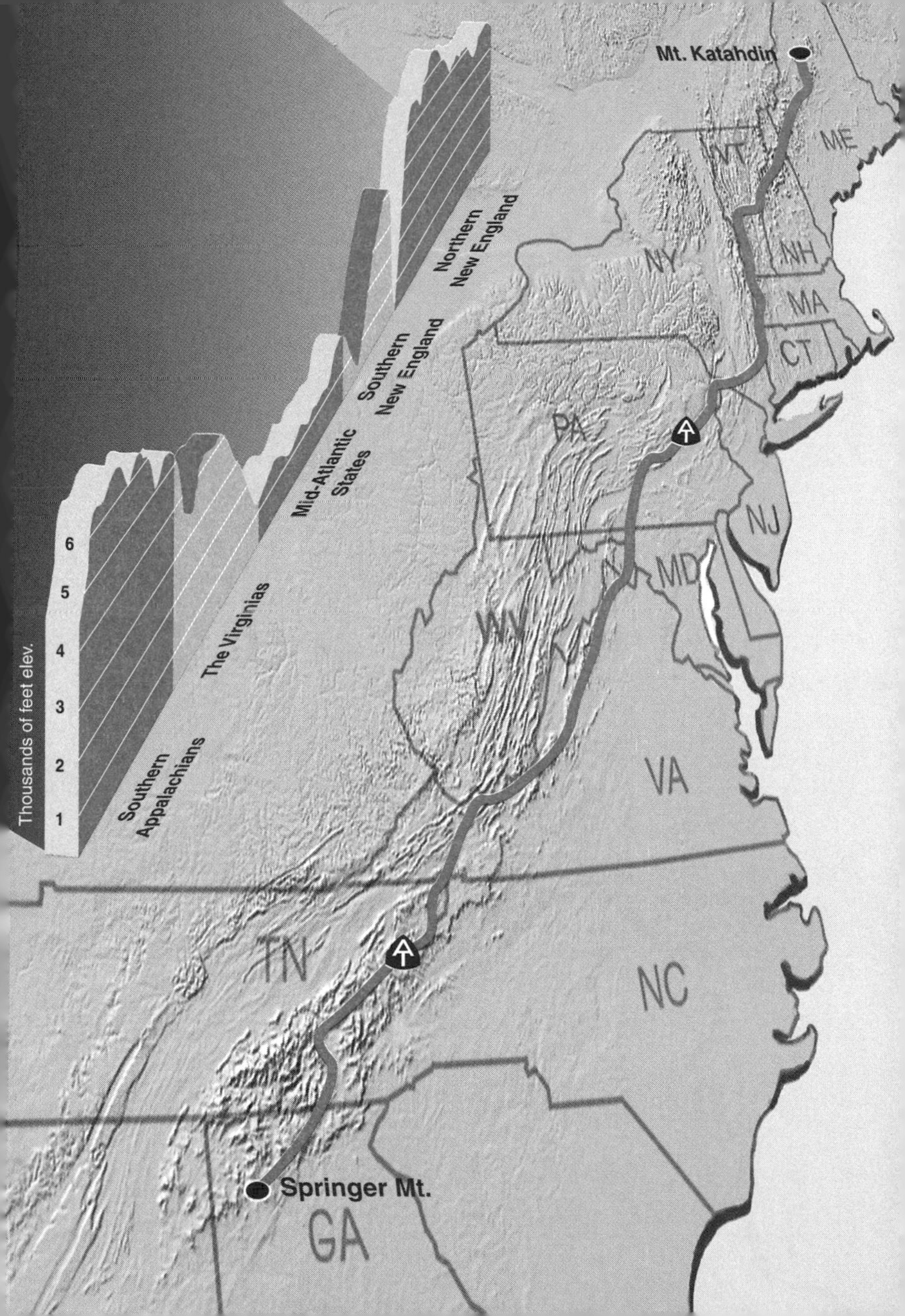

Mt. Katahdin
ME
VT
NH
MA
CT
NY
PA
NJ
MD
WV
VA
NC
TN
GA
Springer Mt.
Northern New England
Southern New England
Mid-Atlantic States
The Virginias
Southern Appalachians
Thousands of feet elev.
6
5
4
3
2
1

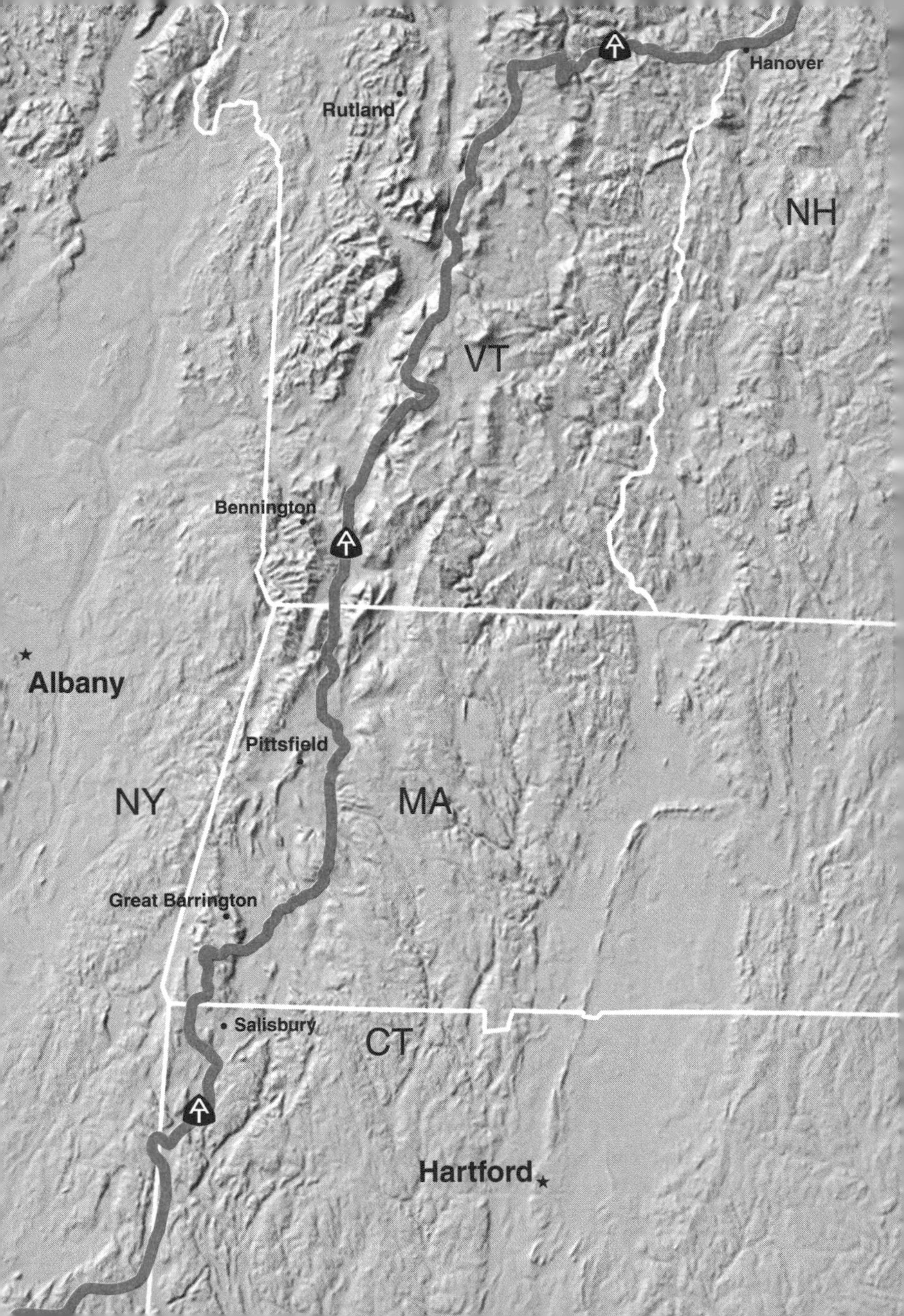
Hanover
Rutland
NH
VT
Bennington
Albany
Pittsfield
NY
MA
Great Barrington
Salisbury
CT
Hartford

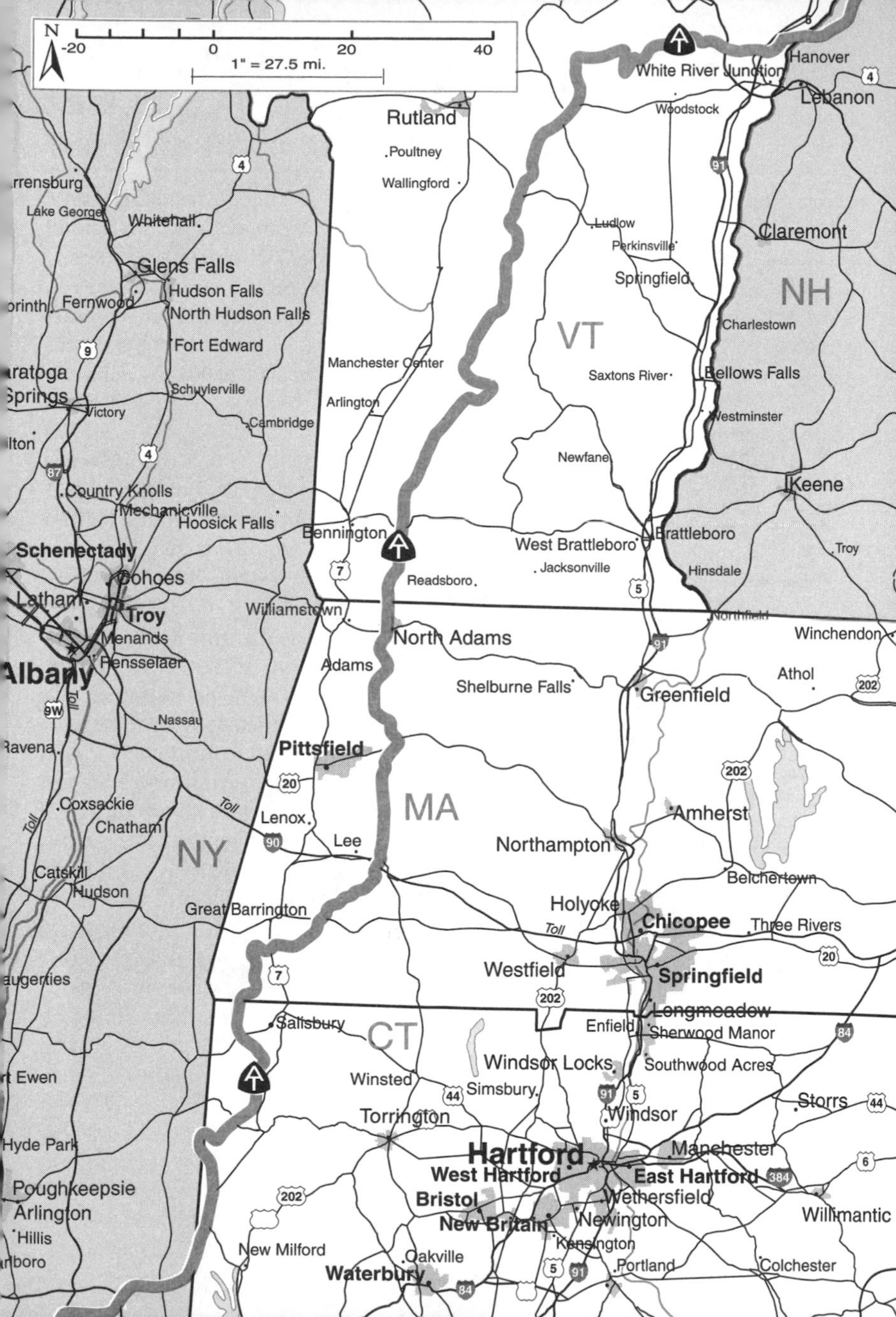
N
-20
0
20
40
1" = 27.5 mi.
Rutland
Poultney
Wallingford
White River Junction
Hanover
Woodstock
Lebanon
Ludlow
Perkinsville
Claremont
Springfield
NH
VT
Charlestown
Saxtons River
Bellows Falls
Westminster
Newfane
Keene
Manchester Center
Arlington
Bennington
West Brattleboro
Brattleboro
Jacksonville
Troy
Hinsdale
Readsboro
Williamstown
North Adams
Adams
Winchendon
Athol
Shelburne Falls
Greenfield
Pittsfield
MA
Lenox
Lee
Amherst
Northampton
Belchertown
Holyoke
Chicopee
Three Rivers
Great Barrington
Westfield
Springfield
Longmeadow
Enfield
Sherwood Manor
Salisbury
CT
Windsor Locks
Southwood Acres
Winsted
Simsbury
Storrs
Torrington
Windsor
Hartford
Manchester
West Hartford
East Hartford
Bristol
Wethersfield
Willimantic
New Britain
Newington
Kensington
New Milford
Oakville
Portland
Colchester
Waterbury
Warrensburg
Lake George
Whitehall
Glens Falls
Hudson Falls
Corinth
Fernwood
North Hudson Falls
Fort Edward
Saratoga Springs
Schuylerville
Victory
Cambridge
Milton
Country Knolls
Mechanicville
Hoosick Falls
Schenectady
Cohoes
Latham
Troy
Menands
Albany
Rensselaer
Nassau
Ravena
Coxsackie
Chatham
NY
Catskill
Hudson
Saugerties
Port Ewen
Hyde Park
Poughkeepsie
Arlington
Hillis
Marlboro
Toll
4
9
87
9W
20
90
7
5
91
202
44
84
384
6

Contents

Connecticut

Massachusetts

Vermont

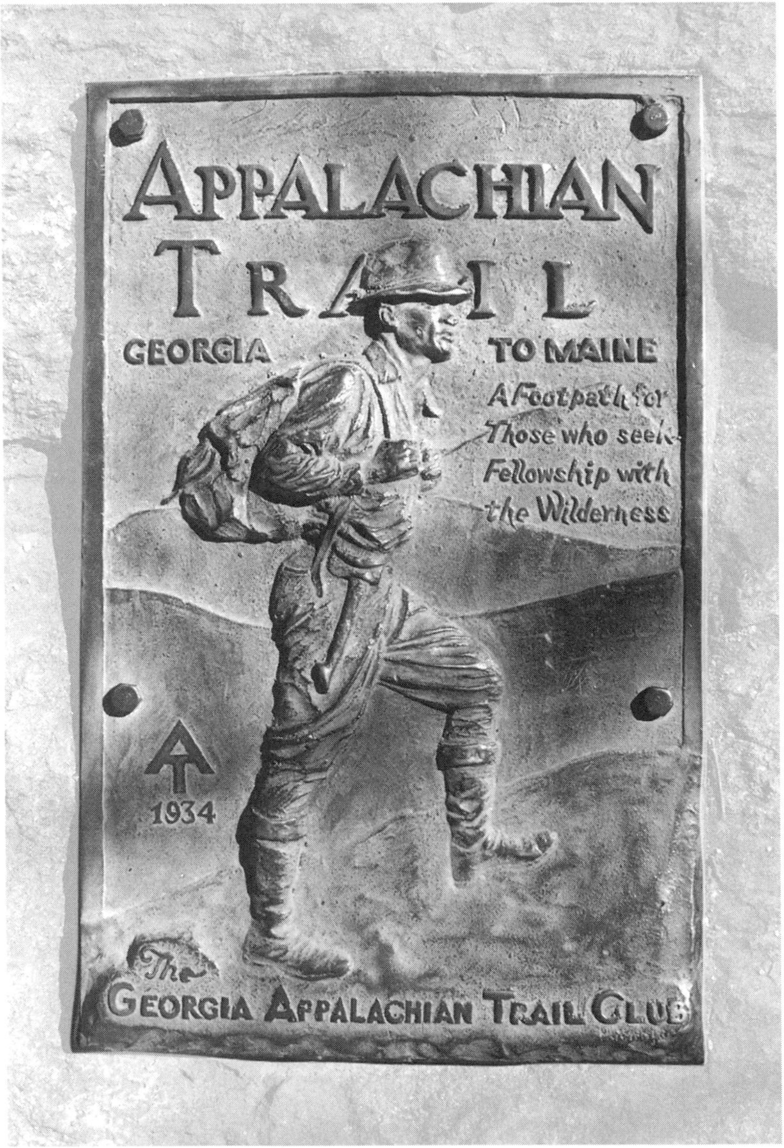

APPALACHIAN
TRAIL
GEORGIA TO MAINE
A Footpath for
Those who seek
Fellowship with
the Wilderness
1934
The
GEORGIA APPALACHIAN TRAIL CLUB

Introduction

Welcome to *Exploring the Appalachian Trail*. We're glad to have you join us for what promises to be a fine outdoor adventure.

You may not have realized it when you bought or borrowed this book, but if the truth be told, it's all about a long-standing love affair. The authors of the hiking guides in this series have been in love with the Appalachian Trail since before we can remember. And we've come to believe that if you truly love something, you will probably act positively to protect it. So when we invite you to join us in walking on the trail, we're also inviting you to let yourself be seduced, indeed to go ahead and take the leap into a sweet and enduring love affair of your own. But then be sure to act on the responsibility created as a by-product of that love. It's called service and support. In the section below called "Joining Up," you can read more about how each of us can contribute to the health and continuing life of the trail. The Appalachian Trail will give you many gifts. Be sure you give some back.

Unlike other good books about walking the Appalachian Trail, this one will encourage you to slow down, to yield to the many temptations offered up freely by nature and by the social-historical world along the trail. Benton MacKaye, considered by most to be the chief visionary of the early Appalachian Trail, once defined the purpose of hiking on the AT as "to see, and to *see* what you see." MacKaye was something of a romantic, and we know he read Emerson, who instructs us all to "Adopt the peace of Nature, her secret is patience." We can't improve on that.

Our intention is to help you plan and carry out a wide variety of hikes on the nation's longest continuously marked footpath, surely one of the most famous walking trails in the world. We'll guide you from point A to point B, to be sure, but as far as this book is concerned, it's what happens for you *between* points A and B that counts the most.

If the goal of hiking on the Appalachian Trail is to come home refreshed in body, rejuvenated in mind, and renewed in spirit, then along with the fun of being outside in the mountains, a little work will be required. The most obvious work is of the muscular variety. Less obvious but just as rewarding is the mental kind, and it's here that the books in this series will help you the most. The famous world traveler Sven-Olof Lindblad said, "Travel is not about where you've been but what you've gained. True travel is about how you've enriched your life through encounters with beauty, wildness and the seldom-seen."

In these AT hiking books, we'll pause to inspect the rocks underfoot and the giant folding and crunching of the entire Appalachian landscape. We'll take time to listen to birds and to look closely at wildflowers. We will deliberately digress into the social history of the area the AT passes through, thinking sometimes about industry, other times about politics, and now and then about a well-known or an obscure but colorful character who happened to live nearby. We'll explore trail towns and comment on trail shelters and campsites (they're not all alike!). And to help make you a savvy hiker (if you aren't already), we will offer up some choice bits of hiker wisdom that just might get you out of a jam or make your load a bit lighter to carry.

This is a participatory book. You will enjoy it and profit from it most if you carry a small notebook and a pen or pencil, if you bring along a camera and perhaps a birding book or a wildflower guide or a guide to some other aspect of the natural world (see the Bibliography for suggestions). Bring a compass and use our maps, or better yet, supplement the maps in this book with the more detailed ones available from the Appalachian Trail Conference and other local sources (see page 9 and the Bibliography).

Chatting with your walking companions is a delightful thing to do some of the time while out on the trail, but the more noise you make, the less wildlife you'll see, and besides, it's hard for anyone to be both in conversation and simultaneously in close observance of the real details of the natural realm. Try hard to make some part of every hike a *silent walk*, during which you open all your senses and your imagination to drink in the marvelous environment of the Appalachian Trail.

The Appalachian Trail in Southern New England: Landscape and Environment

The states covered by this book—Connecticut, Massachusetts, Vermont—make up what the Exploring the Appalachian Trail™ series calls "southern New England." The next volume, *Northern New England*, covers New Hampshire and Maine. In southern New England the AT ranges from a low of about 500 feet above sea level in Connecticut's Housatonic River valley to over 4000 feet at Killington Peak in Vermont. There are about 260 miles of Appalachian Trail in southern New England, walked here in 29 hikes. Hundreds of miles of side trails link with the AT to form a vast network of hiking possibilities.

In this region, contrasts are dramatic in plant and animal life, weather, and degrees of challenge to the hiker. There are woodland walks benign enough for a toddler and mountain climbs ambitious enough to satisfy most robust hikers. The AT spends considerable time in the neighborhood of small towns and villages, making it easy to plan one- or two-car day hikes between road crossings. But there are wilderness sections too, where backpackers can spend a full day or two in deep forest, well separated from the sounds and sights of civilization. In Connecticut the temperate climate supports even dogwood, a flowering tree associated more with southern states, while on Mt. Greylock in Massachusetts and in the Coolidge Range (Killington and other peaks) in Vermont, the forest is boreal (comparable to the tundra hundreds of miles farther north).

The great opportunity and pleasure for a hiker on the southern New England AT is to appreciate the variety of environments and the numerous hiker-friendly towns (many of them graced with lovely historic architecture) where services, supplies, and distractions are readily available. If you have never visited the region, a colorful armchair traveler's introduction awaits you in *The Smithsonian Guide to Historic America: Southern New England.*

Joining Up

We urge you, our fellow hikers, to honor the thousands of volunteers and paid workers who built and who nowadays maintain the Appalachian Trail by becoming a volunteer and a financial supporter yourself. Join your local hiking club and join any or all of the following organizations, each of which contributes to the survival of the Appalachian Trail:

Appalachian Trail Conference, P.O. Box 807, Harpers Ferry, WV 25425

Appalachian Mountain Club, 5 Joy St., Boston, MA 02108

American Hiking Society, 1422 Fenwick Lane, Silver Spring, MD 20910

Walking Lightly on the Land

On behalf of the hiking community, we urge all hikers to manage their behavior in the woods and mountains so as to have a minimal impact on the land. The old adages are apt: *Take only pictures, leave only footprints. Pack out whatever you pack in. Leave no trace.* Indeed, be a sport and pack out some other careless hiker's garbage if you find it along the trail. The National Park Service, which maintains a protective corridor along the Appalachian Trail, estimates that between 3 and 4 million people use the trail every year, and the numbers are growing. In many places the ecology of the AT landscape is fragile. But fragile or not, every one of its 2150 miles is subject to abuse, even if unintended. Leave the trail a better place than you found it, and you'll take home better memories.

Soft Paths: How to Enjoy the Wilderness Without Harming It is a good general introduction to the principles of leave-no-trace hiking and camping. See the Bibliography.

We wish you good weather, warm companionship, and a great adventure, be it for 6 hours, 6 days, 6 weeks, or 6 months on the trail. The Appalachian Trail belongs to all of us. Treat it as you would something precious of your very own.

Reader Participation

Readers are invited to respond. Please correct our mistakes, offer your perspectives, tell us what else you'd like to see in the next edition. Please also tell us where you bought or borrowed this book. Write to: Editors, Exploring the Appalachian Trail™, Stackpole Books, 5067 Ritter Rd., Mechanicsburg, PA 17055.

Acknowledgments

I am grateful to Editorial Director Judith Schnell at Stackpole Books for recognizing the potential of Exploring the Appalachian Trail™ and to Editor Mark Allison for shepherding the books toward publication. The *Berkshire Eagle* (Pittsfield, Massachusetts) published the articles that spawned this project.

Many others have my sincere thanks: Editorial Assistant Marcy Ross, for dogged research and map management with good humor; Kathie Ness, Chief Copy Editor, for admirable competence and grace under pressure; Bill Cooke, designer, for preliminary book design; Walter Schwarz, of Figaro, Inc., Chief Designer, for final book design, map and trail profile production, cover design, and composition (he is a master); also at Figaro, Jean Saliter for Adobe Illustrator work on maps and trail profiles; Kevin Woolley, of WoolleySoft, Ltd., for digital trail profiles; Peter Jensen and Kathy Orlando, of OpenSpace Management, for carefully drawing the corrected AT on our maps; Rodelinde Albrecht, proofreader, for valuable precision; Letitia Mutter, indexer, for great efficiency; Barbara Zheutlin, for keyboarding without tears; and Chris Blair for ever-patient computer support. Thanks as well to each photographer and to all of the authors in this series, each of whom made some contribution to this volume. Special thanks to Doris Gove for sharing her sidebars.

Trail clubs provided important assistance. At the Appalachian Trail Conference: Norman Sills for Connecticut trail information, Pete Rentz for reading parts of the manuscript, and Kevin Peterson, New England Regional Representative, for Vermont trail information. At the Appalachian Mountain Club: Dennis Regan, Mt. Greylock Visitor Center, for Connecticut and Massachusetts trail information. At the Green Mountain Club: Sylvia Plumb, Managing Editor, for Vermont trail information. And at the National Park Service: Don King, AT Project Office, for map advice. Numerous librarians and booksellers led me to facts and anecdotes that enliven this book. In Connecticut, Northeast Utilities offered trail information around Falls Village. Kevin Taft, at the Vermont Institute of Natural Science, introduced me to raptors and wildflowers. Contributors to sidebars, generous people all, are noted in the text.

Thanks to the following for trailhead shuttle rides: Jonathan Hankin and Barbara Zheutlin, Kathie Ness, Bob Riedel, Brendan Handfield, Otter Creek Grocery, Mt. Meadows Lodge, Helen Whybrow, Susan Grace, and several anonymous folks who responded to a hitchhiker's thumb. Casey Sheehan, Merrell Boot Co., provided superb boots. As always, thanks to Sarah and Adam Selzer for happy companionship on the trail.

Such errors as remain in this complicated work are, alas, my own. Such glory as there may be in a finished book, serviceable to the reader and hiker, belongs to us all.

David Emblidge

Author and Series Editor
Great Barrington, Massachusetts
January 1998

HOW TO USE THIS BOOK

USE THIS BOOK as you would the counsel of a wise friend. Absorb the information that seems noteworthy to you; take heed of opinionated statements; consider the logic behind suggested strategies for getting into, and through, the kind of hike you want. But remember that your own personal preferences for length of hike, amount of effort, and things to see along the way will be just as important as—or even more than—any information you may find in these pages. Walking and hiking in the forest and mountains are intensely personal activities. There are few rules to follow, and it's not a competitive game with winners and losers. What works well for Hiker A will be a disappointment for Hiker B. Wallace Stevens gave us a poem called "Sixteen Ways of Looking at a Blackbird." This book should indicate that there are at least that many ways to complete and enjoy a hike on the AT.

How Hike Information Is Displayed Here

INFORMATION BLOCK: The hike's first page, a snapshot of the hike in the form of data and directions. Here you'll find road access information, elevation gain, distance to be walked, names of shelters, and so on. This first section gives an objective overview of the hike.

NARRATIVE: The full story—the hike you're likely to have on this section of the AT. Conditions vary widely depending on season and weather, depending on whether you're a robust 18-year-old, a tottering little kid, or a slow-but-steady octogenarian. Our description of the hike aims for a middle-range hiker, in good shape, with modestly ambitious goals but not with an eye on the stopwatch or the pedometer.

Throughout the hike's narrative we cite mileages at the major way points and landmarks. Occasionally we indicate the amount of time needed to go from one point to another. Generally, however, we stick to mileage as a reference point because each hiker's pace is different.

The narrative also pauses to describe rocks, plants, animals, vistas, and social history seen along the way. . . and then picks up the hike again with further directions toward its destination.

Trail profile: A rendering of the trail's up-and-down travels over the landscape, suggesting graphically how easy or challenging sections may be. The profiles are based on USGS digital elevation maps and were created via cartography software called WoolleySoft created by Kevin Woolley, of Dunblane, Scotland. The linear scale on the profiles does not match the scale on the hike's topographic map (see below). Instead, the profile gives a cross-section view of the mountains and valleys with the trail running up and down as if on a straight line across the landscape. Trail profiles entail a certain degree of vertical exaggeration to make the rendering meaningful, and they do not show every hill or knob in the path.

Topographic map: Based on USGS 1:100,000 scale maps, the hike topo map also draws on information provided on AT maps published by the Appalachian Trail Conference and its member trail clubs. Our scale is usually 1 inch to 1 mile—or as close to that as the page size and the length of the hike will allow. These maps show actual elevations (read about contour lines on page 9), usually in feet. They also show the compass direction (north) and important way points along the trail. See the map legend on page 8. For most day hikes, the maps in this book will serve well. For extended backpacking in the wild backcountry or high mountains, we recommend using Appalachian Trail Conference or Appalachian Mountain Club maps.

Note: Some USGS maps have not been updated for several years and may not show recent trail relocations. Follow the dark green line of the AT on the maps in this book. You may see the old AT outlined in gray on the map. In some cases the old path is open and usable, but in many it's not. Check the narrative and consult local trail clubs before hiking on discontinued sections of the AT.

Itinerary: A summary of the hike in table format, listing important way points noted in the narrative and shown on the topo map and/or the trail profile. Both the narrative and the itinerary describe the hike as either a south-to-north (most common) or north-to-south walk. Thus, in a S-N itinerary, directions to turn left (L) or right (R) mean "left when walking northward on the trail" and "right when walking northward on the trail," respectively. On a N-S itinerary, the reverse is true.

Bear in mind that "north" and "south" as used along the AT are not always literally true. The trail is said to run north from Georgia to Maine, but at any given point, even if you're walking "northward toward Maine," the footpath may veer to the west or east, or even southward to skirt a difficult mountain before resuming its generally northward direction. That's why in the narrative and itinerary we generally use "left" and "right" rather than compass directions. Inexperienced AT hikers simply have to orient themselves correctly at the start of the hike: Make sure you know whether you're following the trail to the north or south, and keep that in mind as you proceed. Then, "left" and "right" in the narrative and itinerary will be easy to follow. In any case, always carry a compass.

Note: In keeping with the tradition of showing north at the top of maps, we structure the itineraries with north always at the top of the table, south at the bottom. Thus, for a S-N hike, you will find the "Start" at the bottom (south) end of the itinerary, and you should read upward. "End" will be at the top (north) end of the table. We give mileage in both directions: the left-hand column goes S-N; the right-hand column goes N-S.

Remember that *access trail* mileage must be added to miles walked on the AT itself. We total both mileages for you in the itinerary. Elevations are given in the itineraries in both feet and meters (feet elsewhere). To construct our itineraries, we relied on walking the trail, taking careful notes, and then verifying by reference to other trail guides, especially the Appalachian Trail Conference and member club trail guides. Published trail guides, USGS maps, and ATC maps sometimes disagree by as much as a few tenths of a mile (distance) or a few feet (elevation).

SIDEBAR: In some hikes, special topics are discussed in a box set off from the narrative. The sidebars are listed in the table of contents.

Abbreviations

Abbreviations commonly used in this book:

AHS, American Hiking Society
AMS, Appalachian Mt. Club
ATC, Appalachian Trail Conference
CCC, Civilian Conservation Corps
GMC, Green Mt. Club
GMNF, Green Mt. National Forest
LT, Long Trail
LT/AT, contiguous Long Trail & Appalachian Trail
USFS, U.S. Forest Service
USGS, U.S. Geological Survey

Geographic Organization

The hikes included in this volume follow the Appalachian Trail from south to north. Most of the hikes are described as south-to-north walks, but many are suitable to walking the opposite way, too. A few hikes are best done from north to south. Pay attention to the suggested direction. We have avoided some wicked climbs by bringing you down, rather than up, certain nasty hills.

Maps: Legends, Skills, Sources

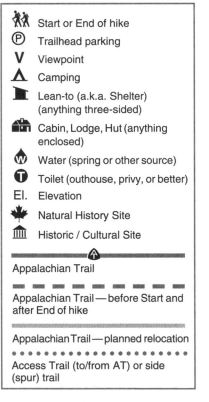

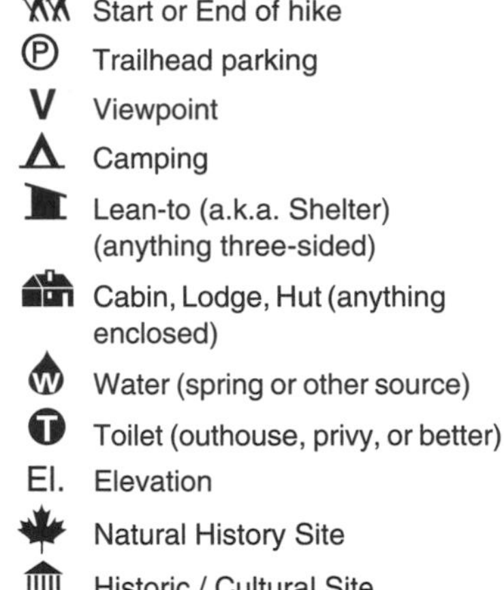

Scale—Unless otherwise noted, approximately 1 inch = 1 mile.

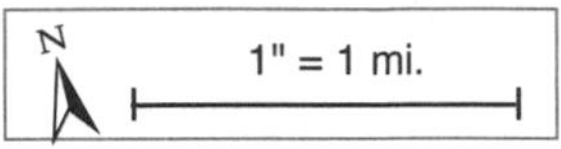

Compass Direction and Deviation—The scale bar also shows the compass direction North. The north shown on the map is "true" or "grid" north, essentially a straight line to the north pole, whereas the north you see on your compass is "magnetic" north, usually a few degrees different due to the earth's magnetic field. Along the AT, magnetic north deviates from true or grid north by several degrees *west*. The farther north one goes, the greater the deviation. At the Vermont–New Hampshire state line the deviation is 15.5° west; throughout Maine it is about 18°.

Contour Interval—See "Contour Lines" below. Contour intervals on the USGS topographic maps used as the base for the hiking maps in this book are either 10 meters (32.8 ft.) or 20 meters (66 ft.), depending on the map (see "List of Maps" under "Useful Information").

Reading and planning your hikes with topographic maps can be fun and is certainly useful. Every hiking party should have at least one competent map reader. Often, if there are children aboard, they will be eager to follow the hike's progress on the topographic map. Here are a few pointers for beginning map readers.

Contour Lines—All the hiking maps in this series of guides are based on official topographic maps which represent the three-dimensional shape of the land with *contour lines* (CLs). Typically, CLs are drawn at fixed intervals, for example, 20 meters, meaning that between each pair of lines in our example there is a rise or fall of 20 meters in the landscape.

In this example, the CLs are close together, suggesting a steep climb or descent:

In this example, the CLs are farther apart, suggesting a gently sloping or nearly flat landscape:

Linear scale—To understand CLs fully, they must be related to the *linear scale* of the map. This relationship gives a sense of vertical rise or fall as it spreads out horizontally across the landscape. Thus, if 1 inch = 1 mile and if there are many CLs clustered in, say, a ½-inch section of trail, then it's safe to assume that this ½-mile section of the trail will be steep, going up or down depending on your direction.

Map Sources— All maps in this series are derived from United States Geological Survey topographic maps. Each of our maps is a small slice of a USGS topo map. We have updated relevant AT information (some USGS maps are 10 or more years old; the AT has moved at several points). The original map scale of 1:100,000 is enlarged here generally to about 1:62,000 (around 1 inch = 1 mile) for readability. A 1:100,000-scale map is not practical to carry on the trail. USGS maps scaled at a more convenient 1:62,000 are easy to read as trail maps, but a day's hike may cut across several maps or use only a tiny portion of one large map, an unwieldy affair when hiking.

For short day hikes, we recommend using the maps in this book. For longer hikes, overnight trips, or serious backpacking, we advise using official AT maps from the Appalachian Trail Conference or supplementary maps from Trails Illustrated, the Appalachian Mountain Club, or the Green Mountain Club (see below).

Bookstores and outdoor outfitters in towns near the Appalachian Trail usually stock the USGS quadrangles (1: 62,500) for the local area. USGS maps can also be ordered by telephone (see "Useful Information" and the Bibliography). If you do not know the USGS map number (see the list in "Useful Information" for maps used in this book), be sure to indicate (a) the portion of the AT you want to hike by providing the names of nearby cities, towns, rivers, or other landmarks and (b) the scale you prefer. Anything over 1 inch = 1 mile will be impractical for hiking.

The Appalachian Trail Conference publishes a set of color-shaded topographic hiking maps for almost the entire length of the trail (excluding the national parks through which the AT passes). The scale is generally 1:38,750. This translates to about 1⅝ inches = 1 mile. In other words, much more detail than on the USGS quadrangles and more than we can show in a book of this size. See your local bookseller or outdoor outfitter, or call the ATC (see "Useful Information"). A catalogue is available. For serious hikers and for any overnight or backcountry hiking on the Appalachian Trail, we strongly recommend these fine maps.

Trails Illustrated (distributed by National Geographic) publishes more than fifty maps of national parks; these include important sections of the Appalachian Trail in Great Smoky Mts. National Park and Shenandoah National Park. These full-color, large-format maps (printed on waterproof, tear-resistant recycled paper) provide detailed topographic information and descriptions of local flora and fauna. A 3-D overview map is an enjoyable bonus. These are metric maps. The scale is 1:100,000, roughly ⅝ inch = 1 mile. A metric conversion chart is provided. See your local bookseller or outdoor outfitter, or contact Trails Illustrated (see the Bibliography).

The Appalachian Mountain Club publishes hiking guides, many of which include fold-out two- or three-color maps. For hiking in New Hampshire's Presidential Range (White Mt. National Forest), these maps are particularly useful: they show not only the AT but many miles of other trails, too. See your local bookseller or outdoor outfitter, or contact the Appalachian Mountain Club (see "Useful Information").

For the AT in southern Vermont, you'll want the fine maps published by the Green Mountain Club in a series called "End to End: Topographic Maps of Vermont's Long Trail." The Long Trail runs from Massachusetts to the Canadian border. The AT and Long Trail are contiguous from Massachusetts to US4 at Killington in central Vermont. From there on, heading eastward toward New Hampshire, use Appalachian Trail Conference maps. The Long Trail / AT maps are four-color, waterproof, and tear-resistant. The scale is 1:62,500, or 1 inch = 1 mile; the contour interval is 20 feet. To order Long Trail / AT maps for southern Vermont, see your local bookseller or outdoor outfitter, or contact the Green Mountain Club (see "Useful Information").

Driving Time to the Trailhead

A factor frequently overlooked when planning a hike is the driving time required to reach the trailhead or to get back to civilization at day's end. When a substantial number of miles must be traveled from a major highway or town to get up into the mountains to the trailhead, we tell you in the information block. You must be sure to leave sufficient time to get to the starting point. Positioning two cars (finish and start) takes even longer.

Remember that many Appalachian Trail access roads are "secondary" at best. Some are decidedly unkind to low-chassis, two-wheel-drive cars. Some are impassable in wet weather (the entire spring mud season). Travel to the trailhead can be slow and dicey. Read our instructions carefully. Plan ahead.

Choosing Your Hike / Effort Required

In this book we rate hikes by three levels of "effort required": easy, moderate, and strenuous. Some hikes are a mix of easy, moderate, and strenuous sections.

If little kids or folks with disabilities might find a hike too rugged, we tell you. If there are difficult water crossings, perhaps varying seasonally, we say so.

But remember, our judgments are somewhat subjective.

Easy: gentle ups and downs, fairly smooth path, few obstacles

Moderate: elevation gain or loss of up to 1000 feet; narrower, rocky path; some obstacles (for example, brook crossings with no bridge)

Strenuous: elevation gain or loss of more than 1000 feet; steep ups and downs; difficult, challenging path; numerous obstacles; possibly unsuitable for young children or the infirm.

Blazing

A "blaze" (from the Old English *blœse*, meaning "torch") is a bright painted mark (about 6 inches x 2 inches) on a tree, post, or rock indicating the path of a hiking trail. The Appalachian Trail is blazed in white (rather easy to see even in fog, though tough to follow in brightly dappled sunlight), all the way from Georgia to Maine. It's the same in each direction, south–north or north–south.

Side trails are often but not always blazed in a different color—generally blue, orange, or yellow. AT blazes are usually spaced 30 to 50 yards apart. In some sections overzealous trail maintainers have blazed at shorter intervals, while in other areas blazing has faded and may be hard to follow. If you haven't seen a white blaze for several minutes, backtrack and make sure you're still on the white-blazed AT, not an unmarked side trail or logging road.

Two blazes, one above the other, indicate a turn coming in the trail. In some states, if the upper blaze is positioned to the left, look for a left turn, and vice versa.

Estimating Hiking Times

An average adult hiker's pace is about 2.0 miles per hour on the flat. For every 1000-foot gain in elevation, add 30 minutes of time to your estimate. Thus an 8-mile hike up a 2500-foot mountain might take you 5¼ hours. This formula does not account for rests, mealtimes, or lollygagging to smell the flowers or talk to the bears. With a full backpack, little kids in tow, or slippery conditions, obviously you would add more time.

We recommend that you keep a record of your time and distance and the hiking conditions for a half dozen hikes, and then compare your averages to ours. You'll soon see whether our numbers match yours and if not, how much time you need to add or subtract from our estimates.

Day Hikes / Overnight Backpacking Hikes

The majority of the hikes in this book can be done as day hikes. Some day hikes can be conveniently strung together to make overnight backpacking trips of 2 or more days' duration. And some hikes are manageable only as overnight backpacking trips. The general rule: the more wilderness there is to traverse, the less likely it is that you can pop in and out for a day hike only. Read the information block carefully, and look at the hike south or north of the one you're considering to see whether a linkage is feasible.

Avoiding the Crowds

A great debate is raging: Is the AT now overused, too busy to be enjoyable, too tough on the land to be justifiable? Are we approaching, or are we already at, the point where reservations will have to be made for floor space in an AT shelter? (In fact, in some southern sections—Great Smoky Mts. National Park, for example—shelters are reserved for thru-hikers or other long-distance hikers only, not the casual weekender.)

We don't mean to equivocate, but the answer seems to be yes and no. Collectively, the authors of this series have hiked thousands of AT miles over several decades. Far more often than not, we have had the trail essentially to ourselves, passing only a few people per day. Inevitably, however, certain sites on the trail (beautifully located shelters, or summits with great views or symbolic significance, for example) attract crowds, especially on weekends, and most especially in midsummer or at fall foliage time. The southern section of the AT is busy with hundreds of would-be thru-hikers in early spring. Don't expect to be alone on Springer Mt. in April.

It does not require a graduate degree in engineering to figure out a plan to avoid these crowds or to avoid swelling them yourself. The best times to be alone on the trail are midweek. No offense to kids or parents (we love 'em all), but June, before the kids leave school, and September, after they're back in, are great times to find warm-weather solitude on the AT. If you can swing it, why not work on Saturday (or even Sunday) and hike on Sunday and Monday (or better yet Monday and Tuesday). We've tried it with success. The most popular shelter in Connecticut is Riga: fantastic cliffside sunrise view. We had it all to ourselves on a Sunday night in mid-August, in good weather.

If you cannot hike midweek and are headed for peaks or shelters likely to be overcrowded, start out early enough to permit you to move on to another site in daylight if your first target has already hung out the "No Vacancy" sign. When the shelter or official tent sites are full, accept the bad news and walk on. Carving out an impromptu tent site is generally forbidden except in extremely bad weather. Carry a detailed map. Study it carefully before leaving home to find the alternative site you may need in a pinch.

Circuit or Loop Hikes / Shuttle Services

Ideally you have a limousine with built-in hot tub and cold drinks awaiting you at the end of the trail. Short of that, you may have to improvise a way to get back to your starting point. Whenever it's convenient and sensible from a hiking viewpoint, we have suggested how to make the hike into a circuit or loop, bringing you back, on foot, to your car or pretty close to it. There are many hikes, however, especially those in wilderness areas, where this is simply not feasible.

It's usually best if you can work out a two-car team for your hike, with one car dropped at the finish line and another driven to the starting trailhead.

Out and back: Most of our hikes are described as linear—from A to B to C. Hikers with only one car available can make many fine hikes, however, by simply going out to a well-chosen point (the mountaintop, the pond) and then reversing direction to the starting point. The mileage indicators in the Itineraries will help you decide on a turnaround point. You may be pleasantly surprised to find that when walked in the opposite direction, the same section of trail yields a very different experience—especially if one direction is steeply up and the other sharply down.

Shuttles: In some areas, and through the auspices of some local hiking clubs, shuttle services are available. For example, the Green Mountain Club in Vermont provides to its members a list of shuttle drivers, although they are few in number and require early notice and modest fees. In this book, when we know there is a reliable shuttle service that is useful on a particular hike, we tell you. If we don't make a shuttle suggestion, it's often worth asking your motel or bed-and-breakfast keeper, or calling the local Chamber of Commerce or even the local taxi company. A hunting-lodge manager helped us one time at a good price. Ask around, make new friends.

Some hikers like to position a bicycle (locked) at the end of a hike so they can ride back to their car at the starting point.

If your hiking group consists of, say, four or more people and two cars, you might swap extra car keys at the beginning of the day and send people, a car, and a key for the other car to each end of the trail. You all meet somewhere in the middle of the hike, trade stories, and perhaps share lunch. And each group finds a car waiting at day's end. Depending on roads and distances to trailheads, this system can shave a good deal of time off the car travel at the start and end of your hiking day. This is especially helpful for very long day hikes and even more so in early spring or late fall when days are short. Besides, meeting friends deep in the forest or on a mountaintop is great fun.

Early Exit Options

Our hikes range from 5 to 15 miles per day. When road crossings and parking facilities permit, we indicate points where you could leave the AT before finishing the entire hike. Sometimes such exits are convenient and safe; sometimes they should be used only for emergencies. Heed our advice. If we do not say good parking is available, don't assume there's a parking lot.

The Early Exit Options can often be used to make a loop hike out of an otherwise longish linear hike. To see your options clearly, study a good local road map.

Camping

Camp only in designated camping areas unless you know for sure that free-for-all camping is permitted. In most sections of the AT the land is too heavily used to permit improvisatory camping. We indicate official campsites. The rules may vary as you pass through state forest, national forest, or national park. In some areas, especially national parks, camping permits may be required and campsite reservations may be possible. See "Shelters and Campsites" in "Useful Information."

Shelters

The names may vary but the accommodations are much the same: Along the AT, about every 10 to 15 miles, you'll find three-sided lean-tos with minimalist interior decorating. Bunk beds or no beds at all, just floor space. Possibly a picnic table, a fire ring, an outhouse, a water source nearby. Many of these shelters have well-maintained facilities, charming names, and equally charming views. Some you wouldn't let your dog sleep in. We tell you which ones we like. Shelters usually have a few tent sites surrounding them.

Except in the two national parks through which the AT passes (Great Smoky Mts., Shenandoah) and in New Hampshire's White Mt. National Forest, where shelters are reserved for thru-hikers (for a fee), the "reservations policy" is first come, first served. Certain rules apply, however: Maximum stay, 3 nights. If it's raining, squeeze in and make room for late arrivals. Clean up after yourself, and respect others' needs for quiet and privacy.

Trail Registers

At shelters and occasionally at trail junctions, you'll find notebooks where you can, and should, write a few words for posterity and for practicality's sake. Logging in your arrival and departure time will help searchers find you if, unluckily, you get lost or hurt on the trail. But the real fun of the trail registers is adding your own thoughts to the collective wisdom and tomfoolery other hikers have already scribbled in the notebooks. The registers make great reading. A whole new literary genre! Go ahead, wax poetic or philosophical. Surely there's at least one haiku in you to express your joy at the view from the mountaintop or the first time you shook hands with a moose. . . .

Trail registers also sometimes provide helpful warnings about trail conditions (recent mud slides or bridge washouts, for example). If the weather has been wild of late, read back a few days in the register to see what previous hikers may have said about what lies ahead of you.

HIKING: THE BASICS

WHILE IT'S TRUE that we go to the woods and the mountains to get away from the trappings of civilization, few of us really want to put our lives in jeopardy. Here are some recommendations every adult hiker (and Boy or Girl Scout–age youngster) should follow.

When the subject is equipment, we suggest you visit your outdoor outfitter to ask for advice or that you read back issues of *Backpacker* magazine, in print or online (see "Useful Information"). *Backpacker*'s annual "gear guide" sorts through hundreds of choices and makes useful recommendations. For the truly hiking/camping gizmo-obsessed, there are on-line chat rooms (again, see *Backpacker*) where you and other similarly gadget-crazed friends can compare notes.

Boots / Shoes

Nothing is more important to a hiker than the condition of his or her feet. From this axiom derives an important rule: Wear the right boots or shoes for hiking, or stay home. Some of the easier sections of the AT can be hiked in firm running shoes or high-top basketball sneakers, but most sections require a tougher, waterproof or water-resistant boot providing nonslip soles, toe protection, and firm ankle support. Shop carefully. Go to an outdoor outfitter rather than a regular shoe store. Try on several pairs of boots, with the actual socks you intend to wear (two pair: one thin, one thick). If you buy boots by mail, trace your foot size with those socks on your feet. Save your pennies and buy the best you can afford. Gore-Tex or one of its waterproofing clones is worth the money. Check the hiking magazines' annual gear reviews (in print or on-line) for ratings of comfort, weight, durability, and price. Think of the purchase as a multiyear investment. Shop long before the hiking season starts, and wear your boots for a good 10 to 20 miles of everyday walking before hitting the trail. Your feet will thank you.

Caveat for kids: The better discount stores carry boot brands that are quite sufficient for a season of hiking by young people whose feet are still growing. Parents, buy your own boots first and then use your shopper's savvy to find inexpensive boots for the kids.

Clothing

Bring sufficient clothes, appropriate for rain and cold. Layers work best. Gore-Tex and other waterproof fabrics are miraculous, but a $3 emergency poncho will do in a pinch. Think about what you would need to get through a rainy night, even if you're just out for a short, sunny day hike.

A visored hat. The top of your head is the point of major heat loss, whether you're bald or not. Inexpensive Gore-Tex hats can be found. Cruise the catalogues.

Sunglasses, in a protective case. Rhinestone decorative motif not required.

Cotton socks, sweatshirts, and T-shirts: avoid them. Blue jeans (essentially cotton): avoid them. Cotton is comfortable until it gets wet (from rain or perspiration). Then it's your enemy. It dries slowly and does not wick away perspiration. There are extraordinary synthetic fabrics nowadays for shirts, underwear, and long johns that will keep you warm or cool and will let the moisture leave your body. Visit your outdoor outfitter for a wardrobe consultation. Money well spent.

Wool is a miracle fabric from nature. Especially good for socks and gloves. Polartec is a miracle fabric from the high-tech world (recycled plastic bottles!). Jackets and pull-overs in these miracle fabrics are what you want.

Food

Hiking eats up calories. Cold weather demands body heat, which demands calories. Diet at home. Eat high-energy foods on the trail. Carbohydrates are best. Sweets are less helpful than you might think, though a chocolate or energy bar to help you up the hill is sometimes right. It's better to eat several smaller meals en route than to gorge on a big one, unless you plan for a siesta. Digestion itself takes considerable energy. You'll find it hard to climb and digest at the same time. The hiker's fallback snack plan: (1) "Gorp," a mix of nuts, granola, chocolate chips, dried fruit, and whatever else you like. Mix it yourself at home —much cheaper than the ready-made variety at the store. (2) Peanut butter on anything. (3) Fruit. Heavy to carry but oh so refreshing. The sugar in fruit is fructose, high in energy but it won't put you to sleep.

And remember the miracle food for hikers, the humble banana. Or dried banana chips (crunch them or add water). High in potassium, bananas are your muscles' best friends because the potassium minimizes aches and cramps.

Planning menus and packing food for extended backpacking trips is a subject beyond the scope of this book. Several camping cookbooks are available, and *Backpacker* frequently runs how-to articles worth reading. Search their Web site for articles you can download. Advice: Whatever you plan to cook on the trail, try it out first, on the backpacking stove, at home. Make a list of cooking gear and condiments needed, and if the list looks long, simplify the menu unless you have willing friends along who will carry a gourmet's kitchen for you. Over time you'll find camp food tricks and tastes to add to your repertoire, such as bagging breakfast granola with powdered milk in self-seal bags (just add water and stir), or choosing tough-skinned veggies like carrots, celery, or snow peas that can be eaten cooked or raw and won't turn to mush in your pack. The ever popular macaroni and cheese (available nowadays in many fancy permutations from Lipton, Kraft, et al.) can be dressed up in countless lightweight, quick-cook ways. The camper's most important kitchen tool is imagination.

Whatever you plan to eat or cook on the trail, be prepared to clean up spotlessly. Leave no mess—indeed, no trace.

Food Storage

You're not the only hungry critter in the woods. Everyone from the bears to the squirrels and mice would like to breakfast on your granola and snack on your Oreos. Never keep food in your tent overnight. It's an invitation for unwanted company in the dark. Use a drawstring food sack, wrapped in a plastic garbage bag, which you hang from a sturdy branch on a nearby tree, keeping the sack several feet out on the branch, about 10 feet off the ground and several feet below the branch. Obviously this means you must carry about 50 feet of lightweight cord (useful in emergencies too).

Don't store your food in your backpack, either, indoors or out. Those cute little chipmunks and their bigger friends will eat a hole right through that expensive high-tech fabric.

Water

Keep drinking a little at a time all day while you hike. Dehydration is the major cause of hiker fatigue. Double or triple your normal daily intake of water.

Sadly, most of the water flowing in streams the AT crosses is polluted to one degree or another, sometimes by industry or agriculture, often by wild animals such as beavers upstream. The most common problem is a nasty protozoan known as giardia from which we get stomach cramps, fever, and the runs. Trust us: you don't want it. The rule is, unless an official sign says the water has been tested and is pure, assume the water must be treated with either iodine tablets or a water filter. Iodine is cheap and lightweight but slow, and it leaves a somewhat unpleasant taste in the treated water (Potable Aqua is an iodine treatment that minimizes the bad taste). Hiker water filters are faster-acting but more cumbersome. They are useful elsewhere too—on boats, at freshwater beaches, and so forth. A good investment. Look for one that screens out most bacteria, is lightweight, and pumps quickly. The most convenient water bottles are (a) wide-mouth, facilitating refill and filter attachment, and (b) equipped with a drinking tube or nipple, eliminating the need to open the bottle itself.

When Nature Calls

Every hiker—day only or overnight backpacker—must come prepared to deal appropriately with disposal of human waste in the woods. At most shelters and many campsites along the AT there are outhouses. Please help to keep them clean. Gentlemen especially are encouraged to urinate in the woods, a few hundred feet off the trail. Urine in the outhouse pit adds to the bad aroma.

Believe it or not, there's an entire book on the subject of defecating in the woods (see the Bibliography). Good reading on a slow day in camp, perhaps. This much you must know to do: Bring biodegradable white single-ply toilet paper in a plastic bag. Bring a little shovel (a plastic garden trowel will do). Bring a strong self-seal plastic bag to carry out used toilet paper, tampons, etc. If the woods is your toilet, get at least 100 feet off the trail and at least 200 feet away from any water. Dig a hole at least 8 inches deep, and cover your waste firmly. A squat is the time-tested position.

Weather

Basic precautions include a careful review of weather forecasts and typical conditions in the area you're hiking—before you pack your pack or leave home. See "Useful Information" for a weather Web site. If you go adventuring outdoors frequently, you'll enjoy and benefit from a lightweight battery-operated weather radio that provides access to several NOAA (National Oceanic and Atmospheric Administration) channels, offering detailed forecasts 24 hours a day, with special recreational forecasts emphasizing conditions at elevations of 3000 feet and above.

Learn to forecast weather yourself by reading the clouds (particularly cumulous clouds with towering thunderheads) and by noticing changes in animal and plant behavior that may telegraph the advent of a storm. Make it a habit to do a 360-degree sky check every hour or so to see what's coming and from which direction. If trouble is heading your way, plan ahead for emergency shelter. Get off the mountaintop or exposed ridge, where high winds and lightning are most likely to hit. Don't sit under a big rotting tree with branches waiting to clunk you on the head. When lightning is likely, avoid all metal objects (fire towers, tent poles, pack frames, etc.). Do find a dry, wind-protected spot (the downwind side of overhanging boulders is good), and lay a plan to make it your home for a few hours.

Wet weather often brings cool or cold temperatures. Wet clothing or a wet sleeping bag can exacerbate your sense of chill. Hypothermia can set in quickly, especially if you're fatigued or anxious. Even day hikers should carry extra clothing and something, if only a big plastic garbage bag, to cover themselves and their pack. Overnight backpackers, anywhere on the AT, must be ready for the worst. Keep rainwear light and simple so you won't resent carrying it on a sunny day.

See "Unfriendly Weather," page 34.

First Aid

Outfitters such as Campmor and REI (excellent catalogues) offer first-aid kits for everyone from the day hiker to the Mt. Everest climber. Buy from them or patch together your own kit, based on the contents listed in the catalogues. A waterproof container is a must. Be prepared for cuts, scrapes, burns, blisters, sprains, headache. Sunscreen if exposure is likely. A very lightweight first-aid manual is not a bad idea either.

One essential is moleskin, a skin-covering adhesive, thicker than a Band-Aid but soft enough to wrap around an unhappy toe. Many a hike has been ruined by blisters. At the first sign (heat, burning, tingling feelings on toes or heels), slap on the moleskin and leave it there until you're back home. Insurance against blisters is cheap: two pairs of (dry!) socks. And break in your new hiking boots *thoroughly* before you hit the trail.

Further insurance: bring a few feet of dental floss. If your teeth don't use it, a sewing job might.

Include a little but loud whistle in your first-aid kit. You might need to call for help.

If first aid is foreign to you, by all means take a course, with CPR (artificial respiration) training, from the local Red Cross. For parents hiking with kids, this is a must. For kids, join the Scouts and earn that First Aid merit badge.

Hiking Alone

There are real pleasures to be had from hiking alone. Generally, however, it's not recommended. Whether you hike alone or in a group, take pains to let someone know your plans (route, estimated times of departure and arrival, what to do if you don't check back in). Often a hiker who wants to walk alone can have that pleasure, letting fellow hikers know that by day's end he or she will rejoin the group.

Hiking in Groups

Keep your group size down to fewer than ten people. Even that many is stretching what the trailside facilities can bear. Large groups tend to overwhelm smaller ones, yet everyone has the same rights to enjoy the space and the quiet on the trail. Don't take a busload of kids on the trail. Find volunteers who will lead sections of a group with at least a mile or 30 minutes between them.

Women Hikers

Statistically, the Appalachian Trail is one of the safest places a woman (or a man) can be in the United States. But there have been some problems with harrassment, and there have been some cases of violence, even a few tragic murders. Play it safe. Don't hike alone. Be sensible—inappropriate clothing may attract the wrong kind of attention. Avoid the rowdy set sometimes found at shelters near road crossings or towns. If you arrive at a shelter and find suspicious people there, move on.

Taking Children on the Trail

By all means, do take the kids. The environment of the Appalachian Trail and the activities of climbing, exploring, and camping will engage the imagination and channel the energies of almost every kid, including those whose regular turf is the city street. Adult hikers just need to remember that a few things are different about kid hikers. Kids' attention spans are (usually) shorter than grown-ups'. Plan to break your hike into smaller units with something special to do in each part—birds here, lunch there, rock collecting next, photography from the mountaintop, writing messages in the trail registers. Give a kid a short-term achievable project linked to today's hike (such as collecting as many different-shaped leaves as you can from the ground beneath the trees), and you'll probably have a happy, satisfied kid hiker by evening.

Most kids love hiking and camping gear. Get them involved in planning, shopping, packing for, and executing the hike, especially the camping portion. Let them make breakfast. Teach them to set up the tent; then get out of the way. Take pictures and make a family hiking photo album: it's a memory bank for years to come. Put a map on your children's wall at home and mark the trails they have hiked, the peaks they have climbed. A sense of accomplishment is priceless.

Be realistic, too, about what kids can endure on the hiking trail. Their pain (and boredom) thresholds are lower than most adults'. Don't let blisters happen to kids; check their feet at lunchtime. Bring a book to read in case of rain, or a miniature chess set if they're old enough to play. Anticipate your own behavior in an emergency situation. If you panic, the kids will. If you're calm, know where to go for help, and know how to keep dry and warm, most kids will rise to the occasion and come home strengthened by the adventure.

See "Of Children, Scraped Knees, and Pride," page 89.

Parking

Do not leave a sign on your car saying where you're going or when you'll return. Try not to leave anything (visible) in your car that might interest burglars. Avoid camping at shelters located very close to easily accessible parking lots. Respect the AT's immediate neighbors by not parking on their private property.

PACKING YOUR PACK

Backpacks and Day Packs

It's not quite a science but it's certainly an art. An incorrectly loaded backpack (badly packed on the inside or poorly fitted or adjusted to your torso and shoulders) can wreck even a sunny day on the world's loveliest trail. Some tips: Fanny packs, worn at hip level, are great for short day hikes as long as you can carry sufficient water, food, clothing, first aid, and map and compass. Less than that and the pack is too small.

Day packs carry proportionately more but without the frame that supports a backpacking pack. For both day packs and true backpacks, similar packing rules apply. Start at the outdoor outfitter. Have a knowledgeable salesperson fit the pack (with realistic dummy weights inside) to your specific torso. Walk around, bend over, squat, and be sure you're comfortable and stable.

At home, make a packing list with items categorized carefully (food, kitchen, first aid, clothes, stove and fuel, etc.). Jettison anything unnecessary. Roll your clothes. Pack one thing inside another (the Chinese box method). Then use the following scheme for stuffing the pack.

Keep weight distributed equally on the horizontal plane, but on the vertical, pack the lightweight items (such as sleeping bag) down low and the heavyweight items (food, water, tent) up high. Keep the heavier items close to your body. But be sure to pad any sharp-edged items so as not to poke you or to rip the pack fabric. Use the pack's outside pockets for a water bottle, fuel bottles, and smelly garbage.

Last, buy a rainproof pack cover or make one from a heavy-duty plastic garbage bag. Your clothing and sleeping bag will be glad you did.

Flashlight

Even a day hiker ought to carry a lightweight flashlight, just in case. In winter, early spring, and fall, daylight can disappear quickly, especially if the weather turns bad or you lose time by being temporarily lost. A slim flashlight that's portable in an elastic headband is a good investment.

Check the batteries before leaving home. Bring an extra bulb.

Matches
Even if you do not intend to cook or camp out and have a campfire, bring a supply of waterproof matches or a cigarette lighter. If you're forced to overnight in the woods, a fire may be good company indeed.

Jackknife
A multipurpose pocketknife will do. It needn't have a built-in chain saw or an eyebrow pencil, but a can opener, a Phillips screwdriver, and a tweezers are handy.

Weapons
We strongly discourage hikers from carrying any kind of weapon.

Cellular Phones
People have been hiking safely and contentedly in the woods for several thousand years without the aid or comfort of cellular phones. This is still possible. Many people come to the trail to get away from the electronic web in which we all are increasingly caught up. Here's a way to win friends on the trail: Keep your cell phone, if you bring one, out of sight, beyond earshot, and out of mind for everyone else. Don't use it except for emergencies, and do use it only when you're far away from other hikers. Domino's Pizza does not deliver to most AT shelters anyway. So why even call them?

FINDING YOUR WAY

Map and Compass
Don't go hiking without a map and compass and the skills to use them. In the fog, in the dark, in a storm, even familiar territory can seem like a directionless wilderness. Many hiking clubs offer map and compass (a.k.a. "orienteering") workshops. Map skills are fun to develop and highly useful. Many of the best natural history observations described in this book depend on your ability to locate a spot on the map and to orient yourself once you're there.

At the very least, be sure everyone in your party knows the compass direction of your intended hike, the cars' locations on the map, and the most likely way toward help in an emergency. *Backpacker* has run articles on map and compass skills (check the index on their Web site). The venerable *Boy Scout Handbook* has a good chapter on these skills. Or see Karen Berger's *Hiking & Backpacking: A Complete Guide.*

Being Lost and Getting Found
If you have studied your map before starting the hike, and if you faithfully follow the AT's white blazes or the access trails' blue (or red or yellow) blazes, the chances of getting lost are just about zero. With a map and

compass in hand, there's no good excuse for being lost while you're on the AT itself. Your group should have a leader and a backup leader, and both should know the route. Because hikers sometimes get separated on the trail, everyone should know the direction of the hike, the major landmarks to be passed, the estimated timetable, and how to use the sun and the clock to keep themselves oriented.

But mistakes do happen. Inattention and inadequate planning are the enemies. Sometimes nature conspires against us. Fog (or snow) may obscure the blazes or the cairns above treeline. Autumn leaves or a snowfall may obliterate the well-worn trail that otherwise would guide your eyes as clearly as the blazes themselves.

If you are lost, the first thing to do is to decide that you will not panic. You probably have not been off the trail for long. Stay where you are and think. Keep your group together. Study the map and note the last landmark you're sure you passed. Get reoriented with the map and compass, and try to go in a straight line back toward the trail. Do not wander. Be especially observant of details until you regain the trail.

If all else fails, let gravity and falling water help you out. Except in the deepest wilderness of Maine or the Smoky Mts., at most places along the AT streams flow eventually to brooks, then to rivers, and where there's a river there will soon enough be a house or even a village. If you have to bushwhack to get out of the woods, and if you're really not sure where you are on the map, follow the water downstream. Patience and a plan will get you out.

Common Sense/Sense of Humor

Taking care of yourself successfully in the woods and on the mountains is not rocket science. It starts with preparedness (physical and mental), appropriate equipment, sufficient food and water. It continues with a realistic plan, guided by a map and compass, a guidebook, a weather report, and a watch. It gets better if you and your companions resolve ahead of time to work together as a team, respecting each other's varying needs, strengths, and talents. And it goes best of all if you pack that one priceless and essential hiker's tool: a ready sense of humor.

AT LEGEND HAS IT that the 2150-mile footpath from Georgia to Maine is an ancient Native American walkway. Not so. In fact, the AT, as a concept, leapt from the imagination of one federal government civil servant who in 1921 had already recognized that Americans were too citified for their own good and needed more nearby, convenient opportunities for outdoor recreation.

In 1921, Harvard-educated forester and self-styled philosopher Benton MacKaye, of Shirley, Massachusetts, published an article ("An Appalachian Trail, A Project in Regional Planning") in the *Journal of the American Institute of Architects*. His was a revolutionary idea: a linear park, extending from Georgia to Maine. The concept germinated in a hotbed of idealistic left-wing social thinking that called into question many of the assumed values of the capitalist workaday world. Look a little more deeply into MacKaye's thinking and the roots lead directly to the 19th-century romantics and Transcendentalists, Thoreau and Emerson. MacKaye had read his John Muir, too.

A whirlwind of self-promoting public relations energy, MacKaye set the ball rolling to develop the AT. Thousands of volunteers and many legislators helped make it a reality. Two other key players were Judge Arthur Perkins of Hartford, Connecticut, who helped found the Appalachian Trail Conference in 1925, and his successor as president of the Conference (1931–1952), Myron Avery, of Maine and Washington, D.C. By 1937, with major assistance from Civilian Conservation Corps workers under President Roosevelt's New Deal Works Progress Administration, the complete trail was essentially in place, though by today's standards much of it was rugged and unblazed.

Thru-hikers are an admirable but increasingly common breed these days. Yet it wasn't until 1948 that anyone walked the entire trail in one season. The first thru-hiker was Earl Shaffer. The first woman to thru-hike in one season was Emma "Grandma" Gatewood, in 1955. By the mid-1990s the National Park Service was estimating that between 3 and 4 million people per year used the trail. In its first 75 years, from MacKaye's brainstorm to today, the AT has gone from a concept about escaping urban crowding to the point where crowding on the trail itself is a big issue.

In 1968, Congress put the AT under the authority of the National Park Service by passing the National Trails System Act. Overall, the story of the AT is a sweet tale of success. Occasionally there has been a sour note when the government's right of eminent domain has been used to take land required to create a 1000-foot-wide corridor of protection for the trail. By 1995 fewer than 44 miles of the trail remained unprotected by the Park Service corridor. In the 1990s, environmental impact concerns (wear and tear, sustainability) and hiker management issues (overuse, low-impact camping and hiking, safety) fill the pages of AT magazines and spark many a late-night campfire conversation. While the educational and environmental protection efforts of the Appalachian Trail Conference, the Appalachian Mountain Club, and all the regional hiking clubs improve yearly, adding strength to an admirable history, the erosion of financial support from Congress in a budget balancing era threatens to undermine many good efforts at a moment when user demands are growing exponentially. It is a time of fulfillment and challenge for all who use and manage the Appalachian Trail.

Note: A more detailed history of the AT can be found in any of the Appalachian Trail Conference's hiking guides. Colorful lore about the earliest days of trailblazing in New England appears in *Forest and Crag: A History of Hiking, Trail Blazing and Adventure in the Northeast Mountains*, by Guy and Laura Waterman. And *The Appalachian Trail Reader*, edited by David Emblidge, contains a diverse collection of writings about the AT.

Appalachian Trail History in Connecticut, Massachusetts, and Southern Vermont

By Benton MacKaye's time, a network of ridgetop trails had existed for decades in Connecticut, the Berkshires, on the Taconic crest, and in Vermont (the "Long Trail"). The Appalachian Mountain Club (AMC) was already almost 50 years old in 1921, when MacKaye conceived the AT (legend says he was atop Stratton Mt., now on the AT/Long Trail, in Vermont). The Green Mountain Club (GMC) in Vermont, founded in 1910, already had the jump in long-distance trail building, with the Long Trail an emerging reality by the time MacKaye thought of the Appalachian Trail. Thus the AMC and GMC had previously cut many of the trails at higher Massachusetts and Vermont elevations. But the trails were not yet linked. In 1928 in Massachusetts, the Berkshire Hills Conference (the tourism board) created a trail committee to push forward the work of joining the Berkshires to the Appalachian Trail in New York and Vermont. (Initially Connecticut was almost left out of the equation.) By 1930, the Long Trail was completed from Massachusetts to the Canadian border.

In the early decades of trail building in southern New England, as now, the problem was: which route to follow? In Massachusetts, for example, the logic of hiking over mounts Everett and Greylock was easy. Yet how to pass through the valleys and close to but not in too many Berkshire towns was less clear. Those who have used the trail for a long time realize that it is somewhat like a sand dune, always subject to subtle and not so subtle moves when erosion or storms or overuse damages the footpath and requires that a new one be cut through the forest. The work continues in the 1990s—for example in Sheffield, Massachusetts (issue: a railroad crossing), and near Killlington, Vermont (issue: ski trails).

Since 1949 the Connecticut chapter of the Appalachian Mountain Club has looked after Connecticut miles. The Berkshire chapter of the Appalachian Mountain Club, founded in 1979, nowadays maintains the trail in western Massachusetts. In Vermont, it's the venerable Green Mountain Club that oversees AT miles from the Massachusetts border to Vermont's Rte. 12, where the equally venerable Dartmouth Outing Club takes over and continues supervision well into New Hampshire. The Appalachian Trail Conference is the umbrella group over all the others, working in conjunction with the National Park Service. Volunteers are welcome and needed.

HIKE #1

Ten Mile River to Bull's Bridge

Maps: ATC Mass. & Conn. #5

Route: From NY/CT border over Ten Mile Hill, to junction of Ten Mile and Housatonic rivers, to Bull's Bridge

Recommended direction: S to N

Distance: 3.9 mi.

Elevation +/-: 400 to 1000 to 350 ft.

Effort: Easy

Day hike: Yes

Duration: 2 to 2½ hr.

Early exit option: None

Natural history features: Junction of two rivers; rapids and gorge

Social history features: Colonial-era covered bridge

Trailhead access: *From NY 22* just N of Wingdale (at Adams Diner), go E on NY 55 to Webatuck section. Watch for Hoyt Rd. on R. *From US 7* at Gaylordsville, go W on NY 55 about 3 mi. Watch for Hoyt Rd. on L.

Follow Hoyt Rd. 0.3 mi., park on R. Cross road and enter AT; head N.

Camping: Ten Mile River Lean-to; Ten Mile River group camping area

Here's a fine short hike for an early season warmup that can easily be combined with Hike #2 for a pleasant overnight outing. This section of the Connecticut AT is the southernmost in New England and the closest in New England proper to the New York metro area. From the city or Westchester County, it's an easy drive to the trailhead with plenty of time for a leisurely hike.

For a modest effort here, you'll see a lovely variety of landscapes. A modest climb will tax but not tire your muscles. Bring a picnic and plenty of water. There are good spots up high (with views), and there is the riverside for a lazy trailside lunch. As part of a longer trek (see Hike #2), this section offers excellent camping sites and a recently built shelter.

Enter the woods off Hoyt Rd., heading north, pick up a trail map from the hiker's info box (a minute up the trail), and look for any trail relocation notices posted here (hiking tip: always carry a pencil and a small notebook). This section (west of the Housatonic River) is maintained by the Connecticut chapter of the Appalachian Mt. Club.

The first mile wanders through woods and fields, still close to civilization. At 0.7 mi. the trail crosses NY 55; no parking here. Shortly the climb begins, never very steep but nonetheless steady. This is Ten Mile Hill, but fear not, you're not doing all ten of them! About midway up the hill (it's a broad, fairly smooth path), take a rest at a small overlook on the left. By now traffic sounds are gone and the feeling of escape from the busy valley below is taking hold. A sense of accomplishment also begins to grow.

With a full backpack, we reached the top of Ten Mile Hill in 50 min., having climbed 600 ft. in 1.8 mi. without pushing very hard. The forest is mixed hardwoods and hemlock throughout. At the top of the hill there are sweet views west into Dutchess County, New York, where the valley of NY 22 runs north-south. The descent is easy, unchallenging, about 30 min., bringing you to Ten Mile River (at 2.6 mi.) and a lovely section of trail on the river's edge.

Hemlocks predominate here, their accumulated needles making a soft bed for quiet walking (all the better to hear the river's music or birds' song). The trail briefly follows some old logging roads. When you first reach the river a tempting sandy spot says "Swim here!" But wait: it gets better. Five minutes along the riverside, a blue-blazed side trail at about 2.8 mi. leads gently uphill to a water supply, a privy, and the new Ten Mile River Lean-to, positioned at one end of a wide meadow, good for morning and evening wildlife watching (if your campmates will sit quietly with you). If you are tenting, carry on to 3.0 mi. and the Ten Mile River group camping area at the Ned Anderson Memorial Bridge.

The campsites are on both sides of the river, though the south side looks preferable for small parties (groups please use north-side campsites).

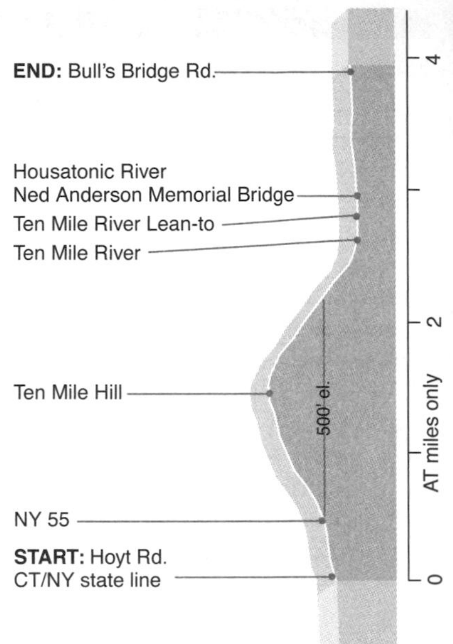

Hand-pumped water here is indicated as potable, a welcome convenience, as is the privy. The campground is likely to be busy. As you'll soon see, there is an easier way to get here. While the location is lovely, privacy and real quiet are unlikely here except off-season.

At the south end of the bridge is a fine sandy spot for both a picnic and a wade in the water. The view here encompasses both Ten Mile River and the Housatonic River, merging. While here, pay your respects to Ned Anderson, a tireless trail planner and builder in Connecticut (see the plaque on the south end of the bridge).

Just north of the bridge, ascend

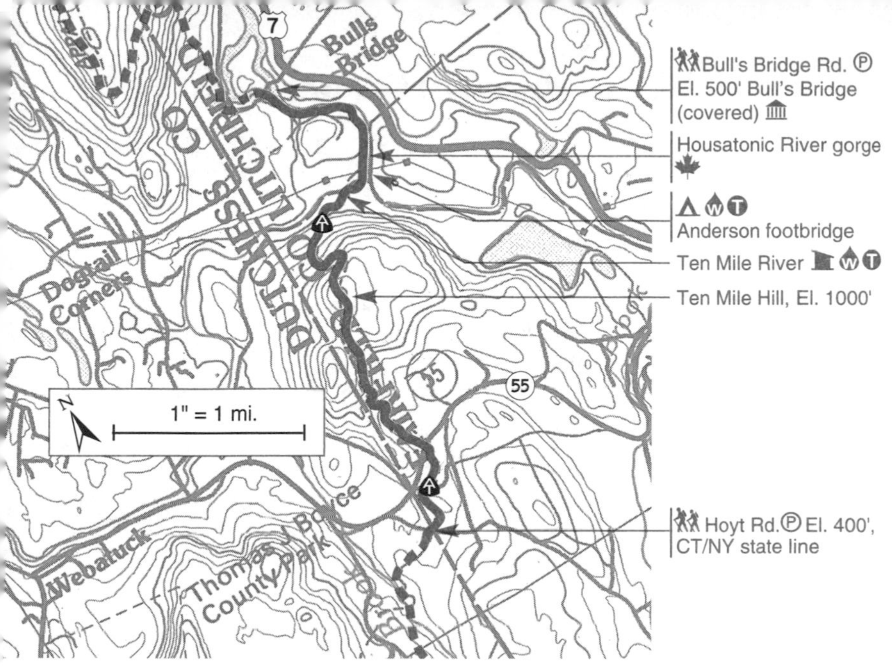

modestly, passing under high-tension electric wires, crackling and humming overhead. You decide: is the sound ominous or thrilling? The AT rises now to the high bank of the Housatonic River gorge, on your right and below. Numerous overlooks tempt the hiker here. Be careful, especially with children. The drop-off is unguarded and precipitous. The hemlock-soft ground underfoot can slip easily off the bedrock, just a few inches below the shallow topsoil. But do pause to enjoy views of the rapids and waterfalls below. The water's melodious music competes with the staccato hammering of pileated woodpeckers, high in the trees. In silent flight here, cruising the gorge (mostly inaccessible to people), was a large blue heron, its 40-in. wingspan beautifully displayed for us as we looked down on its blue-white-gray mottled plumage.

This AT section is a well-worn and wide trail (woods road, actually), running 0.9 mi. from the Anderson footbridge to the parking lot at Bull's Bridge Rd., your destination (3.9 mi. from the start). A second car can be positioned here. US 7 is 0.3 mi. east, at the village of Bull's Bridge. The market there offers short-term supplies and a telephone. Whether terminating here or carrying on, pause to see the charming historic covered bridge just east of the parking lot.

George Washington Rode Here

They say everybody loves a parade. They ought to have added "and a covered bridge." Bull's Bridge is one of three surviving in Connecticut. Only one other is open to traffic. The water below is the Housatonic River, rising near Pittsfield, Massachusetts, flowing to Long Island Sound near Bridgeport. Just upriver from the bridge is an outflow pipe from a hydroelectric dam. A waterfall and rapids, essentially under the bridge, make this a truly scenic spot, great for snapshots and geology enthusiasts. What's more, there's a story attached to the (reconstructed) bridge. En route from the Hudson Valley to Connecticut, none other than Gen. George Washington led his troops across this very bridge at least four times during the Revolutionary War. A perhaps aprocryphal footnote is that Washington lost a horse in the river crossing, though we prefer to think of the general as ever tall in the saddle.

Woodworkers and engineers, take note: much of the original joinery of Bull's Bridge has been preserved. Mortises and tenons, pegs in the timber frame, wide-board flooring—these and other details are worth your inspection.

David Emblidge

Bull's Bridge, Bulls Bridge, CT

One caution: it's a one-lane bridge, and on busy days auto traffic makes walking across rather dicey.

HIKE #1 Itinerary

Miles N	NORTH	Elev. (ft./m)	Miles S
3.9	**End: Bull's Bridge Rd.,** parking. AT turns L.	350/107	0.0
3.6	**Dirt road;** go straight.		0.3
3.1	**High-tension wires** overhead; keep Housatonic River bank on R.		0.8
3.0	**Anderson Memorial Bridge** over Ten Mile River; small campsites S side of river, group sites on N side; privy, pumped water S side.	300/92	0.9
2.8	**Ten Mile River Lean-to,** 0.1 mi. up spur trail, at meadow (privy, water).	325/99	1.1
2.6	**Ten Mile River,** turn R at bank.	300/92	1.3
2.3	Intermittent spring, R.		1.6
1.8	**Ten Mile Hill,** begin descent.	1000/305	2.1
0.7	**NY 55,** cross road (no parking).		3.2
0.0	**Start: Hoyt Rd.** (0.3 mi. N of NY 55). Southern terminus, CT section. CT/NY state line. Cross field, enter woods.	400/122	3.9

SOUTH

HIKE #2

Bull's Bridge to Kent

Maps: ATC Mass. & Conn. #5
Route: From Bull's Bridge Rd., to Schaghticoke Rd., to Schaghticoke Mt. and Mt. Algo Lean-to, to CT 341
Recommended direction: S to N
Distance: 7.6 mi.
Elevation +/-: 350 to 1300 to 364 ft.
Effort: Moderate
Day hike: Yes
Overnight backpacking hike: Optional
Duration: 4½ hr.
Early exit option: None
Social history features: Colonial-era covered bridge; Schaghticoke Indian Reservation
Trailhead access: *Start:* Bull's Bridge Rd., 0.3 mi. W of US 7 in Bull's Bridge village; park (overnight) here. *End:* CT 341, 0.8 mi. W of Kent; limited roadside overnight parking here.
Camping: Schaghticoke Mt. Campsite; Mt. Algo Lean-to and Campsite

A 10-min. road walk (west on Bull's Bridge Rd.) starts this hike and leads to a right turn onto Schaghticoke Rd. for another 5 min. See blazes on utility poles, and watch for oncoming traffic: Bull's Bridge (covered), just yards away, is a tourist attraction (see Hike #1).

At 0.3 mi. into Schaghticoke Rd., the AT turns left and heads uphill into the woods.

"Schaghticoke" (ska-ti-coke) means "the place where the river divides" in Mohegan, a Native American language. You are climbing Schaghticoke Mt. and soon will pass through a reservation by the same name. There are only a few Schaghticokes in Connecticut today, but they are politically active. (The Schaghticokes, originally part of the Pequots of eastern Massachusetts, are an Indian group distinct from the Mahicans of the Southern Berkshires.)

The trail follows numerous switchbacks over the next 2.8 mi. to the top of the mountain at 1300 ft. Though this is a Connecticut hike, the trail crosses the New York state border two times on the way up and on the way down, all on Schaghticoke Mt. You will have to keep a sharp eye out for the trail signs and markings indicating that you are crossing the border.

At about 1.9 to 2 mi. (1 hr. with full backpack), the AT reaches a height of land on the southern shoulder of Schaghticoke Mt., where you'll find a large rock outcropping and fine views to the south. White arrows and blazes on the rocks underfoot turn sharply north here. Take a rest, replenish liquids, or have lunch. You will be in the woods for some time to come. A good eye will pick out high-tension electric lines in the valley below (if you hiked from south of Bull's Bridge Rd., you will have walked under these wires; see Hike #1)—a convenient way to measure your progress visually.

Re-enter the woods. The AT skirts the east side of Schaghticoke Mt., following a gently undulating wide ridge. At 3.3 mi. from the start, see a marker for the state line (your last crossing). In another half mi. at 3.8 mi. (keep a lookout—you'll be moving swiftly here on an easy path), the viewpoint known as Indian Rocks appears. Road noise mars the view somewhat. This is a popular site for views east into the Housatonic River valley, and on busy weekends you may want to seek an alternative for some privacy. In this section of the trail there are numerous possibilities. Explore a little, but keep oriented to the main trail so as not to lose your way.

Rock hounds have a treat coming next. The descent begins sharply, and at 4.1 mi. the trail enters Dry Gulch, a small ravine all tumbled in on itself, with boulders deposited by the retreating glacier about 12,000 years ago. Indeed, many of these boulders would be technically described as "glacial erratics." The gulch may long ago have held water in a pond, when there was still some mountain up above it draining this way. But eons of erosion wore away the ancient watershed, and now Dry Gulch is just that.

The trail briefly rises steeply up and out of the gulch and then affords fine views of the valley below (east). Any of these ledges makes a good rest stop in preparation for the next bit of work. While you gaze into the valley, notice how thickly forested it is, with only scattered farms and houses. Church steeples pop up through the canopy of trees like herons' necks protruding above the tall grass. There was a time in the late 19th century when much of this forest was gone, stripped away for industrial use.

At 4.4 mi., a brook with a small tumbling cascade appears, and a blue-blazed side trail leads uphill (0.1 mi.) to the Schaghticoke Mt. Campsite, one of two overnight possibilities on this hike. Four tent sites, all surprisingly flat and clear of rocks, are well spaced through the woods. Water is generally available from the brook, though you may have to climb up or down a little to reach a sufficient flow. Beware of mossy, slippery rocks. The privy, at least as of summer 1996, was a sit-down toilet *sans* roof over your head, *sans* walls around you. Of dubious merit in the rain, but on our visit the blooming mountain laurel that formed a screen was pleasant to observe while . . .

Some highway noise from US 7 in the valley may disturb your ears at the campsite, but otherwise this spot is off the main thoroughfare. During a sustained rainstorm in June, we hunkered down here for 36 hr. and saw only one other camper. The Mt. Algo Lean-to, a few miles farther

Unfriendly Weather

Fact one: It will happen. Rule one: Be prepared. Get the best weather report you can in the twenty-four hours prior to your hike. Use the Weather Channel, NOAA (National Oceanic and Aeronautics Administration) on the weather radio band, or the newspaper. If the report calls for wet, windy, or cold weather, plan for it to be worse in the mountains and woods. If you get soaked in a downpour, keep a sharp lookout for signs of hypothermia (shivering, disorientation, anxiety, weakness). Wet and cold bring it on; fatigue, discouragement, and fear exacerbate it. Group leaders and hiking partners should watch fellow hikers for signs of hypothermia and take preventive steps (shelter, dry clothes, warm liquids, wrap in sleeping bag, reassurance).

Slipping or falling is another real danger in wet weather. Stay together, talk to one another, lend a hand. Keep focused on the slippery path beneath your feet. Many hikers find a walking stick especially helpful in adverse conditions. Keep your backpack load reasonable and properly balanced (see "Packing Your Pack," p. 21).

If a storm approaches (you should be watching the sky for thunderheads or general darkening, and listening to the wind in the trees or distant thunder), take the following steps:

- Get off mountaintops and exposed ledges. Go below treeline. The deep forest is safest (except directly under large standing dead trees).
- If an official campsite is near, try to get there; set up and take shelter. If not, find a level, well-drained place and set up your tent (you should have rehearsed at home so this takes only minutes even in a stiff breeze or fading light). Position the door away from the approaching storm.
- In fog, darkness, or howling wind,

north, was full to capacity in the same period, we were told. The moral of the story, here as elsewhere along the AT, especially in peak traffic times: carry a tent and seek out some of the less-well-known campsites. Usually you'll end up with room to spare and no strangers snoring in your ear.

Continuing north from the brook, the AT makes a mild ascent over the next 0.8 mi. Then you'll begin to notice numerous viewpoints to the east. At 5.5 mi. from the start, the AT crosses the high point on Schaghticoke Mt.—but it's not the mountain's top, only the trail's high point. Schaghticoke has no prominent peak; it's more like the humped, bony carapace of a sleeping dinosaur. Though US 7's incessant drone may distract you, in fact there is plenty of wildlife to see and listen to up here. A white-tailed deer stunned us as

confusion is easy. Avoid it by carrying a compass and a topo map with the trails well marked. Know where you are at all times.

- Once inside your tent, take inventory. Know where dry clothes, food, light, toiletries, and your first-aid kit are. If you have wet feet or hair, dry off the best you can. Keep your sleeping pad and sleeping bag dry.
- Make a plan: What can you eat without cooking over a stove? If your tent has a vestibule, you may be able to use a stove (with a windshield) at its outer perimeter, but never light a stove inside your tent.
- Before dark, decide how you will handle a run to the privy or pit toilet (keep your camp shovel handy, keep toilet paper dry, and keep a self-seal plastic bag handy, too), and how you will hang your food bag outdoors overnight out of the reach of bears (see "Food Storage," p. 17).

After you have made all these commonsense preparations for storm survival, the fun begins. Indulge in a long nap, or sleep a long night through. Write in your journal, taking time for details, even poetry. Read by daylight (did you pack a lightweight paperback?) or briefly by candlelight (in a safe, protective candle holder, never an open flame in a tent) or by flashlight (but conserve batteries). Play word games, sing songs, tell tall tales, re-engineer society, resolve a philosophical dilemma, or just listen to the music of the storm outside, which may be as delicate as a vibraphone or as muscular as the timpani. Imagine the music is nature's performance for you.

You may be in for a long day or night in the tent. Study your trail guide. Reconsider goals. Look for alternative early exit routes. If you are the leader, keep your own counsel and do not spread anger or anxiety. Patience, calm, good humor, and a plan will see you through most any bad weather. Survival, in good form, makes a great story back home.

it exploded out of brambles and bounded away through more branches, as though absolutely certain of its course. A pileated woodpecker hammered high in the treetops like a percussionist rehearsing some staccato measures.

Two or three smallish brooks appear before the larger but unmarked Thayer Brook (at 6.3 mi., about 1.5 hr. from the campsite).

At this point on our hike we encountered Jessica Brown, a Wellesley College student and Appalachian Mt. Club "ridgerunner." She was checking the section from CT 341 southward, having been holed up with the crowd in the heavy rain the day and night before at the Mt. Algo Lean-to. Garbage bag in hand (in case any hikers had left things behind at the campsite), she also carried a cell phone and showed us how our isolation in the woods could turn, electronically, into an ordinary day at the office (in her case, the AMC Berkshire County office on Mt. Greylock in northern Massachusetts, about 70 mi. distant).

Following Thayer Brook, the trail rises to another high point (but not a mountain peak), this time on Mt. Algo. There are more viewpoints and then a rapid descent through mountain laurel and what on a bright day would be lovely sun-dappled woods. The Mt. Algo Lean-to side trail appears prominently at 7.3 mi. A standard lean-to, Mt. Algo offers plenty of water at a brook only steps away, a good privy, several tent sites, almost guaranteed company, and a quick exit to the highway (CT 341, only 0.3 mi. farther on). Some would say this proximity to the road makes Mt. Algo too easy for unwanted visitors to reach; nonetheless, it's a spacious, well-maintained site.

Minutes later, you step out of the shady woods onto the pavement, at hike's end. If you have time, head into Kent, 0.8 mi. east, for some of its numerous pleasures and services.

Long-distance hikers will do well to reprovision at the Davis IGA in Kent. It's a hiker-friendly town. The presence of the Kent School, a private boarding school, gives the town a somewhat preppy feeling, and the tide of visiting New Yorkers brings on the yuppie influence (boutiques, a coffeehouse), but if all this appeals, or you can stomach it, Kent will not disappoint. Recommendations: the Kent Coffee & Chocolate Co., House of Books (good hiking and local history sections), Stroble Baking Co., Stosh's Ice Cream—all on Main St. (US 7).

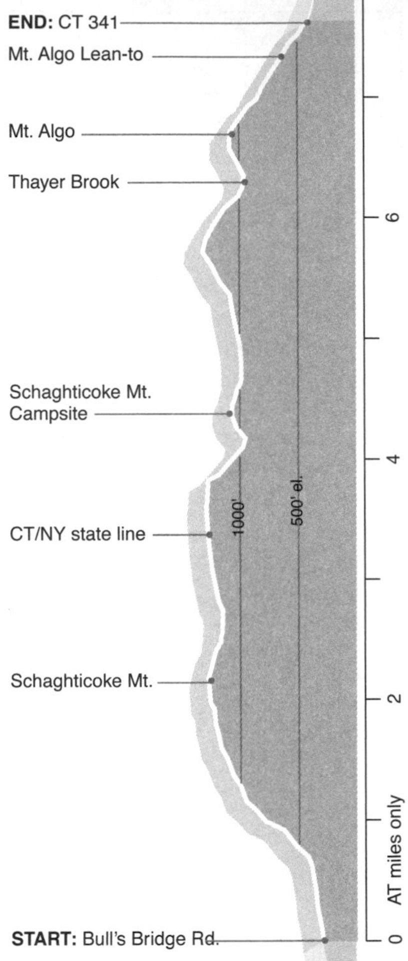

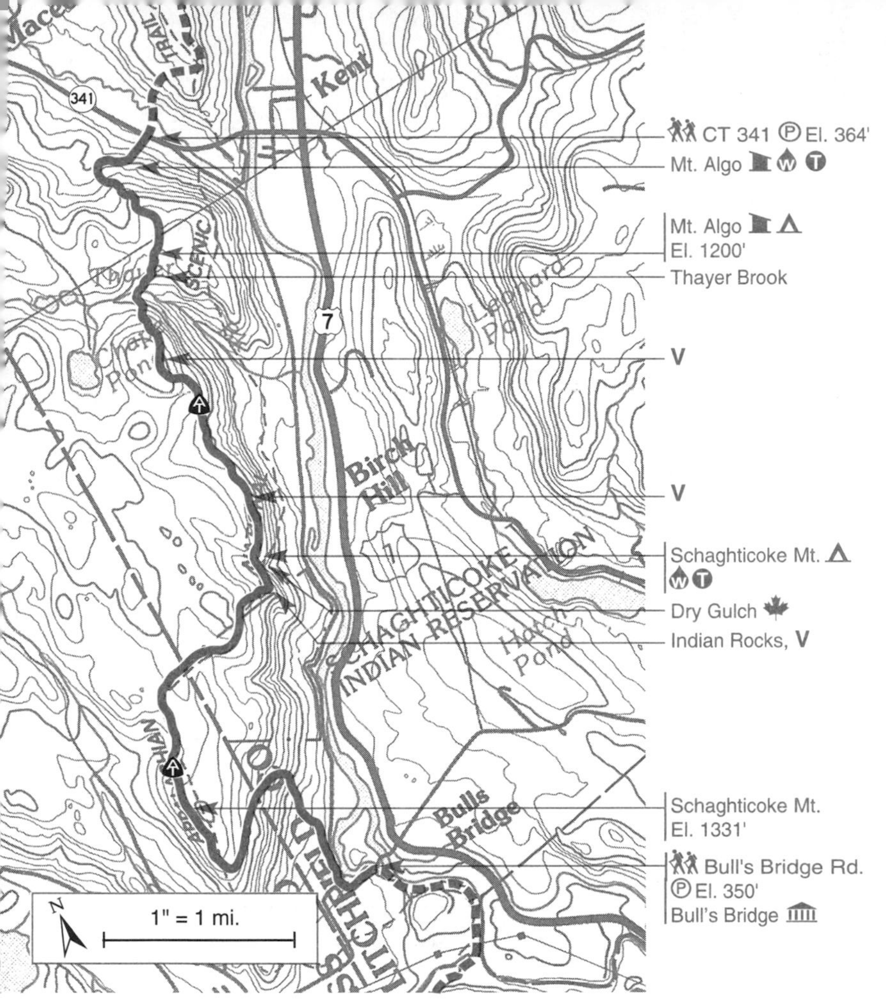

Kent
341
TRAIL
SCENIC
7
Birch Hill
SCHAGHTICOKE INDIAN RESERVATION
Hatch Pond
Bulls Bridge
N
1" = 1 mi.
CT 341 Ⓟ El. 364'
Mt. Algo
Mt. Algo
El. 1200'
Thayer Brook
V
V
Schaghticoke Mt.
Dry Gulch
Indian Rocks, V
Schaghticoke Mt.
El. 1331'
Bull's Bridge Rd.
Ⓟ El. 350'
Bull's Bridge

Hike #2 Itinerary

Miles N	NORTH	Elev. (ft./m)	Miles S
7.6	**End: CT 341,** parking	364/111	0.0
7.3	**Mt. Algo Lean-to,** short spur trail, L; reliable water, privy.	650/198	0.3
6.7	Crest of **Mt. Algo,** wooded.	1200/366	0.9
6.3	**Thayer Brook,** then climb.	900/274	1.3
5.5	**Crest of trail,** wooded.	1300/396	2.1
4.4	**Schaghticoke Mt. Campsite** spur trail, L, heading uphill (0.1 mi.); brook (reliable water), open-air privy.	1100/335	3.2
4.1	**Dry Gulch,** a ravine; then up sharply to ridge top (view), and quick descent.		3.5
3.8	**Indian Rocks** overlook; then steep descent going E.		3.8
3.3	**Cross NY/CT state line** for 2nd (final) time (see special blaze on rocks).	1300/396	3.9
0.5	**Enter forest,** L, and climb gradually during next 2.8 mi., using switchbacks, to Schaghticoke Mt. overlooks to E.		7.1
0.2	**Schaghticoke Rd.,** turn R (N).		7.4
0.0	**Start: Bull's Bridge,** W side, 0.3 mi. W of US 7. Parking (overnight). AT follows Bull's Bridge Rd. W.	350/107	7.6

SOUTH

HIKE #3

Kent to St. Johns Ledges

Maps: ATC Mass. & Conn. #5
Route: From CT 341, Kent, over Fuller Mt. and Caleb's Peak to River Rd., North Kent
Recommended direction: S to N
Distance: 4.9 mi.
Elevation +/-: 364 to 1100 to 450 ft.
Effort: Moderate, with steep descent at end
Day hike: Yes
Duration: 3½ to 4½ hr.
Early exit option: None
Natural history features: Extraordinary geology (rock-climbing opportunity)
Trailhead access: *Start:* CT 341 crosses the AT 0.8 mi. W of Kent; limited overnight parking here. *End:* From US 7 and CT 341 in Kent, go W on CT 341, cross Housatonic River, turn R immediately onto River Rd. (Kent School athletic fields on your L) and follow for 3 mi., keeping river directly on R, to AT parking (day/overnight).

As a day hike this is a gem, with a superb reward at the end in the form of a tremendous tumble of boulders down a precipitous but manageable cliff. Thrills and chills without having to scale the Matterhorn. If you're walking north, gravity will be your friend.

Squeeze through the stile at CT 341, paying attention to the barbed wire (decidedly unfriendly to full backpacks). If the field is flooded, use the bypass trail, blue blazed, 0.3 mi. east on CT 341. Otherwise, welcome to a cow pasture. If the cattle are on the trail, give them a wide berth; this is their home you're visiting. Pay heed to cow flops on the trail or grass. Not only are they a mess to clean off your lugged boots, they're slippery too. Views east and west in the CT 341 valley are sweet. Enjoy the breeze, sunshine, and wildflowers here; the dark and quieter woods will swallow you soon.

Serpentine Macedonia Brook meanders through the pasture. Do not drink the water (or any water with livestock nearby); treat it chemically (iodine) or filter it if you must refill here. Up the trail goes, somewhat steeply for 10 min. or so (use caution here on wet rocks), then more gently into the forest, and the sense of pleasant quietness begins. At 0.7 mi. note the junction with the former AT (it's here that the bypass trail circumventing a flooded Macedonia Brook enters the current AT). The bypass, if taken east from here, leads to Numeral Rock, a popular overlook for Kent area residents and Kent School students.

The first 30 min. of forest walking provide cool shade and a soft bed of

Dale Gelfand

Downy woodpecker

hemlock needles underfoot. Eventually the forest is more mixed, with hardwoods becoming more common. A good stretch for a walk and talk; fine for small kids once they're past the initial climb. Recently blazed and very easy to follow.

On a sunny day, a 12-year-old companion said, "Hey, it's raining!" And it did sound that way up in the leaves and at our feet as large "drops" pelted everything in sight, but not with water. This was a shower of nuts from a grove of American beech trees, with their telltale sawtooth-edged leaves. The nuts in their casings, green as scallions, are sent out into the world to be fruitful and multiply by the exuberant breeze high in the treetops. Black bears are fond of these nuts. We scanned the perimeter of the trail for bear scat but saw none (see "Berkshire Bruins" in Hike #16). One spindly, leaping faun, speckled brown and white and looking too young to be grazing alone, was entertainment enough, however.

Periodically during the first 2.5 mi. of this hike there are overlooks (right) into the Housatonic valley. But press onward—the better viewpoints are still to come. Choggam Brook (a three-stranded watercourse, none of them wide) appears at 2.8 mi., about 1¾ hr. into the hike. The brook may be dry late in the season. Another 0.1 mi. brings you to the Skiff Mt. Rd. crossing (no parking), and then a few minutes of noticeable climbing. By 3.1 mi. great views, worth waiting for, are yours off the east (right) side of the AT.

Caleb's Peak (1160 ft.), with large rock outcroppings dressed in gorgeous lichens, is a fine destination for a rest or a picnic, offering the broadest panorama yet on this hike. We dined in style here and didn't have to tip the maître d' for a table with a view. The Housatonic valley below is busy with traffic and village life, but you would never know it from here. The peak is at 3.7 mi., which we reached after 2¾ hr. The curiosity of a young companion is well worth indulging along the way, though it does slow the pace somewhat. The river winds its lazy way through the long, leafy valley to the south, and white church steeples mark the centers of villages hidden by summer's green canopy. You're looking south toward Kent.

What immortal hand?

"What immortal hand or eye, / could frame thy fearful symmetry?" asked William Blake in his famous poem "The Tyger" (1794), and you might pose the same philosophical question when descending or ascending the rock outcroppings of St. Johns Ledges in North Kent. Geologist Michael Bell says the history of Connecticut's landform can be subsumed in one word: crunch. The third smallest state in the Union was once a territory perhaps thousands of miles wide. We have the collisions of continental tectonic plates to thank for the "crunch" that forced the land into mountains. Hundreds of millions of years passed while the continents and oceans formed and re-formed themselves into what resembles our world today. Here is Bell's summary of the geologic history of Connecticut.

*Much has happened between that time [500 million years ago] and this to redraw geography into today's world, and Connecticut was in the thick of the action. Current geologic thought places Connecticut in the midst of a collision in which all the world's early continents united into a single land mass. Geologists refer to this supercontinent as "Pangea" (from the Greek for "all-lands"). The collision closed the Iapetos [the ocean preceding the Atlantic] with a mighty crunch, and by about 250 million years ago a great weld had formed between the continents, with Avalonia [ancient islands off proto–North America's shore] for solder and sediments from the floor of the Iapetos Ocean for flux. The supercontinent held together for only a relatively short time, and about 200 million years ago Pangea began breaking apart. Many great cracks opened in the weld zone, vying for the right to form a new ocean. Eventually, one crack won out over the others and widened into Atlas's Atlantic Ocean ["Atlantic" is derived from "Atlas"], separating once again Europe, Africa, and North America. Remnants of the weld remain stuck to the edges of the renewed continents. Connecticut is one such remnant; what we now call Connecticut reaches from the edge of the early North American continent, across some sorry scrinched remains of the Iapetos ocean floor, and over to a chunk of Avalonia. Depending on how far offshore our particular Avalonian Japan was, Connecticut may once have been 500 to 3000 miles across. Today it spans about 100 miles.**

The rest, as they say, is history — that is, the history of erosion by wind and water, and grating and scoring by the advancing and retreating glaciers, which created the rivers and lakes we have today.

---

*From *The Face of Connecticut: People, Geology, and the Land,* by Michael Bell. Connecticut Geological Survey, 1985.

Now gravity becomes an ally again, as the descent begins, steeply at first off Caleb's Peak, stepping down ledge after ledge for 0.2 mi. A relatively level section follows, and at 4.1 mi. the trail rises again, though not severely, to reach the top of St. Johns Ledges at 4.3 mi., again with a fine viewpoint over the valley. Both adults and kids must be careful here. The drop-off is precipitous. There are no guardrails.

Pause here and consider how you would negotiate the descent if you were an explorer, hunter, surveyor, or serious rock climber. Give thanks to the trail builders who came before you, and be glad you're not coming *up* this way with a 50-lb. backpack. Continue north on the AT, along the edge, about 300 ft., then over the lip and down a remarkable set of roughly hewn "steps," some magically natural and many levered into place by a muscular trail crew from New Hampshire's White Mts.—where this 500-ft. drop-off might be considered a hop, skip, and jump. On the way down let yourself feel overwhelmed by the gigantic size of the heaped-together boulders that comprise the hillside. The rocks are large enough to shut the sunlight out of your day.

Near the bottom of St. Johns Ledges (named for an 18th-century landowner nearby), the woods finally slopes gently off to the right, toward the river, and the rock face smoothes out to form a kind of vertical carapace for the mountain. In cooler weather, when the rock face

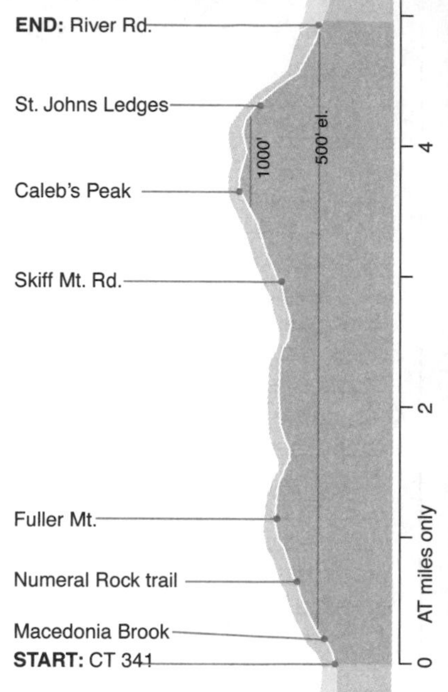

won't overheat unpleasantly, you are likely to find rock climbers clambering up this smooth face, grasping for whatever niche or notch their toes or fingers can grab. Do not try this without proper equipment or experienced guidance.

At 4.9 mi., after a concluding stroll through woods toward the river, the parking lot at River Rd. appears. We arrived after about 4½ hr., including the lunch stop. To return to your origination point, go right (south) on River Rd. The AT turns left (north) here.

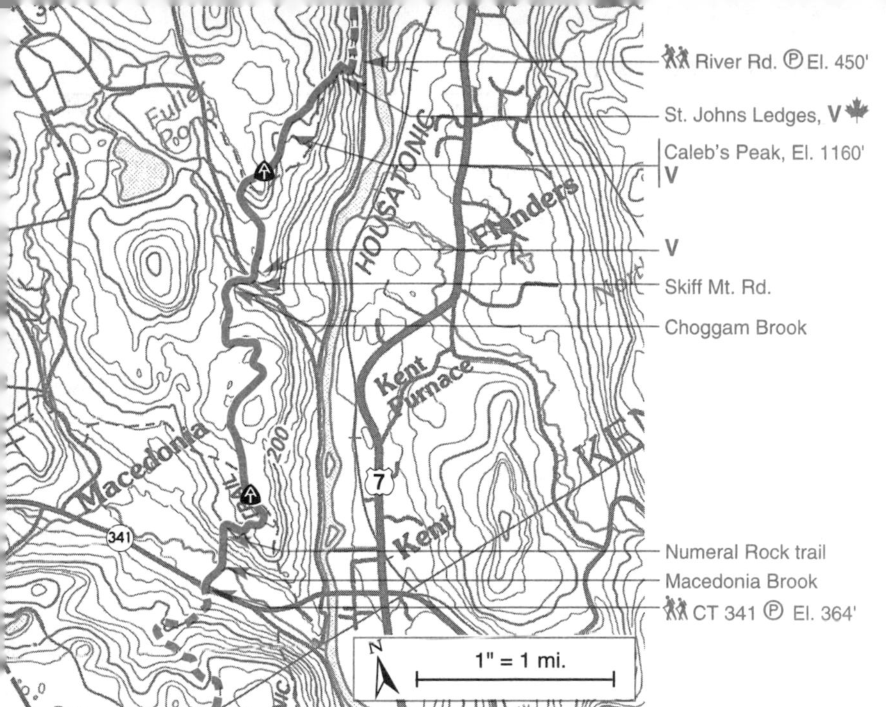
River Rd. Ⓟ El. 450'
St. Johns Ledges, V
Caleb's Peak, El. 1160'
V
V
Skiff Mt. Rd.
Choggam Brook
Numeral Rock trail
Macedonia Brook
CT 341 Ⓟ El. 364'
1" = 1 mi.
N
Fuller Pond
HOUSATONIC
Flanders
Kent Furnace
Macedonia
Kent
341
7
200

Hike #3 Itinerary

Miles N	NORTH	Elev. (ft./m)	Miles S
4.9	**End: River Rd.,** parking (overnight).	450/137	0.0
4.3	**Top of St. Johns Ledges,** severe precipice, exercise caution; fine views of Housatonic River valley. Follow ledge straight for 300 ft., then descend (steeply, 450 ft.) on series of rock steps. AT turns L at bottom, following foot of ledges.	900/274	0.6
4.1	Ascend again in forest.		0.8
3.9	**Rock steps,** descending from ledge; trail levels out.		1.0
3.7	**Caleb's Peak,** good views, then sharp descent on switchbacks.	1160/354	1.2
3.1	**Overlook,** Housatonic River valley.		1.8
2.9	**Skiff Mt. Rd.,** paved, no parking.	800/244	2.0
2.8	**Choggam Brook,** unreliable water late in summer.		2.1
0.9	**Overlook,** L: Housatonic valley, village of Kent.		4.0
0.7	**Trail junction:** former AT, on R (leads short distance to Numeral Rock overlook); end of flood bypass trail.	750/229	4.2
0.2	**Macedonia Brook,** log bridge.		4.7
0.0	**Start: CT 341** (day/overnight parking), N side, enter pasture through stile. Flood conditions: use blue-blazed bypass trail 0.3 mi. E.	364/111	4.9

SOUTH

HIKE #4

Housatonic River Walk

Maps: ATC Mass. & Conn. #5

Route: From River Rd., North Kent, to River Rd., Cornwall Bridge

Recommended direction: S to N (described here) or N to S

Distance: 4.8 mi.

Elevation +/-: 400–450 ft. all the way

Effort: Easy

Day hike: Yes

Overnight backpacking hike: Optional

Duration: 2½ hr.

Early exit option: None

Natural history features: River floodplain and rapids; pine blight

Trailhead access: *Start:* From US 7 and CT 341 in Kent, go W on CT 341, cross Housatonic River, turn R immediately onto River Rd. (Kent School athletic fields on your L), and follow for 3 mi., keeping river directly on R, to AT parking (day/overnight). *End:* AT parking (day/overnight) at Swift's Bridge, 1.5 mi. W of Cornwall Bridge (village) on River Rd.

Camping: Stewart Hollow Brook Shelter and Campsite; Stony Brook Campsite

The Housatonic "river walk" is virtually unique on the AT, probably the longest essentially flat section anywhere between Georgia and Maine (except on roads), affording excellent opportunities to enjoy the river's music and abundant wildlife (some of the latter in the form of white-water kayakers who slip by in the rapids, whooping it up). If you have just come down from the hills to the south or north of this section, your load-weary knees will find welcome relief on the broad, generally stoneless path (an old farming road), and your hamstrings, too, will welcome the stretch that comes with a lengthened stride. This is a good hike on which to time yourself to set your normal rate of speed "on the flat."

For a south-to-north stroll: Starting at the base of St. Johns Ledges, the AT follows River Rd. itself (unpaved) for the first 0.9 mi. You could drive this distance to park temporarily at the road's end, but this is discouraged. Several dirt roads branch off, right, toward the river to sites popular for anglers. In dry conditions some of these riverside sites may be suitable for picnics; camping, however, is not allowed. At 0.6 mi. the road crosses Mount Brook, and at 0.9 mi. the driveable road ends. At this point note the foundations of the North Kent (or Flanders) Bridge, washed away in a 1936 flood.

The original Appalachian Trail crossed the river here and meandered through Connecticut state

Sloane-Stanley Museum and Kent Iron Works

Appalachian Trail hikers are walking through a second-growth forest. Where did the first-growth trees go? The hills of Connecticut (and Massachusetts) were virtually stripped bare to meet the demands of the iron-making and shipbuilding industries in the 17th, 18th, and 19th centuries. Vast quantities of hardwood charcoal fueled the heat-hungry iron-making process. Furnaces burned twenty-four hours a day, weeks at a time. Tree felling created open farmland that until the post–WW II era continued to produce handsomely.

Local geology provided essential ingredients for the furnace: iron ore and flux, a dark gabbro rock containing calcium carbonate (to separate the iron ore from other earthy elements). Mountain streams powered sawmills and all manner of other industrial sites. Iron mining in New England began near the coast at Saugus, Massachusetts, in the late 1640s and spread within a generation to Connecticut and Rhode Island. Kent's iron furnace functioned from 1826 into the 1890s. Among its claims to fame were the iron sheets used on the hulls of the *Merrimac* and the *Monitor,* fighting ships in the Confederate and Union navies respectively during the Civil War.

In the furnace, raw pig iron, mined nearby, turned to liquid under high heat and was cast into long bars (sows). In a forge on the same site, brittle cast iron was hammered into malleable wrought-iron bars. These could be split and shaped into useful objects: nails, machine parts, domestic hardware, farm tools. Slag, the waste product of iron making, was dumped into nearby pits and rivers. Working conditions were dangerous and exhausting. Colliers and blacksmiths, among the strongest of men, were also the most frequently burned and injured.

Connecticut artist, writer, and antique tool collector Eric Sloane donated his extraordinary collection of early American industrial and agricultural tools to this museum, sponsored by Stanley Tool Works of Connecticut and by the state. (The Stanley Co. owned the river walk area of the AT by the Housatonic and sold it to the National Park Service.) Many of Sloane's finest paintings of barns and tools are also on display. A scale model of the iron furnace and samples of the raw pig iron give a good sense of the process. Ruins of the furnace are down the hill behind the museum. Eventually the old millrace will be cleared, exposing the full dimensions of the iron furnace operation. The museum, just north of Kent, is beautifully situated, good for picnics. It's open from mid-May to October; call 860-927-3849 for information.

parks on the east side of the valley, reaching Kent Falls and Mohawk Mt. Some of those trail miles are now part of the Mohawk Trail and can be used for extended loop hikes with good backpacking and camping options. See "Useful Information" for information about maps.

We walked here a day after Hurricane Bertha's rainy aftermath swept over southern New England in July 1996. The river was moiling, churned a rich hot-chocolate brown by the vast amount of silt washed down the brooks from the hills. Normally gentle rapids were in a fury, and at many points the river flowed over its banks. Fragile summer wildflowers clung for dear life beneath the rushing waters, no doubt thinking unkind thoughts about Bertha. The river's tumultuous energy made for an exciting walk.

A barrier marks the end of the official road, but the walk continues on a roadbed beyond the barrier. At 1.6 mi. a mowed field appears, left, with remains of an old farmhouse foundation. The trail meanders through a (dead) pine plantation, the trees being victims of red pine scale. Out of the jumble of fallen and cut pine trees arises new life. Trailside we found abundant red raspberries and the inedible but cheerfully red berries of honeysuckle. Birds go with berries, and so the discouragement of the dying pines is mitigated by an abundance of birds in this section (and along the river's edge, where red-winged blackbirds, startling us by bursting from bushes, are common).

David Emblidge

Creeping bellflower

Zipping or lollygagging along, you'll soon come to the side trail for Stewart Hollow Brook Shelter (2.4 mi.), which we hit after a brisk hour's walking. The brook is sufficient for a cool splash on the face, but it is not a reliable water supply (and the Housatonic itself is generally too muddy and in any case suffers from chemical pollutants). For more reliable water, go north a few moments to the next stream. The shelter, a bit smaller than most and offering no view of the river, is a typical lean-to, built with some of the dying pine trees. There are several good tent sites closer to the river. A privy stands nearby. Stewart Hollow is one of two fine options for an overnight stay on the AT during this short hike.

The trail is so smooth and easy all along here that families with little kid hikers, elderly walkers, or adventurous handicapped people can give it a try. If the older or more ambulatory people try this walk themselves first, they will know what to expect. This section is owned by the National Park Service, to whom we owe thanks for preserving it from development. The only drawback is road noise from just across the river, where US 7 skirts the riverside. The highway is the transportation spine of extreme western New England, from Long Island Sound to Canada. The AT crosses US 7 several times. It's your friend, leading to society and supplies, as well as your nemesis, buzzing in your ear.

Along here from morning through at least midafternoon, there is a nice mix of sunshine and shadow, and thus a mix of wildflowers and mossy places. We spotted bumblebees aggressively at work on the open and as-yet-unopened flowers of creeping bellflower, a non-native plant with stunning purplish-blue five-lobbed nodding bells (see p. 47). Though many gardeners curse this "most insatiable and irrepressible of beautiful weeds,"* we found it handsome and worth pausing to photograph at trailside. Often bellflower is a sign of nearby domesticity, and indeed just uphill from the riverbed we noted ancient remains of early foundations, a farmhouse and barn themselves long gone fallow and to

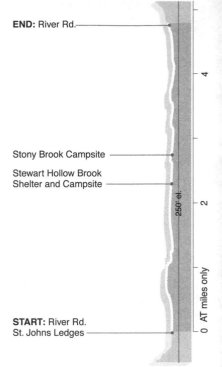

END: River Rd.

Stony Brook Campsite

Stewart Hollow Brook Shelter and Campsite

250' el.

START: River Rd. St. Johns Ledges

0 AT miles only 2 4

seed. Folk legend has it that bellflower was used in Russia to treat hydrophobia. How convenient then to have it blooming in abundance at the river's edge.

While dawdling with our flower book, we heard the familiar honking of Canada geese and looked skyward for the equally familiar flying V-formation. Nowhere to be seen, yet the honking came nearer and intensified. Puzzled, we went back to the flowers and, bending over them, almost at water level, caught from

---

Reginald Farrar, Victorian plant collector, quoted in Strauch, *Wildflowers of the Berkshire & Taconic Hills*, p. 99.

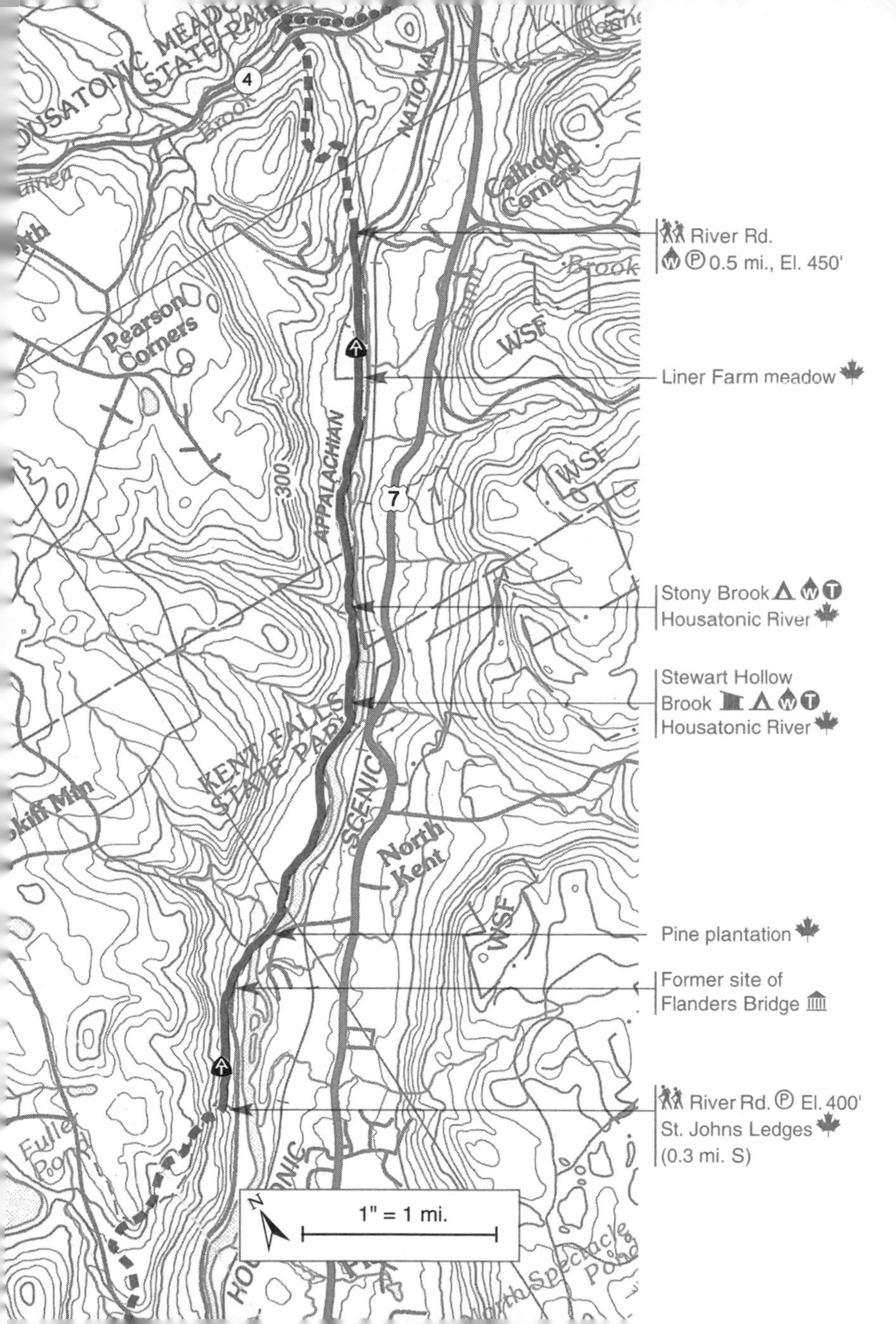

HOUSATONIC MEADOWS STATE PARK
4
Brook
NATIONAL
Calhoun Corners
River Rd.
0.5 mi., El. 450'
Brook
Pearson Corners
WSF
Liner Farm meadow
APPALACHIAN
300
7
WSF
Stony Brook
Housatonic River
Stewart Hollow
Brook
Housatonic River
KENT FALLS STATE PARK
SCENIC
North Kent
WSF
Pine plantation
Former site of
Flanders Bridge
River Rd. El. 400'
St. Johns Ledges
(0.3 mi. S)
Fuller Pond
1" = 1 mi.
N
North Spectacle Pond

the corner of an eye a hilarious sight: a *floating* V-formation, made somewhat ragged by the turmoil of the rapids but a V nonetheless, as a flock of happy geese rode the waves down the river, rafting as it were for whitewater entertainment. Who had this neat idea first? Geese or people?

A mere 0.4 mi. north beyond Stewart Hollow is Stony Brook Campsite (at 2.8 mi.), which we would prefer if tenting (there is no shelter). The tent sites are uphill away from the river, but beautifully situated with respect to the brook. Reliable water, a privy, interesting stone remains of what may have been a mill in the brook's miniature gorge, and a generally sweet setting make this site a tenting option worth waiting for. Group camping at Stony Brook is just slightly farther north.

Another 2 mi. of river walk await you, though the landscape changes little as the trail progresses northward. Handsome stone walls lace the woods rising up from the river (pastured animals would not have been allowed to wander accidentally into the Housatonic, which might easily sweep them away). The old farms are long overgrown with woods by now, but this walk comes toward its end by stepping up a few feet from the river's edge to the hayfield and meadow of the still active Liner Farm for a fine half mile or so with broad views of the hills to the west.

At 4.8 mi. the AT crosses River Rd., your destination on this hike. A piped spring here provides reliable water. We arrived after 2¾ hr. from the start and wished we had slowed the pace considerably to prolong the fun. Turn right and follow the dirt road for a short distance to the AT parking lot. From there it is 1.5 mi. east to Cornwall Bridge.

HIKE #4 Itinerary

Miles N	NORTH	Elev. (ft./m)	Miles S
4.8	**End: River Rd.,** piped spring a few yards N on road (on AT); trail continues steeply uphill; go R to parking (day/overnight) at Swift's Bridge (village of Cornwall Bridge is 1.5 mi. E).	450/137	0.0
4.4	**Liner Farm,** fields and meadow, AT veers L, slightly uphill from river.		0.4
2.8	**Stony Brook,** tent sites, dependable water, privy nearby gently uphill.		2.0
2.4	**Stewart Hollow Brook,** shelter, tent sites, privy uphill about 0.1 mi.		2.4
1.6	**Open field,** L, foundations; enter pine plantation.		3.2
0.9	**End of town road;** barrier; day parking; former site of Flanders or North Kent Bridge (destroyed by flood, 1936); AT uses abandoned road continuing N along river.		3.7
0.6	**Mount Brook.**		4.2
0.0	**Start: River Rd.,** AT parking (overnight); head N following road parallel to river. CT 341 is 3 mi. S on River Rd.	400/122	4.8

SOUTH

HIKE #5

Silver Hill and Pine Knob Loop Trail

Maps: ATC Mass. & Conn. #4

Route: From Housatonic River valley (Cornwall Bridge) up to ridge and Silver Hill Campsite, up Breadloaf Mt., to ridge above Housatonic Meadows State Park, to N junction with Pine Knob Loop Trail; to US 7

Recommended direction: S to N (described here) or N to S

Distance: 4.7 mi.; 4.2 mi. on AT

Access trail name & length: Pine Knob Loop Trail, 0.5 mi.

Elevation +/-: 450 to 1200 to approx. 500 ft.

Effort: Easy to moderate (two steep sections)

Day hike: Yes

Overnight backpacking hike: Optional

Duration: 3 hr.

Early exit options: CT 4 at 1.8 mi. (emergency only); Breadloaf Mt. Trail at 2.1 mi.

Natural history features: Guinea Brook; Housatonic River

Other features: Recreation access to Housatonic River—fishing, canoeing, kayaking, car camping, all at Housatonic Meadows State Park on US 7. Also, access to the blue-blazed Mohawk Trail, formerly the AT, which runs E of the Housatonic River from Cornwall Bridge N to Falls Village, making a 24-mi. loop hike using the old and new ATs. For Mohawk Trail details, see *Connecticut Walk Book,* Connecticut Forest & Park Assoc.

Trailhead access: *Start:* In Cornwall Bridge, from W side of Housatonic River, follow unpaved River Rd. S 1.5 mi. to AMC parking (day/overnight) at site of Swift's Bridge (washed out in 1936); AT is a few moments' walk farther on River Rd.; at crossing, AT turns R (N, uphill). *End:* From US 7 / CT 4 bridge over Housatonic River at Cornwall Bridge, go N on US 7 about 1.1 mi. to parking lot (day only) for Pine Knob Loop Trail, W side of US 7 (overnight parking may be arranged with ranger at Housatonic Meadows State Park).

Camping: Silver Hill Campsite (tent sites plus pavilion); car camping at Housatonic Meadows State Park (reservations 860-424-3200)

Here's a short hike without much up and down (though two brief climbs will have you puffing) that can serve those who happen to be in the Cornwall Bridge area or are car camping at Housatonic Meadows State Park. Two cars are required.

The village of Cornwall Bridge and environs are rife with distracting weekender activities: antiques, boutiques, galleries, and country restaurants. Fly-fishing, canoeing, and kayaking are popular in the Housatonic River here. And so this AT hike can easily be combined with other activities.

Caution: though Hike #5 is a short walk with only modest elevation gains, the path *is* rocky and can be slippery. Wear hiking boots, not street shoes. Bring extra socks (there are *four* brook crossings).

Heading north: At the AT trailhead on gravel River Rd., a piped spring awaits you a few yards north of this crossing. Fill your water bottle. The first leg of the hike is steeply uphill as the trail ascends the ridge on the west side of the Housatonic Valley. Switchbacks help during the climb of 400–500 ft. over 0.8 mi. to Silver Hill Campsite (spur trail, right; keep a sharp lookout for the trail sign—there's no obvious landmark).

The campsite will surprise and may delight you. Its broad over-the-valley view opens onto a breezy hillside looking south and east above the winding Housatonic River. There is hand-pumped potable water from a well—cold and refreshing—but some muscle and, apparently, three hands are needed to manage the pump handle *plus* a tipsy water bottle. Now you see why widemouthed water bottles are recommended. In 1991 the original shelter burned down. The site, managed by the Con-

Michael Warren

Housatonic Valley, Breadloaf Mt., and Silver Hill from Pine Knob, above Cornwall Bridge

Three Forests in One Region

At elevations such as these (about 1000 ft.), we are in the "transition forest" between the "boreal forest" of colder regions (much higher or much farther north) and the "mixed deciduous forest" of warmer areas. The transition forest combines conifers and deciduous trees, the latter liking the longer growing season. There's more sunlight in this forest than in its northern, colder counterpart, and thus the forest floor is drier (due to evaporation) and has a richer understory of shrubs, flowers, smaller trees, and other plants. "Drier" and "richer" are relative terms, and on the north side of some mountains in the transition forest, there are suitable conditions for elements of the boreal forest, right next door rather than hundreds of miles to the north.

The predominant transition forest trees are sugar maple (the winner, hands down); red spruce (a visible link to the boreal forest, where it also thrives); gray birch; white pine and red pine (which thrive in burnt-over areas); red oak, beech, and basswood; and Eastern hemlock (which particularly likes moist, cool, shady areas, often the northern sides of the hills). This varied family of trees is supported by richer, deeper topsoil than is found up north in the boreal forest, and the transition forest generally stands tall over a bedrock of granite, gneiss, and schist. The till, or sediment, left by the retreating glaciers helped to build topsoil here too.

necticut AMC's Trails Committee, feels a bit like a suburban park with its pavilion and picnic tables, charcoal grill, and impromptu sleeping loft. On the edge of the hill, enjoy a separate patio or deck with another table and a view. There is a privy and plenty of flat space for tents, though not much tenting privacy. Even a chair-swing. Not a bad place for a first-time overnight backpacking experience if the roughest spot you've tried thus far is the backyard. After a short though steep hike to get here, you are rewarded with almost all the comforts of home.

The AT continues north another few minutes to a height of land and another good viewpoint (this time looking northwest) that stands at about 900 ft. Given the narrowness and depth of the valley below and the busy weekend traffic, road noise may follow you even up here. Rise above it mentally and think on other things, such as the nature of the forest the AT cuts through in these parts. See "Three Forests in One Region," above.

As the AT heads down now toward its CT 4 crossing (at 1.8 mi. into this hike), see if you can identify the elements of the transition forest hereabouts. This descent is mostly on the northern slope of Silver Hill, through a cool, shady, moist area. A tree-finder handbook is fun to carry along, if it's lightweight. With leaves or needles in hand (gathered only from the ground) and a careful look at tree bark (sometimes the tactile approach helps too), you can identify stand-alone trees and entire groves. Through here the cushion underfoot is composed of fragrant hemlock needles.

At dawn and dusk these woods are filled with birdsong. The Audubon field guide *Eastern Forests* lists over seventy bird species common to the transition forest, though not all are present at any one time of year. Among the more well-known birds we spotted here on a summer's day were chickadee, blue jay, pileated woodpecker, red-tailed hawk, hermit thrush, ruffed grouse, white-breasted nuthatch, turkey vulture, and the common crow. Any serious birder, or even a neophyte with a bird book, binoculars, and patience, can expand on this list. Choose a site where birds will feed or drink in safety, and wait quietly.

One mile beyond Silver Hill, after a steady descent, the AT crosses busy CT 4 at 1.8 mi. (walk diagonally to the left). No parking here, but in an emergency you could walk 5 min. east (downhill) to Guinea Rd. or 15 min. to US 7 and the overnight hiker parking lot and nearby stores. If you must use CT 4 for walking, be sure to walk on the left side, facing the traffic, and in single file.

On the north side of CT 4, descend 0.1 mi. to Guinea Brook, a lively piece of water in a gorgeous setting named after a freed slave from the Guinea coast who settled in the area. This land is owned by the [Izaak] Walton Fishing Club. No camping or fires permitted hereabouts. Fishing permits from Connecticut are required. Trout are a good bet. The brook crossing is likely to be a ford except during a distinctly dry period. You may need that extra pair of socks if you slip into the stream. Use a walking stick or a staff to steady yourself, and lend a hand to other hikers. Remember, a tripod (three-legged) approach is always steadier than a bipod (two-legged) one. Inexperienced hikers will want to take their time looking for a viable set of steps (not leaps!) from stone to stone across the brook. Try to read the shoreline opposite you: a worn-down area suggests that many hikers before you made it across to that point, and you can too. Then look for rocks with dry tops and the promise of friction to steady your boots. Avoid anything with slippery moss or algae or with a bottom you can't see or surmise.

If Guinea Brook is too high for crossing (it can be impassable after a big rain), retreat to CT 4 and walk east, downhill, for 10 min. to Old Sharon Rd. #2, a dirt road entering on the left at an oblique angle. From this junction, you can see the junction of CT 4 and US 7 a few minutes farther east. Follow Old Sharon Rd. for 10 to 15 min., passing several houses, enjoying the roar of Guinea Brook below and to the left, before rejoining the AT on the right, heading uphill into the woods. If you have crossed Guinea Brook itself, the 0.1-mi. ascent to this point will have stretched your hamstrings for sure: it's short but steep.

A blue-blazed side trail at 2.1 mi., right, reaches the top of Breadloaf Mt. in just 0.1 mi., worth the detour. From that summit the blue-blazed trail continues down to the AMC's overnight hiker parking lot on US 7 (0.6 mi.). To continue our hike, return to the AT and head north (right) again.

Some of the best walking on the hike follows, during the next 2 mi. The AT keeps to the higher parts of the ridge, with few strenuous ups or downs. The distinctness of the Housatonic River valley, several hundred feet below, will be evident all along here: the slow work of glaciers, erosion, and geologic folding of the underlying bedrock. Hikers will make good time here, unless there's a stop for more bird watching or to listen to the lichens growing. An unnamed small brook divides this section of the hike more or less in half, but carry on for a better water view.

The south (main) branch of Hatch Brook appears at 3.2 mi., offering several small but pretty waterfalls as the AT briefly ascends along its banks. After crossing Hatch Book the AT descends to its northern and smaller branch, crossing this too, and almost immediately meets the intersection with the south branch of the

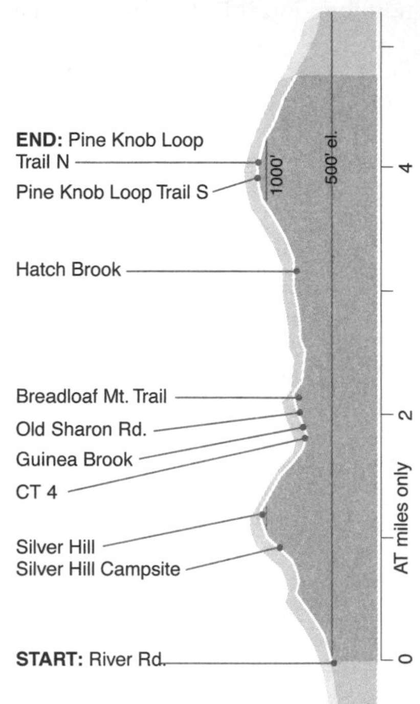

Pine Knob Loop Trail, blue blazed, coming up from the valley. Your options are to turn right, heading down this first branch of Pine Knob Loop Trail, following the blue or the red blazes (the reds appear on the right, a few moments down the blue-blazed trail, and will keep you by the brookside); or to carry on, following the AT northward. We recommend the latter option.

At 4.1 mi., reach Pine Knob Lookout, with fine views and convenient rocks to sit on for a rest or lunch. The thermal updrafts out of the valley may

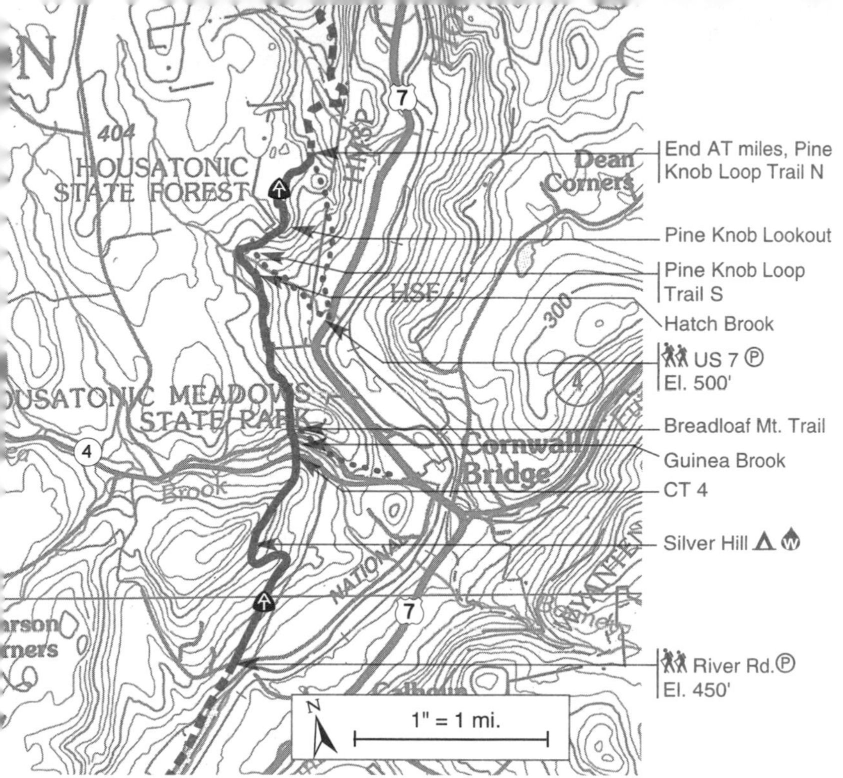

bring hawks or ravens or turkey vultures, or even a heron, into full view.

Just beyond the lookout, at 4.2 mi., Pine Knob Loop Trail's northern branch leaves the AT, right. Take this blue-blazed trail and enjoy the roller-coaster ride in its first section through gullies and rock outcroppings before you begin the actual descent into the Housatonic Valley. En route there are a few handsome overlooks. Anybody unsteady on their feet will want to proceed cautiously during this descent. It's not difficult, but the views are pretty and can distract a hiker from paying attention to safe walking.

At the top of the ridge, along the AT, oaks and other not-too-tall hardwoods predominate, but near the bottom of the descent the forest changes to dramatically taller trees, mostly hemlocks and pines. After the rocky scramble of the descent, the softer conifer forest floor will be welcome. Pine Knob Loop Trail finishes off with a short section (a few minutes) paralleling US 7, now visible through the trees, and partially along an ancient stone wall suggesting that years ago all this was pasture. A last brook crossing (Hatch Brook again) may be fun or a nuisance. Car #2 will be be visible from here. If the brook crossing looks undoable, retreat a few yards away from the brookside and bushwhack to US 7, just steps away. The highway curves decidedly here and traffic moves at a good clip, so be careful: no loose kids or dogs at this point. The broad, rippling Housatonic River is just across the road, likely to be busy with anglers (fly-fishing only for 2 mi. north of here), kayakers, or rafters. Drive south from here on US 7 to collect car #1.

Housatonic Meadows State Park, spread out on the river's floodplain, is a brief car ride or a 10-min. walk north on US 7. The site was developed by the Civilian Conservation Corps in the early 1930s. The park is open mid-April through December for camping but is staffed only on busy warm-weather weekends and in summer's high season. There are ninety-four campsites, many with RV hookups, plus toilets, hot showers, a telephone, and a helpful park ranger (860-672-6772). Fees are modest but have increased annually in recent years. Two miles north of the park, CT 128 crosses the Housatonic River in fine form on a lattice-truss wooden covered bridge in the design patented by the Connecticut architect and bridge builder Ithiel Town. If you go south on US 7, stop at the Cornwall Package Store, just south of the US 7 / CT 4 bridge over the river, and add your name and comments to the proprietor's AT hikers' register. You will read many notes from happy or discouraged thru-hikers, many of whom stop here in hopes of a free cold beer. If you have walked only 4.7 mi. today, you had better pay for yours.

HIKE #5 Itinerary

Miles N	NORTH	Elev. (ft./m)	Miles S
Total: 4.7 mi., with access			
0.5	**End: US 7,** parking for Pine Knob Loop Trail; overnight parking at state campground 0.5 mi. N on US 7.	500/152	0.0
4.2	**End AT mi.** Access: **Pine Knob Loop Trail,** N branch, blue-blazed trail to US 7.		0.5
4.1	**Pine Knob Lookout.**	1200/366	0.6
4.0	**Pine Knob Loop Trail,** S branch, blue-blazed trail to US 7.		0.7
3.2	**Hatch Brook.**		1.5
2.1	**Breadloaf Mt.,** side trail 0.1 mi.; 0.6 mi. down to US 7, parking.	900/274	2.6
2.0	**Old Sharon Rd. #2.**		2.7
1.9	**Guinea Brook.**		2.8
1.8	Cross **CT 4.**	700/213	2.9
0.8	**Silver Hill Campsite** spur trail; pavilion, privy, water.	880/268	3.9
0.0	**Start: River Rd.** just S of site of Swift's Bridge (AMC parking).	450/137	4.7

SOUTH

HIKE #6
Pine Swamp and Sharon Mountain

Maps: ATC Mass. & Conn. #4

Route: From US 7, Cornwall Bridge, up Pine Knob Loop Trail to AT, to Pine Swamp Lean-to, Mt. Easter, Sharon Mt. Campsite, and US 7, Falls Village

Recommended direction: S to N (described here) or N to S

Distance: 10.5 mi. total; 9.8 mi. on AT

Access trail name & length: Pine Knob Loop Trail S, 0.7 mi.; or Pine Knob Loop Trail N, 0.5 mi.

Elevation +/-: 500 to 1350 to 550 ft.

Effort: Easy

Day hike: Optional

Overnight backpacking hike: Yes

Duration: 6 to 7 hr.

Early exit option: W. Cornwall Rd., at 3.1 mi. (including access trail)

Natural history features: Rattlesnakes

Other features: Access to the blue-blazed Mohawk Trail, formerly the AT, which runs E of the Housatonic River from Falls Village S to Cornwall Bridge, making a 24-mi. loop hike using the old and new ATs. For Mohawk Trail details, see *Connecticut Walk Book,* Connecticut Forest & Park Assoc.

Trailhead access: *Start:* CT state park's parking lot, W side of US 7, just moments S of Housatonic Meadows State Park at Pine Knob Loop Trail. *End:* US 7 & CT 112, S of Falls Village (overnight parking permitted).

Camping: Caesar Rd. Campsite; Pine Swamp Brook Shelter; Sharon Mt. Campsite; car camping, Housatonic Meadows State Park

Starting this modest overnight backpacking trip—which can easily be hiked in 1 day, too—you have several options, all of them good. There's more than one way up to the Appalachian Trail from the valley; there are four camping choices; and there are numerous wonderful views both east and west from the ridge tops. In the middle portion of this hike a delicious wilderness feeling surrounds you. It's an easy yet effective getaway.

Heading from south to north, begin at the base of Pine Knob Loop Trail, just south of Housatonic Meadows State Park on US 7 near Cornwall Bridge. Immediately out of the parking lot, cross handsome Hatch Brook; or if the brook is too wide, retreat to US 7, cross the brook on the highway, and bushwhack for a minute to regain the Loop Trail on the brook's opposite (north) side. Follow the blue-blazed Loop Trail a moment or two parallel to US 7 to a sharp left turn heading up the mountain. At this point, make a decision.

The longer and more delightful version of this hike takes you gently up the south branch of the Loop Trail, where Hatch Brook and its small waterfalls entertain and refresh you on the left, before joining the Appalachian Trail after about 0.5 mi. and 500 ft. of climbing that will loosen the muscles and provoke a mild sweat. If you go this way, turn right (north) when joining the AT and follow the white blazes thereafter. The Loop Trail and the AT are contiguous for the next 0.6 mi. Take a rest at Pine Knob Lookout, 0.2 mi. after the junction of the two trails—pretty forested views to the southeast over the Housatonic River valley. Birds ride the warm updraft along the cliff here. Keep the zoom lens or binoculars handy. Alas, highway noise also wafts your way on the warm rising air.

A shorter and equally interesting, though steeper and rockier, access to the AT takes you up the north branch of the Loop Trail. There is no water on this route. At the sharp left turn noted above, go straight, keeping US 7 on the right, and follow the blue blazes up a winding, rocky path for 0.7 mi. to its junction with the AT. On the way up there are at least two good overlooks, though you'll need to stop and turn around to enjoy them. When the AT appears, turn right (north) and follow the white blazes. Mileage calculation for the main part of Hike #6 begins here.

After a brief descent, the Caesar Rd. Campsite appears at 0.4 mi., with six flat tent sites in a nondescript setting. An adjacent brook provides water, and an outdoor privy provides relief. If you have started late, this is a perfectly good though undramatic place to camp.

Cross Surdan Mt. Rd., no longer in use, 1.4 mi. farther on after regaining about 250 ft. If it's a hot day, trudge onward—there's a treat a-comin'. At 2.3 mi., clear, cool Carse Brook crosses the AT under a primitive, slippery log bridge. A swimming hole, shoulder-deep, invites the sweaty hiker. Cool down and replenish water supplies: there's climbing ahead. A tenth of a mile later West Cornwall

Sharon Audubon Center

The 758-acre Sharon Audubon Center (National Audubon Society) is a short drive from the southern terminus of Hike #6 (go west on US 4 about 6 mi. from US 7 & 4 at Cornwall Bridge). There are guided nature walks and self-guided nature trails, exhibits, and a library. Visitors may see raptors (birds of prey), beavers, otters, wild turkeys, and ospreys. Adjacent to the Audubon center is the Injured and Orphaned Wildlife Center, which attempts to save and return to the forest injured and abused wild animals. Call 860-364-0520 for more information.

Rd., with a few parking spaces for day hikers, meets the path.

An early exit here is feasible. The minuscule village of West Cornwall is right (east) about 1.5 mi., mostly downhill. A handsome covered bridge links US 7 to the village center, where you'll find restaurants, gift shops, antiques stores, craftspeople, a bookstore, public toilets, and a library. A few moments south on US 7 is Clarke Outdoors, the leading canoe, kayak, and raft renters in the upper Housatonic Valley.

Continuing the hike, across the road the climb begins, and it continues for half a mile or so with few switchbacks. Just shy of a mile from the road, the geologic oddity known as Roger's Ramp provides a unique experience on the southern New England AT. A narrow passage between two halves of the giant glacial erratic boulder is a 1-min. taste of what thru-hikers will do over hours in the Mahoosucs near the New Hampshire–Maine border. Turn off your claustrophobia switch and squeeze through the corridor. Backpackers may need to adjust protruding horizontal objects, such as tents, before entering the passage. Most kids will love this little adventure.

Continue climbing to a sharp turn to the left, where the AT heads north-northwest. There are fine views along here at several places. On a really clear day the distant Catskills in New York State, beyond the Hudson Valley, rise up over 4000 ft. on the western horizon. A gentle downhill section follows, through abundant oak groves and pleasantly sun-dappled shade.

The side trail to Pine Swamp Brook Shelter (built in 1989), a tidy spot in the woods if ever there was one, appears at 3.8 mi., a half mile beyond Roger's Ramp. This is one of the better shelters in Connecticut, though its immediate environs offer no long-distance views. Right in front of the lean-to, a boulder serves up a geology demonstration with colorful striations outlining the effects of metamorphic heating, cooling, and folding. No less important than geology, a covered privy is nearby. Easy-to-use tent sites are located off the shelter's short access trail. Water can be found at the brook 10 min. farther back in the woods, where the swamp and meadow open up. The wetlands hereabouts are the main reason for choosing this as a shelter site. For those with patience, the edge of the swamp and meadow is a prime wildlife observation point.

Uninterrupted forest continues beyond Pine Swamp Brook Shelter until the trail reaches the out-of-use Sharon Mt. Rd. (dirt) at 4.7 mi. This is not a viable early exit route. There's a tiny, unreliable brook a few yards north of this road. After a brief (0.3 mi.) but noticeable climb on Mt. Easter, stunning views appear, at 1350 ft., where this hike reaches its highest elevation (a trail sign here inexplicably adds 45 ft.). Cast your eyes to the far western horizon, where again the Catskills may be visible. Though a

Hsssssss . . . Alert!

Near Belter's Bump and in similar areas, watch carefully where you sit, stand, or reach in with your hands. The largest timber rattlesnake we have seen on the southern New England AT—about 48 in. long and fat in the belly, presumably from a recent meal (most likely a small rodent) — was sunning himself trailside just north of the Bump. Northern timber rattlesnakes are handsome creatures, varying in color from yellow through brown to gray or black, but all have dark blotches that form rings around the tail section, and the tail is black. These snakes love rocky dens and sun-drenched rocks. They may appear smack in the middle of the trail. If the snake is coiled and still, it's waiting for prey, not for you, but if accidentally a hiker threatens a coiled rattler, the snake will rattle its tail and may strike. Its venom is poisonous. When camping in areas near sunny rock outcroppings, keep your tent door zipped shut. Study snakebite first aid *before* you go hiking, and if bitten, seek medical help immediately.

David Emblidge

Timber rattlesnake

vast river valley (the Hudson) lies between Connecticut and these distant peaks, the Catskills are actually contemporaneous cousins of the Appalachians, pushed farther inland by the ancient geologic folding and crunching of the landscape.

Mt. Easter makes a fine midhike lunch spot. The views here compete well with our Connecticut favorites, at the Riga Shelter and on Bear Mt., farther north on the AT. Listen for road noise here: you won't hear any. Just the wind and the birds. Give thanks to the state of Connecticut for preserving Housatonic State Forest, which surrounds you now.

After another 1.1 mi. of generally level ridge-top walking (in the woods), the AT crosses a small brook (which may be dry in the summer), and 0.1 mi. beyond the brook the trail reaches the spur to Sharon Mt. Campsite, in a sweetly isolated, quiet setting. This idyllic spot (6.2 mi. from the point where you joined the AT, 6.9 mi. from your car) gets our recommendation for a midhike overnight stay. There are four large, well-cleared, well-dispersed tent sites and a few catch-as-catch-can smaller ones. The privy is open to the sky, and the water source, a brook, is plentiful and conveniently adjacent to the major tent sites. Arriving here toward sunset, you'll find the forest is dappled with sunlight, for the campsite is tucked just back from the edge of Sharon Mt.'s western slope. To enjoy the evening light to the fullest, follow the campsite path westward until it emerges from the trees and ends at rock outcroppings with comfortable moss and wild thyme waiting to cushion your seat. (Sharon Mt. is not a specific peak but the entire surrounding area.)

Day #2 (or the next leg of a 1-day hike) begins with a modest climb of 100 ft. over 0.8 mi. to a spectacular viewpoint known as Hang Glider View (7.0 mi.). Linger here to drink in the multifaceted sights. From the north side of the opening, a clear day reveals the Catskills. From the south side, hikers see the Lime Rock (auto) Race Track and its circular practice ring, where drivers whirligig on oil- and water-slick pavement. The Skip Barber Driving School meets here. Its winter course is most interesting: learn to drive on ice with confidence and chutzpah. From the middle of the opening, where the hang-glider ramp stands (stay off: it's steeply pitched!), there's an expansive view of the Taconic Range on the Connecticut–New York border, extending into Massachusetts. With a regional topo map and a compass you can pick out

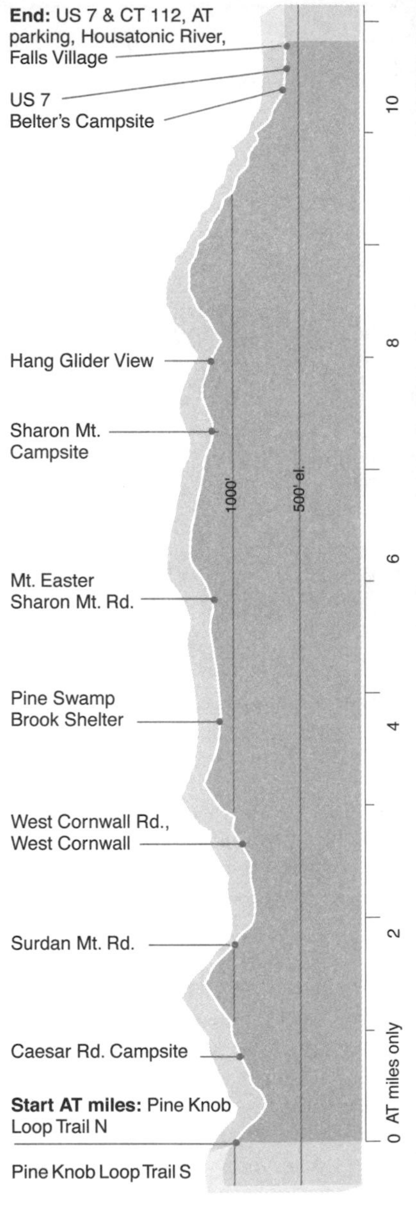

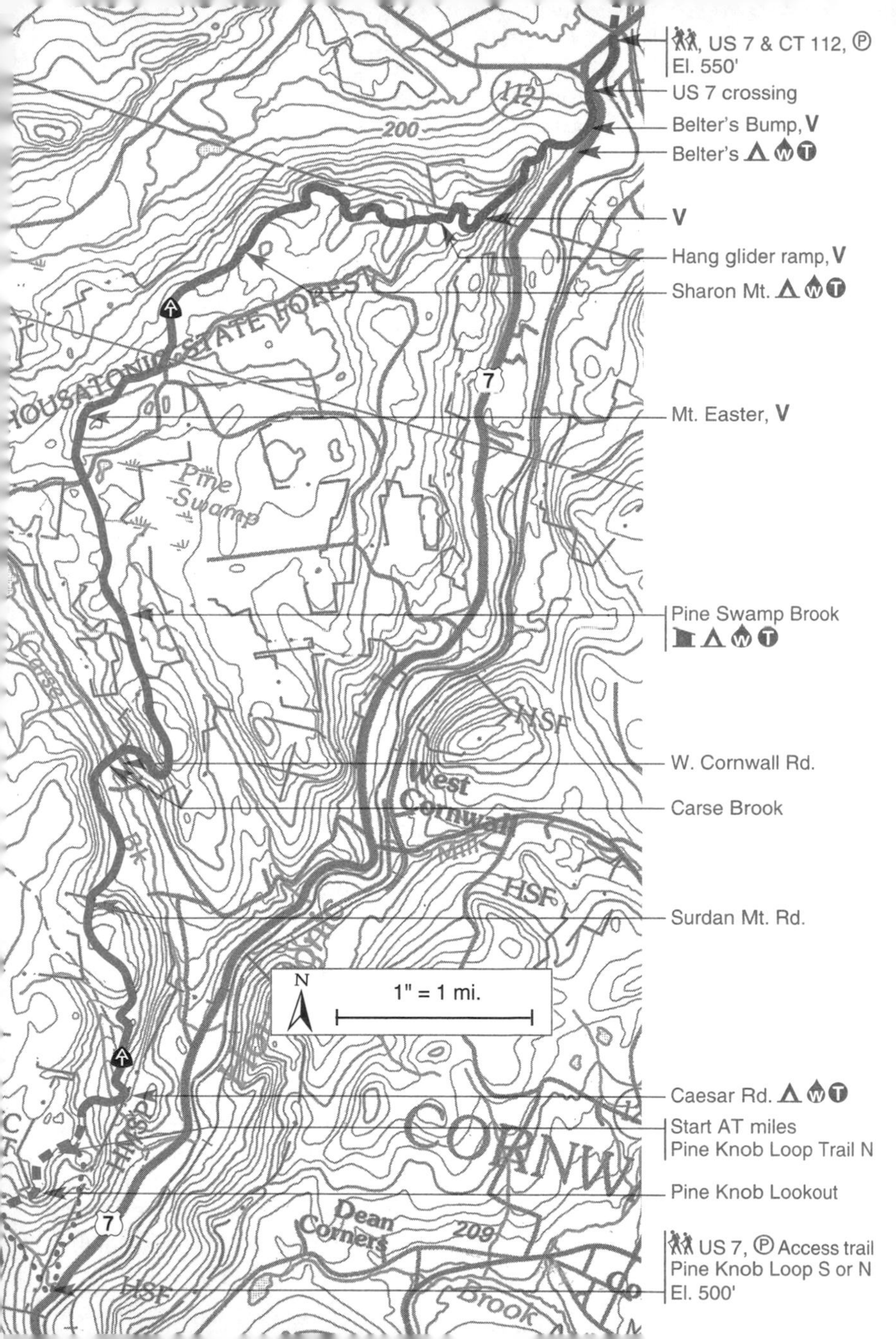
US 7 & CT 112, Ⓟ
El. 550'
US 7 crossing
Belter's Bump, V
Belter's
V
Hang glider ramp, V
Sharon Mt.
Mt. Easter, V
Pine Swamp Brook
W. Cornwall Rd.
Carse Brook
Surdan Mt. Rd.
1" = 1 mi.
Caesar Rd.
Start AT miles
Pine Knob Loop Trail N
Pine Knob Lookout
US 7, Ⓟ Access trail
Pine Knob Loop S or N
El. 500'
HOUSATONIC STATE FOREST
Pine Swamp
West Cornwall
HSF
Dean Corners
CORNW
Brook
112
7
200
209
N

Bear Mt. (highest in Connecticut) and Mt. Everett (highest in southern Berkshire County, Massachusetts), both to the northwest. Take a mental picture of both peaks: if you're hiking from here into the Berkshires, you will ascend and descend both of these mountains.

Following next is a longish descent, easy when you're heading from south to north, not much fun coming up the other way. The AT crosses an old woods road, now more a gully than a road, with stone steps on either side.

The trail meanders along the ridge, with occasional distant views to the west, and eventually crosses over to the east, or Housatonic valley, side of the mountain. If you're hiking here in the morning, you may find pleasant breezes wafting up the hillside as the sunshine warms the valley's air. The birds enjoy this time of day too. Watch for hawks and turkey vultures. The latter have a wingspan of up to 6 ft., almost as big as an eagle's. If you see one up close, the head with its wrinkled red skin is the giveaway. From afar and in flight, these scavenger birds are easier to identify from the rear because of the way they hold a V shape with their wings. The flight pattern is an unsteady rocking or tilting.

Descending the mountain, the AT leaves behind the hardwoods and enters an expansive hemlock grove where the trail may be somewhat harder to follow. Blazing here is less than perfect, and underfoot the path is not as well worn. Soon the remnants of a barbed wire fence appear (right, east), and increasingly road noise from US 7 disturbs the air.

Belter's Campsite is off the west (left) side of the trail in the hemlock forest, at 9.0 mi. from the start. Though the campsite is spacious, it's also noisy due to the highway just over the hill, and water can be in short supply here. A spring located on the opposite side of the AT near the campsite's spur trail is sometimes dry by midsummer. There is no babbling brook hereabouts. Belter's does have a privy, however.

The trail rises a bit over the next 0.4 mi. to Belter's Bump, a rocky outcropping providing good views into the Housatonic valley. (Willie Belter was a local landowner.) By now, most hikers will be spoiled by the quiet and solitude experienced higher up, farther back in the forest. Belter's Bump is easy to reach from the north and is too heavily used, sometimes abused. Why not carry out some trash and help with the maintenance?

US 7 is 0.2 mi. ahead, but you may have to negotiate with a small herd of cattle in the pasture through which the trail reaches the highway. Generally cows are docile, but if frightened they will charge. If they block the trail, wait for them to move rather than barging through. Or make loud noises from a good distance. Cross the highway and continue on the AT through the cornfield and along the riverbank for 10 min. The river view is delightful, but the banks are steep—keep little kids in tow. The AT overnight parking lot, and your car, appear after you have circumnavigated the cornfield (9.8 mi., 10.5 mi. with the Loop Trail access route at the start).

The AT continues northward, briefly on US 7 and then on a side road in front of the high school. To reach Falls Village by car, go north on US 7 for 1 min. and turn left. In this sleepy town hikers can find the P.O., a diner (and a restaurant), cabins for rent, and a convenience store. The hydroelectric plant and the falls themselves are described in Hike #7.

HIKE #6 Itinerary

Miles N	NORTH	Elev. (ft./m)	Miles S
Total: 10.5 mi with S access trail; 10.3 mi. with N access trail			
9.8	**End: Falls Village,** AT overnight parking, US 7 & CT 112.	550/168	0.0
9.6	**Cross US 7.**	550/168	0.2
9.4	**Belter's Bump.**	800/244	0.4
9.0	**Belter's Campsite.**	750/229	0.8
7.8	Ridge, views.		2.0
7.0	**Hang Glider View.**	1300/396	2.8
6.2	**Sharon Mt. Campsite,** side trail.	1200/366	3.6
6.1	Brook.		3.7
5.0	**Mt. Easter.**	1350/412	4.8
4.7	State forest service road (Sharon Mt. Rd.).		5.1
3.8	**Pine Swamp Brook Shelter,** side trail.	1075/328	6.0
3.3	**Roger's Ramp.**		6.5
2.4	**West Cornwall Rd.,** early exit option.	800/244	7.4
2.3	**Carse Brook,** bridge, swimming hole.		7.5
1.8	**Surdan Mt. Rd.**	1000/305	8.0
0.4	**Caesar Rd. Campsite.**	750/229	9.4
0.0	**Start AT miles:** Junction, N branch Pine Knob Loop Trail and AT	1000/305	9.8
0.7	Access: **Pine Knob Loop S branch** trail. Or 0.5 mi. on Pine Knob Loop Trail N.	500/152	0.7

SOUTH

HIKE #7

Falls Village to Salisbury

Maps: ATC Mass. & Conn #4
Route: From AT parking area S of Falls Village (US 7 & CT 112) to the power plant and falls in the village, up Mt. Prospect, to Limestone Spring Shelter, Rand's View, Barrack Matiff plateau, and down to US 44, Salisbury
Recommended direction: S to N
Distance: 9.9 mi. total (10.6 mi. with access to overnight parking at End); 9.4 mi. on AT
Access trail name & length: US 7 and local road portion of AT, 0.5 mi.
Elevation +/-: 550 to 1475 to 750 ft.
Effort: Easy, with a strenuous descent to and ascent from the shelter
Day hike: Optional
Overnight backpacking hike: Yes
Duration: 5 to 6 hr.
Early exit option: Iron Bridge in Falls Village, at 1.6 mi.
Natural history features: Housatonic River; Great Falls; cliffs at Limestone Spring Shelter; Giant's Thumb glacial erratic
Social history features: Hydroelectric plant; industrial 1851 canal; Music Mountain summer chamber music festival
Trailhead access: *Start:* Park (overnight permitted) at US 7 & CT 112, S of Falls Village. *End:* Park (day only) in field off US 44, N of Salisbury village center (overnight parking at AMC lot on CT 41, 0.7 mi. farther on AT on village streets)
Camping: Limestone Spring Shelter

There is so much to see and do on this hike that while the mileage (9.9 overall) suggests that a day hike is feasible, we recommend making it an overnight trip. The setting for the shelter and campsite midhike is extraordinary (and requires special effort to get there). Once at the site, most hikers will want to stay.

Beyond this, both villages (Falls Village on the south end, Salisbury on the north) offer many good reasons to spend at least part of a day in town. This is a historically rich area, with a dramatic landscape traversed by the Appalachian Trail. Come for the weekend, and don't rush through.

Let's begin with the base rock underfoot. We're in the northwest highlands of Connecticut, in what geologists refer to as the Housatonic Highlands Plateau. The plateaus have remained high because their bedrock resists erosion, whereas the bedrock in the valleys below is more vulnerable to erosion. On this hike you will see plenty of tough schists and granites in the highlands, and in the valleys an abundance of colorful, sometimes stunningly beautiful, marble. Marble is indeed a metamorphic rock (which we usually think of as very hard), like schist and gneiss, but in this region it's a softy, being heavily laced with limestone, a softer sedimentary rock made of compressed mud and fragments of marine animal shells. Eons ago this entire area was underwater. It's the remnant limestone aspect of marble that dissolves easily, even in the relatively minor acidity of rainwater (such acidity has risen dramatically in the past 100 years). Thus it's no accident that the AT shelter site on this hike is called Limestone Spring, and that there's a village just west of the Trail called Lime Rock.

Geologists often call the valleys in this region the "Marble Valley," and generally the Housatonic River hereabouts (to about 2 mi. south of Falls Village) has banks and waterfalls of handsomely polished marble. Minor gorges, caves, and various depressions and hollows all are by-products of the easily eroding lime-rich rocks. An aerial view or a broad topographical map shows that this area is dotted with lakes and swamps. But it's the river that offers the first destination of interest on this hike.

From the parking lot at US 7 and CT 112, the AT follows US 7 north over the Housatonic River and immediately angles left past Housatonic Valley Regional High School on Warren Turnpike. This road walk is 0.5 mi., a few minutes. The hike mileage starts at the school (no parking here).

Back across US 7, on the east side, is the road up to Music Mountain, the oldest (1930) and one of finest summer chamber music festivals in the U.S. Gordon Hall is an acoustic wonder, worth the detour (by car) if you have clean duds and $15 to $18 for a ticket. Call 860-824-7126.

Minutes beyond the school, the blue-blazed Mohawk Trail, the old AT, heads east up Barrack Mt. And just beyond the Mohawk Trail the AT slices right, uphill into the woods (0.2 mi.). After a half mile or so of undulating footpath and a crossing of Warren Turnpike (0.8 mi.), the river reappears and by its banks the wide, soft trail passes beneath many giant pine trees. Northeast Utilities, whose power plant the AT is about to pass, has built a self-guided nature walk (an 0.8-mi. loop) adjacent to the AT and the river here.

Stepping out of the woods, hikers see the hydroelectric power plant, and across the road from it the remnant wall of an industrial canal built in 1851 (1.4 mi.). There is a 10-min. road walk now. River water is dammed to the north of the plant and fed through sluices into the turbines. Dan Wingfoot's *Thru-Hiker's Handbook* reports that there's an open-air shower, an AT rarity, "at the small brick building with ivy" just south of the power plant. For drinking water, use the faucet on the front side of the power plant. Just beyond the electric plant is a bridge built by the famed Berlin Iron Bridge Company (1.6 mi.), narrow enough to suggest its 1903 vintage. Across the river, on the left, are picnic tables and a privy in a town park. Do not drink directly from the river.

Tiny Falls Village is about 0.5 mi. back across the bridge and uphill. Services are limited, but you may find the quiet enticing. Dine high or low, at a restaurant or a diner.

The AT turns right (north) after the bridge, paralleling the river briefly until a spur to a lookout in front of the falls goes right. Go see this amazing waterfall, even if the water is not flowing (in dry seasons available water is directed from the dam into the spillway for the power plant). Swimming at the base of the falls is possible, and popular, but ill-considered: broken glass below the falls is threatening.

The trail now parallels Housatonic River Rd., which it eventually crosses (2.5 mi.) near a dam. Not far north of the AT's turn off Housatonic River Rd., to the right of the road, are historic industrial site markers (but no buildings), including a cannon factory and a railroad repair shop. Hikers can make a little self-guided detour out of this section, glimpsing the handsome river at several points.

Up the trail goes now, first through a field of spectacular spring and summer wildflowers, then onward for quite a long stretch. If you need water, keep a sharp lookout for a refreshing cold spring on the right at 3.0 mi. From the road the trail marches on through sun-dappled woods, ascending steadily, for about 2.8 mi. before reaching the top of Mt. Prospect (some maps call it Prospect Mt.), at 1475 ft., 5.3 mi. The climb gains more than 900 ft., passing through sections where witch's hobble and other shrubs make a tunnel along the trail (in damp periods it's mosquito hell). An abundance of beautiful ferns compensates for the buggy annoyance.

At the top of Mt. Prospect everything opens up. The Housatonic valley spreads out below and views to the north take in Canaan Mt.

Now you'll head for the opposite extreme, as the AT descends toward the spur trail to Limestone Spring Shelter (6.0 mi.). The spur, on the left, drops off steeply, soon following a rugged cascading brook called Wetauwanch, plummeting to a hollow that seems worlds apart from anywhere when you arrive. The shelter's elevation is 980 ft., only about 500 ft. down from the top of Mt. Prospect, but it feels like a lot more due to the precipitous access trail with its giant overhanging rock formations.

Tenting sites here are spacious though not private or clearly delineated. The shelter is the basic lean-to, no special amenities. An enclosed privy is nearby, and there is abundant water from a piped spring nearby in the brook. One caveat: in this often windless, sometimes damp place, mosquitoes find a happy home. Hikers should come prepared. One time we challenged a young friend hiking with us to scare the bugs away by repeating a few hundred times, as an incantation, the name of the Anti-Mosquito God, "Godbugbegone." It worked intermittently, or at least as a distraction. Retreating to our tent at sunset, we had plenty of time for a leisurely candlelit game of chess on our miniature board.

Day #2: After overnighting here, the climb back up to the AT in the morning stretches the hamstrings and gets the juices flowing. A mere 0.1 mi. ahead on the AT is Rand's View, one of the sweetest long-distance views in Connecticut, with the Taconic Range on the state's western border outlining the horizon. Mt. Everett, in the southern Berkshires, should be easy to pick out. With a lucky super-clear day, you'll see Mt. Greylock (3491 ft. high and 50 mi. off), at the northern border of Massachusetts, beckoning hikers to walk on toward Vermont. You won't see anything better from the top of the World Trade Center. Day hikers coming through may want to use Rand's View as their lunch spot. No water here or privy. Be prepared. Alas, no camping either. Give the cattle in the meadow a wide berth, and watch where you step.

Children, and adults with a good imagination, will enjoy the strange rock formation known as "Giant's Thumb" that appears on the AT a few moments north of Rand's View (6.5 mi.). A cross between a glacial erratic and a prehistoric monolith, the site may be just what you need for a momentary break and a little yarn spinning. Another good view

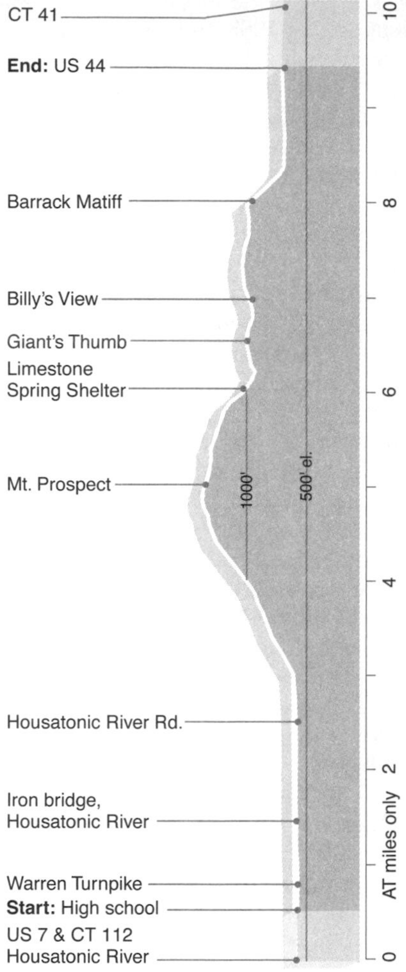

opens up at a woods road, 6.9 mi., this one called Billy's View, offering the reverse panorama from Rand's: this one looks south. The AT is skirting the top of Raccoon Hill.

The trail ambles onward through beautiful mixed hardwood forest,

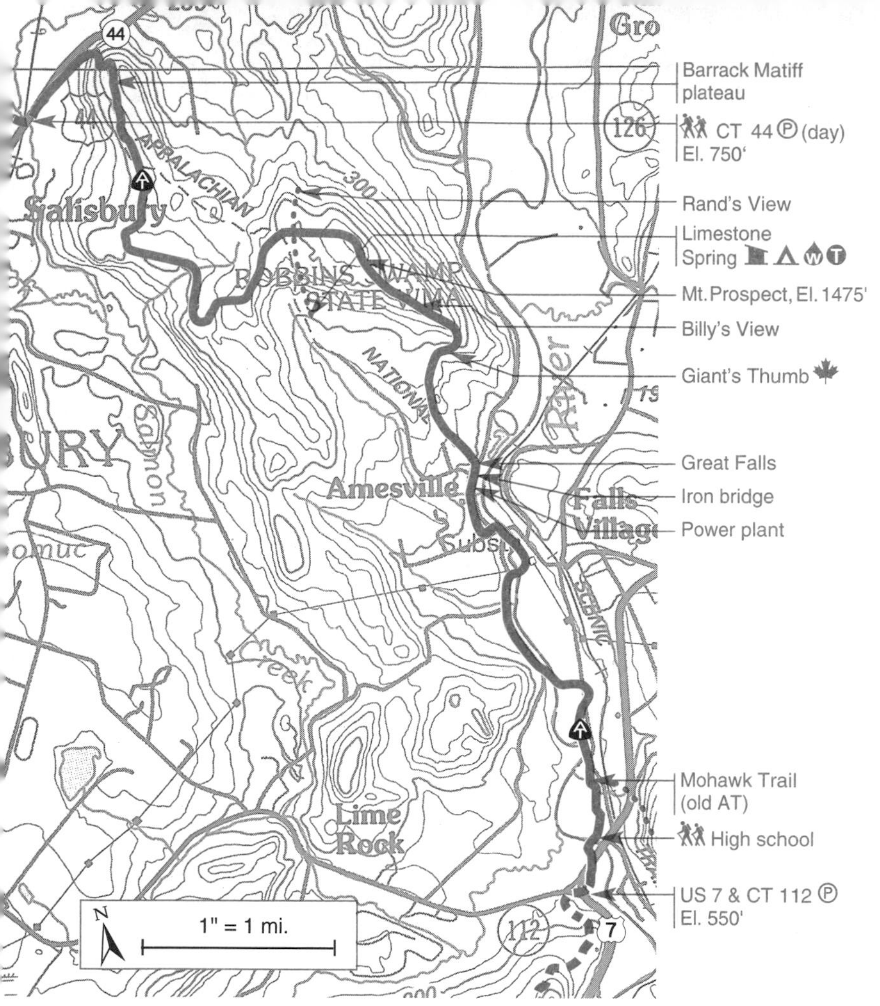

zigzagging along in mostly level territory, crossing an AT&T telephone cable right-of-way at 7.5 mi. Another mile farther on brings hikers to a plateau oddly named Barrack Matiff ("barrack" is possibly Gaelic for "pyramidal" or Dutch for "steep, high cliff"; the origin of "matiff" remains obscure), actually in a town park belonging to Salisbury, which is just at the bottom of the hill. The Native Americans called this Wetauwanchu Mt. ("the mountain bounding the wigwam place"). And what a hill.

Here you will see why we recommend hiking from south to north. The trail is alternately a narrow, crumbling ledge and then a boulder-strewn chaos challenging your concentration and your ankles. As if by magic (in fact with much help from trail builders), there are many good rock steps to help you down the slope. After descending about 350 ft. the AT turns left and enters a hayfield, paralleling busy US 44. The day-only parking area lies dead ahead.

Overnight AT parking is 0.7 mi. away, where the AT crosses CT 41. Follow the white blazes on US 44, briefly on Lower Cobble Rd., then through a field to CT 41. For emergency water, continue on Lower Cobble Rd. to St. Mary's Cemetery (spigot at cross in center).

Salisbury is a town loaded with services and worthwhile distractions: upscale and downscale restaurants, B&Bs, country inns, a sporting goods store, a pharmacy, a bank, a very literary bookshop (Lion's Head), and a marvelous library. As a base for hiking in the Litchfield Hills or the southern Berkshires, it's one of the better choices.

HIKE #7 Itinerary

Miles N	NORTH	Elev. (ft./m)	Miles S
Total: 9.9 mi. with access			
9.4	**End: Salisbury,** day parking, US 44. Overnight parking on CT 41, 0.7 mi. farther.	750/229	0.0
8.6	**Barrack Matiff** plateau.	1100/335	0.8
7.5	AT&T cable right-of-way.		1.9
6.9	**Billy's View.**	1100/335	2.5
6.5	**Giant's Thumb.**	1200/366	2.9
6.1	**Rand's View.**		3.3
6.0	Trail to **Limestone Spring Shelter** (descend steeply approx. 500 ft. to shelter, 0.5 mi.).	1300/396	3.4
5.3	**Mt. Prospect,** views.	1475/450	4.1
3.0	Spring.		6.4
2.5	Cross **Housatonic River Rd.**	600/183	6.9
1.6	**Iron bridge.**	550/168	7.8
1.4	**Power plant & 1851 canal.**		8.0
0.8	Cross **Warren Turnpike.**		8.6
0.2	Junction of AT and **Mohawk Trail** (former AT).		9.2
0.0	**Start: Housatonic Valley Regional High School.**		9.4
0.5	Access: **Falls Village,** AT overnight parking, US 7 & CT 112. AT follows US 7 N over river.	550/168	0.5
	SOUTH		

HIKE #8
Salisbury to Bear Mt.

Maps: ATC Mass. & Conn. #4

Route: From CT 41, Salisbury, to Lions Head, Riga Shelter, Mt. Riga State Park, Undermountain Trail, Bear Mt., and Paradise Lane Trail

Recommended direction: S to N

Distance: 10.0 mi. total; 6.7 mi. on AT

Access trail name & length: Undermountain Trail and Paradise Lane Trail, 3.3 mi.

Elevation +/-: 750 to 2316 to 761 ft.

Effort: Moderate, with brief strenuous sections

Day hike: Optional

Overnight backpacking hike: Yes

Duration: 6 hr.

Early exit option: Lions Head Trail, at 2.8 mi; Undermountain Trail, at 5.1 mi.

Natural history features: Exposed mountaintop rock outcroppings

Other features: Twin Lakes for fishing, boating, swimming

Trailhead access: *Start:* Park (overnight) on CT 41, 0.8 mi. N of Salisbury village center. *End:* CT 41, S of Beaver Dam Rd., 1.5 mi. S of CT/MA line, approx. 2.5 mi. N of Start.

Camping: Plateau Campsite; Riga Shelter and Campsite; Ball Brook Campsite; Brassie Brook Shelter and Campsite; Paradise Lane camping area

Walking northward on the AT in Connecticut, to this point it has been a landscape of sweetly rolling hills and verdant valleys. Now the true mountains begin. Granted, these aren't the Smokies or the Whites, but everything is relative. For northbounders, this hike takes us up over 2000 ft. for the first time since Pennsylvania. With higher elevation comes a package deal: more work, more reward, more wildness, more weather. Hike #8 is an ambitious day hike or a leisurely overnight camping trip. Once you have seen the view from the shelter/campsite we recommend, you will know why we suggest backpacking overnight.

The hike can be done south to north or north to south, but be aware that those walking north–south will encounter a brief, brutish climb up the north slope of Bear Mt., tough in good weather, dangerous when the rocks are slippery. We've chosen to go from south to north. We suggest leaving a car at the AT overnight parking lot at the base of Undermountain Trail on CT 41 (your destination). If you have only one car, the odds are good that at the end of the hike you can get a ride back to the Salisbury trailhead, either from another hiker at this lot or by using your thumb on well-traveled CT 41. There are no pay phones here, so don't plan on calling a taxi.

Fair warning: In dry seasons this can be a thirsty hike, with brooks looking as parched as you may feel. Carry plenty of water if it hasn't rained in a while.

The first water source appears just 0.2 mi. from the start, at Plateau Campsite, a reasonable camping spot if you need to be near town for resupply or repairs. If the spring here is dry, you could backtrack to CT 41, and then to Lower Cobble Rd. (a few yards toward town) and into the cemetery, where at the center there is a water spigot available to hikers.

Those on a 1-night trip will want to go on to the higher, more secluded campsites. This region is laced with old woods roads, many of which were log cutters' routes in the days when the local iron furnaces were hungry for charcoal. As you climb the first 1000 ft. to the Lions Head lookouts (one south, one north), console yourself that at least you're not dragging felled trees out of the woods with ornery oxen in a cold rain. Lions Head is 2.7 mi. from the trailhead, and much of the ascent is gentle, almost unnoticeable, affording a good opportunity to speculate on what the many stone walls in the woods may have walled in or out when this relatively level area was farmed. Before or after this hike you may enjoy reading a fine piece of history, *Sermons in Stone: The Stone Walls of New England and New York*, by Susan Allport (see "If the Walls Could Speak").

On the way up, there is one ravine where in damp weather the ferns are prodigious. If you are not rushed, an interesting exercise, especially in the ravine, is to find one of the large glacial erratics (freestanding boulders) on which there is everything from absolutely bare rock (the origi-

Henry Lafleur

Bear Mt. Tower

nal state after the rock's formation), to the faintest dusting of lichen, to fully developed lichens (they take years to grow), to mosses, grasses, flowers, small shrubs, taller shrubs, and a tree (perhaps embracing the rock with a Medusa-like snarl of exposed roots). Such a rock with its diverse plant community illustrates how the plant world grows tenaciously yet patiently by manufacturing its own topsoil (lichens break down rock to form soil; growth and decay yield humus, the organic matter in which new plant life thrives) and by sinking roots into even the most unpromising of sites.

Just past 2.0 mi. into the hike the real work begins. There's a steep climb for about 0.3 mi. to the Lions Head Trail and to Lions Head itself. The side trail (blue-blazed) could be used as an early exit or to make a short loop hike. Follow it to Bunker Hill Rd. (0.4 mi.), then turn left into Cobble Rd., and follow it to its intersection with the AT where you went up; turn right on the AT (south) to reach the trailhead. (In bygone days the AT used Bunker Hill Rd. as part of its route up toward Lions Head.)

At 2.7 mi. you'll find the Lions Head south lookout and a blue-blazed 0.1-mi. bypass trail for use in bad weather. Gazing southward one sees the villages of Salisbury and Lakeville and the Wetauwanchu Mt. Range (southeast), over which the AT passes en route to Salisbury. Beyond that mountain is the Housatonic River valley. East-northeast may be the best view, however, with Twin Lakes in the middle distance and Canaan and Prospect Mts. beyond. At 2.8 mi. you reach the north outlook and gaze toward Mt. Everett, situated just over the Massachusetts border. Everett is right on the AT and announces itself with its fire tower. This hike's highest destination is Bear Mt., clearly visible below and south of Mt. Everett. Lions Head is a popular day-hike destination and a good rest or lunch spot. The area needs careful treatment. Help the trail maintainers by packing out some garbage if you find any clutter on the site.

Bald Peak Trail (left, blue-blazed) comes up at 3.2 mi. Relatively little used, this is not a viable option as an early exit or a loop hike side trail. It leads 1.0 mi. to Bald Peak, 2016 ft., and then to Mt. Washington Rd. (dirt and often impassable).

Whether you're day hiking or backpacking overnight, be sure to follow the side trail to the Riga Shelter and Campsite, which comes along at 3.4 mi. on your right. The trail to the site quickly approaches the eastern edge of the ridge, and a true "edge" or cliff it is. The drop-off where the woods ends and the sky begins is precipitous. Spreading out before you is almost the entirety of northwestern Connecticut—hills, mountains, valleys, lakes, villages, and sky. No shelter south of here in New England, or north of here until the Goddard Shelter near East Arlington, Vermont, offers anything to compare with Riga's famous view. Linger for

If the Walls Could Speak

In the woods of New England are the ruins of this area's agricultural past, the remains of eighteenth-, nineteenth-, even twentieth- century farms, farms abandoned so recently it is amazing how little evidence of them still exists. Their fields have returned to forest; their barns and houses have rotted. Indeed, al-most all that is left are the stone structures: foundations, old wells, and mile after mile of stone walls, crisscrossing the land, marking old boundaries and pastures, delineating cow runs, and climbing the sides of the steepest hills.

But what this evidence lacks in kind—or diversity—it makes up in quantity. These walls seem endless. They speak, of course, of how extensively New England was once cultivated, that 150 years ago, seventy-five to eighty percent of the area was cleared and farmed. They speak also of how quickly the past is forgotten. Today, when so much is said about protecting the small family farms of the West and Midwest, we barely remember that New England too was a region of small family farms—in 1850, 168,000 of them—abandoned when the various forces of railroad expansion, Western competition, soil exhaustion, farm mechanization, and government price supports made them unprofitable to run. Hikers come across stone walls in the woods and they are surprised, puzzled until they dig back in their minds for the key that opens the lock of these mysterious works of backbreaking effort, as out of place and evocative as a shipwreck on the ocean floor. This was where the country began, and in agriculture, not industry.

*Written in these walls are eloquent reminders of the odds against which the early farmers of this area worked, tilling thinly soiled ground whose main claim to fecundity was the abundant crop of rock that heaved to the surface each winter. . . . There is not a sign of the house and barns that would make sense of this sprawl of rocks on rock, yet that wall is still there to say that these woods were not always so, that they once were fields, and that the walls enclosed not young birches and shaggy-bark hickories but cows and crops.**

*From *Sermons in Stone: The Stone Walls of New England and New York,* by Susan Allport. Norton, 1990, pp. 15–17.

a while or, better yet, stay overnight.

Tent sites are located a few yards behind the shelter, back toward the AT. There is a privy, and a spring is close to the main trail. Raccoons are frequent visitors here (protect your food). Keep young children back from the cliff edge. Two caveats about Riga: the water supply is unreliable in dry times; and as of 1996, the steps at the shelter were dangerously loose.

On our visit, owls hooted plaintively at sunset, perhaps their hour for romance. From the shelter or the edge of the cliff, trace the constellations sliding by in the night sky or track the running lights of boats on windswept Twin Lakes, their outboard motors silenced by the distance. Better yet, be up before dawn to worship the rising sun, directly ahead on the far horizon. Within minutes the entire valley below is set to glowing.

Odell Shepard, a latter-day Thoreau, rambled in the Connecticut highlands for 2 weeks one summer in the late 1920s, and looking west across this valley at Mt. Riga, whose shoulder is the setting for the Riga Shelter, he wrote: "I look out upon a Revelation now in progress, never to be complete. . . . What now shall I save to remember out of this final day and out of the two golden weeks to which it has been the appropriately quiet climax and close? . . . Free for a few hours yet from the clutch of circumstance, glad for the days that have been and gladly facing the days to come, I sit here in the last rays of the sun fulfilled with such a love of the brown earth, my Mother, as I have seldom known before."*

Onward with the AT now, through mixed hardwood forest where some handsome stands of white and silver birch add highlights to the green and brown palette of the forest. A yellow-blazed trail (an old lumber road) crosses the AT at 3.5 mi., leading to Forge (South) Pond (not on most maps; on private property).

*Odell Shepard, *The Harvest of a Quiet Eye*, Houghton Mifflin, 1927.

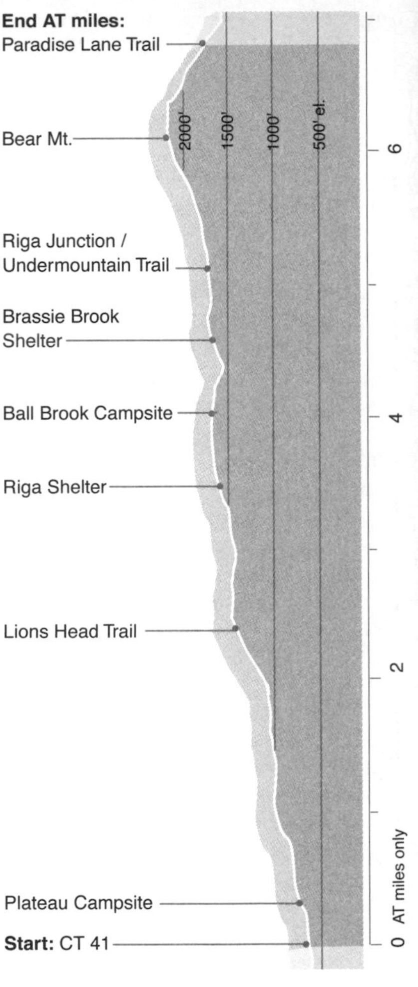

If Riga's shelter and campsites are full, continue on to 4.0 mi. and Ball Brook bridge, with the Ball Brook Campsite and privy just beyond. If you're camping in a large group, this site will accommodate the numbers better than Riga.

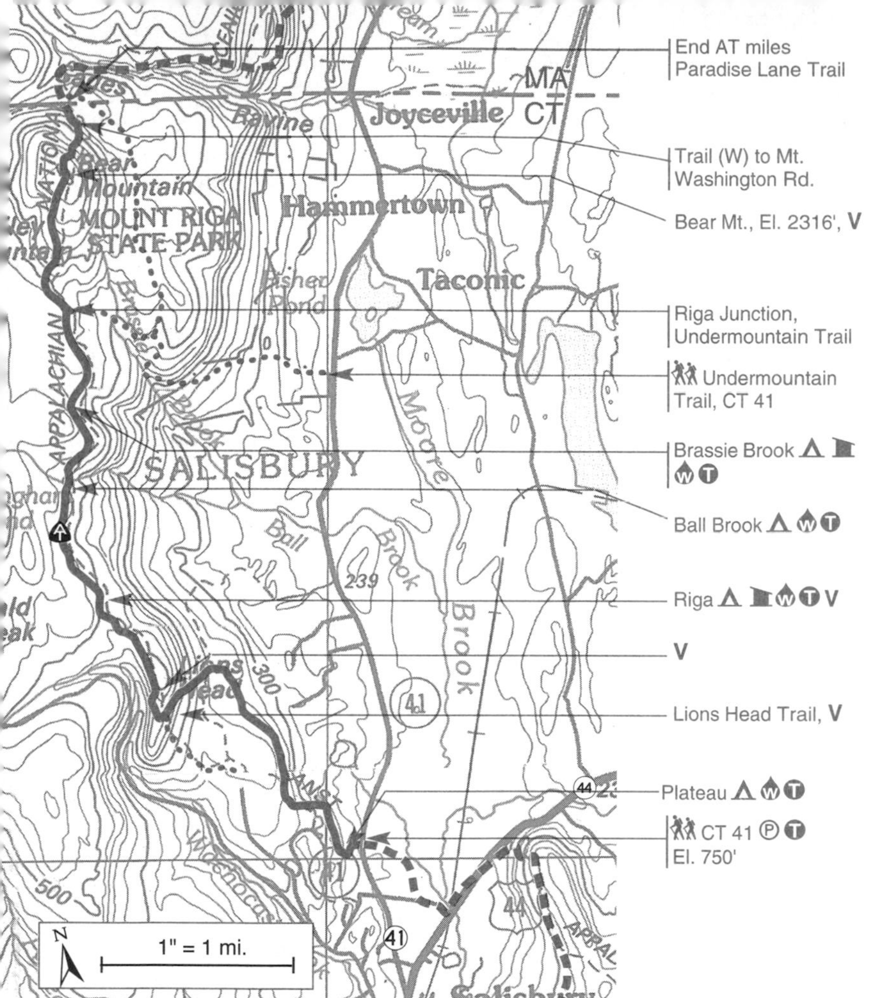

The trail is generally level in these parts, though it's climbing slightly toward the foot of Bear Mt. At 4.6 mi. Brassie Brook Shelter and Campsite precede Brassie Brook bridge. None of these brooks is very active except in spring or after a big storm. The Brassie Brook site can also accommodate larger groups, and it offers the convenience of a picnic table as well as a privy. A few grassy tent sites are invitingly soft and aromatic.

Half a mile farther on (5.1 mi.), the Undermountain Trail enters on the right (east), having ascended from the CT 41 valley. Known as Riga Junction (some maps label this entire area up to Bear Mt. as Mt. Riga), this steeply descending access trail is an early exit opportunity and will bring you out at the same spot as will the planned route in this hike 1.5 mi. ahead, after the ascent and descent of Bear Mt. There is a group camping area reachable via the Undermountain Trail from here (and then a stretch going up and north on Paradise Lane Trail); the same camping area will be passed en route down from Bear Mt., hiking the other way.

Shortly after Riga Junction, unused Bear Mt. Rd. crosses the AT (5.3 mi.), and immediately the climb up Bear Mt. begins, lasting about 0.5 mi., much of it on exposed rock with scrubby evergreens at trailside. Soon good views, then great ones, open up; and at the top (6.0 mi.) the remnants of an 1885 stone monument marking what was then thought to be the highest point in Connecticut invite you to scramble (carefully) even higher. (Mt. Frissel, on the Connecticut–New York border, is slightly higher.) Panoramic views are the payback for making the climb. By now Mt. Everett's fire tower (north on the AT) seems within easy reach. The next hike takes you there.

Warning: This is rattlesnake country, especially on the exposed rocks on sunny days. We have seen them here, on the AT itself, though they were smallish in size and more frightened of us than we were of them.

Before heading down (north), fortify yourself and tighten the laces on your boots. It's a challenging though brief descent off the summit for about 0.2 mi. This steep slope is one reason why we recommend a south-to-north hike.

Just as the trail levels out at the northern foot of Bear Mt., a wide, unmarked side trail, the old Northwest Rd., appears on the left. It runs about 0.5 mi. west to Mt. Washington Rd. / East St. at the Connecticut–Massachusetts state line, where there is an unofficial overnight parking lot (do not park on the road). For road directions to this lot, see Hike #9. The road is often impassable in wet periods.

Carry on another 0.4 mi., somewhat downhill, to the junction with Paradise Lane Trail on the right, well signed. Hike #8's AT miles end here. Just north of this junction the AT enters Sages Ravine, en route to Mt. Everett in Massachusetts; see Hike #9. You follow Paradise Lane down fairly gently until it passes the Paradise Lane group camping area and joins the Undermountain Trail (2.1 mi.), which is then your downhill route, fairly steeply, to CT 41 (another 1.1 mi.). The total mileage from CT 41 in Salisbury, to Bear Mt., and down to CT 41 via the two access trails is 10.0 mi. You will have climbed 1566 ft. and descended 1555 ft., a good effort with commensurate rewards.

HIKE #8 Itinerary

Miles N	NORTH	Elev. (ft./m)	Miles S
Total: 10.0 mi. with access trail			
3.3	Access: **Paradise Lane Trail,** to Undermountain Trail (2.1 mi.), then Undermountain Trail (1.1 mi.) to CT 41.	761/232	3.3
6.7	**End AT miles:** Paradise Lane Trail.	1795/547	0.0
6.3	Unnamed trail (old Northwest Rd.), right (W) to Mt. Washington Rd. and parking.	1811/552	0.3
6.1	Descend Bear Mt.; steep, rocky slope.		0.4
6.0	**Bear Mt.,** monument.	2316/706	0.5
5.4	Begin climb of Bear Mt. at right turn.		1.3
5.3	Former Bear Mt. Rd. (no cars).		1.4
5.1	**Riga Junction / Undermountain Trail,** to group camping (1.9 mi.) and CT 41.	1847/563	1.6
4.6	**Brassie Brook Shelter and Campsite,** privy; then Brassie Brook bridge.	1705/520	2.1
4.0	**Ball Brook bridge,** then Ball Brook Campsite (privy).		2.7
3.5	Yellow-blazed trail crossing.		3.2
3.4	**Riga Shelter Campsite,** spur trail; privy, water.	1610/491	3.3
3.2	**Bald Peak Trail,** to Bald Peak (1.0 mi.), then Mt. Washington Rd.		3.5
2.8	**Lion's Head N,** view.		3.9
2.7	**Lion's Head S,** view; blue-blazed bypass trail (bad weather).	1738/530	4.0
2.5	**Lion's Head Trail,** to Bunker Hill Rd. (0.4 mi.).		4.2
2.2	Former charcoal (woodcutters') road.		4.5
1.6	Ravine.		5.1
0.7	Motorcycle trail crossing.		6.0
0.2	**Plateau Campsite,** privy, water.	790/241	6.5
0.0	**Start:** **Rte. 41,** 0.8 mi. N of Salisbury, AT overnight parking, privy.	750/229	6.7

SOUTH

HIKE: #9

Sages Ravine to Mt. Everett to Jug End

Maps: ATC Mass. & Conn. #4 & #3

Route: Sages Ravine (CT/MA line) to Bear Rock Stream campsite, to top of Mt. Everett, to Glen Brook Lean-to, to Jug End summit, and down to Jug End Rd., South Egremont

Recommended direction: S to N

Distance: 11.2 mi. total; 10.4 mi. on AT

Access trail name & length: Northwest Rd. (unnamed on ATC maps and not signed at trailheads), 0.8 mi.

Elevation +/-: 1811 to 2602 to 800 ft.

Effort: Strenuous

Day hike: Yes (ambitious)

Overnight backpacking hike: Yes (recommended)

Duration: 8 hr.

Early exit option: Race Brook Falls Trail to MA 41, at 5.1 mi.; Mt. Everett summit road to East St., Mt. Washington, at 5.8 mi.; Elbow Trail to MA 41, at 7.6 mi.

Natural history features: Sages Ravine (glacial cirque, waterfalls); Race Brook Falls; cliffs, bird-watching; high peak; true wilderness

Trailhead access: *Start:* East St., town of Mt. Washington, accessible via Mt. Washington Rd. from MA 41, South Egremont (allow 45 min.). For the last few mi., East St. is unpaved but negotiable by 2-wheel-drive, low-chassis cars; may be impassable in wet season; not plowed in winter. Stone marker, L, indicates MA/CT state line; parking here (keep off road). *End:* Jug End Rd., Sheffield, accessible from Mt. Washington Rd., South Egremont, or from Guilder Hollow Rd. (Curtiss Rd. on some maps; it becomes Jug End Rd.), off MA 41, Sheffield. AMC roadside parking at trail crossing.

Camping: Sages Ravine AMC Campsite (summer caretaker, fee); Bear Rock Stream Campsite; Race Brook Falls Campsite; Glen Brook Lean-to and Campsite

---

Even the *drive* to the southern trailhead for this spectacular hike will be a delight, up high in the town of Mt. Washington, smallest (by population) in the commonwealth. The adjacent Mt. Washington State Forest (3500 acres) and Mt. Everett State Reservation (1100 acres), which the AT traverses, are surrounded by thousands more acres of deep forest. Here you will enjoy the highest elevations in southern New England, short of a trip to Mt. Greylock, which is almost in Vermont. The Mt. Everett region is an easily accessible and welcoming area for great hiking and camping. You *will* climb here: this is not a region for folks badly out of shape. But you will also be rewarded with breathtaking vistas, numerous waterfalls in pristine high-mountain brooks, a mountaintop pond surrounded by mountain laurel, and some of the best campsites on the southern New England AT. From Connecticut to Vermont, the Appalachian Trail is 75 to 80 mi. long. From the high point on this hike, you will be able to see almost all of it at once. Hike #9 offers backpackers the chance to spend a couple of days away from it all, and ambitious day hikers a dazzling variety of sights and a definite aerobic workout. There are good ways to break Hike #9 into two or more easier day hikes as well. We predict that once you're up in these mountains, you won't want to come down.

For a south-to-north hike (highly recommended), position car #1 at the AT trailhead on Jug End Rd.: From the junction of MA 23 and 41 in South Egremont, go very briefly south on MA 41, bear right onto Mt. Washington Rd. (pond on your right), then go about 0.9 mi. across the valley and turn left onto Avenue Rd. At the top of Avenue Rd., bear left. You'll reach the trailhead in a little under a mile.

To position a car at the starting point, go back to Mt. Washington Rd., turn left, and head up the mountain. The road evolves into East St. after entering the township of Mt. Washington (in the woods). Follow East St. for about 3 mi., passing Blueberry Hill Farm, left, and then in another 0.3 mi. the Mt. Everett Reservation access road, also left. Shortly, pass the Union Church, at the intersection with Cross Rd. (where a right turn will take you to Bash Bish Falls). Continue straight on East St. for another 1.5 mi., passing the Mt. Washington State Forest headquarters on the right. The road turns to dirt here; continue for approximately 3.4 mi. Keep a sharp lookout for the parking lot, left, near the Massachusetts/Connecticut border (stone marker). The last 2 mi. of road can be rough, especially in spring. Ordinary cars can make it by proceeding slowly. Watch for wildlife in the road.

Overnight parking is permitted at the hiker parking lot. From South Egremont, the uninitiated should leave a good 45 min. to reach the two trailheads. There are no stores, gas stations, or any other commercial establishments in Mt. Washington, and there are no pay phones—so bring what you need with you.

The 0.8-mi. access trail from the East St. parking lot to the AT is called Northwest Rd. on some maps but is generally unnamed and sparsely blazed. Head east from the parking lot, soon coming to a cabin used by AMC trail workers, and continue east and generally downhill, following the brook. It's a well-worn path. At the AT junction you'll be in Connecticut, with the foot of Bear Mt. on your right (a short but very steep climb to a great view if you have the time and energy).

Turn left (we begin Hike #9's AT mileage here) and go north on the AT, soon dropping noticeably downhill and arriving (in about 0.3 mi.) at a sign announcing Sages Ravine, a fragile and hauntingly beautiful wild area (1629 acres) owned by the

David Emblidge

Entering Sages Ravine

AMC, the Massachusetts Department of Environmental Management, the National Park Service (the AT corridor), and private landowners, all working cooperatively to protect and preserve it. Join the effort by being especially careful about low-impact hiking here.

At 0.5 mi. the Sages Ravine Campsite appears, left (fee for camping, caretaker on duty in summer). This is a fine place to stay if you want to explore the ravine in detail, but there are more dramatically situated sites farther on. By now the music of Sages Ravine Brook, pouring off both Bear Mt. (Connecticut) and Mt. Race (Massachusetts), fills the air. These mountains are in the Taconic Range, which is predominantly schist, and the brook has cut a west-to-east watercourse, flowing into Schenob Brook on the Housatonic valley floor in Sheffield (the water cooling you off up here makes its way to the Housatonic River, then Long Island Sound). But not before tumbling more than 400 ft. in a gorge with several delightful waterfalls, at the bases of which you'll find pools with bracing (!) pristine water. The ravine is a bit over a mile long before it drops precipitously into the valley.

In his fine book *A Guide to Natural Places in the Berkshires,* René Laubach explains that a north and south slope configuration makes for sharp contrasts in the two sides of the ravine—one in shade, one in medium light.

The south slope (facing north) is dominated by eastern hemlock, yellow birch, and red maple, all tolerant of heavy moisture. The understory includes abundant wood fern and other ferns in smaller numbers: Christmas fern, polypody fern, and where there is some sun, hay-scented fern. Mosses and lichens abound. The north slope (facing south) is less rugged. American beech, white birch, mountain laurel groves, some witch's hobble, and striped and mountain maples are the most common trees here.

In the ravine and throughout the Mt. Everett region, the mammals a (lucky) observant hiker may see include the elusive bobcat, black bear, and coyote. White-tailed deer are abundant. If you have binoculars, in summer look for the Louisiana water thrush (a warbler)—6 in. long, olive brown, with a loud call—frequenting the brook. The naked eye can easily spot wild turkey and the hairy woodpecker throughout the New England upland forest. Underfoot on the generally moist trail in the ravine, a tiny and charming amphibian may startle you: the red eft may have wandered here from ponds farther uphill. In brook pools tiny brook trout (2 to 3 in.) are fun to watch, but they aren't big enough for dinner. For the truly hardy—winter hikers—Sages Ravine can be extremely beautiful but icy. Try some animal tracking, and along the brook you may see the mink's footprints (paired, five toes, not quite 2 in. long).

The AT crosses to the north side of the brook (0.9 mi.) and eventually leaves the ravine, climbing 400 ft. to Bear Rock Stream (2.3 mi.), where there is a superb campsite (tent platforms) and a waterfall plummeting over the cliff—a great bird-watching and lunch spot, but be careful at the brink: it's a long way down.

At 3.4 mi. those with vertigo begin to have fun. The AT emerges from the woods and follows the edge of a long, treeless, precipitous escarpment, offering spectacular views of the sprawling Housatonic valley. Sheffield's MA 41 is at your feet, way down below. You may well see a solitary hawk, its wing-tip feathers stark against the sky, riding the warm updraft along the mountainside. Toward the southeast, Twin Lakes, in Lakeville, Connecticut, sparkle in the distance. You may be struck by the vastness of uninterrupted forest in every direction. Thousands may be convening in Lenox for a concert at Tanglewood this very afternoon, oozing northward through this valley like relentless lava, but they're all invisible from here.

After a mild in-the-woods ascent comes a cairn (3.8 mi.) that marks the southern peak of Race Mt., then the peak itself (2365 ft.) at 4.0 mi. Out here again on the exposed rocks, note how the pines and oaks are short and gnarled, a little hint of the krummholz to come on higher peaks to the north. On sunny warm days, watch for rattlesnakes on the rocky path. If you see one, admire its colors and the hiss of its rattle if it displays, but don't taunt it, and do give it a wide berth. From Race Mt. views include glimpses to the west as well (over Alander Mt. in the Taconic Range on the Massachusetts / New York state line) and northward toward this hike's highest point, the fire tower on Mt. Everett.

On a summer's day, you'll be perspiring by the time you reach Mt. Race. One time here we had the blessing of a deliciously refreshing downpour, washing us clean of a sticky sheen of sweat and bug repellent. If a thunderstorm sweeps by when you're on the ridgetop, head down into the woods immediately: lightning likes the high places. Now it's back down again, some 450 ft., and onward for a mile through the forest to the junction with Race

Brook Falls Trail on the right (5.1 mi.), which you could take down to MA 41 (1.5 mi. below in the valley, exiting the woods at Race Brook Lodge, a favorite B & B of area hikers; next door to the lodge is the Stagecoach Hill Inn and pub, a bit of olde England in ye olde Berkshires). Another fine campsite is 0.4 mi. down Race Brook Trail, where you'll also find the top of Race Brook Falls, the most spectacular on the mountain. As an early or emergency exit trail, bear in mind that Race Brook has some steep sections but no technical climbing. After the trail junction, the day's biggest ascent begins —0.7 mi. and another 700 ft. up, through a rocky scramble amidst dwarfed, wind-blasted pines, bringing you to Mt. Everett's summit (2602 ft.) at 5.8 mi.

From Mt. Everett, the western horizon can reveal the distant Catskills, and even the Empire Plaza in Albany on a crystal-clear day. You may be rewarded instead with an equally precious gift: successive valleys with a layer cake of dense gray and white cumulus clouds, and sunlight as icing. Once, atop this fine peak (fourth tallest in Massachusetts and highest in the southern Berkshires), a young hiker in our group, age 8 and proud of his nascent spelling skills, pointed out that by changing a "t" into an "s", Mt. Everett turns into Mt. Everest: "Then we can say we climbed the world's highest mountain."

Turn right past the fire tower (closed), and descend into the woods. More fine views come along shortly as the AT wends its way to the old fire-tower road. Where the trail leaves this largely washed-out road, at a right turn in the road, there is a good option for day hikers: A few yards down the road is a parking lot at an unnamed stone shelter. This is the topmost end of Mt. Everett Rd. (paved for all but the last 0.5 mi., where it is steep), which you passed on East St. en route to the Sages Ravine trailhead. If, and only if, you're sure you can be here well before the gate at East St. closes (open dawn to dusk), you may park a second car here to conclude a day hike.

The view from the stone shelter, by the way, is worth a side jaunt by hikers continuing on the AT; from the top of Mt. Everett you have no view to the north. But from here, northward in the foreground is Monument Mt., between Great Barrington and Stockbridge. Forty miles northeast, near the horizon, is double-humpbacked Mt. Greylock, on whose whalelike shape Herman Melville brooded from his study in Pittsfield. That far-off mountain—and whatever going beyond it symbolizes—became a dark obsession for Melville, manifesting itself as *Moby Dick*. For AT hikers, Greylock is a benign, tantalizing goal to be reached and surpassed.

Continuing on the AT (or following the road down from the stone shelter), the Guilder Pond picnic area soon appears on the left (6.5 mi.). People, voices, cars. And a deluxe outhouse.

Of Children, Scraped Knees, and Pride

It has rained off and on for days and the path is slimy-wet, an unpatterned hopscotch of mud and glistening rocks. Your eight-year-old hiking buddy slips, stumbles, scrapes a knee, and moistens the path a little more with some tears. You've just started out, and now he's afraid to go on, sensing that there are hours of this terror ahead of him. You may have reservations about hiking with young kids (low pain tolerance, short attention span), enough to cast a sudden pall over your own sunny enthusiasm. But magically, after a hug with some comforting words, applying no-sting first-aid ointment and a Band-Aid, presto, you're underway again.

A child's chagrin is disempowering, but new knowledge is like an extra set of muscles. For kids new to the sport, you might try deconstructing the action of hiking: what's obvious to adults isn't necessarily so to kids. The trick is first to get the young one to slow down so as to see what he's doing that gets him into slippery trouble. Then maybe he'll be able to speed up, safely, later on.

You could try this: "Lift your feet higher when you're going over rocks or logs or stumps, as if you were marching in the school band for the Halloween Parade. Look for dry spots, so you can use the friction between your shoes and the ground."

"What's 'friction'?" he may ask, sliding again down the shiny wet side of a rain-slicked boulder. Hang in there, even if you can't remember not knowing what "friction" is. Surely there was a time when you, too, had to ask. More power to him for not pretending to know. Do a little physics lesson as you walk: friction, gravity, equilibrium. Keep it concrete. Teach him about onomatopoeia—"friction" is one of those words with a meaningful sound. Show him how to step only where his shoe will make a dry, grating sound underneath. Help him look for natural steps or the ones built into the trail by the AMC. Make a game of identifying and explaining the difference between dangerous spots where concentration is necessary and easy spots where a hiker can be more playful.

Odds are that later on in the same day, your young companion will be doing fine, scrambling over rocks faster than you can keep up with him. He'll probably spout his newly found wisdom about walking safely on the trail. And you will hear pride in his voice and realize that you have accomplished something larger than a few miles of hiking.

A side trail (at 6.6 mi.) circumnavigates the pond (at 2402 ft., the second highest water in Massachusetts). Impromtu swimming is OK, but there's no beach.

The AT rambles gently now, with only a 330-ft. change, downward, in the next 2.8 mi. At 7.0 mi., deep in the forest, a spur trail leads to the Glen

Brook Lean-to and Campsite, a good overnight option for those whose first day of hiking has brought them over the top of Mt. Everett. An easy descent follows Glen Brook, along the wooded eastern slope of Mt. Undine (2203 ft.), whose rounded top you may not even notice. At a distinct left turn, 7.6 mi., the blue-blazed Elbow Trail appears on the right (it's maintained by the students at Berkshire School). It goes down, sharply, about 1.5 mi. southeast to the campus on MA 41 at the bottom of the valley (850 ft. elevation).

Giant strides are easy now, the AT wide and smooth. Coming out soon at the eastern edge of the Mt. Everett ridge, the next 2 mi. deliver prizes for today's effort: repeated excellent views to the north and northeast, as the trail crosses the relatively flat summit of Mt. Bushnell (1834 ft., 8.1 mi.), then two more intermediate, hardly noticeable peaks. In this section the landscape provides the perfect combination of elevation and exposure for a happy result in mid- to late summer: heavily laden wild blueberry bushes. Walk, stoop, pluck, toss 'em down, smile contentedly at Earth's free bounty, then repeat the sequence. But keep an eye out for rattlesnakes if you're reaching into low-lying bushes near rocks.

In his richly informative *Nature Walks in the Berkshire Hills*, Charles Smith notes that these Taconic and Berkshire mountain ridges are frequently forested by pitch pine and bear oak, and the latter tree has an

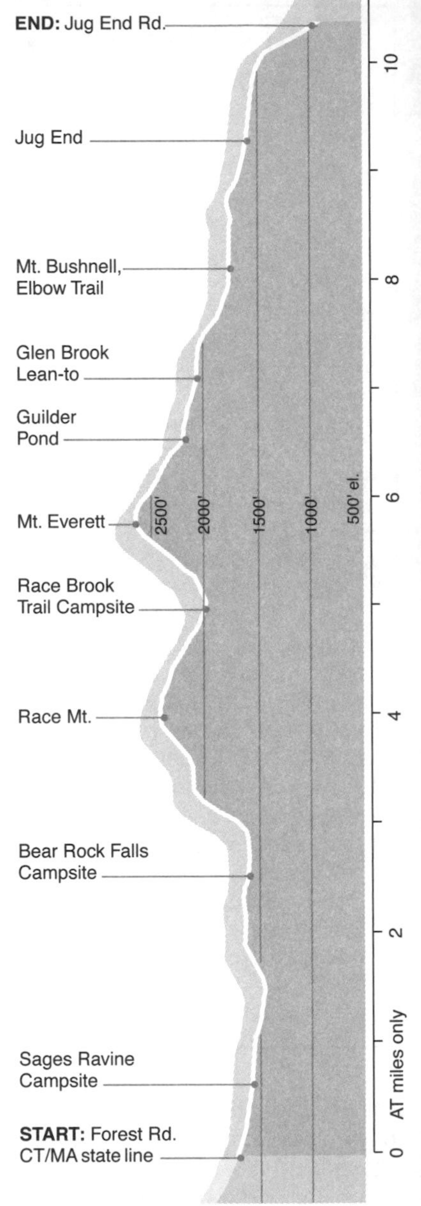

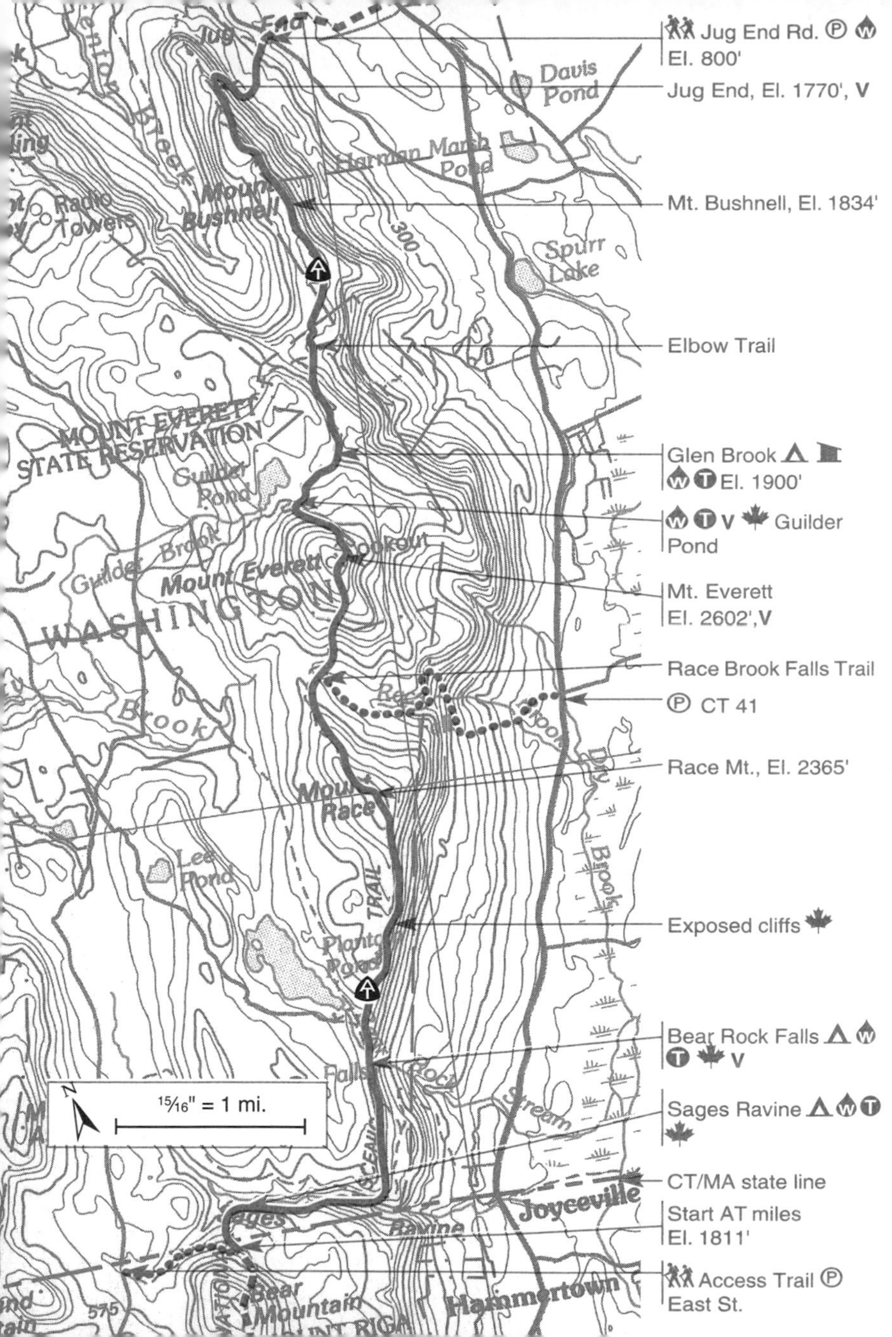

Jug End Rd. Ⓟ
El. 800'
Jug End, El. 1770', V
Mt. Bushnell, El. 1834'
Elbow Trail
Glen Brook
El. 1900'
V Guilder
Pond
Mt. Everett
El. 2602',V
Race Brook Falls Trail
Ⓟ CT 41
Race Mt., El. 2365'
Exposed cliffs
Bear Rock Falls
V
Sages Ravine
CT/MA state line
Start AT miles
El. 1811'
Access Trail Ⓟ
East St.
15/16" = 1 mi.
Davis Pond
Harmon Marsh Pond
Spurr Lake
Radio Towers
Mount Bushnell
Jug End
MOUNT EVERETT STATE RESERVATION
Guilder Pond
Guilder Brook
Mount Everett
Lookout
WASHINGTON
Lee Pond
Mount Race
Plantain Pond
TRAIL
Joyceville
Hammertown
Bear Mountain
Sages Ravine
575

interesting history and chemistry about it.

There are about three hundred different species of oak that grow around the world, thirty-four of which are indigenous to the eastern United States. Historically these trees have been one of the most important sources of high-grade lumber. The bark has been used for tanning and cork and the acorns are a significant source of food for wildlife. In European tradition the tree was venerated by the Druids and used to build English warships, and served as the hiding place for Robin Hood's treasures. In New England the Charter of Connecticut was hidden within a great oak when royal agents demanded its surrender in 1687.

All of this nobility and purpose, however, have managed to elude the little bear oak. While some oaks can reach 100 feet in height, the bear oak is stretching things if it gets 20 feet tall. It is too small for lumber, and its nuts are so full of bitter tannin that almost no animal will eat them. Yet the nobility in nature, if not always obvious, is always present. Bear oaks are celebrated because they can survive where no other oak can.

This little tree thrives in the nutrient-starved soils that often drape the highest Berkshire summits, helping to stabilize these fragile areas. Its small size makes it less prone to wind damage, and the hardy twigs can survive frigid winter winds that would kill other trees. In addition, bear oaks tend to grow in dense thickets which serve as hiding places for wildlife such as birds and chipmunks. Bear oak is recognized easily by its small, sometimes holly-shaped leaves that are dark green above and gray beneath. In autumn the leaves turn a muted red.*

Next, Hike #9's pièce de résistance: Jug End summit (1770 ft., 9.3 mi.).

You will want to pause here, before the knee-crunching downhill work ahead of you. If you meditate a bit on history, you may pick up vibes left by Mahican chief Konkapot, who, it is said, liked to view his vast "Hooestonnuc" valley tribal lands from this spectacular perch. The Mahican people had villages at present-day Great Barrington, Stockbridge, and elsewhere in the river valley. They long ago moved to Wisconsin, after selling (or losing) their land to white settlers. The Mahicans were distinct from the Schaghticokes of the lower Housatonic valley in Connecticut (see Hike #2).

The odd name "Jug End" has nothing to do with endings, geological or otherwise, but rather is a poorly Anglicized version of the Dutch and German *jugend,* for "youth" or "young." The Dutch from the Hudson Valley settled early in what became Mt. Washington and Egremont.

---

*Charles W.G. Smith, *Nature Walks in the Berkshire Hills.* Appalachian Mountain Club Books, 1997, pp. 55–56.

Scramble another 0.4 mi. and over the brink you go on the glacier-smoothed rocks, losing 970 ft. in just 0.7 mi.—which is why, unless they like rock climbing, few hikers go up to Mt. Everett this way. Given the pitch here, a hang glider might be a more comfortable way to get down to the valley, where Egremont Plain awaits you. At Jug End Rd. (10.4 mi.), a reliable spring is 0.2 mi. to the right (south).

Other Trails in the Mt. Everett Region

The South Taconic Trail system (STT), overseen by the New York–New Jersey Trail Conference, maintains several other trails along the New York border with Massachusetts and Connecticut. From the East St. trailhead of Hike #9, the Mt. Frissell Trail goes west to link with the white-blazed STT, which runs south a few miles into Dutchess County (New York) and north all the way to MA 23 at the Catamount ski area on the New York–Massachusetts line. On its northward journey, the STT meets the Alander Trail, which runs back east to the Mt. Washington State Forest headquarters on East St.; from the Alander junction, the STT hooks west to head down the Bash Bish Falls gorge to the famous waterfall in Bash Bish Falls State Park. The falls (the biggest single drop is 80 ft.) are a 10-min. walk from the parking lot on Falls Rd., accessible from East St. in Mt. Washington or from NY 344 in Copake Falls, New York. (The state line is about 1000 ft. below the falls.) Two state parks—Bash Bish in Massachusetts and Taconic in New York—offer car camping here. Convenient, but heavily trafficked.

HIKE #9 Itinerary

Miles N	NORTH	Elev. (ft./m)	Miles S
Total: 11.2 mi. with access trail			
10.4	**End: Jug End Rd.,** Sheffield; parking.	800/244	0.0
9.7	Crest of rocks; begin steep descent.		0.7
9.3	**Jug End summit** (Chief Konkapot's view).	1770/518	1.1
8.9	Cross another intermediate peak.		1.5
8.5	Cross intermediate peak.		1.9
8.1	**Mt. Bushnell.**	1834/559	2.3
7.6	Distinct L turn; **Elbow Trail** enters on R (SE to MA 41 at Berkshire School, approx. 1.5 mi.).		2.8
7.3	Easy descent on E side of Mt. Undine.		3.1
7.0	**Glen Brook Lean-to and Campsite,** short side trail on R.	1900/579	3.4
6.6	Trail from **Guilder Pond** enters L.	2042/622	3.8
6.5	**Guilder Pond** picnic site.	2100/640	3.9
6.4	Dirt road.		4.0
6.1	Old fire-tower road (no vehicles).		4.3
5.8	**Mt. Everett** summit (R turn at fire tower).	2602/793	4.6
5.1	**Race Brook Falls Trail,** enters R; 0.4 mi. to campsite and top of falls; blue-blazed trail continues 1.5 mi. down to MA 41; AT begins strenuous climb to Mt. Everett.	1900/579	5.3
4.0	**Race Mt.,** superb views; descend.	2365/721	6.4
3.4	Southern end of exposed cliffs; views.		7.0
2.3	**Bear Rock Stream;** on R: campsite, falls, view.	1700/518	8.1
0.9	**Sages Ravine Brook.**	1300/396	9.5
0.5	**Sages Ravine Campsite,** N side of trail.	1400/427	9.2
0.0	**Start AT miles:** Turn L onto **AT** and head N.	1811/552	10.4
0.8	Access: AMC parking, **East St., Mt. Washington,** at MA/CT line; follow trail (Northwest Rd. on some maps) E to AT.		0.8

SOUTH

HIKE: #10

Sheffield to Jug End, South Egremont

Maps: ATC Mass. & Conn. #3
Route: From Boardman St. to Sheffield–South Egremont Rd., to MA 41, to Jug End Rd.
Recommended direction: N to S
Distance: 5.4 mi.
Elevation +/-: Negligible
Effort: Easy
Day hike: Yes
Overnight backpacking hike: No
Duration: 2½ to 3 hr.
Early exit options: US 7; Sheffield–South Egremont Rd.
Natural history features: Housatonic River, bog
Social history features: Shays's Rebellion historic site
Trailhead access: *Start:* From Great Barrington follow US 7 S, cross Sheffield town line, turn L onto Kellogg Rd., and follow to its end at Boardman St. Park on Kellogg Rd. or in AMC lot (planned for 1998). *End:* From Gt. Barrington follow MA 23 W to South Egremont, then MA 41 S for 100 yd. Turn R onto Mt. Washington Rd. At about 0.9 mi. turn L onto Avenue Rd., which soon joins Jug End Rd. Trailhead parking, R, is about 0.8 mi. farther on.

Sometimes what's wanted is a stroll, a ramble, and not a climb. If you are so inclined, a hike across the Housatonic River valley in the southern Berkshires can be a real delight. The rewards here are several: the chance of seeing herons feeding in the riverbed, the sight of many wildflowers in fields and bogs, the uplift of impressive mountain views. This short hike can be further shortened at any of several road crossings, but taken as a whole it's a fine morning or afternoon outing. We recommend walking north to south because toward hike's end, the views of the Taconic Range and Mt. Everett to the southwest are excellent and because it's nice to have the road noise of busy US 7 well behind you for most of the hike. However, walking south to north is good as well, and Berkshirites will want to go both ways eventually. One caveat: a few sections are wet and mucky despite recently installed bog bridges and puncheons. Bring extra socks just in case.

At Boardman St. and Kellogg Rd., in Sheffield, the trail heads southward (in AT terms; actual direction is more westerly) along the edge of a cornfield. The first views of Mt. Everett are fine even from here but will improve as the hike proceeds across the valley. Leaving the cornfield, the trail winds briefly through woods before joining Kellogg Rd. to cross the river.

Shays's Rebellion

The Revolution may have been won in 1776, but then the hard work of forming a lasting Union began. For a decade there was as much disunity as unity among the former colonies. Among the worst problems was the regulation of trade. Under the Articles of Confederation, the central government could not tax citizens. The states wanted to keep the central government weak: a remnant fear from pre-Revolutionary days under King George. There were no federal trade laws, and each state could tax as it pleased products coming in from other states. In September 1786 a convention, attended by delegates from only five of the thirteen states, met in Annapolis and adopted plans, using revisions to the Articles of Confederation as proposed by Hamilton and Madison, for a stronger central government.

After the Revolution, the price of goods had risen steadily. Many people were overcome by debt. In August 1781 alone, 165 cases concerning debtors

Henry Lafleur

Shays's Rebellion monument at trailside, Sheffield

Detour: As of early 1998, hikers here faced a somewhat confusing problem. The trail had recently been relocated to the river's edge northward before angling toward US 7 and then crossing the highway, traversing a field, crossing the railroad tracks, and then reentering the woods. But, alas, the Housatonic Railroad Co., owners of the tracks, withdrew their permission for the trail to cross their right-of-way. The AT was thus, temporarily at least, forced back onto its former route, using the local roads as follows: Continue on Kellogg Rd. to US 7, cross it angling toward Lime Kiln Rd., then follow that road, immediately crossing the railroad tracks, and continue a brief distance until the road rises gently, with the lime kilns themselves on the right (private property). A gated drive on the right leads the AT back into the woods.

When the dispute with the Hous-

were heard at the Great Barrington Court of Common Pleas; by 1784, there were even more. The states repeatedly increased their taxes (war debts had to be paid, new roads were required), further burdening private citizens. Many farmers—especially in Massachusetts—lost their land to the banks through mortgage foreclosures. By the summer of 1786, a loosely knit group of landowners in the southern Berkshires, centered in Sheffield and Great Barrington, revolted against the Commonwealth's tax laws. In August, an angry mob of 800 prevented the Great Barrington court from sitting. To stop judges from issuing further foreclosure orders, the farmers seized the courthouse. One Berkshire yeoman reportedly called the court "a Damned Pack of Rascals."

Daniel Shays, who had fought in the Revolution, led a rowdy band of farmers and other landholders on a march past the courthouse and armory in Springfield. Threatened by violence from Shays's people, the state legislature in Boston adjourned. Eventually, Shays's irregular troops were broken up by the state militia, led by Col. John Ashley, in February 1787 in a battle on the Sheffield Plain, now marked by a monument on the Egremont–Sheffield Rd. at the AT crossing. A few men were killed; more than a few were injured.

"Shays's Rebellion," as it came to be called, produced little specific tax relief legislation or court reform, but it brought into sharper focus the country's need for a unified central government, empowered to tax its people and regulate the economy. Thus it contributed to the momentum toward a Constitutional Convention, which took place that year, resulting in a signed document by September. This instrument, for all its ambiguities (debated to this day), still shines as a model to all nations, the backbone of the oldest continuously standing constitutional government in the world.

atonic Railroad Co. is resolved, the AT will again proceed from the Housatonic River bridge on Kellogg Rd. as follows: Turn sharp right on a farm road leading to the river's edge, with more fields on the left. The next 0.5 mi. follows the riverbank and actually carries you northward on this southward walk! Never mind. Remember, this is a meandering stroll.

Those familiar with New England mountain geology will appreciate the smoothness of the grassy path here. The soil in the cornfields is sandy and loamy, relatively free of rocks, and the riverbanks show off the underlying soil structure. Not only has the river spread its sediment over the valley in the floodplain, but the valley itself is the floor of an ancient lake from preglacial times.

These are rich farmlands, in use hereabouts for thousands of years by the Mahican people, who had settlements at river crossings in present-day Sheffield, Great Barrington, and

Stockbridge. The valley and its woodlands were Mahican hunting grounds, and the river provided an abundance of fish and small mammals (keep an eye out for muskrat). You may see fly-fishermen in the shallows, but you may also note the posted warnings about PCBs in the fish. Industrial sites upstream (primarily General Electric Co., in Pittsfield) unwittingly polluted the river. A decades-long debate about how to clean it up and who should pay drags on. The Housatonic River Watershed Association and other regional conservation groups are making headway in cleaning the river. After appreciating its beauty, you may want to join the effort.

Along the river and at cornfield's edge there's a plethora of wildflowers, more common than exotic, but lovely nonetheless. One June day we spotted black-eyed Susans, purple asters, bluets, fragrant honeysuckle abuzz with pollinating bees, buttercups, daisies, Queen Anne's lace (wild carrot), milkweed in the early stage of building its seedpod, and the aromatic wild plum (a shrub with five-petaled purple flowers), reminiscent of the rose family, thorns and all. Armed with a wildflower book, you will discover many more.

At US 7, the Corn Crib farm store is 0.1 mi. north, a source for snacks and drinks if you forgot them. Cross US 7 (0.9 mi.) very carefully, keeping kids and dogs under control. No parking here. After a short field west of the highway, puncheons seem to

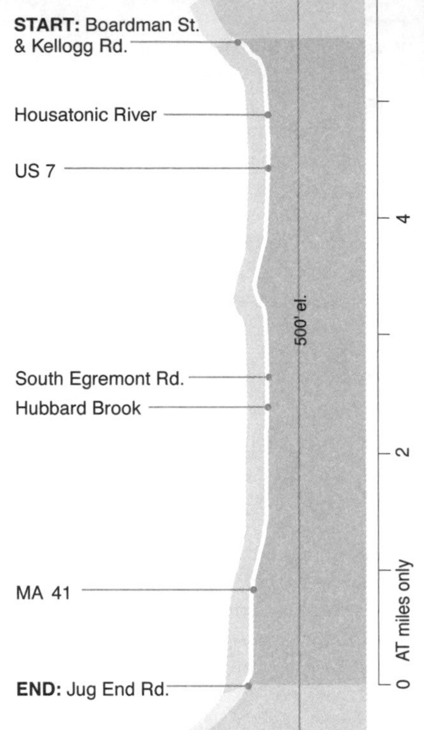

float the trail across a small bog before a little rise takes the AT over the Housatonic Railroad Co. tracks and into a mixed deciduous woodland with abundant wood fern, another small bog, then a 25-ft. rise to a section where the trail rides the bank of a shaded gully with more farm fields just uphill to the left. Leaving the gully, the trail curves left and rises through a brief stand of spindly maples to West Rd. (left, to Sheffield), also called West Sheffield Rd. (right, to South Egremont). No official parking here.

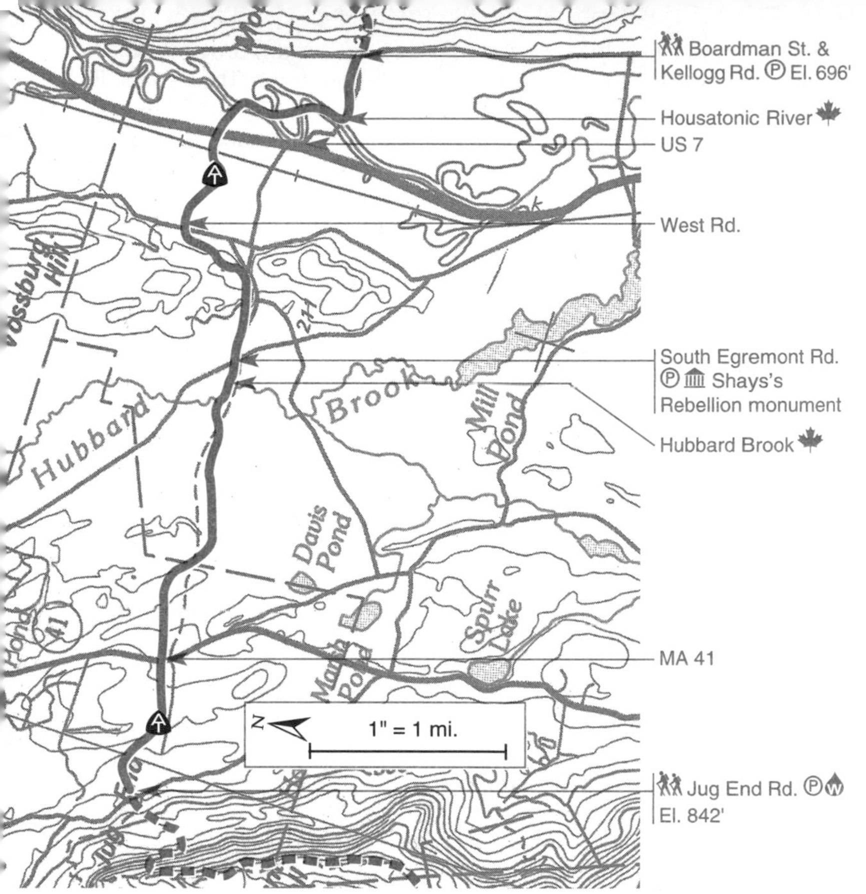

Cross the road, scoot up a tiny hill, and enter another farm field, enclosed by woods. Midfield is a solitary white oak with a magnificent spreading crown. Naturalist Charles Smith *(Nature Walks in the Berkshire Hills)* hangs a tale on this tree:

> In colonial times these great field oaks were sometimes called fairy forts, in reference to the little creatures believed to live beneath them.
>
> To many people of Celtic ancestry, fairies are diminutive folk with supernatural powers.... If you rest beneath the tree, don't be disappointed if you fail to see any fairies, as these shy creatures are primarily nocturnal. On bright moonlit nights, however, they throw caution to the wind and dance merrily beneath the leafy branches. If a fairy takes a liking to you it will fol-

low you home, bringing good fortune to wherever you live.*

Keep to the edge of the field as the AT makes a half-circle around it. Shortly after crossing a dirt driveway and then curving left, the trail veers sharply right, back into the forest. A look backward at this point gives a sweeping view of the mountains to the east (June Mt., East Mt.), at whose foot you began this hike.

A brief rise in the woods leads to a left turn in the AT, marked by a faint double blaze (a woods roads continues straight). Another gentle rise along a mossy stone wall and then a short switchback bring the trail to a (usually) breezy ridge, still in the woods—generally oaks and hickories here. A few minutes of easy downhill walking are followed by a breathtaking view of the Mt. Everett (Taconic) Range when the AT exits the woods at a dirt road. This is where the detour described above rejoins the AT. Turn right to follow a hayfield's border. If you have planned lunch or a snack on this hike, here's your best view and sweetest resting place. Along the mountain range to the south the view sweeps into Connecticut. The AT runs along the crest as far as the eye can see, toward Salisbury. On the range coming northward from the top of Mt. Everett (marked by a fire tower), the mountain gently descends until it reaches Jug End, a sharp drop-off over which the AT plummets. The Taconic Range continues north, out of the picture frame, to Catamount ski area (MA 23) and north all the way along the Massachusetts–New York border.

After leaving these delightful fields, again a fine wildflower area, the trail reaches South Egremont Rd. (2.7 mi.), where the historical marker for Shays's Rebellion stands (see "Shays's Rebellion"). A few yards to the right along the road is an AMC parking lot. The road leads to Sheffield (left) and South Egremont (right), minutes by car in either direction.

Hubbard Brook bridge is next on the trail (2.9 mi.), affording a good look into the aquatic plant life below. Dogs may have trouble here with the bridge's ladders. The next mile or so is often wet. AT volunteers have installed numerous bog bridges made of synthetic wood with a *long* lifespan (recycled plastic bags, provided with help from Mobil and Amoco oil corporations). The swampy areas attract many songbirds, red-winged blackbirds especially. Don't fall in while watching them!

Rising eventually out of the woods, again into farm fields with ancient crab apple trees along the trail, views of Mt. Everett reappear (much closer now), and the MA 41 crossing marks another way point in the hike (4.5 mi., no parking). Traffic is fast here; use caution. With a gentle upward tendency (the beginning of the Taconic piedmont), the land rises as the AT passes through deeply shaded pine

---

*Charles W. G. Smith, *Nature Walks in the Berkshire Hills*. Appalachian Mountain Books, 1997, p.14.

HIKE #10 Itinerary

Miles N	NORTH	Elev. (ft./m)	Miles S
5.4	**Start: Boardman St. & Kellogg Rd.,** Sheffield, overnight parking (new in 1998).	696/212	0.0
5.0	**Housatonic River,** bridge; soon turn R into farm road entering fields (See "Detour," p. 96.)		0.4
4.5	**US 7,** no parking; cross carefully, continue through wet fields and over numerous bog bridges.	674/205	0.9
4.4	Railroad tracks.		1.0
3.9	**West Rd.**		1.5
3.2	Modest ridge, followed by more fields.		2.2
2.7	**South Egremont Rd.,** Shays's Rebellion monument, parking.		2.7
2.5	**Hubbard Brook,** bridge.		2.9
1.7	Series of bog bridges, swamps, a small rise, more bridges.		3.7
1.3	AT uses old road on higher ridge.		4.1
0.9	**MA 41,** no parking; South Egremont village approx. 1.3 mi. N.		4.5
0.6	Stone wall, followed by 0.3 mi. in pine woods.		4.8
0.0	**End: Jug End Rd.,** South Egremont, overnight parking; spring 0.2 mi. S beside road.	842/257	5.4

SOUTH

and hemlock woods, all second or third growth as confirmed by the crisscrossing stone walls (4.8 mi.) that once marked pastures in this area. Put out your antennae and listen for distant whispers from across the decades, from farmers and horses and oxen who labored in these all-but-forgotten fields. In just over another half mile, Jug End Rd. marks the end of this stroll, where you will note how steeply the trail and the mountain rise on the far side of the road. There is parking for several cars along the road here, and a reliable piped spring 0.2 mi. south on the right.

HIKE: #11

Sheffield to Monterey

Maps: ATC Mass. & Conn. #3
Route: From Kellogg Rd. and Boardman St., Sheffield, over East and Warner Mts. to MA 23, Monterey
Recommended direction: S to N
Distance: 7.1 mi.
Elevation +/-: 696 to 1890 to 1024 ft.
Effort: Easy to moderate
Day hike: Yes
Overnight backpacking hike: Optional
Duration: 4¼ hr.
Early exit option: Home Rd., at 1.7 mi.; Lake Buel Rd., at 5.6 mi.
Natural history features: Ice Gulch; Lake Buel swamp; tornado damage
Trailhead access: *Start:* From US 7 about 1 mi. S of the Great Barrington / Sheffield town line, turn L (E) onto Kellogg Rd. Follow Kellogg about 0.7 mi. to its end at Boardman St.; park on roadside; new AMC overnight parking here in 1998. *End:* Go E on MA 23 from Great Barrington to the Monterey / Great Barrington town line, 0.1 mi. W of the MA 57 junction; AMC overnight parking, N side of MA 23. (Note: tornado damage in this area but trail is open.)
Camping: Tom Leonard Lean-to and Campsite

The flat valley bottom is the inauspicious starting point for this delightful hike over a relatively seldom used trail. We recommend this section as one deserving of more attention. It's a good place to have the AT mostly to yourself. On Hike #11 you can anticipate a lazy lunch high up on a rocky ledge with an inspiring view to the south, down the winding Housatonic valley.

Leave the Sheffield cornfields behind you as you step into the woods at Boardman St., where the hills rise from the Housatonic River's eastern shoulder. Out of the sunlight and suddenly into the shade, the climb begins. The effort soon reaps rewards as the valley's mingled human sounds (traffic, farm machinery, backyard voices) are muffled to silence by a spongy ground cover of pine needles, leaves, and moss.

From the river, at about 600 ft., the AT aims for East Mt., which peaks at around 1800 ft., then travels on to Warner Mt. After a gradual decline to the bog feeding Lake Buel, it ends with a short rise to MA 23, at about 1000 ft., in Monterey. A net gain of only 400 ft. overall, but on this walk the relative elevations will be deceptive. Geologically speaking, from the young, sandy soil in the heavily silted Housatonic valley to the ancient marble outcroppings high in the hills, this hike is a journey through time itself.

The Rocks Underfoot

Some Berkshire rocks are "foreigners," having been deposited here by the tumultuous action of shifting, overlapping continental plates, while others were dropped by the advancing and retreating glaciers. In the Cambrian period, some 600 million years ago, Berkshire County was all underwater—ocean water, that is, the seacoast being to the *west!* Waves on the beaches created sandstone that, given time and pressure, metamorphosed into the quartzite found throughout the hills. Limestone evolved from marine crustaceans' coral reefs. Again, with time and pressure, creating enormous heat, the result was something familiar to us now: marble outcroppings that, on the Appalachian Trail, adorn the path underfoot like so many naturally white blazes. The muddy underbelly of the vast sea evolved, geologically, into shale and schist, two crystalline rocks that often split evenly. Much of this rock has been pushed upward. In south Berkshire it's common to see igneous granite, as it will be for eons to come: granite is *durable*.

In terms of seniority, the Taconic ridge, on the west side of the Housatonic valley, considerably antedates all other hills in the region; as young mountains, the Taconics towered skyward. The folding, overlapping continental shelf slid westward toward Berkshire territory, bringing with it the "Berkshire massif" on the east side of the valley (all the upland hilltown area from Monterey to Windsor and Clarksburg at the Vermont border). In a generally north–south direction, the glaciers scored the surface rocks, carved out a few shallow lakes, scattered "glacial erratics" (random boulders) everywhere, but left the already established rivers to flow again, eventually, in their well-established courses (Housatonic southward; Hoosic, surprisingly, northward). Wind, ice, rain, and running water continue to reshape the landscape today. Southern New England has been glacier-free for only a blink in time, just 10,000 years. With a rock hound's book in hand on the Appalachian Trail, you can see back in time to hundreds of millions of years before that most recent geologic event.

The first 1.7 mi. rise and decline over modest June Mt., all in the woods until a crossing at Home Rd. At 2.5 mi., after a large glacial boulder and a cleft with a quietly spouting spring in its bottom, a bad-weather bypass trail veers off to the left. Usually such bypasses on the AT provide an escape from sections that are truly dangerous or scary under wet conditions, but the actual AT miles just ahead make one wonder why such a bypass was needed here. Granted you'll walk on the edge of a ridge, exposed to the southwest (the direction from which most good and bad weather comes), but it's pretty benign all the way.

Your muscles will tell you, if your eyes don't, that the AT is definitely ascending the steep ridge side of East Mt. The topographic map's contour lines squeeze ever more closely together here. The uphill work is steady but not overwhelming. Facing southwest has an advantage now, in that almost always there's a blessed breeze, swooping across the valley and up the mountainside. Birds love such updrafts. Take a rest and break out the bird book and binoculars. Hawks, turkey vultures, ravens, common crows, and uncommon herons (that feed in the river) may put on a show here for observant hikers.

The trail snakes upward with short, then longer, switchbacks (where the path turns back on itself to gain elevation gradually). There is no single exposed peak at the top of East Mt.; in fact, most of the pleasure in this climb comes in the first half mile, once you're on the ridge. For here, along the western edge of East Mt., it's panorama bonanza time. Repeatedly there are lovely overlooks to the south and west. What a pastoral canvas! The foreground is the Housatonic valley; midground is the Taconic Range, including Mt. Everett (2602 ft.) with its long-distance reference point, the fire tower (see Hike #9); and in the background are the Catskills, beyond the Hudson Valley, visible only as a faint horizon on all but the clearest days. Your problem now is a sweet one: which promontory to choose for lunch? Our advice: ramble onward to 3.1 mi. at a ridgetop point where the AT makes a sharp left turn away from the cliff. Here is the best southern view.

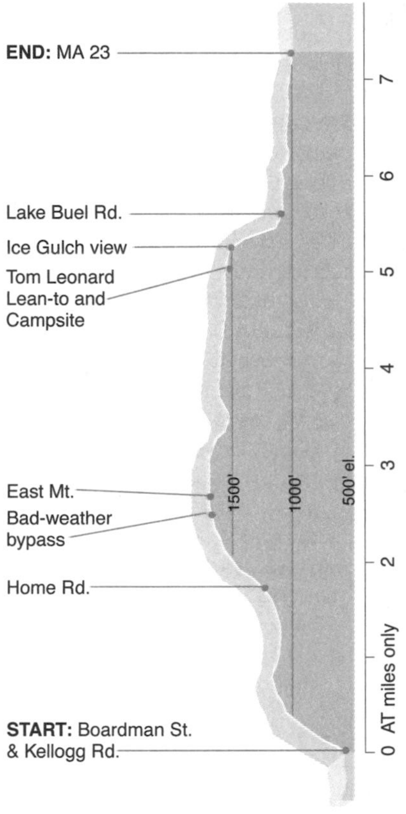

If your timetable allows, a siesta or a little after-lunch reading or sketching in the dappled sunshine here would be delightful.

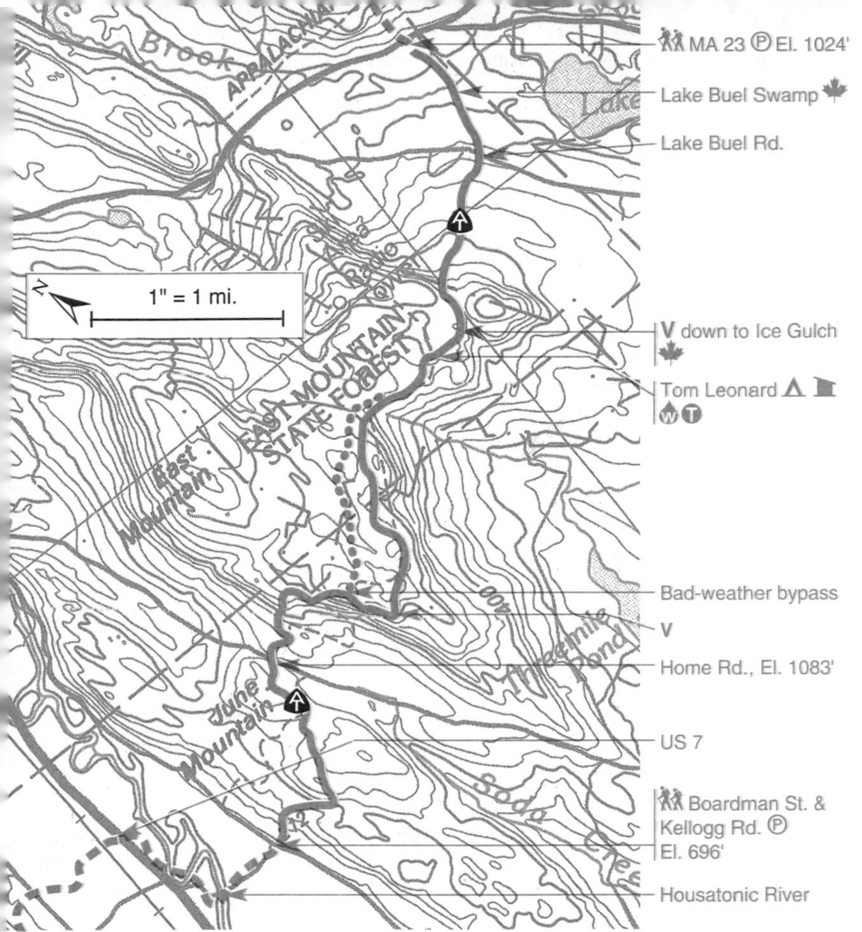

Even if you carry on right after lunch (in a mild digestive stupor . . .), don't worry about the terrain. The next 1.5 mi. atop East Mt. undulate easily. This is the mountain's eastern flank, running north toward Warner Mt. The AT has been shifted up here in recent years; it used to go to the top of Warner Mt., on the back side of Butternut Basin ski area, then down the ski trails to MA 23. Now a seldom used side trail, left, shortly south of the Tom Leonard Lean-to, leads up to Warner Mt. (forested) and over to the top of the ski area, where there are good views. Hikers are welcome to hike in for the look and back out to the AT again, but descending the ski trails is verboten.

Next, at 5.2 mi., the AT passes the (very short) spur trail to the newish Tom Leonard Lean-to (a state-of-the-art affair with tent platform, view to the southeast, picnic table, refreshing spring water down in Ice Gulch, and outhouse). Following the shelter, along this side of East Mt. you'll find yourself peering down into a deep, extended abyss on the right. Down, way down, in the eternally refrigerated shadows is Ice Gulch. Those who've grown jaded about the popular walk at Ice Glen in Stockbridge can here renew their sense of the awesomeness of nature's power. The 19th-century landscape painters of the Hudson River School, with an eye toward what they called the "sublime" (that spine-tingling marriage of beauty and terror found in wild places and gothic stories), would have had a heyday with Ice Gulch. Both the upwardly thrusting tectonic plates and the retreating glacier have left their violent marks, creating a beautiful if spooky place.

Ice Gulch is a mad tumble of huge boulders, with no apparent bottom to stand on—except a subterranean, off-limits world in the chilly darkness below. That inscrutable darkness in the caves makes a cold winter's ice linger throughout the entire summer. Rock climbing here is more akin to spelunking. Be very careful.

After views into the gulch, the AT ambles happily downward to cross Lake Buel Rd. (paved, at 5.6 mi., parking). Things here turn moist and musky, as the trail soon approaches a small dam at the foot of Lake Buel Swamp (6.1 mi.). The bog spreads northwest for 2.5 mi., teeming with life. If the bugs aren't bad, this is a great spot to stay put and watch for everything from birds to beavers to moose. For the latter, you'd better have time to spare. Though moose are showing up in Berkshire towns more often these days, they are still a rarity. Crisscrossing the woods hereabouts are bridle paths and, as you will surmise from the tracks, and perhaps from the sounds, mountain bike and motorbike trails. Several hours in the woods, alone or almost so, gives one a proprietary feeling. This busy network of trails may seem an invasion of your privacy.

Alas, at 6.2 mi., the AT reaches the tornado damage area (May 1995). It was a vicious storm, taking three lives, scores of homes, and thousands of trees. AT trail crews worked feverishly in the summer of 1995 to reopen the footpath. When you give thanks that you weren't hiking here when the twister roared through, give thanks to the trail crew too.

Your car awaits you, minutes later, at the MA 23 AMC parking lot. The road, with its whir of passing traffic, reminds hikers that in the Berkshires, wilderness and society live cheek by jowl and had better remain good neighbors. Busy Great Barrington is a 5-min. drive west.

HIKE #11 Itinerary

Miles N	NORTH	Elev. (ft./m)	Miles S
7.1	**End: MA 23,** Monterey; overnight parking.	1024/312	0.0
6.2	Tornado damage area, 1995.		0.9
6.1	Stepping stones, bog bridge across **Lake Buel Swamp,** outflow.	919/280	1.0
5.7	Cross gravel road (to Lake Buel Camp).		1.4
5.6	Cross **Lake Buel Rd.** (paved), parking; early exit option.	1109/338	1.5
5.4	High point with view down into **Ice Gulch.**		1.7
5.2	Small brook, then spur trail, R, to **Tom Leonard Lean-to and Campsite,** water, privy.	1540/469	1.9
4.8	Another junction with former AT (leads to **Butternut Basin ski area,** views); current AT veers R.	1890/576	2.3
4.4	AT curves R, away from old trail to top of Warner Mt.		2.7
3.3	Cross unused forest road; AT parallels steep drop-off on R.		3.8
3.1	Sharp L turn at large boulder; excellent views.	1723/525	4.0
2.6	Ascend to ridge of **East Mt.;** excellent views to S and W.		4.5
2.5	Large glacial boulder; cross cleft (spring at bottom of cleft); alternate bad-weather bypass heads L (1.5 mi.).		4.6
2.0	Distinct R turn.		5.1
1.9	Join old forest road; head L, climbing ridge.		5.2
1.7	Diagonal left across **Home Rd.;** re-enter woods.	1083/330	5.4
1.3	Brook crossing; shortly head R on unused woods road.		5.8
0.0	**Start: Kellogg Rd. & Boardman St.,** Sheffield; day parking (new in 1998); enter forest, climbing ridge of June Mt.	696/212	7.1

HIKE: #12

Beartown State Forest to Tyringham Cobble

Maps: ATC Mass. & Conn. #3

Route: From MA 23 (Monterey/Great Barrington line), through Beartown State Forest, to Tyringham Valley and Tyringham Cobble, to Tyringham Main Rd.

Recommended direction: S to N

Distance: 12.1 mi.

Elevation +/-: 1024 to 2100 to 1000 to 1250 to 955 ft.

Effort: Moderate

Day hike: Yes

Overnight backpacking hike: Optional

Duration: 6½ to 7 hr.

Early exit option: Blue Hill Rd., at 1.2 mi., no parking; Beartown State Forest, at 1.6 mi.; Beartown Mt. Rd., at 5.8 mi.; Fernside-Jerusalem Rd., at 8.9 mi., limited roadside parking; Jerusalem Rd., at 11.0 mi., overnight parking about 0.2 mi. N at Trustees of Reservations lot

Natural history features: Vast state park, abundant wildlife; Benedict Pond; exposed rock ledges; meadows with numerous wildflowers; Hop Brook

Social history features: Shaker buildings and holy land

Other features: Trustees of Reservations property (Tyringham Cobble)

Trailhead access: *Start:* From Great Barrington go E on MA 23 to the Monterey / Great Barrington town line, just W (0.1 mi.) of the MA 57 junction; AMC overnight parking, N side of MA 23. (Note: tornado damage in this area but trail is open.)

From Tyringham (see *End*), follow Tyringham Main Rd. S, away from village, to R turn onto Monterey Rd. (also known as Tyringham-Monterey Rd.). Cross the valley, go back up over the mountain and down into Monterey village to MA 23. Monterey General Store is good for provisions. Turn R (W) and follow MA 23 to MA 57 (on L). Just beyond is AMC parking, R.

End: From Lee (off MA 102), take Tyringham Main Rd. into and through Tyringham village; AT is 0.9 mi. W of post office; park on shoulder (S side of road). Tyringham, pop. 335, has *no* stores. Center of town is town hall and post office. Don't blink or you'll miss them!

Beartown Mt. Rd. Access: For this early exit option, take Tyringham Rd. (from the center of Monterey village) about 0.7 mi. and turn L onto Beartown Mt. Rd. (paved for the first few mi., then dirt to the AT crossing at, effectively, the dead end). The road dwindles to seldom-used double track. Parking and turnaround space appear, R, just before the AT crossing.

Camping: Beartown State Forest campground (car camping) at Benedict Pond; Mt. Wilcox South and North Lean-tos; Shaker Campsite

Ups and downs, inspiring views, a choice of lean-tos, running and still water: Hike #12's second name is "variety." The tornado of Memorial Day 1995 ripped through the trailhead area, but soon enough the hike leaves the disturbed area behind, entering lovely woods. The first mile or so is easy going, with the fun of bog bridges and steppingstones in a red-maple swamp. At the Blue Hill Rd. crossing (1.2 mi.), the trail suddenly vaults upward the better part of 500 ft. through a glacial boulder field. Have a swig of water before you climb up, for you'll be panting at the top. Take a rest at about 1.5 mi. at a long-gone charcoal burner's fire pit. The role of charcoal in iron-making is discussed in "Sloane-Stanley Museum and Kent Iron Works" in Hike #4.

The AT meanders now for quite some time through 10,870-acre Beartown State Forest, third largest in the commonwealth. At 2.0 mi. the trail passes the inlet to 37-acre Benedict Pond, a glacial pool. For those with unlimited time on this hike, or for a pleasant short ramble another day, there's the Pond Loop Trail, blue-blazed, with plenty of mountain laurel and azaleas, turtles near the shore, a few beaver lodges in less accessible places, and frequent salamanders in the path. The AT and Pond Loop are contiguous briefly at the southeast end of the pond. At the opposite end of the pond are all the facilities that come with easy access—car-camping areas (outhouse, running water, telephone, picnic tables, swimming beach, rental canoes, fees)—and, occasionally, some of the annoyances too (crowds, trash). Muskrat lodges can be seen near the swimming area. Still, Benedict Pond is arguably one of the prettier pieces of Berkshire water, worth a visit any time of year.

Time to climb again, steeply though briefly. At 2.4 mi. a formerly marshy area has been turned into a pond by beavers, whose engineering work you can inspect in the dam just off the trail. After the pond a turn to the right leads you to The Ledges, a favorite hiker's viewpoint (2.6 mi.). The horizon outlines nearby East and Warner Mts., as well as more distant Mt. Everett. The AT has crossed all these peaks, and the ravines and valleys in between, en route to here. The dominant impression is of endless forest, and these days that's true, with the forest claiming nearly 80 percent of the territory. To get a sense of the Berkshires a century ago, reverse the ratio and wonder at the thought of it (a whole new perspective on clear-cutting).

Berkshire historian Gerard Chapman informed us that tall as Mt. Everett looks from here, it ranks as only the ninth highest peak in the county. All of its taller cousins are up north, leaving Everett as the uncontested queen of southern Berkshire peaks. The Catskills, too, loom massively on the western skyline (on a clear day), like mountain-islands floating on the void of the invisible Hudson Valley, obscured by the Taconic Range.

David Emblidge

Tyringham Valley, from Tyringham Cobble

Unless you're a very quiet and very lucky hiker, your chances of seeing the elusive bobcat, coyote, black bear, or moose—all of which live in the state forest—are slim. You can increase your chances by hiking alone or in small groups, at dawn or dusk, by bushwhacking a little to watering places, and by sitting patiently with your binoculars in hand. Keep an eye out for scat in the trail, bear claw marks on beech trees (whose nuts the bears crave), paw or hoof prints in the mud. A mammal identification book is helpful. Berkshire residents will attest to these fascinating animals' presence with stories of moose and bear who come right into town, as if on a shopping errand. Camping here, you're quite likely to hear a coyote calling in the night, or the hooting of an owl. Remember: we are the visitors in the wilderness. Hang your food well out of reach at night.

After The Ledges, a steep descent, another brook crossing, and back up again. At 3.3 mi., pass a spring (right), then the spur trail to the Mt. Wilcox South Lean-to. There's another spring along the short spur. If you're headed for the Mt. Wilcox North Lean-to, tank up on water here: the source there is less reliable. At either shelter take precautions, especially at night, against pesky porcupines, who will eat not only your food but your boots as well (they like the salt left by perspiration).

The climb continues, steadily, up an unnamed mountain from the top of which, at 4.0 mi. on an open plateau, there are more good southerly views. After a brief, steep descent the AT crosses the Mt. Wilcox Trail (go left, then right, on Mt. Wilcox Rd. to reach the high point—with no view—a 2.5-mi. round-trip).

At 4.5 mi., a hauntingly beautiful beaver pond appears (Swann Brook), studded with hundreds of tall, barkless tree stumps, a veritable cemetery of trees drowned by the spreading watery world of the industrious beaver. A chorus of protests from disturbed bullfrogs and green frogs along the edge of the pond will probably welcome you. You may see painted turtles basking in the sun on logs out in the pond. Snapping turtles are common here as well.

Mt. Wilcox North Lean-to, a shelter for eight to ten sleepers, is 0.3 mi. up a side trail at 5.1 mi., at around 2100 ft., in a seemingly endless wilderness. In fact, in only another 0.5 mi., civilization roars back into view. On weekends especially, the growling sounds of motorbikes, rampaging through woodland trails intersecting the AT, announce, rudely, the temporary end of sylvan peace. At 5.8 mi., the AT crosses the dead end of Beartown Mt. Rd. near its junction with East Brook, where day hikers may want to park car #2. Despite the noisy conclusion, a hike to this access point is a highly satisfactory outing.

If you love a hike through a universe of wildflowers and the eerie, if silent, presence of history, then get on board for the second half of Hike #12. The first 0.5 mi. or more of the AT corridor, heading north, is dominated by water, both running and beaver-dammed. Minor acrobatics may be required to keep your boots dry. Kids will love testing themselves, skipping from rock to log to footbridge to rock.

Soon, though, you're on slightly higher, level ground, in a mature stand of hemlocks. Then, at a striking convergence of three long, mossy stone walls (6.9 mi.), the trail leaves the state forest behind. All through the beech and hemlock groves, the muscular stone walls—some perfectly upright, others tumbled by frost heaves—make stoic declarations of borders and delineations, something walled in or walled out by farmers and herdsmen of a century or even two centuries ago. The occasional ancient apple tree (always a domestic plant) signals the likely presence nearby of a cellar hole on an abandoned farmstead, now smothered in moldering needles and leaves. If you fancy yourself an archaeologist, you may want to explore. Hereabouts there's an eerie feeling of trespassing on private land.

Gentle ups and downs and a wide, clear path make for surprisingly quick momentum over the next mile. If you bend down to retie a bootlace, keep a sharp eye out for a diminutive salamander, most likely the shy red eft, which likes the moist woodlands and is one of few that wander in the daylight. Easy walking, such as you have on this portion of the AT, is an opportunity to pay more attention to the surroundings—rocks, plants, and animals. So break out the field guide and do some exploring. If it's fall, see how many colors the red and sugar maple leaves have turned (see pages 223 and 246 for more on maples). Striped maples, in the understory, are identified by the whitish stripes in their greenish bark; their other name, "goose-foot" maple, derives from the shape of the leaf. Or look for all three birches: yellow,black, and white. As you cross the marshy areas, underfoot you may find spongy tussock sedges, "carpeted stepping-stones." Among the prettiest flowering plants in spring is the yellow marsh marigold, most often seen in the bogs. The patient birder might find all five species of woodpeckers here, might be startled by a ruffed grouse thumping, then exploding from the bushes, and might also see squadrons of Canada geese and a variety of ducks on the ponds. These suggestions barely scratch the surface. For a complete guide to the wildlife of Beartown State Forest, see Laubach, *A Guide to Natural Places in the Berkshire Hills*, or Smith, *Nature Walks in the Berkshire Hills*.

At about 8.1 mi. the trail reaches the lip of the hill forming the southern side of the Tyringham Valley (800 to 1000 ft. below), and here you get your first glimpse, through the hemlocks, of this incomparably pastoral hidden gem, decidedly off the beaten track. Down you go, and quickly now, surrounded by vast expanses of delicate wood ferns, as you clamber amidst the boulders and fallen, twisted trees of a cool, darkened gulch that looks promising for spelunkers (at 8.4 mi.). The trail loses considerable altitude here, as you switchback down the southern slope of the valley and soon cross Jerusalem-Fernside Rd. (unpaved, 8.9 mi.). A piped spring is located on the road, 0.1 mi. east.

At 9.2 mi., not far above the valley floor but still in shady forest, Shaker Campsite (with a privy) appears, right, with two tent platforms and a few other ground spaces for tents. Behind the campsite in the woods are the foundation remains of a 19th-century Shaker barn. Next, in quick succession (and possibly indistinct in a dry season), three small brook crossings occur. Explore a little up the largest of the three to see a pretty waterfall (100 yd. upstream).

At 9.5 mi. the trail crosses the Tenneco Gas Co. pipeline (a 50-yd.-wide swath), which offers another good overlook (north) of the Tyringham Valley: a great rest spot. If you're lucky you'll sit amidst freshly mown, aromatic hay and buzzing bees, besotted with pollen. A sweet sequence of hayfields and wooded sections follows the gasline crossing, leading to Hop Brook, a Housatonic River tributary. With its sun-dappled twists and turns and several miniature waterfalls, the brook pleases both eyes and ears.

A stile climbs over a barbed wire fence (10.1 mi.), bordering the Trustees of Reservations' property, Tyringham Cobble. The trail rises again, easily. In the dark woods—hemlocks, once more—fallen trees are home to extraordinary colonies of fungi. In another 10 to 15 min. (at 10.7 mi.), branching off left is the trail to the top of the cobble, a 30-min. (round-trip) walk and scramble, well worth the detour. If you go up to the top, you'll want to linger, perhaps basking in the sun on the warm exposed rocks. Quartz, gneiss, and marble give the cobble its rocky

The Tyringham Shakers

In 1792 several families here united all their farmland to form the Tyringham Shaker settlement. They clustered along Jerusalem Rd., between Hop Brook and Beartown, in an area the AT traverses. Only a few Shaker houses remain standing today, and none are open to the public. However, elegantly crafted stone walls, a sure sign of the Shakers' well-deserved reputation for attention to the marriage of form and function, cut through the surrounding woods.

In their heyday (the early 1800s), the Tyringham Shakers numbered over a hundred souls. Their landholdings were extensive, nearly 1500 acres, and they prospered, much like their Shaker brethren at the larger settlements at nearby Hancock, Massachusetts, and Mt. Lebanon, New York. At Tyringham the specialty was seeds, hundreds of varieties packaged in envelopes with eye-catching colorful labels that won them a large market throughout the East. The seed house was the biggest Shaker building in Tyringham, boasting even a freight elevator. Luddites the Shakers were not—Henry Ford would have loved their efficiency. At harvest time the crops were so bountiful that scores of "world's people" (outsiders) were called in to work.

There were two large Shaker families here, each an extended band of men, women, and children, not necessarily blood-related. Mother Ann Lee, the Shakers' messianic founder, never visited Tyringham, and an unexplained upheaval in the community in 1858 began its disintegration. By 1874 the Tyringham Shakers were all but gone.

Like other Shakers, those in Tyringham had a holy place for spiritual retreats, theirs known as Mt. Horeb (uphill, toward Beartown Mt. State Forest), an open summit at that time. Legend has it that when a visiting Elder from Hancock was leading a prayer meeting, the Devil himself appeared in the room, and the Shakers rallied courageously to rout old Satan, first into the basement and later up the hill to their holy place. Eloise Myers, the late Tyringham librarian-historian, passes on the story: "Here they buried him, face down, with clam shells in his hands, so that if he dug he would go deeper instead of digging out."* The Tyringham Shakers: practical even under duress.

---

*From *Tyringham: A Hinterland Settlement*, by Eloise Meyers. Self-published, 1963, 1989.

crest. The fine views of the Tyringham valley you have here on the AT are measurably better at the top of the hill.

Carrying on, the AT wanders now through a botanist's paradise. Down the far side of the cobble, the trail intersects with Jerusalem Rd. (11.0 mi.; piped spring a few hundred feet left; post office and phone 0.6 mi. left) and crosses another stile before marching out across the valley floor, with Hop Brook always nearby. Swish through asters, Queen Anne's lace, goldenrod, juniper bushes, black raspberry patches, and stands of staghorn sumac while following hedgerows along narrow puncheons over squishy fields. If you brought a wildflower guide along on this hike, you'll be flipping from pictures to index and back again during this stretch. Wild thyme, often underfoot here, willingly yields its soothing perfume.

Hike #12 climaxes at a striking wooden bridge over Hop Brook (12.0 mi.), affording a summarizing view of all the colors in the palette of the cobble and low-lying fields of both wild and agricultural Tyringham. It's just 0.1 mi. from the bridge to Tyringham Main Rd., your destination, but in another sense, if you have surrendered by now to the peace and beauty of this valley, you will have already arrived, not quite at your car but definitely in heaven.

Culture note: A few minutes away from pastoral Tyringham, the Berkshires are alive with capital-C culture of all kinds. Why not build an AT hiking trip around visits to Hancock Shaker Village, west of Pittsfield; the Norman Rockwell Museum, near Stockbridge; and in Lenox, The Mount (Edith Wharton's home) and Tanglewood, summer home of the Boston Symphony and of much other music too. Local papers list performances at Berkshire Theatre Festival, Shakespeare & Co., and many others.

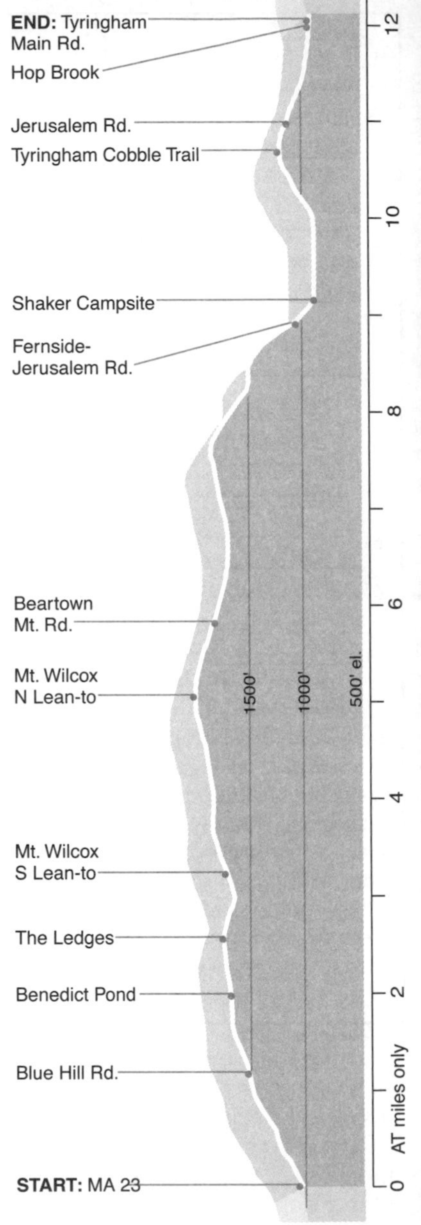

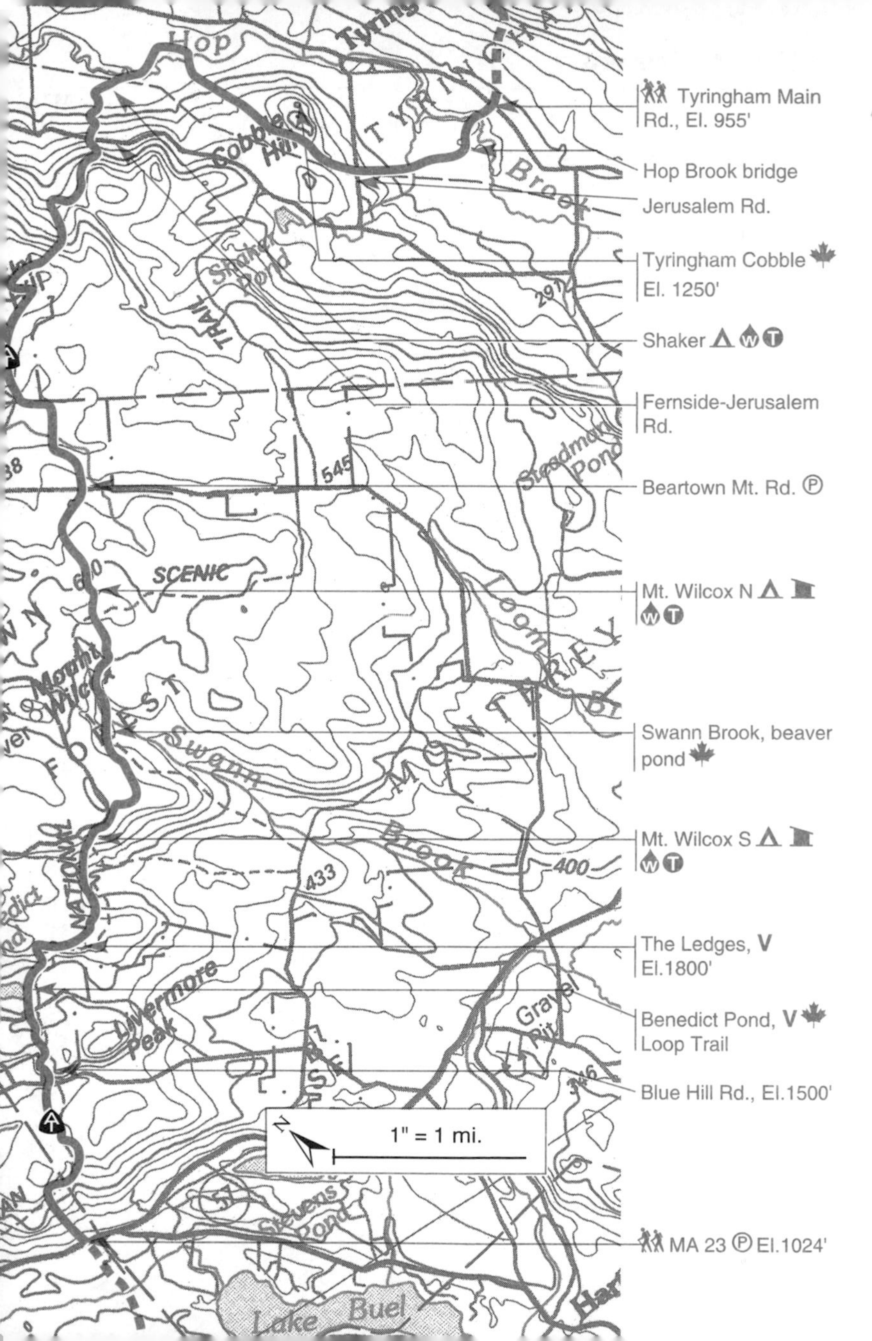

Tyringham Main Rd., El. 955'
Hop Brook bridge
Jerusalem Rd.
Tyringham Cobble El. 1250'
Shaker
Fernside-Jerusalem Rd.
Beartown Mt. Rd.
Mt. Wilcox N
Swann Brook, beaver pond
Mt. Wilcox S
The Ledges, V El.1800'
Benedict Pond, V Loop Trail
Blue Hill Rd., El.1500'
1" = 1 mi.
MA 23 El.1024'
Hop
Cobble Hill
Brook
Shaker Pond
TRAIL
545
Stedman Pond
SCENIC
Mount Wilcox
FOREST
Swann
Brook
NATIONAL
433
400
Livermore Peak
Gravel Pit
Stevens Pond
Lake Buel

HIKE #12 Itinerary

Miles N	NORTH	Elev. (ft./m)	Miles S
12.1	**End: Tyringham Main Rd.,** overnight parking; village, L, 0.9 mi.	955/291	0.0
12.0	**Hop Brook** bridge.		0.1
11.0	**Jerusalem Rd.** (village, L, 0.6 mi.); stile; then mixed forest and fields with footbridges over wet areas.		1.1
10.7	Spur trail, L, to top of **Tyringham Cobble** for superior views; AT descends gently.	1250/381	1.4
10.1	Stile over wire fence, enter **Tyringham Cobble;** climb in hemlock forest.		2.0
9.5	Gas pipeline, fine valley views; then woods, followed by farm fields and woods road, then **Hop Brook,** L.		2.6
9.2	**Shaker Campsite,** R, privy; then three little brooks (waterfall; old foundation 100 yd. upstream).	1000/305	2.9
8.9	Switchback downhill on former logging roads, then cross **Fernside-Jerusalem Rd.** (dirt) and descend again steeply.		3.2
8.4	Pass through gulch with giant boulders and caves.		3.7
8.1	Through hemlocks, small cutaway view toward Tyringham Valley.		4.0
6.2	Beaver pond inlet and outlet; then swampy area; then modest rise through hemlocks.		5.9
5.8	**Beartown Mt. Rd.** (dirt); unofficial day parking.	1788/545	6.3
5.1	Spur trail (0.3 mi.) to **Mt. Wilcox N Lean-to;** unreliable brook for water; AT goes L and continues down.	2100/640	7.0
4.5	Beaver pond outlet at **Swann Brook.**		7.6
4.0	Cleared high point with southerly views.	1985/605	8.1

Miles N	NORTH	Elev. (ft./m)	Miles S
3.3	Spring, R; then spur trail to **Mt. Wilcox S Lean-to;** second spring on this spur.	1800/549	8.8
2.6	**The Ledges,** excellent views to S and E; leaving ridge, go L, descend.	1800/549	9.5
2.4	Beaver dam outlet; go R.		9.7
2.0	After **Benedict Pond** inlet, go L, then over bridge, then R.	1598/487	10.1
1.6	AT on woods road, then footpath; cross **Beartown State Forest** road (left, to campsites, privy, water, phone, swimming, picnic tables).		10.5
1.5	Pass former charcoal burners' fire pit; follow ridge; ignore junction with former trail.		10.6
1.3	Abrupt rocky climb to cliff; views.		10.8
1.2	Bridges bring AT to **Blue Hill Rd.** (dirt).	1500/457	10.9
0.4	Tornado blowdowns through here; small stream.		11.7
0.0	**Start:** MA 23, Monterey; overnight parking; trail begins in field N of road.	1024/312	12.1

SOUTH

HIKE: #13

Tyringham to Goose Pond to Becket

Maps: ATC Mass. & Conn. #3
Route: Tyringham Village, to Upper Goose Pond Cabin, to US 20, Becket
Recommended direction: S to N (described here) or N to S
Distance: 8.6 mi.
Elevation +/-: 955 to 1778 to 1385 ft.
Effort: Easy
Day hike: Yes
Overnight backpacking hike: Optional
Duration: 4½ to 5 hr.
Early exit option: Webster Rd., at 1.9 mi.; Goose Pond Rd., at 4.3 mi.
Natural history features: Knee Deep Pond (swamp); Cooper Brook
Social history features: Tyringham Shakers (see Hike #12)
Trailhead access: *Start:* From Lee (off MA 102), take Tyringham Main Rd. into and through Tyringham village; AT is 0.9 mi. W of post office; park on shoulder (S side of road). Tyringham has *no* stores. Center of town is town hall and post office. Don't blink or you'll miss them! *End:* From Exit #2, Mass. Turnpike (Lee), follow US 20 E for 5 mi., crossing Becket town line to trailhead shortly beyond Gaslight Motel; AT overnight parking, roadside, 100 yd. W and off road 0.3 mi. W.
Camping: Upper Goose Pond Cabin and Campsite

The trailhead is just a small white blaze on a post and a thin cut into the woods, heading north from Tyringham Main Rd.—a characteristic Tyringham understatement. If you have never been to Tyringham before, be sure to add to your plans a hike going south from here as well. Behind you is the peaceful Tyringham Valley, famous for its wildflowers and gentle hills as well as its Shaker history. See Hike #12 for details.

There are many ways to do Hike #13, all rewarding. The basic plan is a day hike from Tyringham village to the Upper Goose Pond Cabin for a short visit and then out of the woods to US 20 in Becket, 8.6 mi. A particularly enjoyable strategy is to split your party in two, launching half by canoe on Lower Goose Pond, heading for the cabin on Upper Goose Pond (no portage), and sending the other half a-walking on the Appalachian Trail, with the cabin also as destination. When you all meet—for lunch—at the cabin, you trade paddles for hiking boots and out you go, retracing your companions' strokes or strides. A third strategy entails an overnight stay at the cabin (or its campsite). A fourth would be a combination of the hiking, canoeing, and the overnight at the cabin. We'll give you one guess as to which is our favorite.

At the trailhead, parking is 50 yd. north. Into the woods the trail goes immediately, up from the Tyringham valley (up over 800 ft. to the top of overgrown Baldy Mt.) and down, steeply, over the first 1.9 mi. to Webster Rd. These first 2 mi. are the only strenuous part of the hike, which we rate as "Easy" overall. At 2.2. mi. the AT crosses the inlet to Knee Deep Pond (left), actually a marsh, providing a good spot to take a breather by sitting still to watch the wildlife. A cooling hemlock grove follows, and at 3.4 mi. a side trail leads to a sometimes reliable spring (0.1 mi. off the AT). Be smart: bring plenty of water with you, or at least bring a water filter or iodine tablets if you have to purify water found en route. Most of the marshes and bogs in the Berkshire uplands have beavers in residence, not to mention other wildlife using the water supply. Where there are animals, there are bacteria in the water, and hikers must take precautions.

Gentle ups and downs through mixed hardwoods bring the AT to Goose Pond Rd. (4.3 mi., unpaved) and a few moments' contact with civilization—cottages and homes within earshot, and the hum of outboard motors on the big pond a few hundred yards away and downhill. The AT crossing here is tough to find if you're driving, unless other hikers have already parked near the trailhead. Indeed, it's not really an official trailhead, though it can be used

David Emblidge

as an early exit option in a pinch (MA 8 in Becket is 3.0 mi. east). The proximity of houses reminds us that in many places the National Park Service's Appalachian Trail corridor is minimally 1000 ft. wide, and the trail cannot always be built in the middle of the corridor. On a 2150-mi. footpath, it's no surprise that occasionally one can see or hear a homeowner cutting the backyard grass, just off the trail.

Within the next 0.5 mi. hikers here walk through fern heaven, the various green tones and leaf shapes almost surreal in their subtlety. Wood fern, hay fern, polypody fern, and others abound. A good wildflower identification book would serve well for the truly curious observer. At 4.5 mi. another dramatic marsh lies smack in the path of the AT. Cooper Brook runs through these apparently still waters. A handsome, recently rebuilt footbridge (the work of trail volunteers) crosses the teeming marsh, and storm-tossed trees, some with complete giant root balls turned up from the mucky ground, lie

Trail Food—Do's & Don'ts

Packing a lunch or snack for a day hike? Miriam Jacobs, cookbook author, food columnist, and Berkshire hiker, offers these time-tested rules:

- Lots of calories and little weight carries you farther with less effort.
- Eat often and eat lightly. Don't let your blood sugar drop too low. Accidents happen more often when you're either too hungry or too full.
- Plenty of water (2 quarts per person per day when it's hot) reduces fatigue and stiffness. Water is better than fruit juice. Sugary soft drinks and alcohol are not what you need.
- Trail mix ("gorp"): Why pay a lot to buy it when you can fine-tune it cheaply at home? Buy the ingredients in bulk (nuts, raisins, sunflower seeds, dried fruits, carob or chocolate chips) and mix away. A small bag for each hiker lets leaders and laggards feed themselves en route.
- Hard foods travel better than soft: crusty bread, tough-skinned fruits, carrots, celery, all fare well in a stuffed knapsack. Bring a miracle banana, your best source for potassium, to ward off muscle cramps.
- If a food needs refrigeration, leave it at home.
- A little candy, or a cookie or brownie, makes a good reward for a steep hill just climbed, but a lot of sugar sends you into an energy tailspin.
- Equipment: a multipurpose pocketknife, a few paper towels, bottled water or a water filter or iodine tablets.

Low-impact-hiking reminders:

- If you carry food into the woods, carry out your garbage too. Leave nothing behind. Use sturdy self-seal food bags (not twist ties) for good housekeeping inside your pack.
- Bring toilet tissue (rapidly biodegradable camper's tissue is available at outfitter's stores); a tiny gardener's trowel; a self-seal bag for waste. Urinate or defecate at least 200 feet from the trail or any water, burying your waste at least 8 inches deep. For a complete treatise on the subject, see *How to Shit in the Woods* by Kathleen Meyers.

beside the bridge. Anyone with a camera or field glass tripod would be smart to set up here and linger. Birds and beavers are never far away.

A short, entertaining scramble up and over some large rocks follows immediately. A sign for Upper Goose Pond marks the entry to a 700-acre protected habitat (no camping, fires, or hunting) overseen by the National Park Service, the AMC, and other agencies. A quick, steep descent brings the trail to pond level (1483 ft.), where the terrain is easy and the views of water and hillsides are sublime. The surrounding hills rise about 300 ft. from the shoreline, giving the pond a protected feeling.

Upper Goose Pond is as pristine a navigable piece of water as you'll find these days in the Berkshires. From this (east) end of the pond (6.2 mi.), look down toward the distant channel connecting to Lower Goose Pond, almost 1.5 mi. of water away. The breadth of the pond isn't much, perhaps 0.3 to 0.5 mi. A gorgeous expanse of water and not a house to be seen on it, anywhere. Motorboats are welcome but must adhere to a strict speed limit. The isolation of the pond almost begs for silence: canoes, kayaks, and rowboats belong here. Lower Goose Pond, by contrast, is surrounded by cottages and year-round homes.

Crossing Higley Brook, the pond's inlet, in summer, you will see a dazzling array of aquatic plants. One of the loveliest is the flower of the Canada lily (yellow-orange petals). The yellow bullhead lily grows here too. René Laubach's *Guide to Natural Places in the Berkshire Hills* points out that canoeists may want to investigate bladderwort (yellow snapdragon-like flowers on the water surface in summertime), whose "bladders" capture minuscule water fleas the way praying mantises catch flies. An equally strange animal canoeists might find (especially in the channel between upper and lower ponds) is the gelatinous egg-like mass known as a bryozoan colony, seen clinging to waterside branches. They feed by filtration and have not evolved much over hundreds of millions of years.

The AT skirts the north side of the pond and luckily basks in the afternoon sun. You may have trouble deciding which picnic spot is ideal. Break out the binoculars: bird-watching here is excellent. In addition to common waterfowl, you may be lucky enough to see a great blue heron or an osprey (the latter in the fall). In the woods hereabouts, the drumming of the ruffed grouse (his romantic call to her) can be an exciting surprise on a springtime day. If you have come in with fishing gear, you're in luck: both Upper and Lower Goose ponds are home to many varieties (pickerel, bass, trout, perch).

At 6.7 mi., still at pondside, the AT passes a lonesome chimney, minus the lodge that stood here when the Mohhekennuck fishing and hunting club used this territory. Soon the trail turns sharply right, uphill, away from the water's edge, and at 7.0 mi., the side trail to Upper Goose Pond Cabin branches, left. It's 0.5 mi. to the cabin, a bit uphill.

Canoeing to Upper Goose Pond Cabin

Put in at the Lower Goose Pond boat ramp, off Forest St. in East Lee. Head northeast for the narrow end of the pond. Depending on wind and shipmates' paddling abilities, the 1.5-mi. voyage takes 30 to 45 min. (Canoes can be rented from Main St. Sports & Leisure, Lenox; 800-952-9197.) On a calm day, enjoy the middle of the pond. In windy conditions, keep the bow of your canoe pointed into the wind; avoid turning the canoe's port (left) or starboard (right) side to the wind. Feather your paddles (blades turned horizontal to the water) and pack your gear low in the canoe to further reduce wind resistance. The windward shore, where trees and hills provide some buffer, will have calmer water. Though the trip will be longer by distance, it will also be easier and faster near this protected shore.

Entering Upper Goose Pond (45 acres) is a transition from one world to another. Under the delicately arching white birches you glide, through a silent nautical cathedral, magically leaving the buzz of cottages and water-skiers behind. Turn to port (left) after the connecting channel and aim for the cabin's primitive dock. You will need a good length of rope (clothesline will do) to tie your canoe to the dock, a tree, a rock, or other canoes (there is no beach).

Though it's not Tahiti, once ashore you may have the sense that you have arrived in paradise.

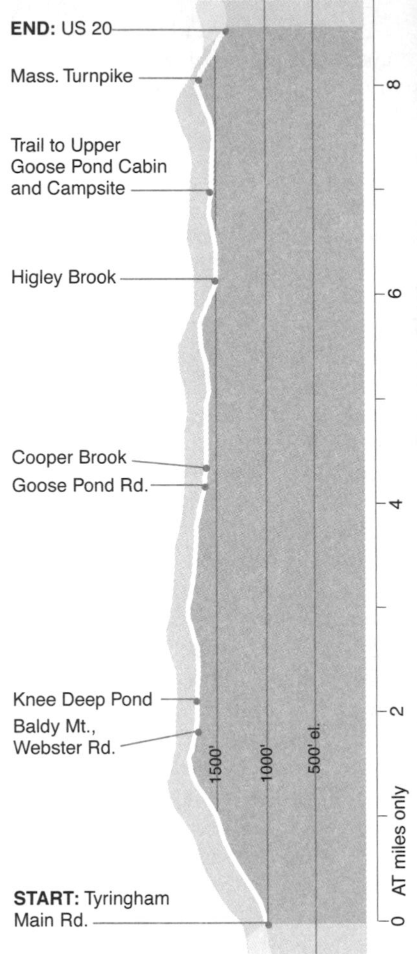

Upper Goose Pond Cabin may be "the Hilton of Huts," but the prices are better: $4 per person per night (donation) in the cabin; $2 per person for tent platforms. A minute's climb from the dock and you're on the cabin's front porch. Volunteers from the Berkshire chapter of AMC maintain the old cabin with considerable help from the Osgood family; extensive renovations were done in 1995–96. Upper Goose Pond Cabin resonates with history. Countless hikers have contributed large and small conveniences and comforts to make what was an austere site a surprisingly accommodating stopover.

The kitchen is well equipped with a mélange of cutlery, dishes, pots and pans, enough to handle all of the two dozen visitors who can make up a

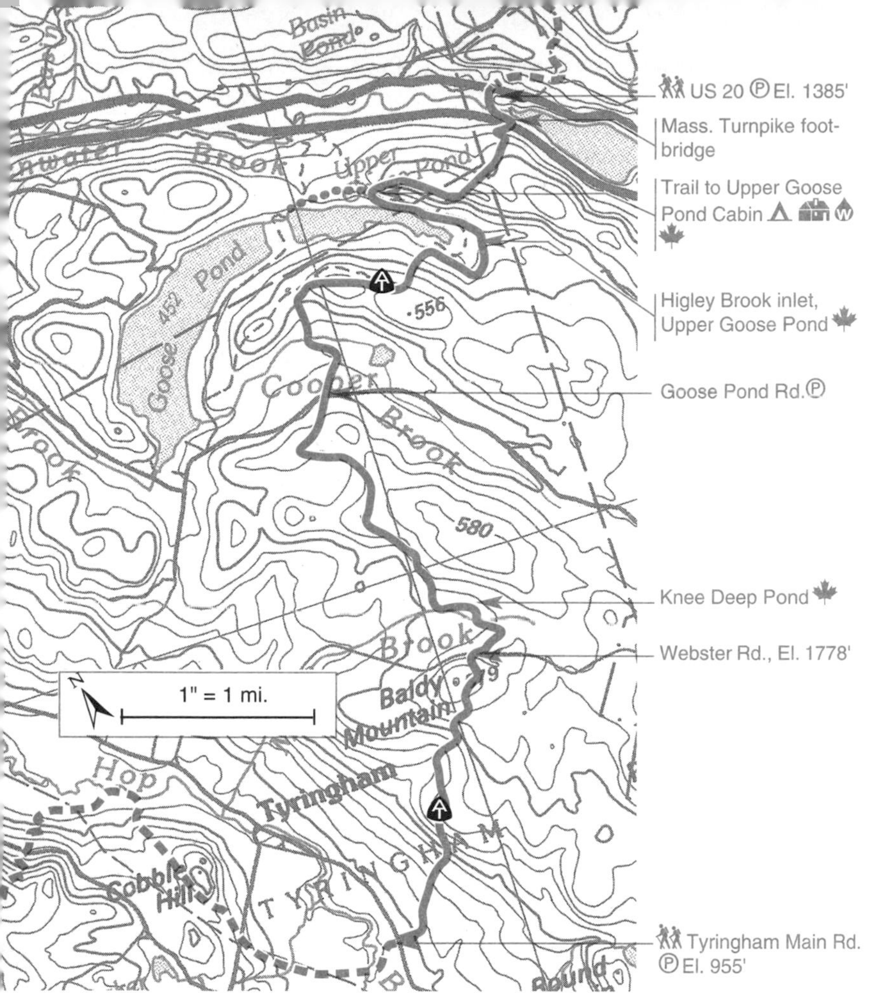

rainy night's full house. There are several tent platforms in the surrounding woods and two outhouses as well, a real luxury. Caretakers lug in propane canisters for the three-burner stove and white gas for the lanterns. There is evening light for the big dining room table and for cards or board games. There's a small library of well-worn paperbacks, but as usual the best books here are the hikers' logs, filled with exclamations of gratitude for this shelter or with expletives aimed at the weather gods who wouldn't cooperate with hapless souls out on the trail.

Outdoor cooking is restricted to a fireplace, where late evening fire-fussing is popular. Inside, in the cheery sitting room, a massive fieldstone fireplace is the cabin's heart. On cool evenings, the caretaker kindles a blaze and everyone gathers 'round.

Bunks are upstairs, enough for about twelve, some with mattresses, some not. It's first come, first served, no reservations; on holiday and summer weekends, you'd best arrive early. It's always smart to carry a tent, in case the inn is full. Bring a sleeping bag and a pad for a cushion.

Try your luck casting for trout from the landing as evening bugs dance on the glassy water, tempting fish toward the surface. Bats will swoop by to take their fill of the bugs. On a fish chain underwater at the landing we once saw a brown, a brook, and a rainbow trout: the caretaker's afternoon catch.

Go for a sunset paddle, exploring the miniature island across the pond. Be careful not to disturb nesting birds. From a canoe you'll have an even better look at aquatic shoreline wildflowers than from the trail, and the chances of spotting a muskrat, beaver, or mink are better too. At the skinny east end of the pond, where beaver dams are common, fat long-necked Canada geese silently roost for the night. Their pearl-gray chests and dark wings blend in camouflage against the rocks (gneiss, with bands of light and dark minerals).

Enjoy a some stargazing over the pond; spin a few yarns or spook yourself with ghost stories; indulge yourself with "s'mores" or another high-calorie snack. You're away from it all, but this isn't an AT site with a Spartan attitude. Only the faint sound of highway traffic, from the turnpike not far over the hill, breaks the spell of crackling fire and forest solitude. In the pitch-black dormitory, ambitious hikers, intending to cover a sizable distance tomorrow, will provide a muted snoring soundtrack for your dreams by the time you slip into your sleeping bag.

Canoeing out? You know the route. Hiking onward, to US 20? You have 2.1 mi. to cover. Return to the AT by the spur trail; turn left (north); and begin a modest ascent through the hardwood forest over rocky ledges. At 7.6 mi. an AT trail register invites you to sign in. Soon the descent toward the increasingly audible highway begins. The footbridge over the Massachusetts Turnpike comes at 8.2 mi. Compensating for the noise is a good view of Greenwater Pond. US 20, Becket (parking), is 0.4 mi. ahead.

CULTURE NOTE: One of America's most prestigious summer dance festivals, Jacob's Pillow, is a few miles farther east, just off US 20 in Becket. Spruce up, go picnic on the lawn, and during the performance, be glad you're not doing all that leaping after a long day's hike.

HIKE #13 Itinerary

Miles N	NORTH	Elev. (ft./m)	Miles S
8.6	**End: US 20,** Becket; town of Lee 5.0 mi. L (W); AT overnight parking 0.3 mi. W on US 20.	1385/422	0.0
8.2	**Mass. Turnpike** (footbridge); view of Greenwater Pond.		0.4
7.6	AT trail register.		1.0
7.0	Spur trail (0.5 mi.) to **Upper Goose Pond Cabin and Campsite;** caretaker, privy, water.	1490/454	1.6
6.7	Abandoned chimney.		1.9
6.2	Higley Brook, inlet to **Upper Goose Pond**.		2.4
6.0	Double white blaze: go L, not uphill.		2.6
5.9	Spring near L side of trail.		2.7
5.5	Relatively level terrain leads to views of **Upper Goose Pond**.		3.1
4.5	**Cooper Brook,** marsh area; extensive bridge; then moderate rise into forest.		4.1
4.3	**Goose Pond Rd.** (unpaved), small parking area; AT re-enters woods; MA 8 is 3.0 mi. E.	1634/498	4.3
3.4	Spur trail to spring (0.1 mi.).		5.2
2.2	Inlet to **Knee Deep Pond** (marsh).		6.4
1.9	Quick descent from Baldy Mt. to **Webster Rd.**	1778/542	6.7
0.0	**Start: Tyringham Main Rd.;** overnight parking; village, L, 0.9 mi.; begin hike through forest and into substantial climb.	955/291	8.6

HIKE: #14

Finerty Pond and October Mt. State Forest

Maps: ATC Mass. & Conn. #2
Route: From US 20, Becket, to Finerty Pond, to October Mt. Shelter, to Pittsfield Rd., Washington
Recommended direction: S to N (described here) or N to S
Distance: 9.4 mi.
Elevation +/-: 1385 to 2220 to 2000 ft.
Effort: Easy
Day hike: Yes
Overnight backpacking hike: Optional
Duration: 5 hr.
Early exit option: County Rd., at 5.4 mi.
Natural history features: Finerty Pond; wetlands and marsh; beavers
Social history features: Stone walls in the woods; 18th- to 19th-century farming
Trailhead access: *Start:* From Exit #2, Mass. Turnpike (Lee), follow US 20 E for 5 mi., crossing Becket town line, to trailhead shortly beyond Gaslight Motel; AT overnight parking, roadside, 100 yd. W. *End:* From Pittsfield, follow Williams St. to Division Rd., keep R onto Washington Mt. Rd., following it for several mi. (becomes Pittsfield Rd.); AT crosses Pittsfield Rd. at unpaved Beach Rd., L; parking along road, L.
Camping: October Mt. Shelter and Campsite

Like so many Berkshirites, I have long been an enthusiast for both south and north county, casting aspersions on the central section for its industrial and suburban sprawl. Besides, there aren't any memorable mountain peaks in the midsection of the Berkshires, so how good could the hiking be?

There's nothing like a slow walk through unexplored territory to change your presuppositions. From Becket to Cheshire the elevation doesn't change much—a bore to some hikers, a blessing to others. Especially for those who love the quiet woods and a lot of solitude, mid-Berkshire is the place to walk.

An ambitious hiker can cover all 9.4 mi. of this AT section in 5 hr., but there's a convenient break at County Rd. if you have only a half day's time or energy available.

Head north from the US 20 trailhead. This is a particularly colorful hike in mid- to late autumn due to the plethora of maples and birches in the forest. When the leaves are coming down here, you may find that the white blazes of the AT are frequently lost against the backdrop of yellow and burnt-umber. If you wander off the trail, carefully retrace your steps until you see a white blaze (and remember your intended direction, north or south). The visible footpath you're accustomed to may be shrouded in fallen leaves, as may be the slippery rocks and tree roots (and holes just the right size to swallow an inattentive ankle). All this can cause considerable trouble in keeping a steady pace.

At the hike's beginning, road noise is an unwelcome companion. With the Massachusetts Turnpike and US 20 immediately behind, the sound of tires whirring on the pavement creeps up the hillsides and lingers amongst the trees for a disconcertingly long time. The first mile is a steady climb but nothing perilous. At 0.7 mi. the trail crosses Tyne Rd. (a lovely way to drive into October Mt. State Forest, where much of this hike occurs). Less than an hour into the hike, at 1.3 mi., comes the overgrown summit of Becket Mt. (2180 ft.), some 835 ft. above the trailhead. Snack time, of course. Free entertainment pours forth from the AT hikers' logbook that lives here in a birdhouse-size box, perched on a tree trunk.

The messages will range from the mundane to the poetic. "Guy in white van: Your lights were on. Red Nissan has jumper cables. Will be back about 3 p.m." Or, "Just got married two days ago. . . . Looking for the perfect spot to consummate our marriage." Or, "I am never, never, NEVER doing this again. . . . More of a workout than a Jane Fonda tape. But it's been fun." Add your own immortal words!

At 2.3 mi. another overgrown summit, Walling Mt. (2220 ft.), the day's highest point, comes and goes. You will hardly notice that you have bagged another peak.

David Emblidge

Checking the trail register

The trail is in the extensively forested town of Washington now, a far cry from that other Washington, where power and money are always the issue. Here it's a different agenda. Over 14,000 acres of woods and hills comprise October Mt. State Forest, largest in the commonwealth. A half mile farther on (2.8 mi.), the pièce de résistance of the hike, Finerty Pond, pops into view. Whatever color the leaves may be, they will be reflected in the rippled waters of this magnificently quiet place—reflections as evocative as those of the colorful flowers at Monet's Giverny. But Monet, step aside; this is Winslow Homer territory. Except for an old logging road and the AT, there is no access to Finerty Pond, and its pristine qualities make it well worth the effort to walk here. Notably absent from the shore near the AT is the

Woodland Chateaux

Spaced every 10 to 12 miles along the AT are lean-to shelters designed to provide a haven from storms and a welcome hello to short- and long-distance hikers. Most of these sturdy huts are far from any convenient access road. How did they get there, in the middle of undeveloped wilderness?

Rick Wagner, chairman of the construction committee for the Berkshire chapter of AMC, says the lean-tos were built with the generous help of a lot of folks who labored "like the elves in *Snow White*." The first task is deciding where to build, and the issue, explains Wagner, is primarily water. "Federal and state regulations require us to rely on surface water only—brooks, springs, ponds," says Wagner. There's also a need to keep foot traffic out of environmentally sensitive areas, Wagner notes.

Road access, if it's too easy, brings vandalism with it, though it can make construction simpler. Dennis Regan, local director of the AMC, cites the Kay Wood (Dalton) and Tom Leonard (Becket) shelters as "almost road accessible," but others are way beyond reach. Thus the need for elves (who may tote a single plank uphill for several miles) and for the modern miracle of helicopters to airlift building supplies to lean-to sites.

The Connecticut Air National Guard, which sometimes conducts maneuvers on Mt. Greylock, has provided the aircraft, capable of lowering loads of 2 tons or more, including lumber and dry cement, right into the forest clearing.

One of the youngest Berkshire AT shelters is Kay Wood; the oldest is Glen Brook on Mt. Everett. Wagner recalls that a few years ago it cost about $1800 to build Kay Wood Shelter, but that's materials only. Nobody wants to think about the cost of donated labor and machinery, such as a motorized wheelbarrow or power auger.

One invaluable contribution was Wagner's own new design (evolved with help from other AT committee members). The plan Wagner likes to call generically the "Massachusetts AT Shelter" provides a nifty cantilevered loft over a spacious open floor, with extra-large bunks permitting hikers to spread out their gear and feel comfortably uncramped. Still, on popular weekends when bad weather hits, sleeping space in the shelters can be cheek by jowl—not for the shy or the claustrophobic.

AT shelters frequently need repairs, and new shelters are sometimes added. Wagner laments the red tape that slows bureaucratic decision-making. Nonetheless, his enthusiasm is infectious. When it's time to do the work, the call for more load-bearing elves will go out to Berkshire hikers.

dreaded European milfoil weed, which is choking so many other New England lakes where fertilizer runoff and septic tank seepage have caused excessive eutrophication of the water. Instead, mountain laurel rims much of the shore, and you may find yellow pond lilies blooming at your feet amidst the stepping-stones.

Birders will love Finerty Pond. A host of waterfowl use the pond for stopovers. The shallow waters are a favorite haunt of great blue herons, whose long legs let them hunt for fish and other food by standing stock-still in the water until lunch unwittingly arrives. If you're lucky enough to see a fully mature heron in flight (often seen coasting at treetop level), you'll catch a glimpse of the widest wingspan of any bird in the Berkshires, sometimes exceeding 6 ft. A conveniently flat, table-size rock may tempt you to linger here for a waterside lunch. Keep the binoculars handy.

The trail zigzags over a rough-hewn bridge at the pond's inlet and heads back up into the woods. About 1500 ft. north of the pond (just before an old hiking trail crosses), there are some old-growth hemlocks to the left of the trail, standing tall, strong, and stately against time and the wind. In the 4.5-mi. section of the hike there are several gurgling brooks, but don't even try to treat this water—use Finerty Pond water: there are beavers galore in these parts. The next mile, to County Rd. (5.4 mi.), through marshy territory, proves wet underfoot. Not the best for hiking, but there can be rewards, such as the wild turkey we have seen here, feeding in the puddles.

Cross County Rd. and carry on. The AT is now on the generally level crest of the Berkshire plateau (also called the Berkshire massif), meandering through the Pittsfield watershed. Only the first 0.2 mi. north of County Rd. requires some climbing (up to forested Bald Top Mt., 2040 ft., which has found the secret of growing new hair . . . or trees), and even this is more like a walk through a fern and rock garden. The next 3.8 mi. are a level stroll in breezy, sun-dappled woods. Here and there the trail hops over an ancient stone wall, where you may find a mixed forest on one side and nothing but evergreens on the other. Something more rational than Mother Nature worked this land years ago.

This is damp territory, with many narrow bog bridges over wide patches of pitch-black primordial ooze.

At 7.2 mi., a short spur trail leads left in a hemlock grove to the handsome and tidy October Mt. Lean-to, with an outhouse and water source (creek, south of lean-to). A picnic table makes a covenient lunch spot. Some tent sites surround the shelter. This is the only camping option on Hike #14. It is particularly easy to get here, especially from the north, off Pittsfield Rd., and for brand-new campers or backpackers, this might be a good practice location as a warm-up for more challenging hikes elsewhere. One caveat: Porcupines aplenty hereabouts. Protect your food and boots. And don't bring the dog. Plucking stinging quills out of a too-curious canine is no fun for you or your pet. The porcupines are not shy. You may see them or their shedded quills right on the footpath.

Before you know it, paved Pittsfield Rd. / Washington Mt. Rd. appears (9.4 mi., or 4.0 mi. from County Rd. if you have cut this into two shorter hikes), with parking roadside. Go left to return to Pittsfield; right leads 5.0 mi. to the village of Becket.

Bonus: Just 0.1 mi. right toward Becket is the Wiley family's blueberry farm. They are sympathetic to hikers (water, cheerfulness, and the occasional cookie).

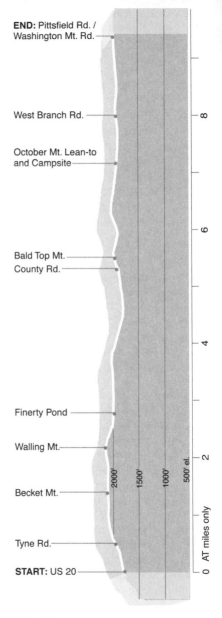

END: Pittsfield Rd. / Washington Mt. Rd.
West Branch Rd.
October Mt. Lean-to and Campsite
Bald Top Mt.
County Rd.
Finerty Pond
Walling Mt.
Becket Mt.
Tyne Rd.
START: US 20
2000'
1500'
1000'
500' el.
0 AT miles only
2
4
6
8

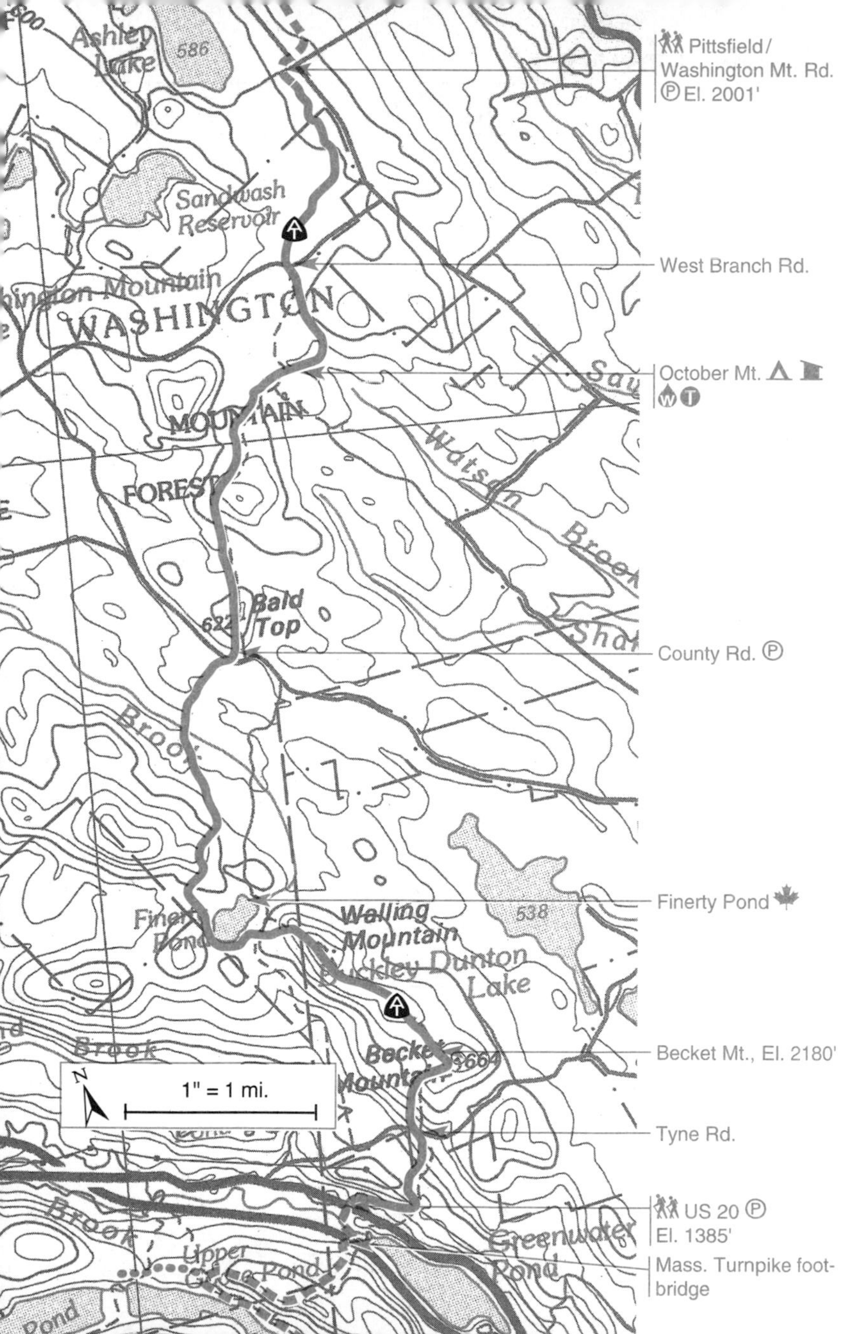

Pittsfield / Washington Mt. Rd.
Ⓟ El. 2001'
West Branch Rd.
October Mt.
County Rd. Ⓟ
Finerty Pond
Becket Mt., El. 2180'
Tyne Rd.
US 20 Ⓟ
El. 1385'
Mass. Turnpike foot-bridge
Ashley Lake
586
Sandwash Reservoir
Washington Mountain
WASHINGTON
MOUNTAIN
FOREST
Watson
Brook
Bald Top
622
Brook
Finerty Pond
Walling Mountain
Buckley Dunton Lake
538
Becket Mountain
Brook
1" = 1 mi.
N
Upper Goose Pond
Greenwater Pond

HIKE #14 Itinerary

Miles N	NORTH	Elev. (ft./m)	Miles S
9.4	**End: Pittsfield Rd.** (paved); parking along road.	2001/610	0.0
9.3	Pittsfield Water Co. unpaved service road; N turn.		0.1
7.9	**West Branch Rd.** (unpaved); begin swampy, wet section.	1929/588	1.5
7.2	Brook, then spur trail N to **October Mt. Lean-to and Campsite;** privy, water.		2.2
6.1	Motorcycle trail.		3.3
5.6	**Bald Top Mt.,** summit, no view.	2040/622	3.8
5.4	**County Rd.** (unpaved), parking; early exit option; AT soon climbs steeply for 0.2 mi.	1887/575	4.0
4.4	Stream from Finerty Pond; upper end of Washington Mt. Brook.		5.0
3.9	Former logging road.		5.5
2.8	**Finerty Pond;** AT follows edge of pond for 0.2 mi.	1916/584	6.6
2.3	**Walling Mt.,** summit, no view.	2220/677	7.1
1.3	**Becket Mt.,** summit, trail register.	2180/664	8.1
0.7	**Tyne Rd.** (paved).	1772/540	8.7
0.0	**Start: US 20,** Becket; AT overnight parking 0.3 mi. N on US 20; town of Lee 5.0 mi. N; AT follows former woods roads, climbing modestly.	1385/422	9.4

SOUTH

HIKE: #15

Washington to Dalton

Maps: ATC Mass. & Conn. #2

Route: From Pittsfield Rd. / Washington Mt. Rd., Washington, to Kay Wood Lean-to, to Housatonic and Depot Sts., Dalton

Recommended direction: S to N (described here) or N to S

Distance: 9.1 mi.

Elevation +/-: 2000 to 1200 ft.

Effort: Easy

Day hike: Yes

Overnight backpacking hike: Optional

Duration: 5 hr.

Early exit option: Blotz Rd., Washington, at 3.2 mi., overnight parking; Grange Hall Rd., Dalton, at 6.9 mi., limited overnight parking

Natural history features: Fern fields

Social history features: Zenas Crane and other paper mill owners; Crane Paper Museum; Dalton church thru-hiker hostel

Trailhead access: *Start:* From Pittsfield, follow Williams St. to Division Rd., keep R onto Washington Mt. Rd., following it for several mi. (becomes Pittsfield Rd.); AT crosses Pittsfield Rd. at unpaved Beach Rd, L; parking along road, L. *End:* In Dalton, follow Main St. (MA 8) E, passing junction with High St., L, and North St., R, to Depot St.; turn R, following Depot St. to end at Housatonic St.; overnight parking on street (caution: lumber trucks).

Camping: Kay Wood Lean-to and Campsite

From start to finish on Hike #15 you're not far from 2000 ft. in elevation. On the Berkshire massif, which lines the eastern flank of Berkshire County, the Appalachian Trail is a generally level walk. Most of the way the trail is blessed with cooling shade and good exposure to westerly breezes, at least where the trail is on the windward (west) side of the hills. A breeze is a springtime or early summer hiker's friend: it wafts away the bugs and provides air conditioning to boot.

A short and simple AT walk can be carved out of this hike in its first 3.2 mi., ending at Blotz Rd., where parking space is available. During these 3 easy miles the trail provides a good look at old stone walls, a brook and bridge crossing, and a modest rise on a cliffside to a ridge, but alas, no long-distance views. An overhanging boulder on the cliff could provide fine shelter in a pinch. It's a good "photo-op" too.

Beyond Blotz Rd., after a climb of less than 200 ft., a stunningly pretty reward for your efforts appears. Myriad ferns here undulate like waves on a lime green sea. The fern fields on Warner Hill are some of the best in

Henry Lafleur

Beaver lodge

the Berkshires. You will want to take off the pack and sit a while for a daydream or a snack amidst the sweetened air and gracefully waving fronds.

The AT passes over the gently rolling top of Warner Hill (2050 ft.) at 3.9 mi. It's a tough call as to which of several beauties here ranks first. Views out over the valley are sensuous, even in a haze. White marble outcroppings, which may sweat in humid air, make an elegant if intermittent pavement underfoot, often in near-perfect steps on the hillside. Wildflowers abound, reveling in full sun and a moist, loamy soil. Buttercups and daisies wave on their long, skinny stems. Most arresting in late spring to midsummer are the solitary clumps of wild iris, in sharp purple contrast to the vast hilltop sea of ferns. The flowers stand proudly like a gaggle of Victorian ladies of a certain age, a bit past their prime but still dressed to the nines. The woods here is a mix of birches and scrub oaks.

It's about 2.5 mi. to the spur trail leading to Kay Wood Lean-to and Campsite, at 6.6 mi. The picnic table under the overhanging loft of the shelter is an inviting place for dinner. Perched on a small cliff, the shelter looks out into treetops, alive with birdsong. There are a few tent sites beyond the shelter, but no space big enough for a group. A trickle of a stream 50 ft. below yields just enough water, in a dry season, to rinse faces and necks. You will certainly want to filter the water for drinking.

Kay Wood, a senior citizen of Dalton, is a longtime friend of AT thruhikers. At age 73 she decided it was about time she did the whole trail herself. Over two summers (1989–90) she marched all 2143 mi., recovering from a nasty fall in the midst of it. The shelter named for her by the Berkshire chapter of AMC has sleeping space for about a dozen hikers, more if you don't mind rubbing elbows. A privy is close by. A primitive fireplace is just fine for outdoor cooking or fire gazing. There is a delicious sense of woodsy isolation here at Kay Wood, but in fact the site is only 0.3 mi. from Grange Hall Rd. (6.9 mi. on this hike; limited overnight parking; also called Robinson Rd.), making it easily accessible from the north.

Following the road crossing, a modest ravine with a few streams, all belonging to Barton Brook, appears. Nothing difficult. About 1 mi. after Grange Hall Rd. and after a 150-ft. rise, there are charming views of the town of Dalton, essentially due north, from the top of Day Mt. (7.7 mi., 1800

Of Rivers, Trees, and Dollar Bills

Where does the Berkshire rainwater go? To the sea, of course, but by routes more circuitous and historic than you might imagine. Today's Berkshire traveler may believe US 7 is the county's spine, but long before the highway existed, two rivers shaped the decisions about travel, investment, and social development in the Berkshires.

The Hoosic River, rising in Cheshire, runs (surprisingly) northward, through the Adamses and Williamstown, then into Vermont and on to the Hudson River, north of Troy, New York, where it joins the seaward flow. The Housatonic River, rising in Dalton and Pittsfield, meanders southward through the Berkshires and Connecticut to Long Island Sound near Bridgeport. Though the Housatonic is the more famous (or infamous, due to pollution) of the two, it drains only about two-thirds of the county's watershed.

The downward-spilling energy of Berkshire rivers has been critical to the region's history, a fact nowhere more evident than in Dalton. To this hamlet in 1799 came one Zenas Crane, looking for a site for a paper mill. Crane surmised that at Dalton the Housatonic River ran fast enough to turn a mill's waterwheels, but more important, he saw that the water was unusually pure. En route to Dalton, Crane had crossed the path of today's AT, high on the Berkshire plateau, noting that unlike most limestone valleys, the upland Berkshires were mostly quartz. The springwater running down from the hill country was almost as pure as distilled water, free of calcium, iron, and magnesium — good news for a paper maker. Mineral-laden water would stain Zenas Crane's new paper, but pure water would leave it clean.

The story of Crane's success is a proud one for the Berkshires and for Dalton. As the first paper mill in western Massachusetts and the oldest continuously operating business in the region, Crane's reputation has spread worldwide, mostly through the manufacturing of the rag paper used to make currency (U.S. and other governments') and fine stationery. A visit to the (free) Crane Paper Museum is well worth the detour. The museum, open weekdays from June to mid-October, is within walking distance from the AT crossing at MA 8 and 9 in Dalton.

The museum building is a throwback to the stone construction techniques of the Industrial Revolution. The entire history of papermaking is displayed in one well-arranged room. A short video shows how currency papers are marked to prevent counterfeiting, and how watermarking and paper finishing are done. Fine Crane stationery has been used by the White House and many important world figures. Often the museum guide hands out a sample of Crane stationery to visitors at the end of the self-guided tour.

ft.). These are the last long-distance views on this hike, and there is a brief but steep descent coming next; so rest a while and enjoy.

The trail switches back and forth among large boulders on the way down, then levels off, and you will see that this section has been heavily forested in times past. Old logging roads crisscross the area, and none of the trees look ancient. At 9.0 mi. the AT steps over railroad tracks, and given the bend in the track to the west (left), caution is advised. Look twice and listen. You're in town now, Dalton looming dead ahead. The hike terminates officially at Housatonic and Depot Sts., 9.1 easy miles from the start.

CULTURE NOTE: If you have time, or on another day, be sure to visit the Crane Paper Museum in Dalton, just off the trail, one of the finest single-topic museums we know. But don't get your hopes up, for although Crane Paper Co. has been the country's sole manufactuer of currency for over a century, the museum does not give out free samples of dollar bills. (See "Of Rivers, Trees, and Dollar Bills.")

If a rainy day spoils your Pittsfield area hiking plans, take a walk *inside* at the Berkshire Museum (fine art and natural history), South St., or at Arrowhead, writer Herman Melville's home and home base for the Berkshire County Historical Society, 780 Holmes Rd., both in Pittsfield.

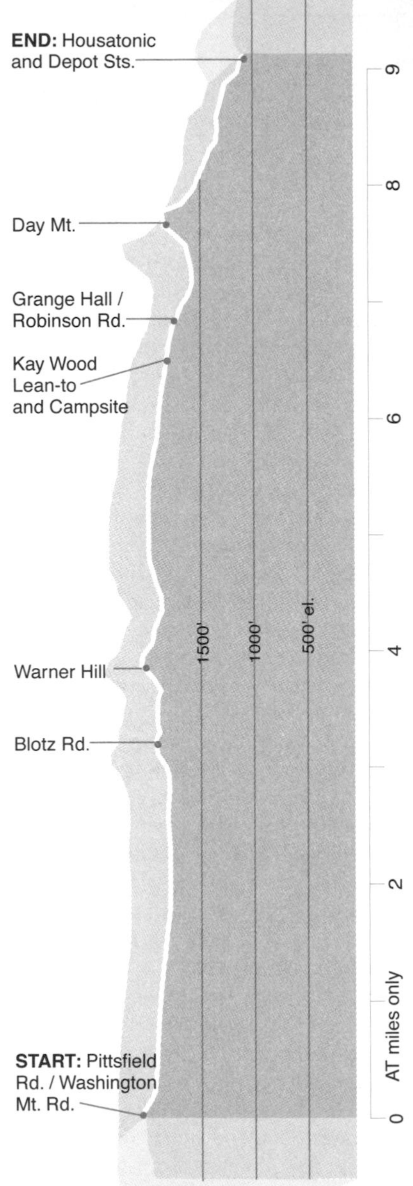

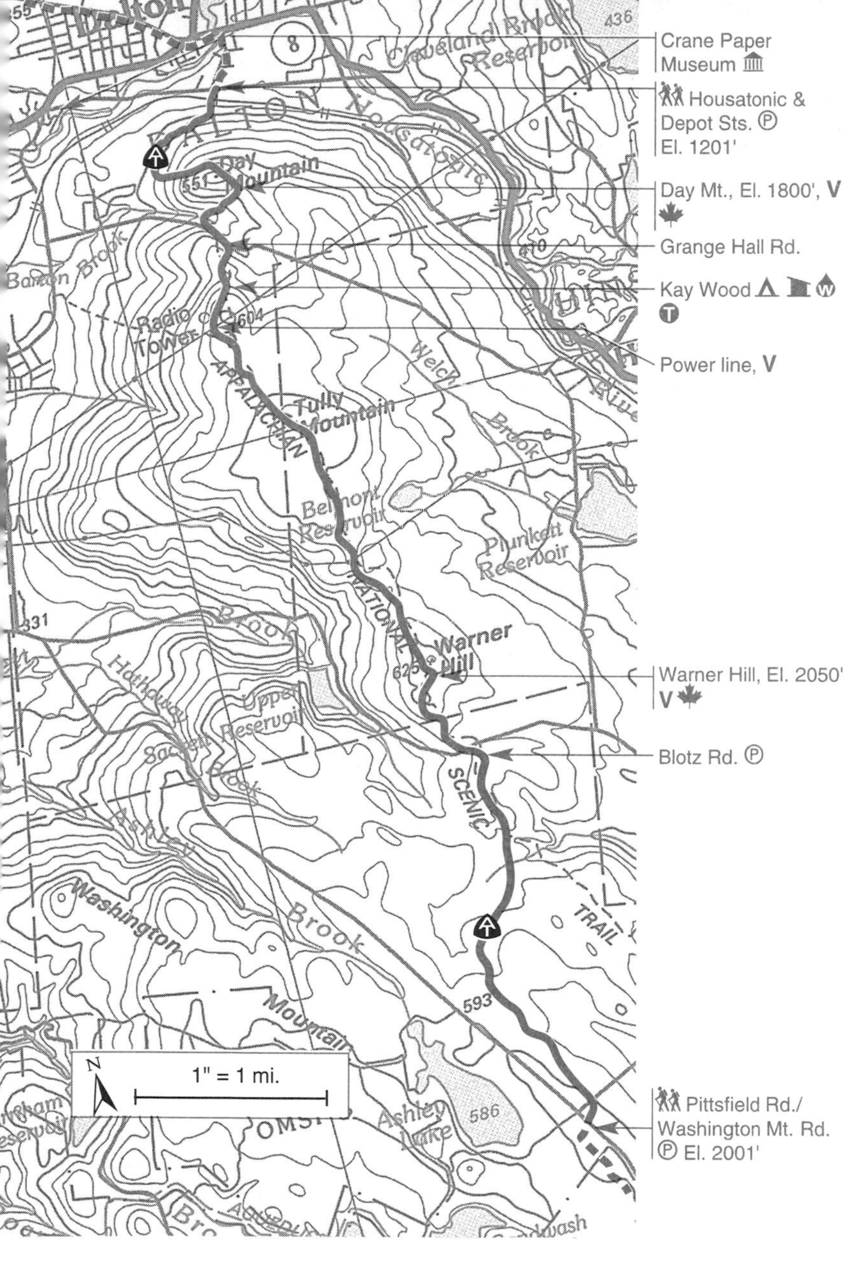

Crane Paper Museum
Housatonic & Depot Sts. Ⓟ El. 1201'
Day Mt., El. 1800', V
Grange Hall Rd.
Kay Wood
Power line, V
Warner Hill, El. 2050' V
Blotz Rd. Ⓟ
Pittsfield Rd./ Washington Mt. Rd. Ⓟ El. 2001'
1" = 1 mi.
N
Dalton
Day Mountain
Tully Mountain
Warner Hill
Belmont Reservoir
Plunkett Reservoir
Upper Sackett Reservoir
Ashley Lake
Washington Mountain Brook
Radio Tower
APPALACHIAN NATIONAL SCENIC TRAIL

HIKE #15 Itinerary

Miles N	NORTH	Elev. (ft./m)	Miles S
9.1	**End: Housatonic and Depot Sts.,** Dalton; day parking on street; overnight parking at Gulf Rd., AMC lot, about 1.8 mi. farther through Dalton streets on AT.	1201/366	0.0
9.0	Railroad tracks: Caution, especially to W (L).		0.1
8.9	Numerous old forest roads in this section.		0.2
7.7	**Day Mt.;** views of Dalton below; AT makes steep zigzag descent among boulders; then trail descends more gently.	1800/549	1.4
7.6	Ridgetop and then off-road-vehicle recreation road.		1.5
7.1	AT skirts edge of ravine, then passes through ravine, crosses Barton Brook (tributaries), descends ravine.		2.0
6.9	**Grange Hall Rd./Robinson Rd.**	1650/503	2.2
6.6	Spur trail (0.2 mi.) to **Kay Wood Lean-to and Campsite,** privy, water; AT follows steep hillside.	1867/569	2.5
6.5	Electric power lines overhead; view of Pittsfield.		2.6
3.9	**Warner Hill,** summit cairn, R; ensuing 2.5 mi. descend, rise (over Tully Mt., 2100 ft.), descend moderately.	2050/625	5.2
3.2	**Blotz Rd.,** parking; early exit option.	1864/568	5.9
2.4	AT negotiates modest cliff to ridgetop; L turn.		6.7
2.1	Brook and bridge.		7.0
1.6	Stone wall.		7.5
0.0	**Start: Pittsfield Rd. / Washington Mt. Rd.** (paved), parking along road.	2001/610	9.1

SOUTH

HIKE: #16

Dalton to Cheshire

Maps: ATC Mass. & Conn. #1

Route: From Gulf Rd. and High St., Dalton, to Furnace Hill St., Cheshire

Recommended direction: S to N

Distance: 7.4 mi.

Elevation +/-: 1168 to 2100 to 922 ft.

Effort: Easy to moderate

Day hike: Yes

Overnight backpacking hike: Optional

Duration: 4½ hr.

Early exit option: None

Natural history features: Gore Pond; The (Cheshire) Cobbles

Social history features: Crane Paper Museum, Dalton (see Hike #15); Cheshire Cheese Monument

Trailhead access: *Start:* In Dalton, from junction of Main St. (MA 8), North St. (MA. 8A / 9), and High St., take High St. about 1 mi. to just beyond Park Ave., which enters from L, to beginning of Gulf Rd. and AMC overnight parking. *End:* In Cheshire, from MA 8 turn E on Church St. and go about 0.5 mi. to Furnace Hill Rd.; turn R, drive to end of street, and park on street (day only), being careful to avoid private property. For overnight parking, continue past Furnace Hill Rd. (Church St. becomes E. Main St.) to the Cheshire Highway Department shed.

Camping: Crystal Mt. Campsite

Unless you're an AT thru-hiker, determined to trod every step of the path from Georgia to Maine, there's no point in walking the streets of Dalton or Cheshire as the trail passes through these towns, pretty and hospitable though they are. In Dalton, however, a side trip to the Crane Paper Museum, just off the trail, is recommended (see Hike #15).

Hike #16 may be less than dramatic, compared to what lies just north of here on Mt. Greylock, but it is calming, lovely, and pleasantly undulating. Try to buy *that* in a store! This makes a fine day hike or an easy overnighter (bring a tent), without substantial climbing. There is a rise of 900 ft. over the first 3.7 mi., but it's hardly noticeable. From the start at Gulf Rd. to the Crystal Mt. Campsite spur (3.7 mi.), there are few distinct landmarks (except power lines overhead at 3.3 mi.). The trail wends its easy way over numerous small ridges, often on the edge of wet areas likely to be teeming with birds, beavers, or flower blossoms. Given the ease of walking here, this is a good hike for wildflower photography, for bird-watching, or for a quiet chat with your hiking partners along the way.

The transitional forest here (on the cusp between mixed deciduous and boreal forest; see Hike #5) has plants and wildlife of both lowland

Berkshire Bruins

Who is the black bear (*Ursus americanus*) frequenting New England woods—and gardens—more and more often these days? This bear is wild and shouldn't be toyed with. He (or she) is not an actor in costume for the U.S. Forest Service, nor a cartoon character from children's TV, nor a huge, aggressive beast likely to eat your dog for a snack. Nonetheless, if provoked, frightened, or unduly hungry, black bears can be dangerous. They weigh 200 to 300 pounds, and upright, the male is a good 5 feet tall.

Male bears may roam hundreds of miles, crisscrossing their territory in search of mates. Generally the black bear likes to feed at night, but don't be surprised to see a daytime wanderer, especially in northern Berkshire or Vermont. Being abroad in daylight, however, doesn't mean a bear wants to give you a photo opportunity, especially if it is a mother with her cubs. Steer clear.

A dry summer can reduce the supply of skunk cabbage, chokecherries, and berries in the woods (staples in a bear's warm-weather diet), inducing bears to forage more widely.

The best way to see a bear up close, unless it accidentally wanders into your path or garden (they love sweet corn), is through a telephoto lens or binoculars. Do not chase a bear: she can turn on you and give you chase at 30 mph.

Two land-use factors play a part in the upsurge of the New England bear population: farmland is dwindling rapidly (often returning to forest), while suburban development spreads ever more deeply into forested land. The *Boston Globe* reported a year or so ago that wildlife biologists estimated there were 700 to 750 bears in Massachusetts, mostly west of the Connecticut River. Vermont authorities estimate a bear population of 2000 to 2500 in the state. Some may live to be 20 years old.

Hiking with a group is fun, but the collective impact of human scent and footstep noise may keep wildlife out of your way. In the Smoky Mts. of North Carolina and Tennessee, the Green Mts. of Vermont, the White Mts. of New Hampshire, and throughout Maine, however, bear sightings are common despite the hiker foot traffic (and sometimes because of unprotected food and improperly disposed-of garbage). In fact, black bears appear from time to time in all fourteen AT states.

If the bruins come visiting, don't feed them, especially not with garbage. A dependent bear can grow frustrated when the easy supply disappears and then may become a nuisance or a danger. The best thing to do with bears is to admire them in respectful stillness. If a bear appears intent on harming you or your pets, clanging a few pots and pans together should quickly send the curious beast up a tree or back into the cover of his homeland woods.

and upland varieties. Here and a bit higher up, in the town of Windsor, birders are delighted to find over-wintering species such as shrike, crossbills, grosbeak, and of course, chickadees. There are stark contrasts between the dark and sometimes damp conifer forest, so deeply shaded by hemlocks and spruce that very little grows on the soft ground beneath, and the more open areas—marshes and sedges—where there is plenty of sunlight. In these brighter, wetter places, look for red maples and the speckled alder at waterside. As everywhere else in southern New England, keep an eye out for white-tailed deer, whose behavior switches from standing stock-still to rapid, bounding leaps through thickets and fields. René Laubach's *Guide to Natural Places in the Berkshire Hills* notes that in upland meadows and former pastures there are numerous meadow voles (dark brown mouse, short tail). If you see them, especially at early morning or evening, look also for their predators: red foxes, coyotes, red-tailed hawks (daytime), great horned owls (at night).

Crystal Mt. Campsite, although equipped with a privy, is otherwise deliberately bare. It's just a few flat tenting spaces 50 yd. apart, in a gorgeous forest of towering mixed hardwoods, many of them mature white birches over 60 ft. tall.

If you camp here, you're likely to make new friends. The campsite layout is generous with space but conducive to neighborliness. Once, by a sweet summer's night campfire here,

David Emblidge

Young hiker below Cheshire Cobble

we found conversation flowing easily. A financial writer from deepest Brooklyn told a story: One day he made a business call to somebody in Abu Dhabi (United Arab Emirates), was put on hold (!), and while waiting he heard—fiber-optically, no doubt—a watered-down Muzak rendition of "Home on the Range." Truth once again outdoes fiction.

The pileated woodpecker, jackhammering away in the treetops, may break your reverie or wake you in the morning. Absent the woodpecker, you may want a cup of Java the way we've heard camp coffee should be: "hot, black as a bat cave, strong enough to walk on its own."

The AT now rises and falls easily, ambling northward toward Cheshire. At 4.1 mi. the trail travels alongside Gore Pond, evidently growing these days due to an impressive beaver dam, inspectable at close range. At 4.6 mi., cross the pond's outlet. The mixed woods hereabouts can be cheerfully dappled in sunlight where the AT intersects a maze of old logging roads, many of them posted with bright red warning signs, urging motorbikes to keep out.

A granite Dalton/Cheshire boundary marker is just off the trail at 5.9 mi., but don't be surprised if you miss it. After a wandering, uninterrupted ramble of another 30 to 45 min., the trail rises gently to The Cobbles, a rocky outcropping. There are two viewpoints, southern and northern. In season, you can pick blueberries galore. Much of the cobble is

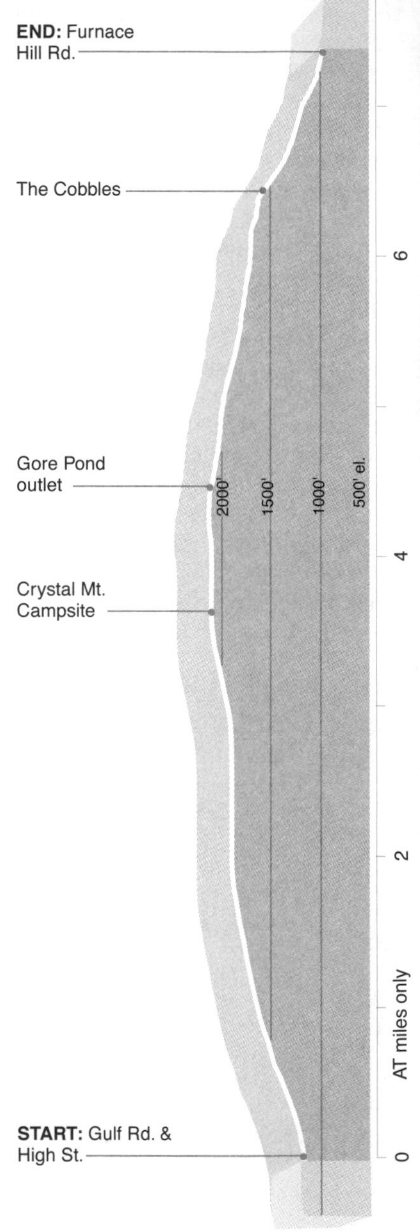

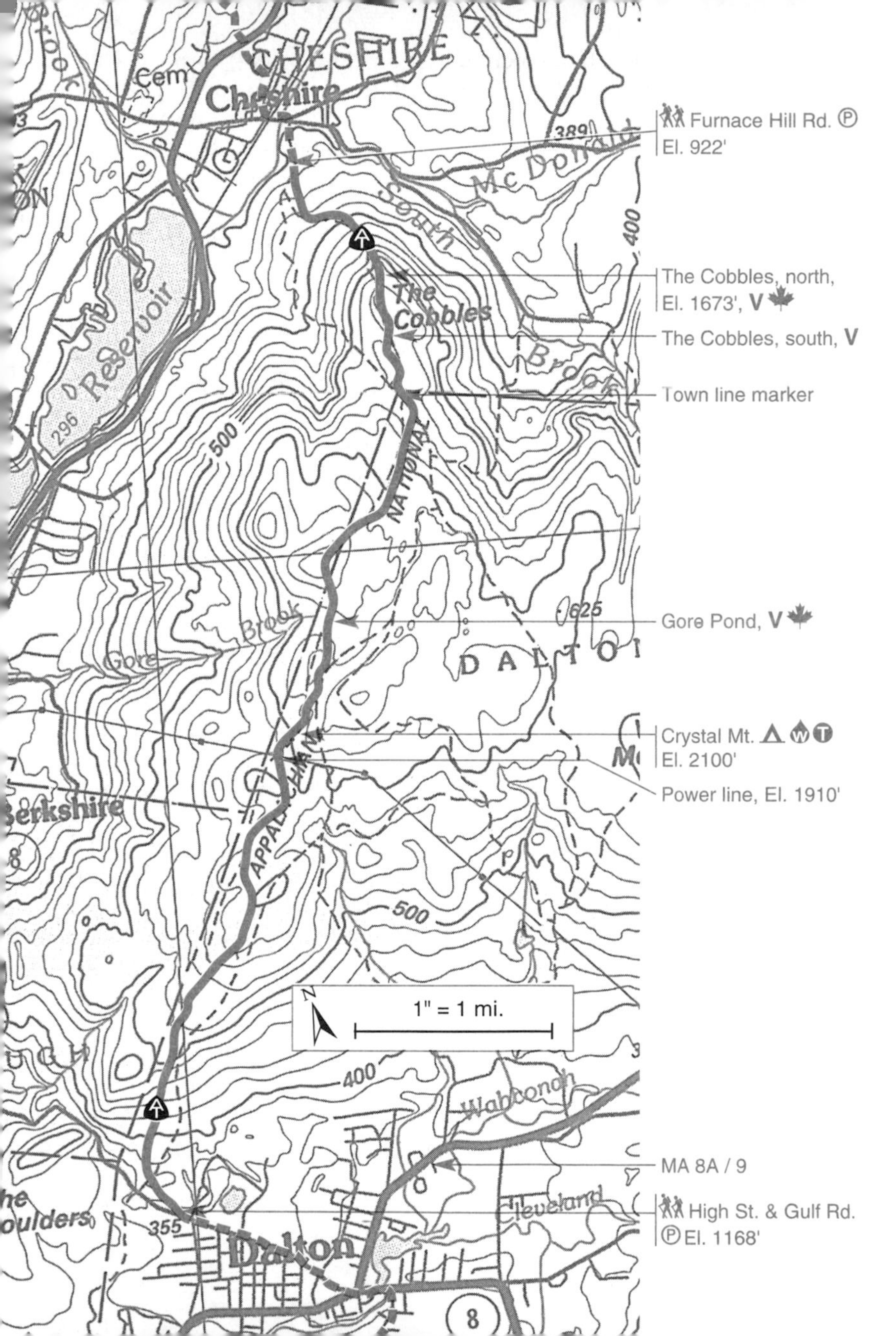

CHESHIRE
Cheshire
Cem
Reservoir
296
McDonald
South
Brook
The Cobbles
Gore
Brook
DALTON
NATIONAL
APPALACHIAN
Berkshire
Wahconah
Cleveland
Boulders
Dalton
355
389
500
400
625
1" = 1 mi.
N
Furnace Hill Rd. Ⓟ
El. 922'
The Cobbles, north,
El. 1673', V
The Cobbles, south, V
Town line marker
Gore Pond, V
Crystal Mt.
El. 2100'
Power line, El. 1910'
MA 8A / 9
High St. & Gulf Rd.
Ⓟ El. 1168'

exposed limestone with thin patches of mossy topsoil, where the berry bushes (close to the ground) thrive in full sunlight.

Shale and other rocks obtrude hereabouts as well, and even an amateur geologist can spot evidence of the undersea past of northern Berkshire. What's more, the cataclysm of colliding tectonic plates that thrust up these mountains eons ago is plain to see. As easily eroded limestone washes away, more obdurate rocks, their fault lines nearly perpendicular to the ground, strain skyward.

From the northernmost overlook on The Cobbles (accessible by a short side trail), drink in the sight of the southern ascent of Mt. Greylock (see Hike #17) and of Cheshire Reservoir and Cheshire village, its white church steeples poking up through the verdant forest. The reservoir is the longest of Berkshire's northern lakes (3.5 mi.), and it flows north into the Hoosic River, which eventually finds its way to the Hudson in New York State. There is no public beach (the lake is sadly choking with weeds), but birders will want to stop at the Farnums Rd. causeway, off MA 8, to watch for migrating waterfowl.

From The Cobbles it's steeply but briefly downhill for the hike's last leg. Soon, just above Furnace Hill St., familiar village sounds—church bells, whirring lawnmowers, and barking dogs—signal your re-entry into the world of human habitation.

In Cheshire, a particularly hiker-friendly village, St. Mary of the Assumption Church (on Church St., a short distance from the trail), welcomes several hundred long-distance hikers per year with Spartan hostel-style accommodations (floor space, toilets, no showers); call Father Tom Begley at 413-743-2110.

For a good historical laugh at the end of this hike, cruise by the Cheshire Cheese Monument, on Church St. in the center of town. President Thomas Jefferson had loyal supporters in these Berkshire woods, who sent a giant wheel of cheese (1235 lb., 4 ft. in diameter) to Washington as homage to their leader. Jefferson, a Virginia planter himself and always impressed by agrarian achievements, exhibited the Cheshire cheese (a cheddar) in the brand-new White House in a room later used for an exhibit of mammoth fossils from the West. But as the *Appalachian Trail Thru-Hiker's Companion* notes, it was the giant cheese, not the fossils, that gave the room its nickname, "Mammoth" (today's East Room).

HIKE #16 Itinerary

Miles N	NORTH	Elev. (ft./m)	Miles S
7.4	**End:** R turn, private drive, into **Furnace Hill St.,** day parking (overnight parking: Cheshire Highway Dept. shed, E. Main St.).	922/281	0.0
6.6	Spur trail to **The Cobbles,** N viewpoint.	1673/510	0.8
6.5	**The Cobbles,** S viewpoint; USGS metal marker.		0.9
5.9	Dalton/Cheshire town line marker (stone).	1811/552	1.5
4.6	Cross **Gore Pond** outflow, then modest climb to forested hilltop.		2.8
4.1	View of **Gore Pond,** R, through trees.		3.3
3.7	Spur trail (0.2 mi.), R, to **Crystal Mt. Campsite,** privy, water.	2100/640	3.7
3.3	Electric power line overhead.	1910/582	4.1
0.0	**Start: Gulf Rd. and High St.,** Dalton; overnight parking in AMC lot; enter forest, going N; AT rolls over undulating terrain for first several mi.	1168/356	7.4

HIKE: #17

Cheshire to Mt. Greylock

Maps: ATC Mass. & Conn. #1; AMC relief map of Mt. Greylock

Route: From MA 8, Cheshire, to summit of Mt. Greylock, Adams

Recommended direction: S to N

Distance: 7.6 mi.

Elevation +/-: 1102 to 3491 ft.

Effort: Strenuous

Day hike: Yes

Overnight backpacking hike: Optional

Duration: 5 to 5½ hr.

Early exit option: Outlook Ave., at 0.8 mi.; Jones Nose Trail, at 5.0 mi.

Natural history features: Boreal forest; highest mountain in MA

Social history features: Literary Greylock

Trailhead access: For a one-day, one-way hike, the ascent of Greylock is a two-car operation requiring at least an hour's lead time to position the vehicles. For a round-trip hike to the summit, leave early in the morning. Your total distance will be 15.2 mi. on this route, and you'll want to allow for time spent exploring the summit. For those with only one car available, a potential turnaround point, mid-mountain, is described here; but the total mileage is such that altogether the time involved is the same as or greater than climbing to the top and driving back down.

Newcomers are advised to consult a road map. Going the wrong way around Mt. Greylock can eat up a big piece of your day. The Greylock range runs roughly SSW to NNE. Along US 7 on the W are Lanesborough, New Ashford, Williamstown; along MA 8 on the E are Cheshire, Adams, North Adams. MA 2, on the N end of the range, connects Williamstown and North Adams.

End: The summit of Greylock is accessible by car (usually from May 15 through Nov. 1) from either North Adams (N approach) or Lanesborough (S approach). Overnight parking is permitted at the summit.

From North Adams, use Notch Rd., off MA 2 (between North Adams and Williamstown). It's 9 mi. to the top.

From Lanesborough, N of the village center, watch for the Greylock Reservation sign on the E side of US 7; enter North Main St. here, leading to Rockwell Rd. Early on, pass Greylock Visitor Center (R), a good place for maps and current trail information. Rockwell Rd. continues to the summit (10 mi.).

For early- or late-season road conditions (it's often icy near the summit), call the Visitor Center (413-499-4262, open all year) or call Bascom Lodge at the summit (413-743-1591, open early May to late Oct.).

Start: Assuming you have just positioned car #1 atop Greylock, descend Rockwell Rd. from the summit (10 mi.), passing the Visitor Center (L) near the foot of the mountain; then, shortly, turn L (E) onto unpaved Quarry Rd. (Greylock Rd. goes R here, out toward US 7). Proceed cautiously through woods on Quarry Rd., cross the town line into Cheshire, join West Mountain Rd., proceed to MA 8, turn N (L), pass Coolidge Rd. on L, and reach AT (day only) parking on W side of highway. (For overnight parking: From MA 8 go E on Church St., which becomes E. Main St., to the Cheshire Highway Department shed.)

If you are approaching on MA 8 from the N, watch for Richardson St. on the L, then the AT crossing.

Camping & lodging: Mark Noepel Lean-to and Campsite (on AT); Sperry Rd. Campground (car camping, off AT); other lean-tos at considerable distance off AT (see description); no camping at summit; Bascom Lodge at summit, on AT

Words to the wise: Traffic jams at the summit notwithstanding, Greylock is a wilderness area. If you're hiking on Greylock, wear firm-sole shoes, carry water / map / compass / flashlight / first-aid kit, stay on the trail, don't hike alone, let someone know where you're headed and when you should be back, and be prepared (with rain gear and sweater) for quick and dramatic changes in the weather. Hikers have gotten seriously lost here, sometimes suffering life-threatening hypothermia and occasionally requiring expensive rescues. Enjoy your hike, guided by common sense. Don't become a Greylock statistic.

Mimi MacDonald

Bascom Lodge atop Mt. Greylock

Overnight at Bascom Lodge

Feeling self-indulgent? A grand way to conclude a day's hike to the top of Mt. Greylock is to stay overnight at Bascom Lodge. In car #1, which you positioned on the summit before the climb, you can now invade the cache in the trunk for clean socks, toothbrushes, and champagne and paper cups for your celebratory toast.

To secure a high-season weekend reservation at Bascom Lodge, telephone weeks in advance. Compared to the famous Red Lion Inn in Stockbridge, Bascom is Spartan, and that's its charm; compared to a tent or a lean-to on the Appalachian Trail, Bascom is the Red Lion Inn. To accommodate thirty-six guests, Bascom offers four private rooms (double or twin beds) and four coed bunk rooms (six to nine people each). Bathrooms are shared. Bedding and linen are provided. Overflow hikers may be relegated to the hardwood floor of the glassed-in porch.

Bascom is famous for its good-humored staff, who seem to be able to solve any problems, making hikers —stiffening, hungry, and tired— happy again.

When the dinner bell rings at the foot of the stairs, the best part of the evening is about to begin (well, maybe the stars are best). Supper is served family-style in a dining room that boasts one of the lodge's several massive fieldstone fireplaces, this one presided over by Bullwinkle the Moose. He is mute, but your fellow diners at the long tables will be chatty. Meals (breakfast is also served) are hearty. Bascom's kitchen serves up neither pheasant under glass nor cans of cold Spam, but instead the ever-satisfying golden mean, delivered by agile, smiling waiters: soup, meat, carbo, warm veggie, salad, home-baked bread, and dessert. Mom will be glad you ate here.

On many summer nights, Tuesdays

The best place to begin climbing Mt. Greylock is in your mind. Take a leap of the imagination, as Herman Melville did from his study at Arrowhead in Pittsfield, where he positioned his writing desk so he would have a window-framed view of the mountain: in Greylock Melville saw the haunting mass of the great white whale itself. Or take the empirical approach: Count the myriad lines on the topographic map as you ponder your hiking route. To hike from your armchair, read *Most Excellent Majesty* (Stevens and Burns) on the mountain's social and natural history. Better yet, make a junket to the Mt. Greylock Reservation Visitor Center, on Rockwell Rd. in Lanesborough, to admire the scale-model relief map of the entire Greylock massif, noting the rise and fall of the mountain's rippling, sensuous spine.

Make *contact* with Greylock. Pay your respects. Everest it isn't, and Mt. Washington it isn't. Still, at 3491 ft.,

especially, AMC offers naturalist-led programs (evening hikes, indoor slide shows); on Friday and Saturday nights there's likely to be an open stage for music or storytelling. In the spacious central lounge, a blaze may be crackling in the biggest of the fireplaces, the mantel head-high and 12 feet long. Settle in for some quiet conversation or reading, better yet some fire-gazing and a welcome torpor.

Bascom Lodge has a staff of fifteen, annually serving thousands of day visitors (as many as 6,000 may come up on Columbus Day alone), more than 2,500 overnight guests, including about 150 Appalachian Trail thru-hikers. The lodge is named for John Bascom, one of the original commissioners of the Greylock Reservation in the late 1880s. Built of native schist, with beams taken from Barnard Farm near the bottom of Notch Rd. (and rafters from hand-hewn tree trunks, according to Greylock historian Lauren Stevens), the lodge was a Civilian Conservation Corps project in the mid-1930s. Serving the varied needs of AT thru-hikers (mail drop, showers, moleskin, messages, boot laces) has been the heart of Bascom's mission. For hikers short on cash, there's a *quid pro quo* invitation: $10 and 2 hours labor gets you bed and board.

Nowadays, Bascom Lodge is owned by the Commonwealth of Massachusetts and operated by the AMC. For 8 weeks in the summer, a trail maintenance crew lives at the lodge, caring for 35 miles of footpaths crisscrossing the Greylock range—but not including the Appalachian Trail, which is maintained by the Berkshire chapter of the AMC. In 1998 the summit and its buildings were nominated for inclusion in the National Register of Historic Places.

Lodging (as of 1997) per person, per night: bunk rooms, $25; private rooms, $62; AMC members, approximately 25% discount. Meals: breakfast $6, dinner $12. Children's prices lower. Season: early May to late October.

Greylock is the highest point in Massachusetts. It's also the first mountain that confronts northbound thru-hikers with a botanical zone comparable to the far reaches of Canada and to the higher peaks of Vermont and New Hampshire. Greylock is Massachusetts' richest wilderness area, simultaneously boasting a proud history of literary associations. And, practically speaking, Greylock tests the muscles of every hiker.

From MA 8 the AT starts the climb right away, rising up on a farm track into a field from which, if you look behind you, there's a pretty view of the Cheshire Cobbles to the southeast. This first section of the hike is on or near farmland. The mountain's forest looms ahead.

At the Outlook Ave. crossing (0.8 mi.), by a handsome stand of birch, scramble over a stile bridging a massive stone wall, with Reynold's Rock on the left. The trail proceeds westward along a hedgerow in a lovely

David Emblidge

Sea of clouds in valleys around Mt. Greylock

hayfield, then along a swampy area. A few hundred yards in and the woods envelop you, as the trail crosses a brook and then rises quickly along a cliffside (1.6 mi.).

Even on a cool day in late October, the ascent from here, on Saddle Ball ridge, will warm you. In summer, you'll be stripping down to T-shirt and shorts. It's nearly a 900-ft. climb in the first 1.6 mi. Heavy breathing, of the hiker's kind. But don't leave the warm clothes at home. Like any mountain over 2500 ft., Greylock can turn positively chilly (and stormy) as you approach the top, which may be in damp clouds (or raining, even snowing) while in the valley below it's just an ordinary day. Some say that the mountain gets its name for the gray cast of the clouds frequently swirling around the summit.

The mountainside (beginning at about 1.6 mi.) drops off precipitously to the west, into dark Kitchen Brook Valley, thick with hemlocks. Once you achieve 2000 ft. (at around 2.0 mi.), the AT levels off. Take a short break for a southeast view (near 2.5 mi.) from a ledge just off the right side of the trail. In another 0.5 mi., the boundary of the Mt. Greylock Reservation appears, under towering red spruces, and then the AT's junction with Old Adams Rd. The reservation is the crown jewel of the commonwealth's state park system, encompassing 11,611 acres, with 43 mi. of trails (7.8 on the AT).

As another mile passes the AT gains more altitude, but easily now. The map's contour lines have light between them again, a sign of relief. At 4.1 mi. you twist and turn amidst hulking boulders (some of them glacial erratics) and then climb a set of natural rocky steps. Did the kindly glacier know you'd be coming this way?

By now it's time to picnic. Scout anywhere along here to choose a satisfying perch with a grand view to the west, perhaps near the 0.2-mi. side trail to Mark Noepel Lean-to (4.4 mi.). Convenient rocks and logs can make seats and a table. There is almost always a breeze wafting up from the valley below.

A more protected picnicking spot, to leeward, can be found behind the huge rocks, but then you'll miss the view. The deep-throated call of hawks fills the treetops along Saddle Ball ridge. The birds swoop up on warm drafts along the mountainside to your left.

Moving on again, you're climbing now, but almost imperceptibly compared to the morning's heart-pounding effort. The trail passes through a beech grove, then a lovely stand of aromatic balsam fir. A good viewpoint comes along at 4.9 mi., a few hundred feet off the AT. Watch for the side trail, left.

By the time you reach the Jones Nose Trail (5.0 mi.), the AT has gained another 900 ft. and is now on top of Saddle Ball ridge (3238 ft.), where the new Appalachian Trail has a junction with an older AT route.

If you have the time and inclination, a detour out to Jones Nose (0.6 mi. round-trip, also accessible from Rockwell Rd.) will give you an unobstructed long-distance look at the Catskills way over to the west, beyond the Hudson Valley—assuming you have a sunny day. The Nose used to be pastureland; hence the clearing.

This location may be an appropriate turnaround point, also, for those making a round-trip hike with one car. Including the detour out to the Nose, the round-trip is 10.6 mi. There is parking on Rockwell Rd., out at the Nose, so a shorter two-car day hike can terminate there as well.

Continuing on the AT, even from the present vantage point, familiar Berkshire landmarks are easy to pinpoint toward the southwest: glistening Pontoosuc and Onota lakes, plus north-facing Bousquet ski area (all three in Pittsfield); Monument Mountain (between Stockbridge and Great Barrington); and dome-topped Mt. Everett (in the town of Mt. Washington, almost 50 mi. distant on the Connecticut line). The Taconic Range, directly to the west, marks the nearby Massachusetts–New York border. Binoculars are a good tool to bring on this mountain hike, or try a camera with a telephoto lens to drink in the view. Don't worry if you miss or skip the side trip to Jones Nose: you'll see all the same sights and much more from the Greylock summit—except that up there, you may have to share the view with a crowd.

As the hike continues, the rhythm of walking may lull you into a pleasant reverie, but then suddenly it may break. Large white-tailed deer may leap across the footpath just above you. A pheasant or wild turkey or grouse may explode out of the bushes. Now and then Greylock hikers see a bear or even a moose (the latter at lower elevations, usually near water). The deer and other wildlife, just as startled as you, will dematerialize, almost instantly if not quite silently, into the underbrush.

Clothing on, clothing off. Level stretches; short, intense climbs. The rhythm is herky-jerky as you march toward the summit. The higher you go, the wetter it gets underfoot. Around 5.4 mi., there's a balsam swamp on the eastern rise of Saddle Ball ridge. At 5.8 mi., hopscotch across two more brooks. Boggy patches (with intense sphagnum moss), bridged by narrow rough-hewn logs, appear frequently during the mile to the AT's first intersection with Rockwell Rd. (at 6.7 mi.), at a hairpin turn where day parking is available. Be careful crossing the road; it's busy on weekends.

Hereabouts the AT slips past an invisible border and enters the boreal zone, comparable to Canada's northern woodlands many hundreds of miles away. You are now at about 3100 ft. (On a late October Greylock hike, the first frost-burned plants of the season appeared at this point, and soon we sidestepped a puddle with a lacy apron of ice crystals.) And it's not just your eyes that notice the changes: your ears will tell you that the sound of your footsteps on the trail has changed, too. The topsoil at this elevation is only inches thick, and the ledge just beneath you makes each step sound as though you're walking on a thinly insulated roof. Indeed you are—on the roof of the Berkshires.

Recreational use of Greylock Reservation is similar to that at the beaches of Cape Cod. If you can avoid the beach on the Fourth of July, you do; if you can go there during the week, when everyone else is at work, you do—and it's heavenly. On Mt. Greylock, holiday weekends and prime leaf-peeping season (mid-September to early October) can attract daunting crowds at the summit and a steady flow of short-distance hikers on all but the most difficult of trails (this south-to-north Appalachian Trail approach is, in fact, about the easiest way up the mountain). Predictably, Columbus Day weekend is the most congested, primarily because of the annual "Greylock Ramble," when thousands of hikers climb the various trails to the summit all at once. If you love a party, join in. But off-peak, say midweek or on a non-holiday weekend, you'll have the trail essentially to yourself.

At 7.0 mi. there's a kind of superhighway cloverleaf of trail intersections: the AT meets Cheshire Harbor Trail on the right (leading east, down to Adams, 2.6 mi.) and the Hopper Trail on the left (leading west, down to Sperry Rd. Campground, 1.1 mi., then down to the US 7 valley). En route to Sperry Rd. Campground, Hopper Trail meets Deer Hill Trail (a loop), leading to Deer Hill Lean-to, about 1.5 mi. from the AT and a significant descent and re-ascent (about 1200 ft.). There is a grove of old-growth hemlocks near the lean-to. Here also the AT crosses winding Rockwell Rd. for a second time. Sperry is a busy state-run campground, popular with motorists (thirty-four sites, three lean-tos; no showers, flush toilets, or RV hookups; fee).

Berkshire Rhapsody

Mt. Greylock's charms and challenges have attracted the literati for well over a century. In the mid-1800s, Melville and Hawthorne rambled here when the mountain was still entirely wild. By the 1920s, a certain degree of civilizing had been done to the mountain peak by tourism promoters, and even as chic a society lady as novelist Edith Wharton drove up the rocky road to take the air and admire the view. No one, however, has surpassed Henry David Thoreau in describing the emotional and spiritual impact of seeing the valleys and the sky from atop Greylock. Oddly buried in Thoreau's "other masterpiece," *A Week on the Concord and Merrimack Rivers,* is a report about his walking trip across northern Massachusetts and into the Hudson Valley. Thoreau ascended Greylock by way of Bellows Pipe, a steep trail on the mountain's precipitous eastern slope, so named for the sound of the wind in its woods. He spent one night, alone, on top, sleeping beneath boards at the foot of the Williams College observatory tower, and the experience left an indelible impression, which the master naturalist turned into an unforgettable hymn of praise.

As the light increased I discovered around me an ocean of mist, which by chance reached up exactly to the base of the tower, and shut out every vestige of the earth, while I was left floating on this fragment of the wreck of a world. . . . As the light in the east steadily increased, it revealed to me more clearly the new world into which I had risen in the night, the new terra firma *perchance of my future life. There was not a crevice left through which the trivial places we name Massachusetts, or Vermont, or New York could be seen, while I still inhaled the clear atmosphere of a July morning,—if it were July there. All around beneath me was spread for a hundred miles on every side, as far as the eye could reach, an undulating country of clouds, answering in the varied swell of its surface to the terrestrial world it veiled. It was such a country as we might see in dreams, with all the delights of paradise.*

At 7.2 mi., the AT passes the old water supply pond dug by Civilian Conservation Corps workers in the 1930s, near another junction of the AT with Notch and Rockwell Rds. The Gould Trail descends eastward from here, 1.0 mi. to Peck's Brook Lean-to and Campsite. The hiking foot traffic coming down from Greylock's summit suddenly gets busy. Crossing Rockwell Rd., the main automobile and bicycle access route to the summit from all points south, your woodland idyll on Greylock is more or less over. Now you must watch out for traffic and make your peace with chattering humanity again. Fortunately the rewards of the panoramic views from the top are so potent that it's well worth the compromises of this hike's final half hour.

Another camping option at this point is to descend the Gould Trail for 1.0 mi. (600 ft. down the east side of the mountain) to Peck's Brook Shelter.

Underfoot, the excessive use of the trail up here is evident and worrisome. The path is unnaturally wide and badly eroded. Trees and shrubs along its sides are fatigued and forlorn, their surface roots worn bare, the surrounding topsoil too compacted. Yet, blessedly, the trail is usually litter-free. At 7.5 mi., the trail leaves the woods for good as it skirts the incongruous broadcast tower and approaches the summit parking lot.

The effects of Greylock's elevation (3491 ft.) on plant life are most evident right near the summit. Throughout New England, indeed throughout much of the Appalachian chain, the 19th century's insatiable need for timber and charcoal led to virtual clearcutting of most of the densely forested mountains. Greylock's summit was no exception. If you read Thoreau's luminous, ecstatic report on his ascent of Greylock and his overnight stay on top (see "Berkshire Rhapsody"), you'll note that in his day (the 1850s), Greylock was thickly forested right to the peak. Thoreau had to scale a tree to get any view at all!

Nowadays, following the industrial exploitation and the development of the mountaintop for tourism, it would seem that Greylock's summit is actually above treeline, but not so.

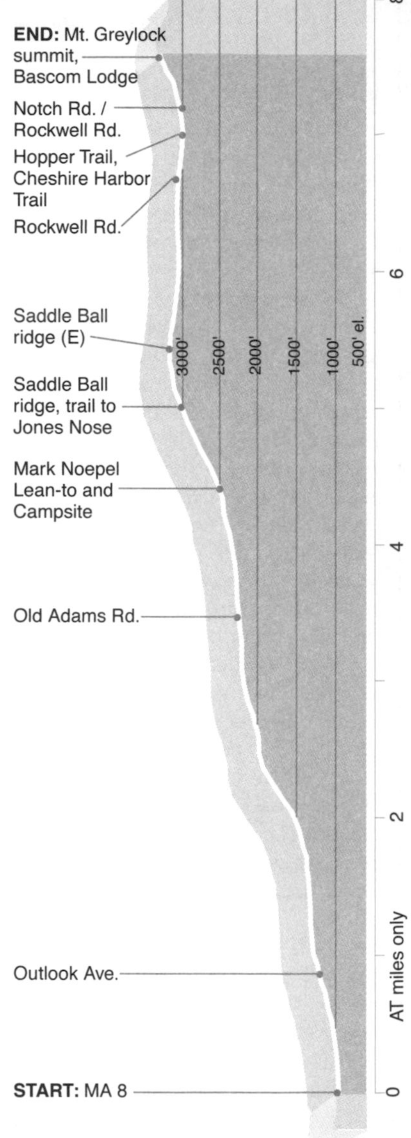

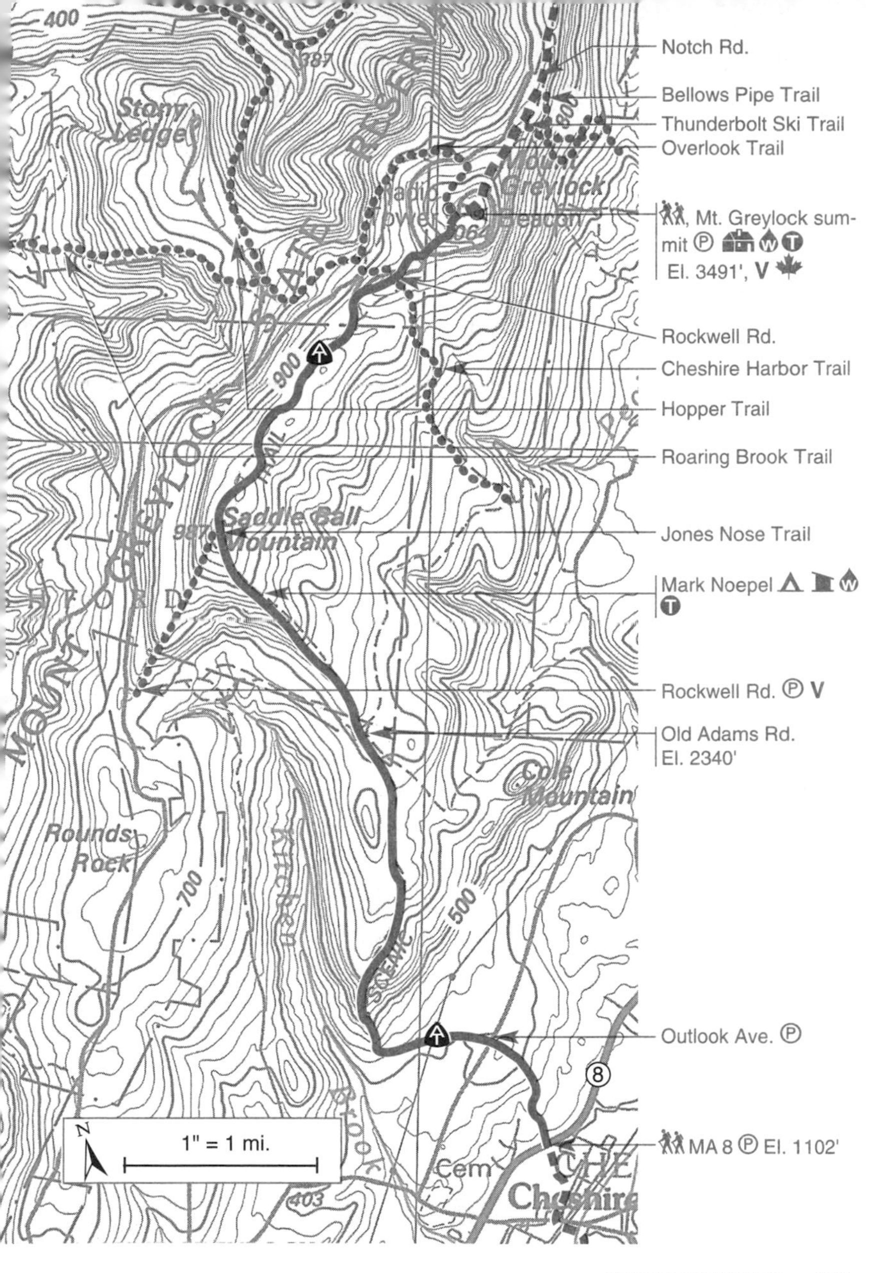
Notch Rd.
Bellows Pipe Trail
Thunderbolt Ski Trail
Overlook Trail
Mt. Greylock summit
El. 3491', V
Rockwell Rd.
Cheshire Harbor Trail
Hopper Trail
Roaring Brook Trail
Jones Nose Trail
Mark Noepel
Rockwell Rd. V
Old Adams Rd.
El. 2340'
Outlook Ave.
MA 8 El. 1102'
1" = 1 mi.
Stony Ledge
Mount Greylock
Saddle Ball Mountain
Rounds Rock
Cole Mountain
Kitchen Brook
Cheshire
Cem
400
500
700
900
403
N

For that you'll have to climb the higher peaks in the White Mts. of New Hampshire (see Vol. 5 in this series, *Northern New England*). On Greylock there is a large treeless area at the summit, but it's not natural. If this fact lowers your spirits, let the extraordinary views afforded by the opening lift them higher again. The outlook is truly unsurpassed in southern New England.

Mountains in five states are visible (Massachusetts, Connecticut, New York, Vermont, New Hampshire). Greylock is sufficiently taller than most of its neighbors to deserve the label "monadnock" (René Laubach's *Guide to Natural Places in the Berkshire Hills* defines this as "a residual mountain mass that stands alone and above the surrounding terrain"). Here, in the last 500 ft. or so of elevation near the top, the nearly constant winds and prolonged intense cold are harsh enough to stunt the growth of evergreens (balsam fir, black spruce, hemlock), twisting them into bonsai-like shapes, sometimes hauntingly beautiful. Such tree miniatures are called krummholz ("crooked wood").

The rounded Greylock summit, 7.6 mi. from today's first steps, is an expansive grassy area with the look of a "bald" in the Great Smoky Mts., but this is an artificial clearing for tourism. You will see a quiver of radio/TV and weather towers, a bumper-to-bumper parking lot, the 100-ft.-high War Memorial Tower, and the welcoming Bascom Lodge. Be sure to explore the lodge, which is operated by the Appalachian Mt. Club. The bookshop offers a fine selection of trail guides and natural history titles as well as maps. Casual food is available in the dining room until 5 p.m., and vending machines provide drinks and munchies. Toilets and telephone are inside.

If you are caught on the summit in bad weather when Bascom Lodge is closed (November to early May), emergency shelter from the elements is available in a stone and timber pavilion just below the low end of the parking lot where the AT goes north. This is an open-sided affair with a fireplace in the middle. No regular camping is allowed here, however.

Note: Hikes #17 and 18 together, in either direction, make an excellent though decidedly ambitious overnight backpacking trip. Or you can do both as day hikes, with a comfortable overnight stay at Bascom Lodge atop Mt. Greylock (see "Overnight at Bascom Lodge"). Extend the trip even further by day hiking around the summit trails, using a different shelter or campsite each night. Contact the AMC Visitor Center at Mt. Greylock, 413-499-4262, for details.

For additional Mt. Greylock hikes (longer or shorter hikes on the AT and other trails), see Hike #18.

HIKE #17 Itinerary

Miles N	NORTH	Elev. (ft./m)	Miles S
7.6	**End: Mt. Greylock** summit, Bascom Lodge, toilets, water, telephone, overnight parking, meals, lodging, bookshop, AMC staff, outdoor skills programs; War Memorial Tower (89 steps to top, 5-state panoramic views).	3491/1064	0.0
7.5	Broadcast tower, then cleared open mountaintop.	3400/1036	0.1
7.2	Former CCC water supply pond, L; then cross junction of **Notch Rd. / Rockwell Rd. and Summit Rd.**; Gould Trail (R) descends steeply 600 ft., 1.0 mi. to Pecks Brook Lean-to, water, privy.	3169/966	0.4
7.0	Convergence of trails: **Hopper Trail** (to **Sperry Rd. Campground,** W, 1.1 mi., toilets, water, parking); **Cheshire Harbor Trail** (to Adams, E, 2.6 mi.).	3100/945	0.6
6.7	Bog (footbridges, mosses); **Rockwell Rd.** at hairpin turn; caution crossing road; day parking.	3100/945	0.9
5.4	Following balsam swamp, eastern rise of **Saddle Ball ridge,** good views.	3228/984	2.2
5.0	**Saddle Ball ridge;** spur trail (0.3 mi. on former AT) to **Jones Nose** (excellent westerly views); continue on spur (1.0 mi. overall) to day parking, Rockwell Rd.	3238/987	2.6
4.4	Spur trail (0.2 mi. E) to **Mark Noepel Lean-to and Campsite;** privy, water (spring), fire permitted.	2750/838	3.2
4.3	View(s), 50–75 yd. apart, to S (L) from ridgetop.		3.3
4.1	Massive boulders lead to stone steps, ascending through mixed hardwoods.	2650/808	3.5
3.5	**Old Adams Rd.**; junction with Old Red Gate Coach Rd. 150 ft. E.	2340/713	4.1
3.0	**Mt. Greylock Reservation** border amidst red spruce.	2340/713	4.6
2.5	View (if trees are bare) to SE (R) from exposed ledge.		5.1

(continued on next page)

Miles N		Elev. (ft./m)	Miles S
2.0	Swamps on both sides; then descend and cross rocky stream.		5.6
1.6	Approach cliffs, then go R by brook; climb steeply to hemlock forest on ridge; sharp drop to Kitchen Brook Valley now L (W).	1969/600	6.0
0.8	**Outlook Ave.,** overnight roadside parking; Reynolds Rock, L; cross hayfield, then swampy area; pass under electric power line.	1319/402	6.8
0.6	Stile at wire fence, followed by farmland.		7.0
0.3	Begin brief period of steep climb.		7.3
0.0	**Start:** MA 8, Cheshire, day parking (overnight parking: Cheshire Highway Dept. shed, E. Main St.). AT follows farm track and begins climb.	1102/336	7.6

SOUTH

HIKE: #18

Mt. Greylock to North Adams

Maps: ATC Mass. & Conn. #1
Route: From the summit of Mt. Greylock, to Mt. Williams and Mt. Prospect, to North Adams
Recommended direction: S to N
Distance: 6.0 mi.
Elevation +/-: 3491 ft. to 630 ft.
Effort: Strenuous
Day hike: Yes
Overnight backpacking hike: Optional
Duration: 4 to 4½ hr.
Early exit option: Notch Rd., at 2.9 mi.
Natural history features: Summit of Mt. Greylock; milky quartz on trail; grove of old red spruce
Social history features: Wilbur Clearing (early settler's farm)
Trailhead access: *Start:* The summit of Greylock is accessible by car (usually from May 15 through Dec. 1) from either North Adams (N approach) or Lanesborough (S approach). Overnight parking permitted at the summit.

From North Adams, use Notch Rd., off MA 2 (between North Adams and Williamstown). It's 9 mi. to the top.

From Lanesborough, N of the village center, watch for the Greylock Reservation sign on the E side of US 7; enter North Main St. here, leading to Rockwell Rd. Early on, pass Greylock Visitor Center (R), a good place for maps and current trail information. Rockwell Rd. continues to the summit (10 mi.).

For early- or late-season road conditions (it's often icy near the summit), call the Visitor Center (413-499-4262, open all year) or call Bascom Lodge at the summit (413-743-1591, open early May to late Oct.).

End: MA 2 and Phelps Ave. in Blackinton section of North Adams, moments E of the Williamstown town line. Overnight parking sometimes available at Greylock Community Club, MA 2, North Adams, 100 yd. E of AT crossing: inquire at 413-664-9020. Overnight parking also on Phelps Ave.

Camping: Wilbur Clearing Shelter and Campsite

Odd to start a hike at the top of a mountain, isn't it? This mountaintop you can drive to or reach on foot. In either case, we recommend that you read Hike #17 before executing #18. You will find useful general information about the mountain there, including notes about the summit, where this hike begins. A full traverse of Mt. Greylock makes a terrific though challenging 2-day backpacking trip.

Before you plunge downward from the top of Greylock, the highest point in Massachusetts, be sure to explore the summit. It offers extraordinary

David Emblidge

Mt. Greylock War Memorial Tower

views in nearly every direction. On truly clear days, pieces of five states can be seen. Improve your odds by climbing the War Memorial Tower for an even better view. Bascom Lodge provides full facilities; see Hike #17 for details. When you're ready to hike, return to the lodge (mileage starts here) and descend to the parking lot, locating the AT exit at the lower end, and pass by a stone pavilion built by the CCC in the 1930s to serve the Thunderbolt ski trail.

Out of the chute, like a ski racer bursting from the starting gate, you will feel gravity's pull immediately. Of course one can hike up here from MA 2 in North Adams, but in a few hours you'll see why relatively few do so.

The mountaintop trail is boggy yet rocky: a walk requiring concentration. Midsummer, every plant is intensely green as the sunlight reflects off the sheen of lingering moisture. No sign of summer drought on cloud-bedecked Greylock. Wildflowers run rampant. Disconcertingly, airplanes buzz overhead, close enough to crewcut the treetops (North Adams's Harriman Airport is at the foot of Greylock).

Just 0.1 mi. from the start, cross Summit Rd., and shortly reach a spur trail that leads again across Summit Rd. and beyond (steeply down, 0.3 mi.) to Robinson Point Vista, where there are more fine views (particularly of The Hopper, Greylock's famous glacial cirque, on the western slope).

A bit farther along the AT, two famous trails descend steeply on the mountain's eastern flank. The Thunderbolt ski trail was a CCC project in 1934, in the fledgling years of American recreational skiing. Burns and Stevens's *Most Excellent Majesty* observes that a 90-min. climb with skis on your back was the lift ticket price for a thrilling 2-min. run, covering 1.6 mi. while dropping 2175 ft. Eastern U.S. ski championships were held here in the 1930s, but the absence of a lift and the inconsistency of the snowfall relegated Mt. Greylock to the ski resort might-have-been category. Most hikers are glad for that. You can hike on the Thunderbolt Trail, but it is precipitous and not thoroughly maintained. The second trail, called Bellows Pipe, follows a route used by Thoreau when he climbed Greylock. The name derives from a wind effect in a spruce and pine grove in the saddle between Ragged Mt. and Mt. Greylock. The AMC Bellows Pipe Shelter is 1.0 mi. steeply down this trail.

Continuing on the AT, progress is rapid, in a jolting, often slippery downhill ramble. At 0.9 mi., the trail passes the almost unnoticeable forested top of Mt. Fitch (3110 ft.), where beautiful milky quartz seems to blaze the trail underfoot. Down next into the saddle between Mt. Fitch and Mt. Williams, where a spur trail at 1.8 mi. leads west out of the woods (0.3 mi.) to Notch Rd. and a water source. The first of this hike's many payoffs, a breathtaking overlook from the peak of Mt. Williams (2950 ft.), arrives at 2.0 mi. after you have regained a bit of altitude. In the valley, pastoral farmland and an orderly village (Williamstown) signify man's dominion, while at your feet a precipice inspires delicious gothic vertigo and distant views (Mt. Haystack in Vermont, the Taconic Range on the New York border) evoke awe at Nature's scope. Romantic landscape painters of the 19th century would have loved this viewpoint. One can sense here how immersing themselves in Nature became for them a spiritual experience. The Victorian art critic John Ruskin said, "Mountains seem to have been built for the human race, as at once their schools and their cathedrals." The Mt. Williams vista may make you agree. Add your own philosophical postulations in the AT logbook on Mt. Williams.

Descend now, steadily, for nearly a mile through mixed forest of hardwoods and evergreens. The trail crosses Notch Rd. at 2.9 mi.; within minutes, in the woods again, it reaches the junction with Money Brook Trail. If you're overnighting on this hike, follow Money Brook's blue blazes for 0.3 mi. to the spur sloping downhill a few yards to Wilbur Clearing Shelter and Campsite. There is no pot of gold at the end of Money Brook Trail, but there is a good story, told well in *Most Excellent Majesty,* about an alleged band of counterfeiters who secreted themselves in the depths of the woods along the brook in The Hopper. Massachusetts pine-tree shillings or, perhaps, Spanish dollars were made here. No evidence has ever been found, but ghosts are said to have given the ne'er-do-wells cover.

A Spider's Web of Trails

You'll need more than fingers and toes to count all the trails on Mt. Greylock. The AT runs south-to-north over the entire mountain. There are many midmountain access points to the AT from Rockwell and Notch Rds., if you haven't the inclination to start at the bottom. Study the Itineraries for Hikes #17 and #18.

Guided walks leave Bascom Lodge almost daily throughout the summer and fall, some at sunrise, and are led by enthusiastic, knowledgeable naturalists from the AMC or the Massachusetts Department of Environmental Management. There's something for everybody. Call Bascom Lodge (413-743-1591) or the Greylock Visitor Center (413-499-4262) for information.

The Appalachian Trail is blazed white. Most trails feeding into the AT or otherwise traversing the mountain are blue-blazed.

Trails on Mt. Greylock

Jones Nose Trail and AT (a triangular loop): On Rockwell Rd., park at Jones Nose. Head east on Jones Nose Trail, shortly veer right onto Old Adams Rd., turn left onto AT (north), turn left onto Jones Nose Trail, returning to your car. Distance: about 3 mi.

Overlook Trail and AT: Park at the summit of Greylock, descend on Overlook Trail, which crosses Notch Rd., then turns south and southwest, continuing to the Hopper Trail; turn left, ascend to the AT, turn left and ascend to the summit. Distance: 2.5 mi.

Brook Loop Trail: This short hike does not include the AT. Park at the Greylock Visitor Center, Rockwell Rd., near the foot of the mountain (Lanesborough side). From the far eastern end of the parking lot, head north into the woods. The loop is about 2.3 mi.

Stony Ledge: This short hike does not include the AT. Park at the upper hairpin turn on Rockwell Rd. Follow the Hopper Trail to Sperry Rd. (unpaved), pass by the campground, and continue on the road out to Stony Ledge, a picnic area with magnificent views down into the Hopper. Return by the same route. Distance: about 2.6 mi.

Mt. Prospect: Park on Notch Rd. at AT crossing. Follow AT north, climbing to junction with Mt. Prospect Trail (left), then along ridge to Mt. Prospect. Return by same route. Particularly pleasant when the leaves are down. Distance: 1 mi.

Trails Ascending Mt. Greylock

Cheshire Harbor Trail: From West Mt. Rd., Cheshire, to Rockwell Rd. and AT. Distance: 6.6 mi.

Bellows Pipe Trail: From Notch Rd., North Adams, to AT. Distance: 4 mi.

The Hopper Trail: From Hopper Rd., off MA 43, Williamstown, to AT at Rockwell Rd. Distance: 8 mi.

The tale is now almost 200 years old.

Jeremiah Wilbur (1753–1813) was perhaps Greylock's most enterprising pioneer farmer. His land included 1600 acres between Notch Brook and Mt. Williams—plus the forested Greylock summit itself, to which he cut a passable trail. Campfires at the lean-to must be short and sweet. There is precious little firewood nearby, picked over by frequent visitors. You will probably see porcupine visitors too, rustling in the groundcover, spitting distance away. Flashlight beams will scare them off for a moment, but porkies are smart. They bide their time until campers are asleep, then scavenge for scraps or fresh food in any pack mistakenly left within their reach. Hoist your pack, with all your garbage and food, on a line strung over a tree branch nearby (several feet from the trunk). This should foil any inquisitive bears, too, who do not want you but who may want a snack from your pack. Water from the small stream at this lean-to is iffy; bring a good supply. There is, however, a privy.

Continuing along the AT, through red spruce alive with warblers' songs, 20 min. of steep climbing brings you to another outstanding view to the northwest from a precipice (3.2 mi.) on Mt. Prospect (2503 ft.). There is a pleasant side trip opportunity here for those with extra time. The Mt. Prospect Trail (on your left) runs gently up to Mt. Prospect (2690 ft.), then down toward The Hopper (sweet views through the trees to the west en route), where a left turn puts you on the ascending Money Brook Trail, which will bring you right back past the spur to the Wilbur Clearing Shelter and thence to the AT (where a left turn continues your hike northward, retracing the 20-min. climb noted above). Allow a couple of hours or more for this diversion. The best reason for making the loop: old-growth red spruce as you pass through the upper Hopper.

Back on the AT, hikers may feel like deep-sea divers, sinking feet-first for the ocean floor, as they drop overboard from the Mt. Prospect Trail junction. The AT plummets to North Adams. Even in dry spots the soil is slippery due to the grade. A full backpack may make you top-heavy, your center of gravity too high. The effort of staying safely in control will bring on the perspiring brow. Quadriceps burn. Ankles wobble. A blister may hatch as downhill steps jam feet into the toes of boots. Isn't this fun? Give your sympathies to all who climb *up* this path.

This is the north slope of the Greylock Range, where moisture lingers. A by-product is numerous colonies of fungi. Take a break to examine them: they can be giants, bright as Day-Glo orange, like an undersea coral. From Mt. Prospect the trail descends 1850 ft., mostly in the first mile. From Greylock's summit, it's 2841 ft. down to MA 2. But it does not go on forever. City sounds soon filter through the woods. You are walking through "pretend" wilderness now, the outskirts of North Adams. At Pattison Rd. (5.1 mi., limited parking), notice a steel-frame building (left), North Adams's water filtration plant. Passing between two watersheds (Williamstown and North Adams), the hike smoothes out, winds down on a braided string of defunct logging roads and driveways, and finally emerges on city streets (Catherine St., then Phelps Ave., at 5.6 mi.). Dead ahead: fine views into northernmost Massachusetts (Pine Cobble), beyond which the AT soon passes into Vermont. Just across MA 2 (6.0 mi.), the AT jumps up again, hungry for more hills.

CULTURE NOTE: Williamstown (west on MA 2) and North Adams (east on MA 2) offer several fine museums and other attractions to add to a Greylock hiking holiday. In Williamstown, the Clark Art Institute has an extraordinary collection of Impressionist paintings, works by Winslow Homer, silver, and contemporary paintings (413-458-9545). The Williams College Museum of Art emphasizes modern and contemporary art (413-597-2429). Sawyer Library at Williams College is a good rainy-day reading place; adjacent is the Chapin Rare Book Library, where you can see a fair copy of the Declaration of Independence and other treasures (413-597-2501). The college also offers Hopkins Forest Museum, with numerous hiking trails (413-597-2346), and Hopkins Observatory, a planetarium (413-597-2188). Williamstown Theater Festival, one of

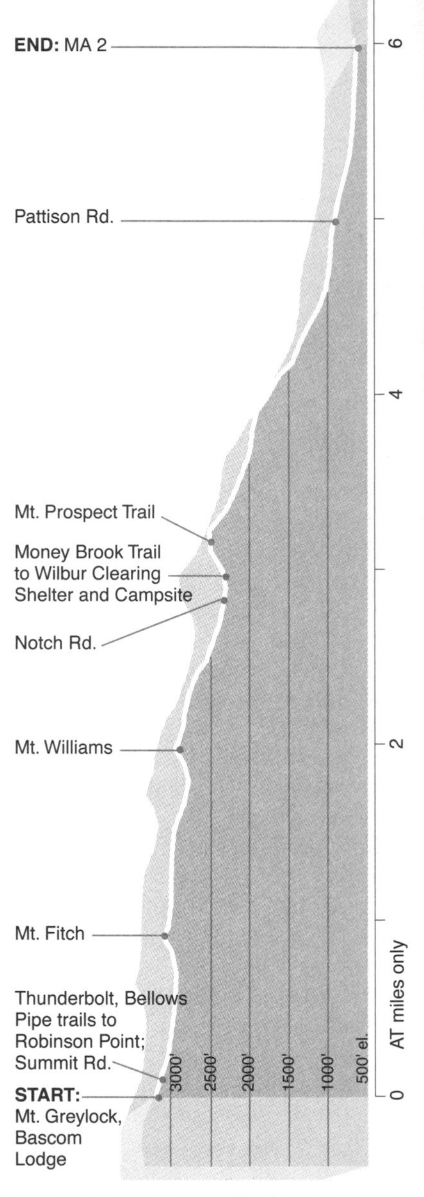

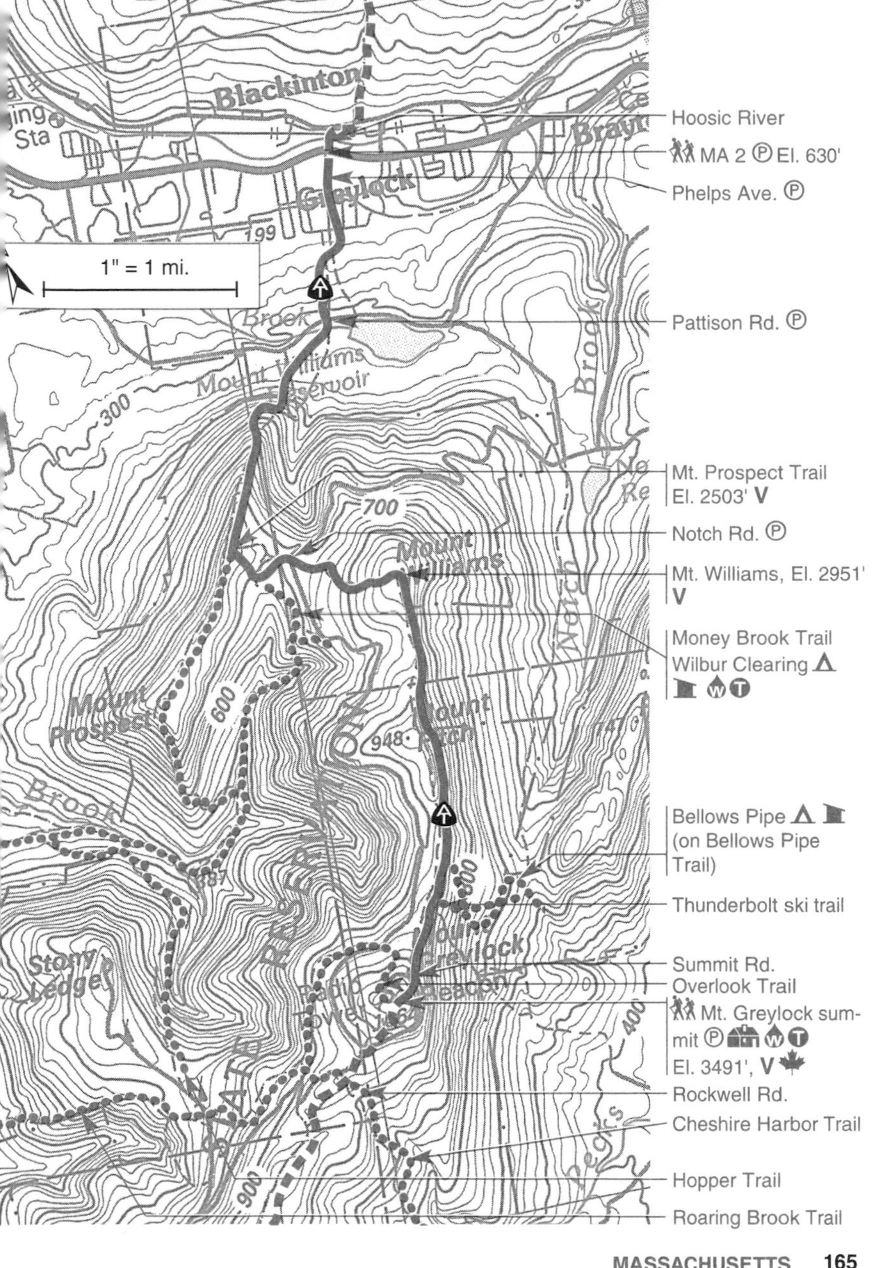
Blackinton
Greylock
Sta
199
1" = 1 mi.
Brook
Mount Williams Reservoir
300
700
Mount Williams
Notch
Mount Prospect
600
Brook
948
Mount Fitch
Stony Ledge
Radio Tower
Mount Greylock
Beacon
800
400
900
Hoosic River
MA 2 Ⓟ El. 630'
Phelps Ave. Ⓟ
Pattison Rd. Ⓟ
Mt. Prospect Trail
El. 2503' V
Notch Rd. Ⓟ
Mt. Williams, El. 2951'
V
Money Brook Trail
Wilbur Clearing
Bellows Pipe
(on Bellows Pipe
Trail)
Thunderbolt ski trail
Summit Rd.
Overlook Trail
Mt. Greylock summit Ⓟ
El. 3491', V
Rockwell Rd.
Cheshire Harbor Trail
Hopper Trail
Roaring Brook Trail

America's premier summer-stock theaters, has Broadway stars in excellent productions on the main stage and in the cabaret (413-597-3400).

In North Adams, there's the Western Gateway Heritage State Park, all about the Hoosac Tunnel, a railway engineering feat of the 1850s (413-663-6312). The Massachusetts Museum of Contemporary Art ("MASSMoCA"), located in a massive old factory complex, is new and full of promise but offers only a few short-term exhibits as of early 1998; keep an eye on this multimedia extravaganza in the making (413-664-4481).

HIKE #18 Itinerary

Miles N	NORTH	Elev. (ft./m)	Miles S
6.0	**End: MA 2,** North Adams; overnight parking on Phelps Ave. or at Greylock Community Club, MA 2, E of AT (ask first).	630/192	0.0
5.6	Good views N to Pine Cobble, Eph's Lookout (Hike #19), and VT.; cross Catherine St., follow Phelps Ave.; overnight parking on street.	653/199	0.4
5.5	After two streams, AT veers E and enters driveway (now in North Adams).	689/210	0.5
5.1	**Pattison Rd.,** limited parking.	1004/306	0.9
4.3	Cross North Adams watershed access road as AT levels out.		1.7
3.2	After tall red spruces, climb briefly to cliff and fine view (W, over Williamstown to Taconic Range); **Mt. Prospect Trail** goes L; begin long, steep descent.	2503/763	2.8
3.0	Trail junction: **Money Brook Trail** goes L (W, 0.3 mi.) to **Wilbur Clearing Shelter and Campsite;** privy, unreliable water, fires permitted.	2325/709	3.0
2.9	**Notch Rd.,** day parking.	2323/708	3.1
2.0	After significant climb, reach **Mt. Williams;** fine N views, trail register.	2951/899	4.0
1.8	Spur trail (0.3 mi. W) to **Notch Rd**. (water); spur also goes E (+/- 1.0 mi.), steeply down Mt. Williams, crosses Notch Rd. at gate.	2795/852	4.2
0.9	Milky quartz underfoot near forested summit of **Mt. Fitch**.	3110/948	5.1
0.1	Following quick descent, cross **Summit Rd.;** then reach spur trail L (W) to Summit Rd. (no parking; spur continues, climbing, 0.3 mi. to Robinson Point, view); then junctions with Thunderbolt and Bellows Pipe ski trails (descending to E).	3100/945	5.9
0.0	**Start: Mt. Greylock summit, Bascom Lodge**, toilets, water, telephone, overnight parking, meals, lodging, bookshop, AMC staff, outdoor skills programs; War Memorial Tower (89 steps to top, 5-state panoramic views); head N from end of parking lot, passing Thunderbolt ski shelter.	3491/1064	6.0

SOUTH

HIKE: #19

North Adams (Eph's Lookout) to Harmon Hill and Bennington

Maps: ATC Mass. & Conn. #1; ATC Vt. & N.H. #8

Route: From North Adams up East Mt. to Sherman Brook, to Pine Cobble, to Eph's Lookout, to Seth Warner Lean-to, to Mill Rd., to Congdon Lean-to, to Harmon Hill, to Bennington

Recommended direction: S to N

Distance: 18.1 mi.

Elevation +/-: 630 to 2890 to 1360 ft.

Effort: Strenuous

Day hike: Optional (see "Early exit options")

Overnight backpacking hike: Yes

Duration: 10½ hr.

Early exit options: Pine Cobble Trail, at 2.6 mi; Broad Brook Trail, at 6.4 mi; Mill Rd., at 6.9 mi.

Natural history features: Northern end of Berkshires, southern end of Green Mts.

Trailhead access: *Start:* MA 2 and Phelps Ave. in Blackinton section of North Adams, moments E of the Williamstown town line. Overnight parking available at Greylock Community Club, MA 2, 100 yd. E of AT crossing; inquire at 413-664-9020. Overnight parking also on Phelps Ave. *End:* VT 9, Bennington, VT; GMC/AMC overnight parking; 5.0 mi. E of Bennington (US 7), 2.8 mi. west of Woodford, 4.8 mi W of Woodford State Park.

Camping: Sherman Brook Campsite; Seth Warner Lean-to and Campsite; Congdon Lean-to and Campsite

At either end of this 2-day backpacking hike there are justifiably popular day hikes, described below. If you're not inclined to go backpacking, don't let the 18.1-mi. total distance scare you away from this wild and beautiful section of the AT. Read on and carve your own shorter hike out of the total.

Backpackers have choices to make as well. You can cover 6.6 mi. on day #1, climbing about 1800 ft. and overnighting at Seth Warner Lean-to; then hike 11.5 mi. on day #2. Or, on day #1 you can hike 13.8 mi. to Congdon Lean-to, climbing 2800 ft.; then day #2 is just a 4.3-mi. walk. A north-to-south hike works well here too.

The AT rises immediately from MA 2 in North Adams, on a footbridge across the B&M Railroad and the Hoosic River. The beginning of Hike #19 is a steady climb up the flank of East Mt., until the trail levels off near the junction with Pine Cobble Trail, coming up from neighboring Williamstown. Once up on the ridge, the going is easy and the views—mostly to the south, back over the Berkshires—are a magnificent and nifty reversal of what hikers south of Mt. Greylock are accustomed to seeing. To your right, for a good distance as you march uphill, there's the delightful sound of babbling Sherman Brook. At 1.4 mi. Pete's Spring, a reliable source, gurgles quietly, east off the trail. Just ahead a spur trail leads 0.1 mi. left (west) to Sherman Brook Campsite (a deluxe affair, with tent platforms and privy); the spur rejoins the AT 0.2 mi. north.

At 2.2 mi., there is a 10-min. scramble steeply up through an amazing tumble of rocks, a geologist's showcase of granite, marble, and quartz. Kids will love it, but adults with fully loaded backpacks may find their center of gravity a bit confused as they tilt from side to side. It's a tipsy, deliciously unnerving walk through the boulder field. If this sounds unappealing, take the alternate route, a 0.3-mi. bad-weather bypass to the south around this section of the AT. In slippery conditions, a hiker might want to be more safe than sorry.

The AT reaches Pine Cobble (and the trail of the same name) at about 2.6 mi. Take a rest, and if the season is right, treat yourself to a snack of wild blueberries, everywhere low to the ground on the marble-topped mountain. What is a "cobble"? We know cobblestones, which paved city streets in the old days. Generically, a cobble is a place where similarly small stones are found in abundance, formed by freezing water and cracking ice over the centuries. Much of the rock here is quartzite. Many trees are stunted due to the continuous winds. Roam about a little to find your favorite viewpoint. Mt. Greylock dominates the southern horizon, the Taconic Range is to the west, the Green Mts. to the north. Take some blueberries home to make blueberry cobbler from Pine Cobble. Impress your friends.

David Emblidge

Giant oyster mushroom

Pine Cobble Trail descends 1.5 mi. to Pine Cobble Rd. (off North Hoosic Rd.), Williamstown, making a fine day-hike loop (about 4.0 mi.).

Better yet, carry on for another half hour of easy walking—you're on the East Mt. ridge now—to Eph's Lookout (3.0 mi., 2254 ft.), named for Ephraim Williams, the founder of Williams College. The vista here improves upon the Pine Cobble views by a good 20 percent—as if one could measure beauty. The lookout is bare rock and blueberry bushes, with hardly a level spot to set your canteen. Turn around here to begin the day-hike loop back to

Hikers' Aches and Pains

Stretch first and last: Five minutes of good stretching exercises before you hit the trail (or after lunch or a long rest) and again at the end of the trek helps muscles, ligaments, and tendons cope with the unusual stresses of ups, downs, tilts, and slides common to mountain walks. Loosen thighs, calves, and lower back. Warm muscles are supple and less likely to strain.

Protect your feet: Kenyan marathoners may train in bare feet, but that doesn't mean you need to punish yourself while hiking with the inadequate protection of tennis or street shoes. Expensive hiking boots are not required for safety or comfort, but something with a tough sole and firm uppers to support your ankles and Achilles tendons will save you from many a sore spot. Blister insurance: a thin pair of cotton socks under a heavier pair of wool or synthetic socks. If a blister starts (a hot, tingling sensation is the warning), cover it immediately with adhesive moleskin—dramatically better than Band-Aids, which bunch up and slip as you walk, exacerbating the problem.

Drink water: It's not just thirsty throats that crave a drink; it's tired muscles too. Even modest dehydration (which you may not notice during the endorphin-enriched pleasure of a strenuous hike) makes it hard to sweat off pain-causing toxins stored in muscle tissue. Carry a plastic water jug on your hip or in an outside pocket of your daypack so you can sip while you stroll.

Avoid a chill: In the dugout between innings, the pitcher wraps his throwing arm in a towel; hikers should

town, using the AT or Pine Cobble Trail.

Even at this distance from the city below, the incongruous sounds of railroad cars shuttling about in the yard down in North Adams may ripple faintly over the mountain. How hard it is in the Berkshires truly to get away from the mechanical music of industry. Vermont, coming soon now, has more wildness to offer.

The last stretch of AT in Massachusetts is a mostly flat 0.8 mi. to the Vermont line, not too far to carry a split of champagne for those who fancy a celebration at the border. The AT log book at the state line is usually peppered with comments from long-distance hikers, many starting or finishing Vermont's Long Trail, but it's the AT thru-hikers' words that put things in perspective: "Eleven states down, three to go." If it weren't for an "AT/LT" (Long Trail) marker at the border, you would never notice the state boundary. In the woods, political lines are fictions, invisible and meaningless. This point too can be the turnabout of a day hike up from North Adams or Williamstown. Like a

follow suit. Even in hot summer weather an overheated hiker can cool off quickly during a rest or a trailside lunch. A chill may bring on cramps. Pack a sweatshirt for the upper body and drape a jacket over legs that will thank you for keeping them warm.

Take precautions: After an unfortunate, bruising fall, halfway into a 6-mile hike with no way out but to walk, you'll be glad you carried a few aspirin, a knee brace, and an ankle brace—a few ounces of security.

Experiment with walking sticks: More AT thru-hikers than not carry chest-high walking sticks to help them keep their balance in slippery or narrow footage conditions. Day hikers with far less weight on their backs have less need for a tall staff, but many hikers use a shorter walking stick in all conditions. The walking stick is a shock absorber against sudden lurches or slides that stretch surprised, uncooperative muscles. Over lunch or a campfire, whittle a masterpiece of totemic folk art on your stick handle. High-tech spring-loaded adjustable trekking poles are a good investment for frequent hikers.

Secret weapons #1 and #2: Pack a banana and eat it as you walk. Potassium-rich bananas help the body break down stored lactic acid (a by-product of digested fructose, or natural sugar). Retention of lactic acid causes muscle pain. When you're working hard, your body consumes your normal intake of potassium more quickly and hungers for more. Sesame seeds, eaten at the end of the hike or the day, provide abundant, readily digestible calcium, which, like the bananas' potassium, helps throw off lactic acid. Bonus: calcium is a soporific (remember that comforting warm milk Mom gave you before bed?), and so you can better sleep your hiker's stiffness away.

swimmer touching the wall between laps in a pool, a hiker can reverse direction and head for home on a wave of satisfaction.

Or . . . welcome to Vermont! From this point northward, to Maine Junction, just north of US 4 near Killington, the AT and the Long Trail are contiguous, looked after by both the Green Mt. Club (GMC) and the AMC.

The following section to Mill Rd. is largely even terrain, deep in the mixed hardwood forest. At 4.2 mi., cross a small brook. Then up again to a ridge (partially exposed bedrock), arriving at 6.4 mi. at the junction with Broad Brook Trail (left, an unpaved woods road). This point can also be used as the turning point for a somewhat longer day hike: Broad Brook Trail runs southwest 4.0 mi. (at first on the woods road, then on a footpath) back to Massachusetts (White Oak Rd., Williamstown), for a total of 10.4 mi. from North Adams.

Just 0.2 mi. beyond the junction with Broad Brook Trail, a spur heads west (left) 300 yd. to Seth Warner Lean-to and Campsite. Built in the 1960s, the shelter accommodates eight, and there are primitive (unofficial, therefore unmaintained) tenting sites nearby. The water source, a brook, is unreliable in dry weather.

Rising slightly, the trail reaches Mill Rd. at 6.9 mi. (a few unpatrolled parking spaces here). Heading west from the AT, Mill Rd. is known as County Rd. and leads to Bennington; it is not passable for automobiles this far up, however. Heading east on Mill Rd., Stamford (VT 8/100) is 4.2 mi. away. High-chassis vehicles (preferably with four-wheel drive) can make it here from Stamford in all but the wettest season. Mill Rd. is difficult to locate in Stamford; you'll need a good local map.

An uneventful but sustained climb follows Mill Rd. A brief but handsome southerly view of the Berkshires provides a good mid-climb resting place. At 8.0 mi. a short side trail east (right) leads to Ed's Spring, not reliable in dry times. The trail—always in the woods here—continues over an unnamed mountaintop that seems more like a lengthy ridge. At the highest point a sweet grassy shaded spot invites picnicking or a snooze. Some long-distance views off the left side of the trail (to the west and south) are the reward for the climb from Mill Rd. At 8.7 mi. a power line runs overhead at a breezy opening in the woods. A plunge downhill follows (the trail loses 420 ft.), to a beaver pond with a lovely vista (Scrub Hill) and some admirable hydroengineering in the beaver dam. The flooding has killed many trees, leaving an eerily beautiful landscape. Herons are frequently spotted along the shore here. Roaring Branch flows out of the pond; the AT/LT crosses the brook on a log bridge at 9.6 mi.

Continued on p. 174

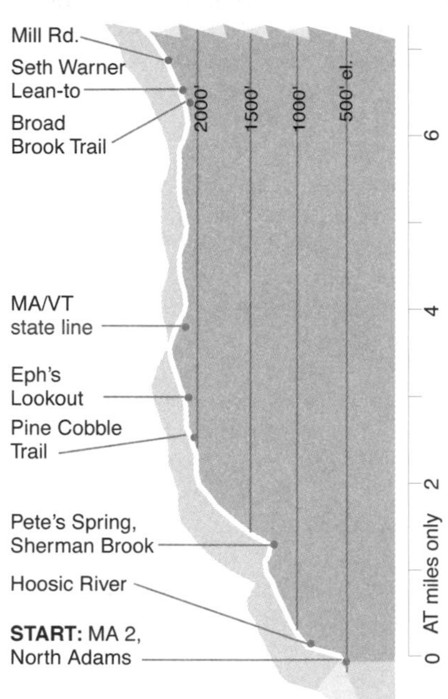

It's up and down over minor knobs during the next mile, regaining about 350 ft., to the forested top of Consultation Peak at 10.8 mi. GMC's *Long Trail Guide* says that trail maintenance volunteers assigned the name because it's a strategic place for planning their work. Downhill from here the AT/LT intersects a woods road leading 0.1 mi. west (left) to Sucker

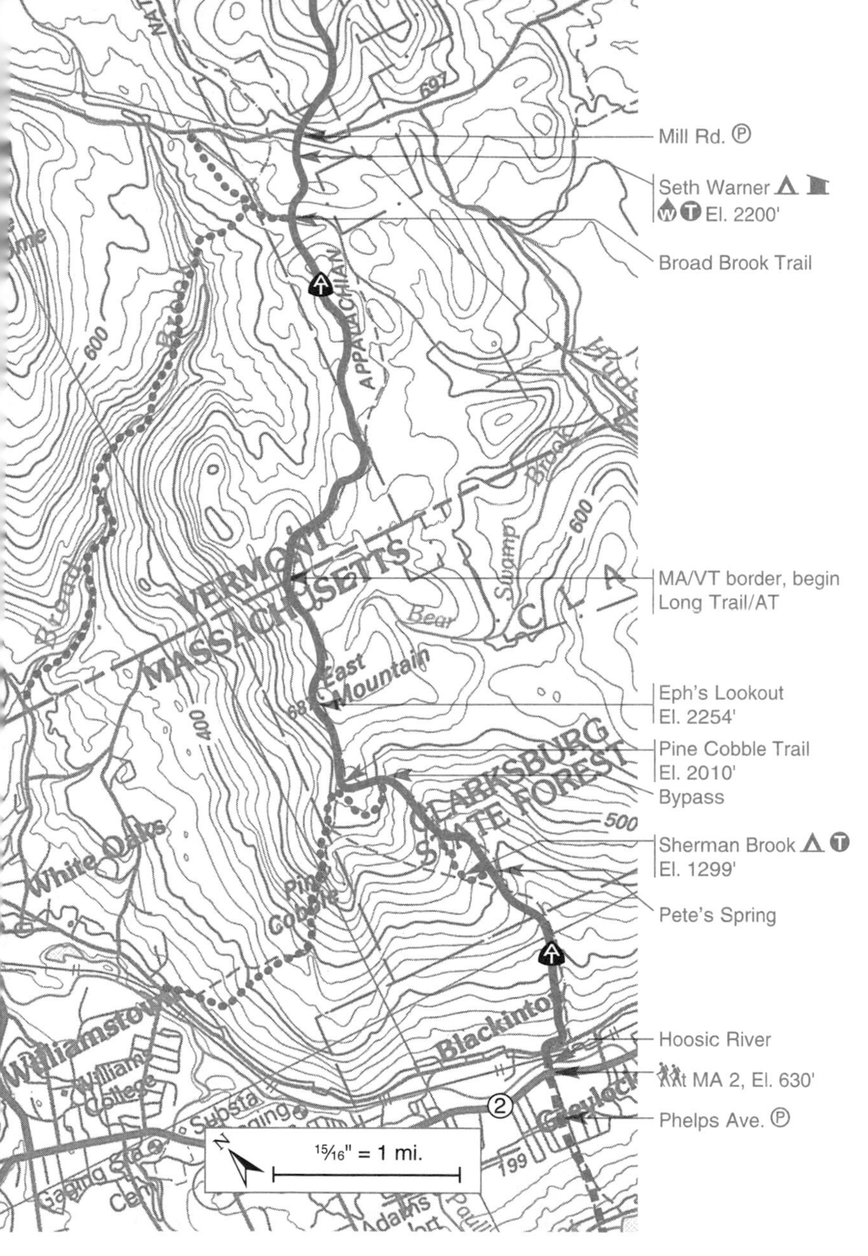
Mill Rd. Ⓟ
Seth Warner
El. 2200'
Broad Brook Trail
MA/VT border, begin Long Trail/AT
Eph's Lookout El. 2254'
Pine Cobble Trail El. 2010'
Bypass
Sherman Brook
El. 1299'
Pete's Spring
Hoosic River
at MA 2, El. 630'
Phelps Ave. Ⓟ
15⁄16" = 1 mi.
VERMONT
MASSACHUSETTS
APPALACHIAN
East Mountain
CLARKSBURG STATE FOREST
White Oaks
Pine Cobble
Williamstown
Williams College
Blackinton
Bear
Swamp
Brook
600
400
500
697
199

Pond, Bennington's reservoir (no swimming or camping). The area near the pond is abused: off-road vehicles and pickup trucks bring in revelers who have trashed the site. It should be closed off. Sucker Pond outlet is at 12.2 mi., with a wet area (and bog bridge) following.

Keep an eye out on the right as the trail rises gently, soon after the wetland. The cellar hole of a 19th-century tavern is prominently visible. From its presence here, you can try to deduce what the path (an old road or even a highway?) and the surrounding woods might have looked like 150 years ago. Are there trees or shrubs that signal domestication, such as crab apple? Does your road map or topo map give clues as to why this was a traveler's route in the old days?

At 13.2 mi. the beautiful and musical Stamford Stream begins to parallel the trail. This is a particularly sweet section, easy underfoot due to a carpet of evergreen needles (primarily hemlock) and generally level. The downstream rush of the water seems to add welcome energy to what by now may be tired strides. It's a cool, deeply shaded place with not much else growing in the understory.

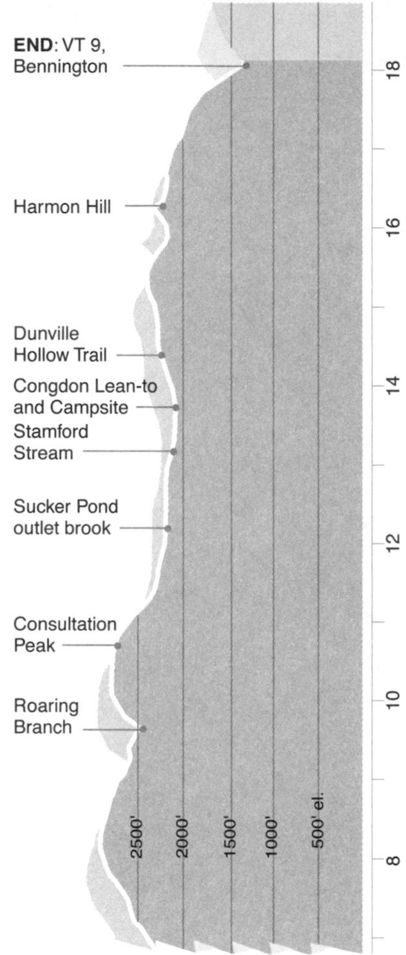

Congdon Lean-to and Campsite appear, right, on the AT/LT at 13.8 mi. Herbert Wheaton Congdon was an early Long Trail builder and cartographer. Although the shelter dates from 1967, it looks older, due no doubt to heavy use. The area in front, with a picnic table, needs restoration. The stream provides an excellent water supply (though purification is as always advised). Tent sites, some not very level, are scattered in the woods on both sides of the stream: it's a bit catch-as-catch-can. On a midsummer visit here we found the site filled with

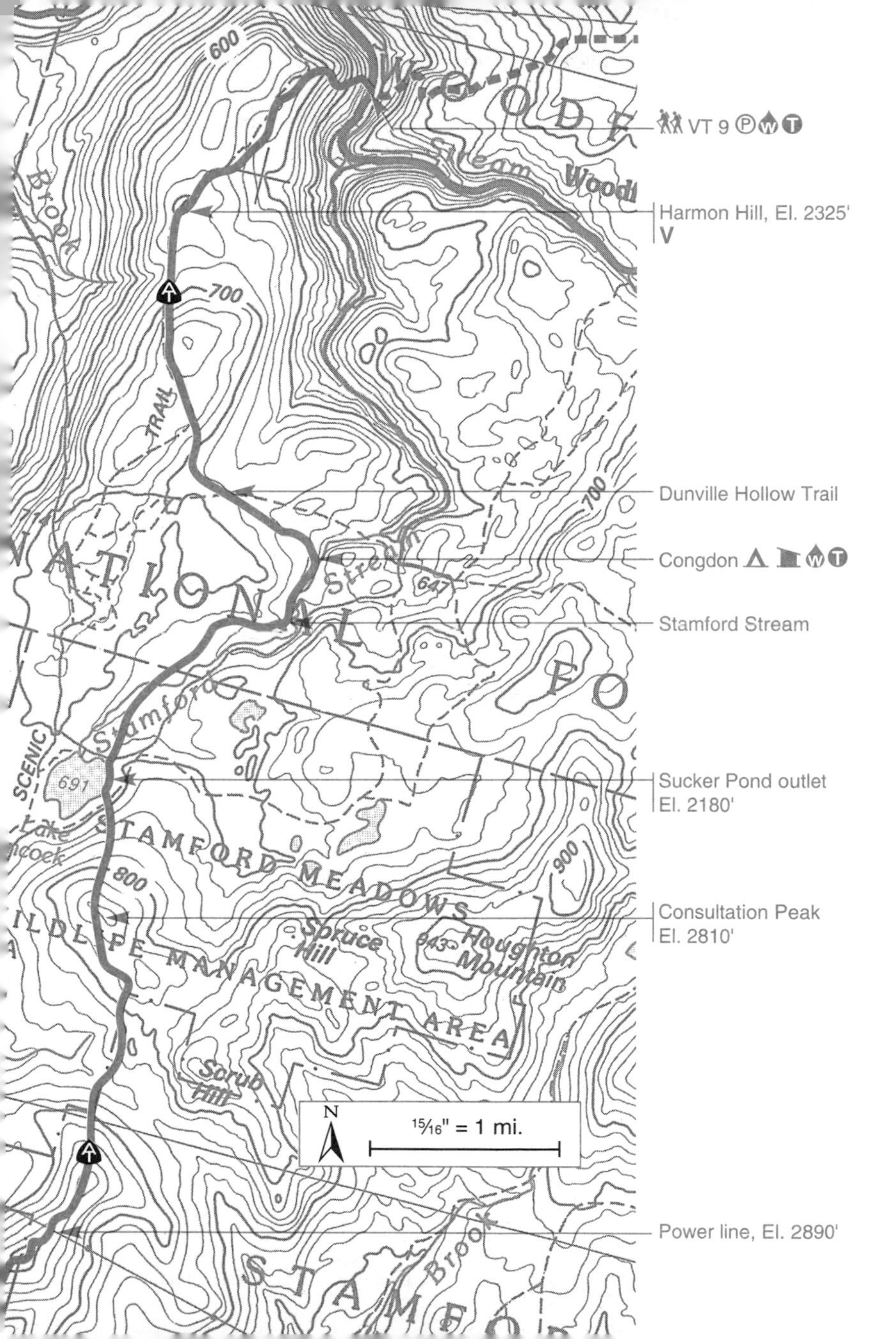

VT 9
Harmon Hill, El. 2325'
V
Dunville Hollow Trail
Congdon
Stamford Stream
Sucker Pond outlet
El. 2180'
Consultation Peak
El. 2810'
Power line, El. 2890'
15⁄16" = 1 mi.
N
STAMFORD MEADOWS
WILDLIFE MANAGEMENT AREA
Spruce Hill
Houghton Mountain
Scrub Hill
Stamford Brook
Stamford Stream
Stream
Brook
TRAIL
SCENIC
NATIONAL FO
WOODF
600
700
800
900
647
691
843

laughter and storytelling by a swarm of thru-hikers who were pleased to act as hiking gear consultants: they had tested the products and could speak with authority. Warning: stock up on water at Congdon. Sources beyond here are unreliable.

Following Congdon, the AT/LT rises briefly before crossing the old Dunville Hollow Trail, also called Old Bennington–Heartwellville Rd. (no longer in use due to heavy ATV traffic). Basically flat terrain rolls onward, with woods road crossings, for almost 2.0 mi. now.

Probably the loveliest views of this entire hike, competing well with those at Eph's Lookout back in Massachusetts, come along at the crest of Harmon Hill (2325 ft.), at 16.3 mi. Foresters use controlled burning to keep several acres open at this summit. The results are dramatic, and the ease of reaching this point on a day hike from Bennington makes it a popular destination. Songbirds love it. Wildflowers love it. You will, too. Look west to see Mt. Anthony and Bennington, with its Revolutionary War monument (an obelisk). Look north for a partial view of Glastenbury Mt. (see Hike #20). At the crest a helpful GMC trail sign notes: "Springer Mt. 1563 mi., Katahdin 557 mi." You won't make either one by dark, so you might as well linger here.

Back into the green woods (dotted with trailside trillium in late spring and early summer) north of Harmon Hill, the descent to VT 9 is at first gentle, then precipitous, losing 965 ft. over 1.8 mi. Slip on the knee brace if you brought one. Truly impressive rock steps wind through switchbacks on the way down, especially the final 0.6 mi. Give thanks to the Herculean trail workers (and the glacier) who wedged the steps in place. Obviously this climb up from VT 9 would be the price of admission for day hikers going to Harmon Hill on the AT/LT. Taking your time, it's doable. GMC estimates the round-trip time to Harmon Hill at 2½ hr.

At VT 9 (very busy traffic), cross carefully to the large GMC parking lot (with privy). Bennington is downhill to the west (5.0 mi. to US 7).

HIKE #19 Itinerary

Miles N	NORTH	Elev. (ft./m)	Miles S
	Note: Mileages differ slightly between hiking guides for this section. The distance from MA 2 to the MA/VT line is 0.3 mi. longer in the ATC's *Appalachian Trail Guide to Massachusetts-Connecticut* than in the GMC's *Long Trail Guide.* Starting at MA 2, we use *Long Trail Guide* mileages northward to the MA/VT line and throughout VT.		
18.1	**End: VT 9,** Bennington, VT; overnight parking, privy, water. Town and US 7 are 5.0 mi. W; Woodford 2.8 mi. E, Woodford State Park 4.8 mi. E.	1360/415	0.0
16.3	**Harmon Hill,** excellent views; gentle descent for 1.2 mi., then steep, rock-stepped descent to VT 9.	2325/709	1.8
14.4	**Old Dunville Hollow Trail,** also called **Old Bennington–Heartwellville Rd.** (unpaved woods road).	2221/677	3.7
13.8	**Congdon Lean-to and Campsite,** water (stream, E of lean-to), privy, fires permitted.	2080/634	4.3
13.2	**Stamford Stream,** on R for 0.5 mi.		4.9
12.2	**Sucker Pond outlet;** wetlands.	2180/665	5.9
10.8	**Consultation Peak** (forested, no views).	2810/857	7.3
9.6	**Roaring Branch,** log bridge.	2470/753	8.5
8.7	Power line overhead; descend sharply to beaver pond; good views.	2890/881	9.4
8.0	Spur trail (E, 100 ft.) to **Ed's Spring**.		10.1
6.9	**Mill Rd.** (unpaved, rough); begin substantial climb, entering Stamford Meadows Wildlife Management Area.	2290/698	11.2
6.6	Spur trail (W, 300 yd.) to **Seth Warner Lean-to and Campsite,** privy, unreliable water.	2200/671	11.5
6.4	**Broad Brook Trail,** (L, unpaved road).	2130/649	11.7
4.2	Brook.		13.9

(continued on next page)

Miles N		Elev. (ft./m)	Miles S
3.8	**MA/VT state line,** southern end of Long Trail (forested, no view); AT soon enters Green Mt. National Forest.	2330/710	14.3
3.0	**Eph's Lookout,** excellent view S to Berkshires; primitive campsite.	2254/687	15.1
2.6	Brief, steep switchbacks to **Pine Cobble Trail,** L; excellent view just S on Pine Cobble Trail.	2010/613	15.5
2.2	Boulder field (blue-blazed bad-weather bypass, 0.3 mi.).		15.9
1.4	**Pete's Spring,** R (E); followed by spur trail L (0.1 mi. W) to **Sherman Brook Campsite,** tent platforms, privy, fires permitted (spur trail rejoins AT 0.2 mi. N).	1299/396	16.7
0.1	**Hoosic River;** bridge over river and B&M railroad tracks, followed by climb along Sherman Brook.		18.0
0.0	**Start: MA 2**, North Adams; overnight parking on Phelps Ave. or at Greylock Community Club, MA 2, E of AT (ask first).	630/192	18.1

SOUTH

HIKE: #20

Glastenbury Mt.

Maps: ATC N.H. & Vt. #8; GMC LT #2 & #3
Route: From Bennington to Glastenbury Mt. to Arlington–West Wardsboro Rd., West Wardsboro
Recommended direction: S to N (described here) or N to S
Distance: 22.6 mi.
Elevation +/-: 1330 to 3748 to 2200 ft.
Effort: Strenuous
Day hike: Optional shorter round-trips
Overnight backpacking hike: Yes
Duration: 13 hr.
Early exit option: None
Natural history features: Glastenbury Mt.
Social history features: Historic Bennington
Trailhead access: *Start:* VT 9, 5 mi. E of downtown Bennington and 8.8 mi. W of VT 8, Searsburg; overnight parking, N side of VT 9; AT/LT heads N over City Stream on MacArthur Bridge. *End:* Arlington–West Wardsboro Rd. (Kelly Stand Rd.), overnight parking. Eastern approach: From VT 100, West Wardsboro, go W on Arlington–West Wardsboro Rd. to Stratton village, then another 3.4 mi. to AT/LT crossing (6.8 mi. total). Western approach: In Arlington, use exit #3 off US 7; go 0.1 mi. W on VT 313; turn R onto South Rd.; go 0.6 mi. to end at Old Mill Rd.; turn R, go 0.7 mi. to fork just after bridge; follow right-hand fork (Kelly Stand Rd.) 10.5 mi. to AT/LT parking on N side of road, just after bridge over east branch of Deerfield River.
Camping: Melville Nauheim Shelter; Goddard Shelter (Glastenbury Mt.); Kid Gore Shelter; Caughnawaga Shelter; Story Spring Shelter

The hike over Glastenbury Mt. covers a remote and hauntingly beautiful wilderness. The entire backpacking hike of 22.6 mi. provides long walks, a choice of camping sites, and plenty of climbing (over 3000 ft. in several ascents). There are some day-hike options as well, and less experienced hikers can enjoy this area too. The long-distance view from one of the shelters (read on) is spectacular. Hiking hereabouts is as good as it gets on the AT in Vermont. A north-to-south hike works well here too, but we're heading from south to north.

From the AT/LT parking lot on VT 9, a spur trail goes a few yards east along the incongruously named City Stream (left), passing a privy, then meeting the AT/LT as it heads north (left) over MacArthur Bridge. The trail then runs downstream briefly before starting a decidedly steep climb for about 30 min., worth the effort to put VT 9's road noise behind you. At 0.7 mi. a large fissured boulder, probably split by freezing ice, which has tremen-

The Long Trail

Appalachian Trail aficionados must doff their hats to the Green Mt. Club and its early members, who started building the Long Trail up the mountainous spine of central Vermont between Massachusetts and Quebec in 1910—over a decade before the AT was even conceived. Indeed, the Long Trail as a vision and a project was one of the inspirations that moved Benton MacKaye, who first proposed the AT, to put his thoughts into action. Though the story may be aprocryphal, it has a good ring to it: MacKaye is said to have conceived the AT while hiking over Vermont's Stratton Mt. (see Hike #21).

GMC today is 6500 members strong, with an active pro-environment policy and outdoor recreation ethic at its heart. New England hikers who use Vermont trails, including the contiguous AT/LT, will want to join up, lend a hand at trail maintenance, contribute funds, or attend natural history and social programs. Membership brings with it a subscription to *Long Trail News* as well as discounts on GMC books, of which *Green Mountain Club Long Trail Guide* is most highly recommended.

Long Trail thru-hikers are called "End-to-Enders," and the title can be used by those who do it in pieces as well. GMC's headquarters, in Waterbury Center (north of AT territory), can provide answers to most hiker questions about trail conditions, trip planning, shuttles, etc. Call 802-244-7037.

The Long Trail was completed in 1927 but has been evolving ever since. Generally the length is thought of as 265 miles. There are shelters every 8 to 10 miles. Much of the northern third is decidedly rugged and less well traveled. The highest peaks are Mt. Mansfield (4393 ft.) and Camel's Hump (4083 ft.), both in north central Vermont, and Killington (4241 ft.), on the AT. The Long Trail is contiguous with the AT for about 100 miles from Massachusetts to Sherburne Pass, just north of Killington in central Vermont.

dous force, appears. This is aptly named Split Rock, and is easily identified by a straight vein of 2-in.-thick white quartz, half on each side of the split. The AT/LT passes through the split, or you can use this as a turnaround point for a pleasant 1.4-mi. woodland walk.

Over the next section, just shy of a mile, the trail rises slowly through mixed hardwoods. At 1.6 mi. the short spur trail to Melville Nauheim Shelter goes east (right). It's a standard lean-to with eight bunks. There's water from the stream by the spur. Tent sites are few in number here. No views, but the woodland setting is sweet. If you want a good view at a rest or lunch stop, carry on another 0.5 mi., and another 330 ft. up, to

Maple Hill, where a power-line cut provides a vista of Bennington and Mt. Anthony on the west, and on the east Mt. Snow and Haystack (ski mountains) and the Hoosac Range, which extends northward from Massachusetts into Vermont.

The next mile is a gradual descent to Hell Hollow Brook, at 3.2 mi., where a bridge offers pretty views of the stream and a good place to dip tired, hot feet in the cooling waters on a summer day. Stock up on water here: there are no reliable sources between the brook and Goddard Shelter. No camping in Hell Hollow area (Bennington's water source).

In the spruce and balsam forest coming next, a wet area, the trail rides on puncheons (narrow footbridges). A stop along here and a close examination on bended knee can reveal a variety of mosses and tiny wildflowers forming the ground cover. There may well be scat near the trail, too: bear or coyote or, more likely here, porcupine. For you are soon to arrive at Porcupine Lookout, 4.4 mi., 2815 ft. up on an unnamed ridge, where you will notice the much-increased perspective that an additional 500 ft. of elevation affords. A vast green panorama spreads out to the east and south. The equally vast silence of Green Mt. National Forest surrounds you — that is, if you arrive on a windless day and in the midafternoon, when the birds tend to be quiet. Whether the porkies cut the trees to make this lookout we don't know, but thank them anyway. Look around for quills. If you do see a

Dale Gelfand

Mountain laurel

porcupine (they scamper up into trees for protection, their black and gray fur camouflaging well against the bark), admire it from afar, and by all means keep dogs away. An encounter can be painful. A roundtrip to Porcupine Lookout is a worthwhile day hike (8.8 mi. total), with a climb of 1455 ft. to its excellent views.

A mile later, after a modest climb, the AT/LT passes the forested top of Little Pond Mt., 3100 ft., then drops down a few feet to Little Pond Lookout (5.8 mi.) for a repeat of the previous views, only better. The dense green of the mixed deciduous forest spreading away in all directions tells you why this state is called *vert mont*. The pond appears about 0.5 mi. below, generally east.

There's now an up and a down over a nameless peak, with some noticeable climbing on either side of

New England's Largest Mammal

Ungainly as moose may appear to be, they can run at 35 mph; they are, after all, the largest deer in the world. The most likely areas to see moose are moist if not flooded. You may spot their hoofprints (cloven, 7 inches long, spaced 2 to 5 feet apart) in a muddy footpath. Moose thrive on aquatic plants, and their long legs and necks allow them to wade into deep ponds or the muck of a bog to forage. If you encounter a moose, give it a wide berth or sufficient time to wander off on its own. Weighing up to 1400 pounds and growing to 7 feet in height, the fully mature moose is a behemoth. A moose can crush a car, so think what it can do to you. Like most wild animals, however, the moose is not aggressive unless threatened, and it is a thrill to see one in the forest. The thrill is only slightly diminished when an errant moose saunters through your New England backyard, munching on tulips and daisies. Moose have been spotted as far south as southern Berkshire County, Massachusetts.

it during the next 1.8 mi. before you reach a third viewpoint, Glastenbury Lookout, at 7.6 mi. This small clearing is a bit inhospitable, offering few comfortable rocks as resting seats. From here you will see the tower on the mountain. To reach Goddard Shelter, about 200 vertical ft. below the Glastenbury summit, more muscle and stamina are required. Press on for the next 2.5 mi. and 640 ft. of climbing. It's worth it, though you may wonder in the final stretch, which is steeply uphill over stone steps set into the trail. Just before the shelter a piped spring offers refreshment.

Goddard Shelter, at 10.1 mi. and 3560 ft., is arguably the best camper's lodging on the AT in southern New England, recommended as the midpoint on a 2-day backpack in this section. Although there are no bunks in this log-style lean-to, there are two floor levels, one for sleeping (twelve people), one as porch (dining room, etc.). GMC's *Long Trail Guide* notes that the Air National Guard airlifted materials to the site (1985), a story repeated at shelters elsewhere up and down the AT. The shelter's name pays homage to Ted Goddard, a past president of GMC. The views to the south—of the Taconic Range on the New York border of Vermont and Massachusetts, and of Mt. Greylock in Massachusetts (its white signal light flashes all night)—are inspiring and wide open. Sunset-lovers and star-gazers will think they're in the heavens up here. A Philips' "Planisphere," a 5-in.-diameter plastic disk that shows the principal stars visible for every hour in the year at 42 degrees north latitude, is inexpensive, almost weightless, and fun to bring on an overnight hike.

There's a price to be paid, however, for the open exposure of Goddard Shelter. A cold wind from the southwest or west will make this shelter uncomfortable. Goddard is a good place to practice your weather forecasting skills (by reading cloud formations to windward). Rain is associated with cumulonimbus, cirrostratus, altocumulous, and stratocumulus clouds; fair weather with cirrus and cumulus clouds. To learn these cloud types, find a weather book in the library, photocopy the relevant pictures, and bring them along on your hike. Sailor's wisdom applies here too: red sky in the morning, hikers take warning (rain's a-comin' within a day); red sky at night, hikers' delight.

There are a couple of tent sites east of the shelter near the fire ring (beware of sparks). The privy is downhill, south of the shelter, off the old AT/LT.

West Ridge Trail (blue blazed) goes west from Goddard Shelter, following a ridge of Glastenbury Mt. 7.8 mi. to Bald Mt. Trail, which can then be used to walk east 1.8 mi. to a road in Woodford Hollow (limited parking) leading another 0.8 mi. to VT 9 (no official parking) at a point about 1.0 mi. west of the AT/LT crossing where Hike #20 begins, making a 20.5-mi. loop. A walk back up heavily traveled VT 9 to the AT/LT is not advised for children or pets. Warning: carry water from Goddard spring; there is none on the bottom part of West Ridge Trail.

From Goddard Shelter the AT/LT climbs another 188 ft. to the wooded top of Glastenbury Mt. (10.4 mi.). In good weather, try the observation platform on the tower, maintained by the U.S. Forest Service. The scope of the surrounding Green Mt. National Forest is awesome—in every direction. Among the AT/LT destinations visible here is Stratton Mt. to the north (see Hike #21). Somerset Reservoir sparkles, due east.

It's an easy cruise now, gently down along a ridge (with beautiful boggy areas where scat along the trail may hint at coyote, bear, or even moose, but deer most likely) to Big Rock (13.7 mi.). Another 0.5 mi., falling off sharply now, and the spur trail (right/east) to Kid Gore Shelter appears. Kid Gore is on a loop trail: from the southern end (at 14.2 mi.) it's 0.1 mi. to the shelter, but from the northern end, it's only 60 yd. Take your choice. Practically next door on the AT/LT, at 14.4 mi., is Caughnawaga Shelter. Most campers will prefer Kid Gore, of more recent vintage (1971 vs. 1931), although water at the stream in front of Caughnawaga is more dependable than at the spring a few yards north of Kid Gore. Caughnawaga is small and cramped, offering minimal protection from a driving rain.

Over the next 3.7 mi., brief ups and downs amount to a few hundred feet of gain and loss, with brook crossings for refreshing splashes on sweaty brows. There is some effort required here, but the loveliness of the deep wilderness is distraction while you work. Keep an eye out. We saw a bull moose in this section, though only briefly after he saw us and then bolted, crashing pell-mell through the undergrowth, fortunately away from us.

At 18.1 mi. South Alder Brook appears, in two streams. The beaver ponds that follow make a good lunch spot. The pond on the left (west) side of the AT/LT had a wonderful dam and lodge in 1997, though in beaver territory, nothing is permanent despite the fine engineering. A midday visit is the least likely time to see beavers, who prefer early morning or late evening for work and food gathering, but you might get lucky. Binoculars are helpful, as is patience.

Story Spring Shelter, at 19.0 mi., follows a generally level section. Nondescript, the lean-to has room for eight sleepers but no porch as at Goddard. But there is a picnic table, plus a privy, fire ring, and flat tent sites. About 150 ft. farther north on the AT/LT is a spring.

The final climb of Hike #20 ensues, a challenging though brief reminder that these are indeed real mountains. Then it's down toward civilization again, a descent of about 500 ft., gradually, to USFS Rd. #71 (20.6 mi.) —which is not an appropriate place to call it quits. There's no official parking and practically no traffic, though it is a well-maintained dirt road, occasionally patrolled.

The evidence of extensive logging is everywhere here. Trees are clearly second- or third-growth. A lacework

Continued on p. 186

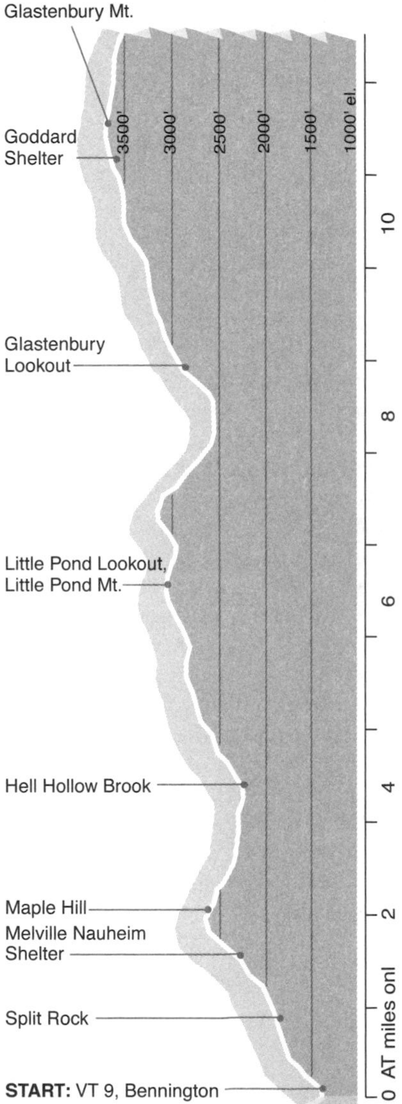

Glastenbury Mt.
Goddard Shelter
Glastenbury Lookout
Little Pond Lookout, Little Pond Mt.
Hell Hollow Brook
Maple Hill
Melville Nauheim Shelter
Split Rock
START: VT 9, Bennington
3500' 3000' 2500' 2000' 1500' 1000' el.
0 AT miles only 2 4 6 8 10

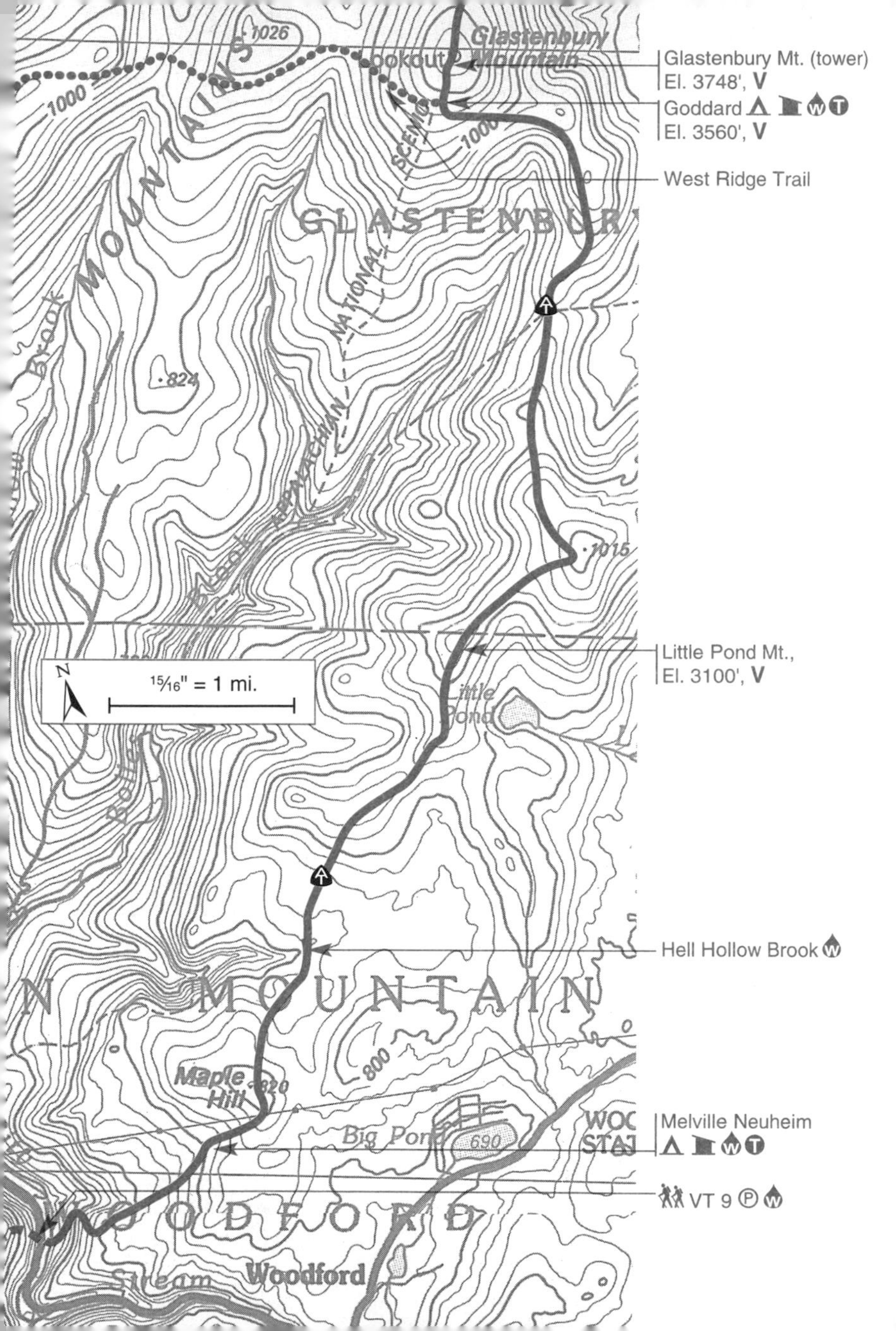
Glastenbury Mountain
Lookout
1026
1000
MOUNTAINS
SCENIC
GLASTENBURY
NATIONAL
APPALACHIAN
Brook
824
1015
Little Pond
Bolles
N
15/16" = 1 mi.
N MOUNTAIN
800
Maple Hill
820
Big Pond
690
WOODFORD
Woodford
Stream
Glastenbury Mt. (tower)
El. 3748', V
Goddard
El. 3560', V
West Ridge Trail
Little Pond Mt.,
El. 3100', V
Hell Hollow Brook
Melville Neuheim
VT 9

of woods roads intersects the trail. There are more beaver ponds during the easy descent to Black Brook bridge (21.7 mi.), then a handsome view of Little Stratton Mt. (we climb the higher Stratton Mt. on Hike #21). Soon the east branch of the Deerfield River appears on the right (east); the trail crosses the river on a road bridge and reaches the trailhead parking, at 22.6 mi., on the Arlington–West Wardsboro Rd. (Kelly Stand Rd.)

HISTORICAL NOTE: A short distance to the east from the parking lot, you'll see the Daniel Webster Monument, marking the spot where in 1840 the great orator spoke to a crowd of 1600 at a Whig Party rally. Thank goodness it's quieter in the woods these days. On your way back west to Arlington, 4.9 mi. from the AT/LT crossing, the road passes the site of Kelly Stand, a stagecoach stop when the wilderness must have been even more magnificent than it is today.

ABOUT BENNINGTON: Bennington, pop. 14,400, has much to offer. It's a good town for provisions and hiking equipment, with a couple of large supermarkets and sporting goods stores. For books and maps, visit Bennington Bookshop, 467 Main St. There are restaurants galore, including low-end pizza and burgers. More interesting are The Brasserie at Bennington Potters Yard, 324 County St.; Madison Brewing Co., Main St.; and Blue Benn Diner, US 7 north of town (the latter is a classic, often full to capacity). Supplied and fortified, you

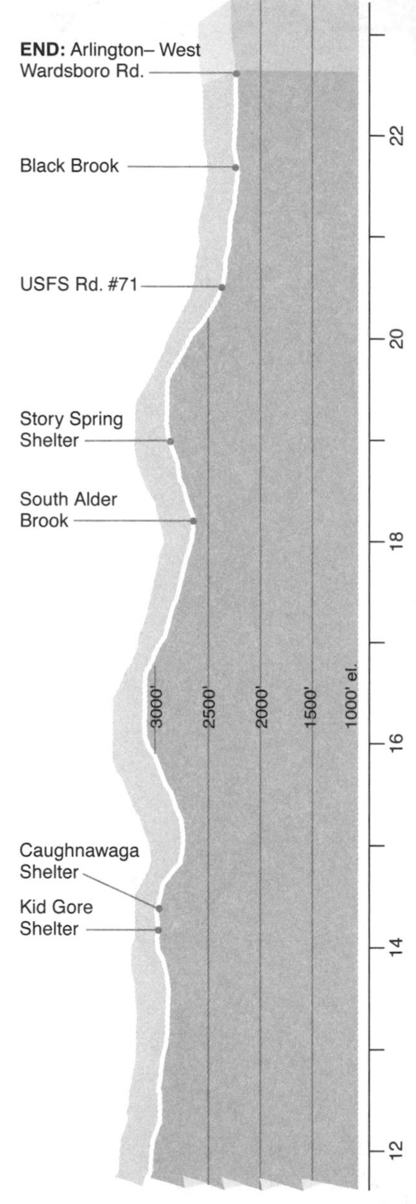

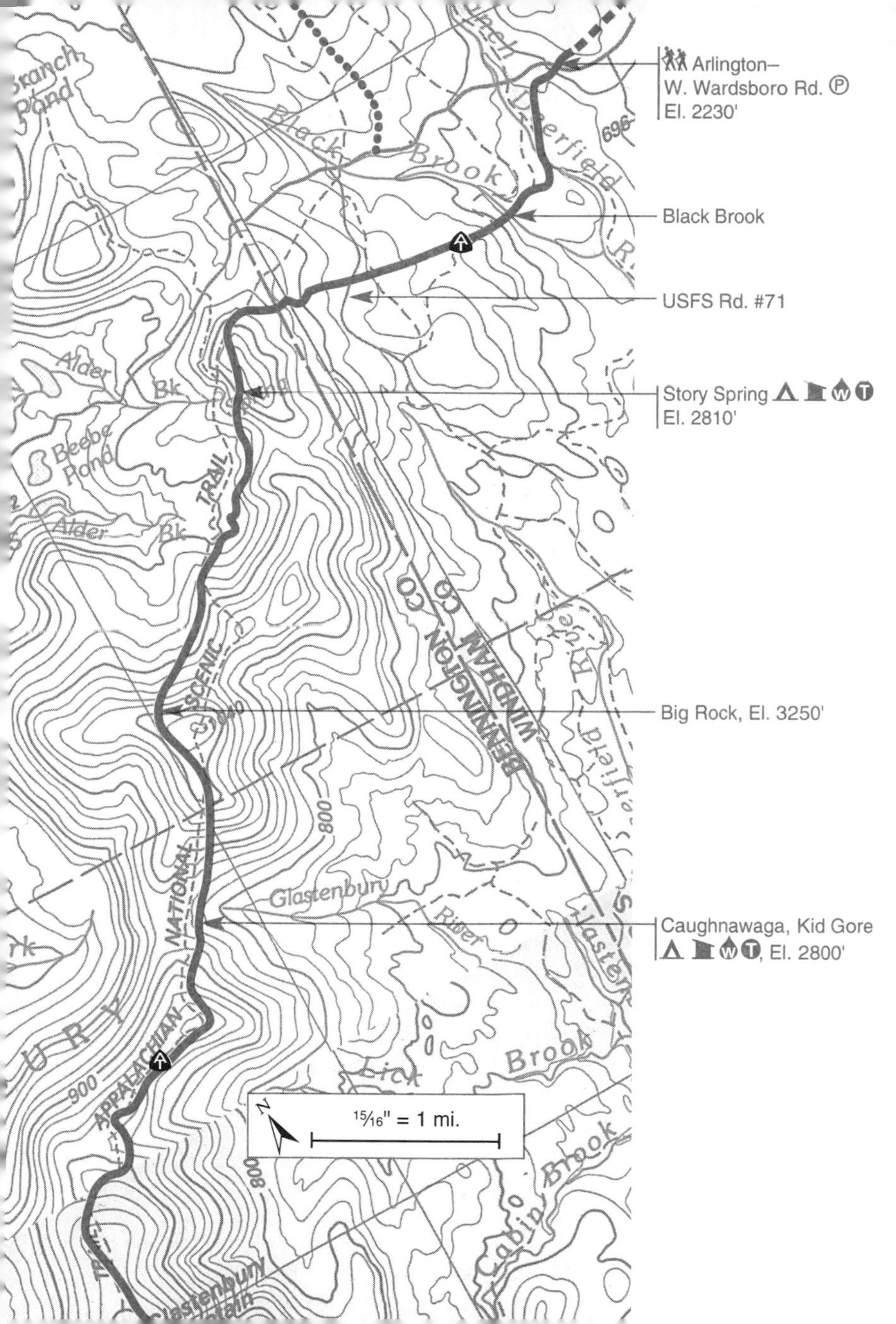

Arlington–
W. Wardsboro Rd. Ⓟ
El. 2230'
Black Brook
USFS Rd. #71
Story Spring
El. 2810'
Big Rock, El. 3250'
Caughnawaga, Kid Gore
, El. 2800'
15/16" = 1 mi.
N
APPALACHIAN NATIONAL SCENIC TRAIL
BENNINGTON CO
WINDHAM CO
Black Brook
Deerfield
Alder Bk
Beebe Pond
Glastenbury River
Brook
Cabin Brook
Branch Pond
800
900
696

can tackle the town's museums: the Bennington Museum, on West Main St., features American furniture and crafts, with a special collection of Grandma Moses' paintings; Hemmings Motor News, an antique filling station and vintage vehicles, 216 West Main St.; Park-McCullough House, a thirty-five-room Victorian mansion with period furniture and clothing, off VT 67A in North Bennington. Revolutionary War buffs will want to visit the Bennington Battle Monument, a 306-ft. stone obelisk with an elevator to an observation point up top, plus a diorama showing the battle (in the summer of 1777, Gen. John Stark and Vermont's famous militia, the Green Mt. Boys, defeated the Hessians who were support troops for General Burgoyne; it was a turning point in the war); it's off West Main St. in Old Bennington. Bennington College, the Old Castle Theater Co., and the cineplex offer entertainment; check the local papers.

In Arlington, pop. 2300, canoeists find nirvana on the Battenkill River; rentals and guided trips are available at BattenKill Canoe, Ltd., US 7A.

For newcomers to New England, a ride through some covered bridges is fun: there are three off VT 67A in North Bennington. Ask the locals for details.

HIKE #20 Itinerary

Miles N	NORTH	Elev. (ft./m)	Miles S
22.6	**End: Arlington–West Wardsboro Rd.,** overnight parking.	2230/680	0.0
21.7	**Black Brook bridge;** followed by woods road to ridge with views of Stratton Mt.	2220/677	0.9
20.6	**USFS Rd. #71,** no parking.	2380/726	2.0
19.0	**Story Spring Shelter;** water from spring 150 ft. N on AT/LT.	2810/857	3.6
18.1	**South Alder Brook,** two crossings.	2600/793	4.5
14.4	**Caughnawaga Shelter;** water from reliable stream.	2800/854	8.2
14.2	Spur trail E to **Kid Gore Shelter,** 0.1 mi.; unreliable spring 10 yd. N of shelter.	2800/854	8.4
13.7	**Big Rock,** after long, gentle ridge; turn L (N).	3250/991	8.9
10.4	**Glastenbury Mt.,** fire tower with observation deck, views.	3748/1143	12.2
10.1	**Goddard Shelter,** piped spring 40 ft. E, view, tent sites, privy; **West Ridge Trail** (to Bald Mt. Trail) goes SW; ascend N beyond shelter.	3560/1085	12.5
7.6	**Glastenbury Lookout,** view.	2920/890	15.0
5.8	Summit of Little Pond Mt. (3100 ft.); then **Little Pond Lookout,** views.	3060/933	16.8
4.4	**Porcupine Lookout,** on ridge, views, primitive camping.	2815/858	18.2
3.2	**Hell Hollow Brook,** bridge; last water until Goddard Shelter.	2350/716	19.4
2.1	**Maple Hill,** power line, views.	2630/802	20.5
1.6	**Melville Nauheim Shelter,** 250 ft. E on spur; heading N, AT/LT crosses Black Brook.	2300/701	21.0
0.7	After following stream and then a sharp uphill section, reach **Split Rock,** fissured boulder.	1900/579	21.9
0.0	**Start: VT 9,** 5.0 mi. E of Bennington; head N over **City Stream** on **MacArthur Bridge.**	1360/415	22.6
	SOUTH		

HIKE: #21

Stratton Mt. and Stratton Pond

Maps: ATC N.H. & Vt. #7; GMC #4 & #5

Route: Arlington–West Wardsboro Rd., to Stratton Mt. and Stratton Pond, to VT 11 / 30 between Manchester Center and Peru

Recommended direction: S to N (described here) or N to S

Distance: 17.5 mi.

Elevation +/-: 2230 to 3936 to 1800 ft.

Effort: Strenuous

Day hike: Several shorter loop options

Overnight backpacking hike: Yes

Duration: 10 hr.

Early exit option: None

Natural history features: Stratton Mt., Stratton Pond

Social history features: Daniel Webster Monument; Benton MacKaye on Stratton Mt.

Other features: Manchester Center shopping

Trailhead access: *Start:* Arlington–West Wardsboro Rd. (Kelly Stand Rd.), overnight parking. Eastern approach: From VT 100, West Wardsboro, go W on Arlington–West Wardsboro Rd. to Stratton village, then another 3.4 mi. to AT/LT crossing (6.8 mi. total). Western approach: In Arlington, use exit #3 off US 7; go W 0.1 mi. on VT 313; turn R into South Rd.; go 0.6 mi. to end at Old Mill Rd.; turn R, go 0.7 mi. to fork just after bridge; follow right-hand fork (Kelly Stand Rd.) 10.5 mi. to AT/LT parking on N side of road, just after bridge over east branch of Deerfield River. *End:* VT 11/30 (Manchester–Peru Hwy.), parking (overnight) N side of road. Eastern approach: In township of Peru, S of Bromley Mt. ski area, go 0.5 mi. W from junction of VT 11 & 30 S. Western approach: In Manchester Center, go E for 5.8 mi. from US 7A.

Camping: Stratton Pond tenting; Bigelow and Vondell shelters; Douglas Shelter; Spruce Peak Shelter

---

The AT/LT section between Arlington and Manchester offers a host of possibilities for both day hikers and backpackers, with two gems in the middle: Stratton Mt. and Stratton Pond. It's a good trip in either direction; this narrative goes from south to north.

First, an historical note: A short distance east of the AT/LT parking lot on Arlington–West Wardsboro Rd. (at this point also called Kelly Stand Rd.) is the Daniel Webster Monument, marking the spot where in 1840 the great orator (at this point U.S. Senator from New Hampshire) spoke to a crowd of 1600 at a Whig (conservative) Party rally. The issues: business (protective tariffs) and ethics (slavery).

Day Hikes

From the southern end (Arlington–

West Wardsboro Rd.), the trail climbs 1706 ft. over 3.8 mi. to Stratton Mt., where a fire tower offers superb views. A return by the same route makes a 7.6-mi. hike, and this is a popular option. Continuing north from Stratton Mt., the AT/LT goes 3.2 mi. to Stratton Pond, a lovely, isolated haven where swimming is feasible. The Stratton Pond Trail, in the lowlands (thus more level), runs 3.7 mi. back to Arlington–West Wardsboro Rd. at a point 0.9 mi. west of the AT/LT parking lot. With a car at each trailhead, this makes a day hike of 10.7 mi. (with one car, 11.6 mi. back to AT/LT parking). Allow plenty of time for lingering at both the summit and the pond.

From the northern end, VT 11/30, a hike with an easy climb of 350 ft. over 4.9 mi. brings you to Prospect Rock, with pleasant views to the west; the return trip on the AT/LT makes it a 9.8-mi. hike. With two cars an alternative return route from Prospect Rock would be Rootville Rd. (now an old woods road), 1.8 mi. to a public road, and then 0.2 mi. to VT 11/30. You will come out on VT 11/30 1.8 mi. east of Manchester and 4.0 mi. west of the AT/LT trailhead.

Backpacking

Now the full trip, south to north, up the mountain, for those with camping in mind. The first mile is generally level, passing through stands of white birch. On this often moist trail, keep an eye out underfoot for the red eft, a reddish salamander who is friendly enough to be held in the hand for a moment. After crossing the dirt road (International Paper Co.) at 1.4 mi., the climb begins. Switchbacks work their winding way up the mountain, with two or more vistas (look back occasionally so as not to miss them) during the next mile or so. The trail first reaches Little Stratton, then the col between it and Stratton Mt., where you still have some work to do. From the vistas, you'll be looking southeast toward Somerset Reservoir and, from higher up, south to Mt. Greylock in Massachusetts.

David Emblidge

Stratton Mt. fire tower, Green Mt. National Forest

At 3.1 mi. the former AT/LT enters on the right; the current trail bears left. A piped spring follows almost immediately (3.2 mi.). In the damp places clintonia (in the lily family), with yellow-green bells (and later in the cycle, bitter blue-black berries), decorates the trailside.

Arrival at the top of Stratton Mt. may come somewhat surprisingly. This ascent is neither terribly long nor difficult. Yet Stratton Mt., at 3936 ft. (southern peak), is one of the highest on the AT in Vermont. The forested top is equipped with a well-maintained fire tower (it's a big one: six tiers of steps), from whose observation deck there is a superb panorama. Look east to New Hampshire's White Mts. Look northwest to New York's Adirondacks. Southwest you'll see the Taconic Range along the New York border with Vermont and Massachusetts, and Mt. Equinox in the Vermont foreground. To the south Mt. Pisgah, the southern Green Mts, and Mt. Greylock. And to the north and northeast, more Green Mts., including, on a clear day, Camel's Hump and Mt. Mansfield. In spring and fall, the White Mts. and Mt. Mansfield may be snow-capped. Be sure to take a map up the tower with you, and binoculars or a telephoto lens. But hold on to your hat, map, and any kids: it's breezy up there.

Green Mt. Club history buffs proudly report that one of their founders, James P. Taylor, was hiking here when the idea of the Long Trail was hatched (1910), and that Benton MacKaye, godfather of the Appalachian Trail, had his vision of the world's longest footpath when he climbed Stratton (1917). Perhaps you will have a vision too (more likely, no doubt, on a weekday when visitors are few), but probably you will share the mountaintop experience with a small crowd of enthusiasts. During the summer and early fall, GMC caretakers are present to assist hikers with directions and advice. Their white cabin appears, right, as you emerge from the woods at the summit. The caretakers love to tell stories about the mountain, including the one about MacKaye's dream, while camping here, that giants had stepped from peak to peak in the Green Mts. MacKaye himself was to become a giant in the trail-building community of his day.

Water is generally available from brooks or springs 10 min. south and north of the summit, but treat it even up here.

From the fire tower a 0.7-mi./ 20-min. walk on a wide woods road, running north, leads to the north peak and the ski area gondola, which operates for hikers in the summer and fall foliage season ($10 in 1997). The gondola can be used up, down, or round-trip, facilitating visits to the top by people who choose not to make the climb. Day hikers in the area, coming up on the gondola from Stratton ski area, could then visit isolated Stratton Pond, climb back up the north side of the mountain, and ride down. The gondola closes at 4:00 p.m., however, and bad weather or special activities at its base (concerts, etc.) can close it all day. Call 800-STRATTN to check.

The descent (turn left past the fire

Thru-Hiking Lab Report

Hiking in the spring is glorious, but there is a substantial risk that you will catch whatever seasonal virus it is that drives people to think they should hike all the way from Georgia to Maine. This insidious disease has a long incubation—so long that you may think you have escaped. However, here are some symptoms that may precede the onset:

- The victims (you or a loved one) start collecting maps and guidebooks.
- They ask everyone they meet about tents, Gore-Tex, and water filters.
- They start introducing themselves by a funny new name.
- They insist on knowing the weight, to the nearest gram, of everything they buy.
- They don't like their 100% cotton underwear and socks anymore.
- They develop an obsessive interest in weather, day length, elevation gains and losses, and how far they can hike in a day.

The most severe form of this syndrome was first described in 1936, but it was rare until the 1960s. Supreme Court Justice William O. Douglas succumbed in 1958. By 1982 there were 1000 cases on record; that number doubled in only 7 years. In the 1990s it became a major epidemic, with thousands coming down with it each year. The virus respects neither age, sex, physical handicap, nor nationality. An 86-year-old got it in 1975, and a 6-year-old got it just 5 years later. Some people get it several times, and many victims write books about their struggle. Several dogs and at least one cat have also fallen prey to it.

More men than women suffer from the disease, but, as with many other conditions, the women are catching up. The causative agent has not been identified; there is some evidence of a tiny parasite that burrows through brain tissue, causing major behavioral changes but minor permanent damage. No remedy has been found; victims harbor the ailment for the rest of their lives and seem to be highly infectious. However, many victims can lead lives that are surprisingly close to normal if they can acknowledge their affliction and get the hiking done, either all at once or in sections. Many self-help books are available, and support groups exist in some communities.

—Doris Gove

tower) is generally easy switchbacks and a long section of rolling woodland (hardwood forest except at the top, where firs predominate), arriving eventually at Stratton Pond Trail (left, at 6.9 mi.). This popular trail runs 3.9 mi. south to Arlington–West Wardsboro Rd. and parking (see "Day Hikes," above).

At 7.0 mi. the AT/LT reaches Stratton Pond, at Willis Ross Clearing, where in summer a caretaker's tent is on your left, pondside. If the caretaker is home, inquire about space in the shelters or tenting areas, and pay your fee for lodging here. Stratton Pond was carved out of bedrock by the glaciers and is nowadays surrounded largely by a spruce forest. The Lye Brook Trail goes left around the pond, leading to Bigelow Shelter (0.1 mi.), then Vondell Shelter (0.2 mi.), both with views over the water. From the AT/LT, Lye Brook Trail runs 9.7 mi. west to Manchester and is used not only for short day hikes from town but also as a link to provisioners in town by thru-hikers who want to avoid the highways. The two shelters at Stratton Pond are highly popular sites and may be full by late afternoon in summer or early fall. Bring a tent and consider the camping option on the north shore, where 0.5 mi. ahead (on AT/LT, then North Shore Trail), numerous sites are cleared in the mixed deciduous woods (though not with much privacy). Some have tent platforms. There is a privy. And the swimming or stargazing, a little farther west along the trail at a grassy opening, is fine. Just beyond the grassy area is a spring. (Stratton View Shelter, shown on recent ATC and GMC maps, has burned down.)

Stratton Pond, the largest body of water on the AT in southern New England, is blessedly clear, clean, and warm (by July, anyway). From the west end, the views of Stratton Mt. are beautiful. But the pond is also the most heavily trafficked place

Continued on p. 196

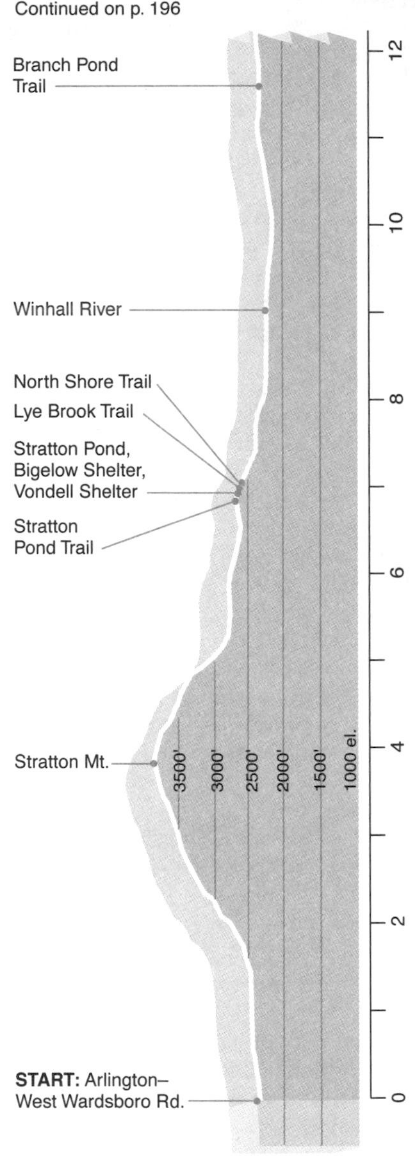

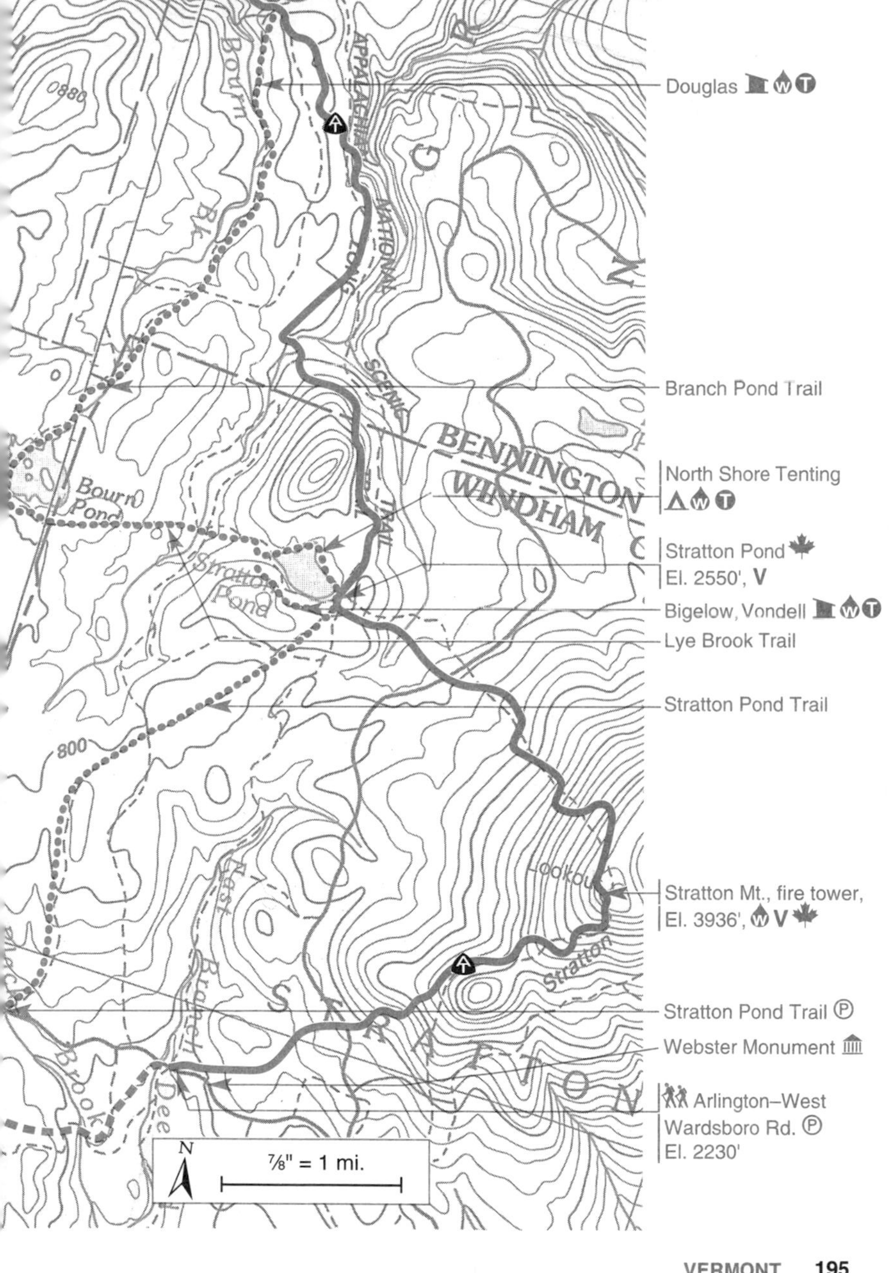
Douglas
Branch Pond Trail
North Shore Tenting
Stratton Pond
El. 2550', V
Bigelow, Vondell
Lye Brook Trail
Stratton Pond Trail
Stratton Mt., fire tower,
El. 3936', V
Stratton Pond Trail Ⓟ
Webster Monument
Arlington–West
Wardsboro Rd. Ⓟ
El. 2230'
BENNINGTON
WINDHAM
APPALACHIAN NATIONAL SCENIC TRAIL
Bourn Pond
Stratton Pond
Bourn Bk
Stratton
Lookout
East Branch
Deer
Brook
800
N
⅞" = 1 mi.

on the AT/LT in Vermont. If you can schedule your visit off-peak (weekdays), you will enjoy it more. The shoreline in particular, due to foot traffic, demands careful respect: Stay on the trail. Use minimal firewood, if any. Bring a stove. And clean up. This is a place really worth preserving in its still-pristine state.

There is plenty of wildlife to observe. At dusk and sometimes after dark, barred owls call across long distances with their easily mimicked "Who cooks for you?" Ducks and geese frequent the pond. In the shallows herons are common. At dusk the rippling laughter of the loon makes a haunting sound. Along the shore, wildflowers, visited by songbirds, bees, and butterflies, create a handsome display. En route to the tenting area, the North Shore Trail crosses a wetland on bog bridges, a good place for a patient look at the birds. Fishing, with a Vermont license, is permitted. If you're really ambitious, bring a small inflatable kayak and be queen or king of the pond, enjoying a perspective few visitors ever see.

Deep in the woods as you are here, it makes sense to expect hungry nocturnal visitors. Be sure to hang your food bag and garbage bag over tree branches, well out of reach of bears, porcupines, and other climbers or crawlers.

The Lye Brook Trail continues west from Stratton Pond 2.2 mi. to Bourn Pond, with overnight options at South Bourn Pond Shelter and North Bourn Pond Tenting Area. From

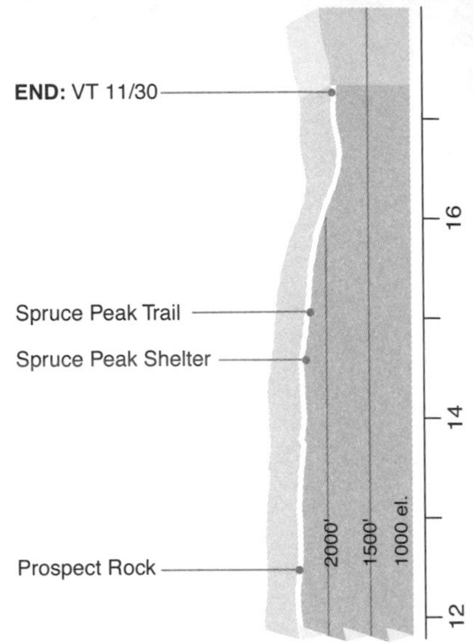

there, heading north, the Branch Pond Trail reaches Douglas Shelter in 6.0 mi. and finally rejoins the AT/LT in 6.5 mi. It's then 4.6 mi. back to Stratton Pond, heading south on the AT/LT. For hikers camping at Stratton Pond, this loop and the climb up (and back down) Stratton Mt. make excellent day hikes, requiring no cars and keeping you in the wilderness all the way.

From Stratton Pond, the AT/LT is mostly level as it heads north, descending gently toward the Winhall River footbridge at 8.9 mi., a good rest stop. The area is former farmland. Shortly after crossing the river, the trail enters Lye Brook Wilderness (federal, in the national forest). A wet section ensues, with puncheons over sphag-

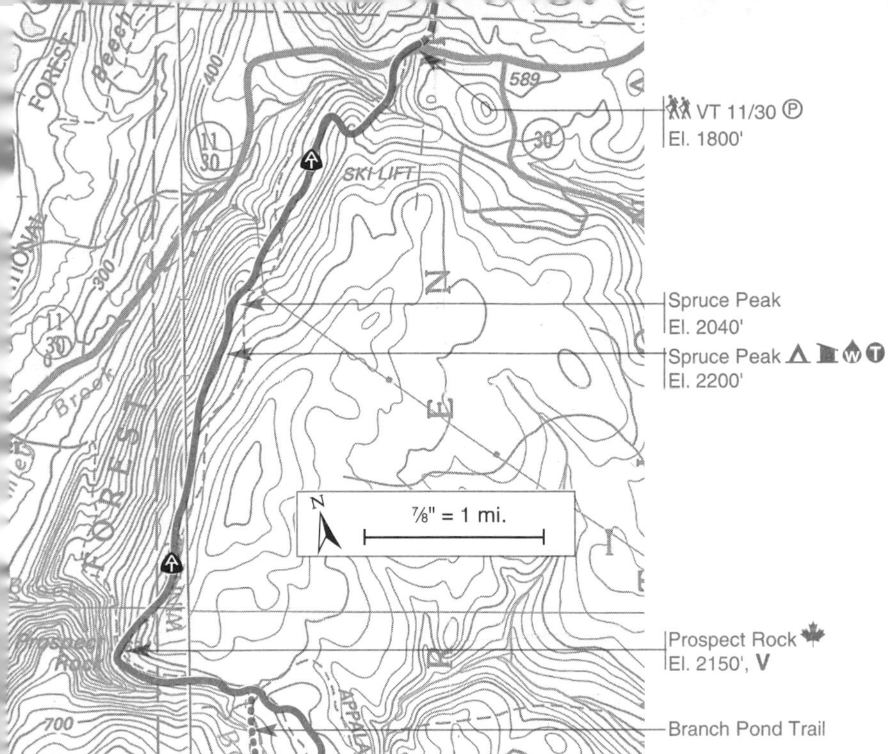

m moss and skunk cabbage tches, as the trail meanders briefly stward, reaching Branch Pond Trail 1.7 mi. (south to Bourn Pond). The uglas Shelter is a mere 0.5 mi. wn this trail, with bunk space for and a spring nearby.

n another fairly level mile, mostly unpaved Rootville Rd., the short e trail down to Prospect Rock pears (12.6 mi.). "The Rock" is an official geological marker of the artzite western boundary of the een Mts. Rootville Rd. continues rth 2.0 mi. to VT 11/30. Hikers walking northward to Prospect Rock will be aware of elevation lost since leaving Stratton Mt. and therefore may be surprised at the fine views from the Rock (2150 ft.). (Hikers walking southward from VT 11/30 get a big reward for a modest effort.) To the southwest is Manchester and beyond it Mt. Equinox, with its small summit house. Far below Prospect Rock is Downer Glen. Civilization (and its road noise) is now not far away. This overlook is a popular destination, requiring everyone's help to keep it clean.

Following a ridge line, mostly level, the AT/LT carries on to a spur trail (left, at 14.7 mi.) for Spruce Peak Shelter, a bigger-than-average bunkhouse (enclosed, sixteen spaces), with a fancy outhouse using the latest composting techniques. Water is from a spring just beyond the shelter.

Spruce Peak is still to come, incongruously at a lower elevation (2040 ft.) than the shelter. The peak, at 15.1 mi., is reached by a little spur on the left, providing another satisfying valley view to the west. It's a gradual, modest descent now most of the way to the end of Hike #21, passing a brook, a power-line clearing, and a woods road. After a short ascent to a ridge with brief outlooks (west), then crossing another brook, old Rte. 30, and one last brook, the trail arrives, at 17.5 mi., at the Manchester–Peru Hwy., known as VT 11/30. Here, at 1800 ft., you are 2100 ft. below the top of Stratton Mt. and a world away from the sylvan silence of Stratton Pond.

Manchester and Stratton Villages

Manchester and Manchester Center, down to the west in the US 7 valley, have elegant 18th- and 19th-century homes, the towns' inheritance from earlier prosperous times. Business is still booming. Known as a shopper's paradise, Manchester today is a mall without a mall, where countless designer factory outlets offer everything from shoes to dishware. With the stores, many of which are indeed handsome and well stocked, come traffic, high prices at local lodgings and restaurants, and an air of unreality in a country town. Still, hikers should not shy away. The Northshire Bookstore is always worth a browse. History and gardening buffs will enjoy visiting Hildene, home of Robert Todd Lincoln, son of the president, with gardens by an apprentice of Frederick Law Olmstead. The Vermont State Craft Center on US 7A, facing the historic Equinox Hotel, is worth a look for its stunning colonnaded architecture alone. Zion Episcopal Church Hostel, on Main St. in Manchester, accommodates long-distance hikers from June 1 through Labor Day. There are good sporting goods stores, a bagelry, better-than-average pizza, and an old-fashioned breakfast joint upstairs in an old house on Main St., where a stack of blues will fuel you up for a day's hiking.

Stratton, east of the AT/LT, is a double village: the older one sweet and quiet, and the newer one built at the base of the ski lifts. It's the latter village (vaguely Tyrolean, or is it Disney?), with upscale boutiques, entertainment, and lodgings, that claims the most attention. As a vacation resort—if you like to be with lots of other people amidst a plethora of activities (golf, tennis, horseback riding, swimming, the Vermont Symphony)—Stratton is hard to beat.

HIKE #21 Itinerary

Miles N	NORTH	Elev. (ft./m)	Miles S
17.5	**End: VT 11/30,** Manchester, overnight parking.	1800/549	0.0
15.1	**Spruce Peak,** via short spur, L.	2200/622	2.4
14.7	**Spruce Peak Shelter** via spur, L, 0.1 mi., spring, privy.	2040/671	2.8
12.6	**Prospect Rock,** L, via short spur; Rootville Rd. continues N 2.0 mi. to VT 11/30.	2150/655	4.9
11.7	**Branch Pond Trail,** L, **Douglas Shelter,** 0.5 mi.	2280/695	5.8
8.9	**Winhall River,** footbridge; soon enter Lye Brook Wilderness.	2175/663	8.6
7.1	**North Shore Trail,** L, 0.5 mi. to **North Shore Tenting Area,** privy; continues to **Lye Brook Trail** at 0.7 mi. for pond loop.	2555/779	10.4
7.0	**Stratton Pond,** GMC summer caretaker, spring. AT/LT turns R at shore. **Lye Brook Trail** (S shore, L) to **Bigelow Shelter** (0.1 mi.), **Vondell Shelter** (0.2 mi.).	2555/779	10.5
6.9	**Stratton Pond Trail,** L, 3.9 mi. to Arlington–West Wardsboro Rd.	2620/799	10.6
5.8	Dirt road.		13.7
3.8	**Stratton Mt.,** S peak: fire tower, views, GMC seasonal caretaker; no camping; spur trail (0.7 mi.) N on unblazed woods road to Stratton Mt. N peak and ski area gondola. AT/LT goes L just beyond tower, descending.	3936/1200	
3.1	Former AT/LT enters on R; current AT/LT bears L and soon passes spring.		14.4
1.4	Dirt road.		16.0
0.0	**Start: Arlington–West Wardsboro Rd.,** overnight parking.	2230/680	17.5
	SOUTH		

HIKE: #22

Bromley Mt.

Maps: ATC N. H. & Vt. #7; GMC LT #6 & #7

Route: From VT 11 / 30 in Manchester, to Bromley Mt., Mad Tom Notch, and Peru Peak, to Griffith Lake, to Danby-Landgrove Rd. (USFS Rd. #10), Danby

Recommended direction: S to N

Distance: 17.3 mi.

Elevation +/-: 1800 to 3429 to 1530 ft.

Effort: Strenuous

Day hike: Several shorter loop options

Overnight backpacking hike: Yes

Duration: 10 hr.

Early exit option: USFS Rd. #21 at Mad Tom Notch, 5.2 mi.; Lake Trail (3.3 mi. to road), 10.6 mi.; Baker Peak Trail (2.9 mi. to road), 12.5 mi.

Natural history features: Bromley Mt., Griffith Lake

Trailhead access: *Start:* VT 11/30 (Manchester–Peru Hwy.), parking (overnight), N side of road. Eastern approach: In township of Peru, S of Bromley Mt. ski area, go 0.5 mi. W from junction of VT 11 & 30S. Western approach: In Manchester Center, go E 5.8 mi. from US 7A. *End:* USFS Rd. #10 (closed in winter), overnight parking. Western approach (easier): From US 7, Danby, follow USFS Rd. #10 (also called Mt. Tabor Rd.) E, continuing 3.4 mi. to USFS AT/LT parking. Eastern approach (more difficult): From Londonderry, take VT 11/30 W briefly to Reilly Rd. and turn R, continuing to North Landgrove; follow Weston Rd. to Little Michigan Rd. (also called USFS Rd. #10) and turn L; go about 10.5 mi. to AT/LT parking. (*Note:* GMC warns hikers about vandalism at this trailhead. Leave no valuables in your car. Inquire about overnight parking at USFS Mt. Tabor Work Center in Danby; call Green Mt. National Forest ranger at 802-362-2307.)

Camping: Peru Peak Shelter; Griffith Lake Campsite; Lost Pond Shelter; Big Branch Shelter

---

Hike #22 leaves the highway about 6 mi. east of bustling Manchester. Amidst the plethora of designer outlets in the village, there are numerous services and distractions for hikers, not the least of which is a U.S. Forest Service information center where Green Mt. National Forest maps and advice can be obtained. If you need hiking gear, The Mountain Goat and CB Sports are two stores worth a visit. Hikers with an interest in botany may enjoy a pre-hike stroll on the Boswell Botany Trail at the Southern Vermont Art Center in Manchester Center (802-362-1405). More than thirty types of ferns and eighty types of wildflowers grace the pathways here, far more than one is likely to see along the AT. The plants commonly seen on the trail are here too, labeled for your edification—trillium, clintonia, trout lily, hepatica, lady's-slipper, and the many ferns. A 250-year-old sugar maple makes a stately centerpiece in the art center's sculpture garden. For more about Manchester, see Hike #21.

An overnight backpacking trip with at least four shelter or camping alternatives, Hike #22 also offers several day-hike options. The trek from the south begins with Bromley Mt., known widely as a ski resort, and traverses many miles of fine wilderness, affording a deep escape into the woods. For those with two cars or an arranged shuttle ride, the hike can be shortened with an early exit at Mad Tom Notch.

Entering the woods beyond the parking lot on VT 11 / 30, the trail soon crosses a brook on a narrow I-beam: use your circus skills here. After a power line and some modest climbing, much of it near Bromley Brook, a bridge crosses the brook. Near here, until 1997, was the old Bromley tent site. (As of early 1998 plans were afoot to build another tent site, and possibly a shelter, about a mile north of here; call GMC for an update.) The climb continues, your legs doing the work of the ski lifts not far away. At 2.0 mi., watch for a small brook and a distinct left turn. Refill water bottles here; it's your last chance for the next 7.6 mi. More climbing ensues, gradually steeper, until the AT/LT emerges from the forest and veers left onto a wide, grassy

Dale Gelfand

American woodcock eggs

ski trail where in summer wildflowers are rampant (see "Killington's Boreal Summit," in Hike #25). Blazes are more or less absent here, but the footpath is obvious, heading toward the summit. At 2.7 mi. the chairlift and ski patrol cabin mark the summit of Bromley Mt. (3260 ft.).

Detour from the trail 100 ft. to the right for the Bromley observation tower, a wooden affair with steps sufficient to lift you above the treetops without inducing vertigo. On a clear day you will enjoy fine views, particularly to the south (Stratton) and west (Mt. Equinox and the Taconic Range). The ski patrol cabin, named for Nadine Justin, is not an AT/LT shelter, though there's a hikers' log outside and the door is often left unlocked. In a pinch you may be able to ride out a storm here.

Big Bromley's chairlift operates from mid-June to mid-October, weather permitting, so expect company at the summit. In the summer, the lift goes only halfway up the

Green Mt. National Forest

Split into two halves, one stretching south of US 4 to the Massachusetts state line and the other to the north, Green Mt. National Forest (GMNF) is home to 72 miles of the AT/LT—many of the best miles of Appalachian Trail in southern New England. The Middlebury and Rochester Districts comprise the northern section of GMNF. The northern border is near the state capital, Montpelier. The southern section is the Manchester District, including many of Vermont's AT miles. A GMNF day-hikes brochure for the Manchester District lists twenty other trails to explore, most of them blue-blazed and many in truly remote areas, less well traveled than the AT/LT. Dozens of all-in-the-wilderness loop hikes can be executed with careful planning.

Camping is permitted in most areas of GMNF, with an emphasis on the policy of "leave no trace." Although small fires are permitted, they are discouraged; backpacking stoves are recommended, especially for hikers using the shelters and established tent sites. Camping permits are not required—except for larger, organized groups—although overnight fees are collected in high season at some popular sites (Little Rock Pond, Griffith Lake, and a few others).

GMNF, a watershed for scores of Vermont communities, is home to hundreds of species of plant and animal life, from the humblest of wildflowers to the broadly antlered moose. Hikers with a serious interest in either botany or zoology should ask for specific suggestions about viewing sites at the GMNF offices. Rangers are well informed and glad to help.

GMNF is deep wilderness—over 350,000 acres of it—and some trails are not well marked. Carry a topographic map and compass. There are six wilderness areas (totaling 58,539 acres) within GMNF covered by the federal Wilderness Act of 1964: Big Branch, Breadloaf, Bristol Cliffs, Lye Brook, George D. Aiken, and Peru Peak. In these remote and often hauntingly beautiful and fragile places, trail maintenance is done without power tools, and even on the AT/LT the trail may be somewhat primitive, with less blazing and more frequent unremoved blowdowns. In Aiken Wilderness, for example, there are no marked trails: hikers must bushwhack with compass and map.

Hiking trail maps (500 miles' worth!) are available at USDA Forest Service, Manchester Ranger District, RR 1, Box 1940 (on VT 11/30, east of town), Manchester Center, VT 05255; 802-362-2307. Or at GMNF, P.O. Box 519, 231 North Main St., Rutland, VT 05701; 802-747-6700.

mountain, meeting the Bromley Alpine Slide, which can be an amusing distraction. In foliage season, the lift goes to the summit, near the AT. Caveat: Tickets (no one-way discount) for rides up or down must be purchased at the bottom of the lift (802-824-5522).

The trail continues across the windswept Bromley summit, keeping the terminus of the chairlift on the right (privy just off the AT/LT north of the summit), then veers left and downhill, passing a dilapidated privy on the right. The drop-off from the summit is steep and wet in spots. Bromley has another summit, too, more northerly, reached as the AT/LT cross the col between the peaks and climbs again. An overlook near this summit may offer respite from weekend chairlift crowds.

The AT/LT rolls down into the notch for another 0.6 mi., through mixed hardwoods, to unpaved USFS Rd. #21 (at Mad Tom Notch, 4.2 mi.) and a parking lot usable for day or overnight hikers. A sometimes-working water pump is north of the road at this junction. From this early exit waypoint, VT 11 in Peru is 4.0 mi. east.

The climb begins anew and continues in earnest for 2.5 mi.—almost 1000 ft., the steep sections made manageable by rock steps. False summits may deceive you: press on until the rocky exposed summit of Styles Peak is yours at 6.8 mi. and 3394 ft. The payoff is a sweeping north-to-south view over Green Mt. National Forest. New Hampshire's southern White Mts. are on the far eastern horizon. Hikers who started early in the morning will find this a great spot for lunch.

Just under 2 mi. farther on is Peru Peak (8.5 mi.), the highest point on this hike at 3429 ft., and while there is an outlook from a clearing in the woods (on a spur, off the east side of the AT/LT), the summit is wooded and less dramatic than Styles Peak. Between the two peaks the trail rises and falls several times, but modestly. The winding descent from the summit of Peru Peak is rocky, sometimes wet and slippery. There is a piped spring 0.4 mi. below the peak. Peru Peak Shelter, at 9.8 mi., offers a standard lean-to with a bit of history, having been constructed by the CCC in 1935 and refreshed by the Youth Conservation Corps in 1979. A brook with plentiful water is out front, its ice-cold flow deep enough for a midsummer wallow. A tent platform is adjacent to the shelter, and there are some tent sites as well.

There is no long-distance view in this spruce, hemlock, and hardwood forest, but the brook provides music. Griffith Lake Campsite is not far off, and the GMC caretaker there may visit here to collect a small lodging fee. Although Peru Peak Shelter will hold ten (plus the tenters), your chances of solitude and quiet are better here than at the popular lake up ahead. In 1997 the privy here offered philosophical graffiti written on a USFS flyer: "Entering the forest without moving the grass; entering the water without raising a ripple. Alan Watts, *Tao: The Watercourse Way.*"

Three handsome bridges during the next half mile cross more musical water. At 10.3 mi. the trail reaches glacial Griffith Lake (on the left), passes the caretaker's tent (check in if planning to camp here), and soon arrives at the tenting area. Camping is limited to four tent platforms. The trail here is mostly on puncheons (to protect fragile soil and plant life) that can be slippery when wet. If you want to fish for dinner or to take a swim (both in deeper waters), proceed north to the junction with Old Job Trail (10.5 mi., just past the lake) and head left. The GMC caretaker advises exploring the west shore of the lake for these activities.Old Job trail runs northeast 3.4 mi. to USFS Rd. #30 and then continues north to rejoin the AT/LT shortly before USFS Rd. #10. Thus it makes a convenient loop for a day hike coming *south* from USFS #10 to Griffith Lake and back.

At 10.6 mi. the Lake Trail branches off the AT/LT to the left (west), heading 3.3 mi. down (steeply) to a road in the hamlet of South End on US 7 (2.0 mi. south of Danby). This short trail also makes Griffith Lake easily accessible.

Griffith Lake's beauty and clarity are magnets, attracting the crowds, particularly day hikers approaching from the north. If you can schedule your visit on a weekday, do so. In fall

Continued on p.206

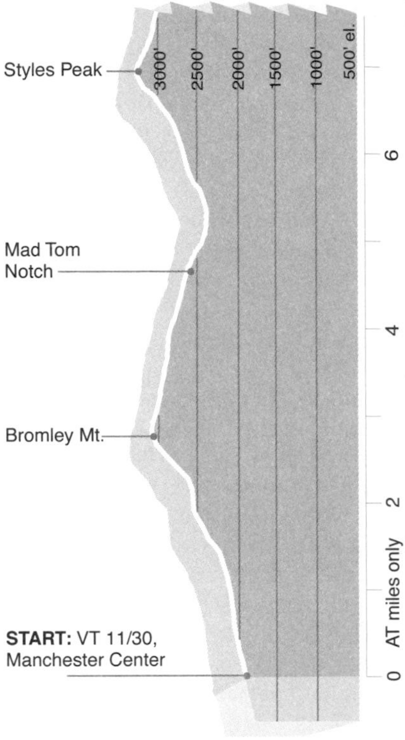

Styles Peak
3000'
2500'
2000'
1500'
1000'
500' el.
6
Mad Tom Notch
4
Bromley Mt.
2
AT miles only
START: VT 11/30, Manchester Center
0

foliage season, pretty as it is here, hike elsewhere so as to minimize impact in this area.

The AT/LT, level but bumpy due to rocks and roots, carries on northward. At 12.4 mi. Baker Peak Trail heads off to the left, connecting with Lake Trail (see above). Glacial scarring is evident on the exposed rock during the brief ascent to Baker Peak, an exciting scramble gaining only 90 more ft. but exposing hikers

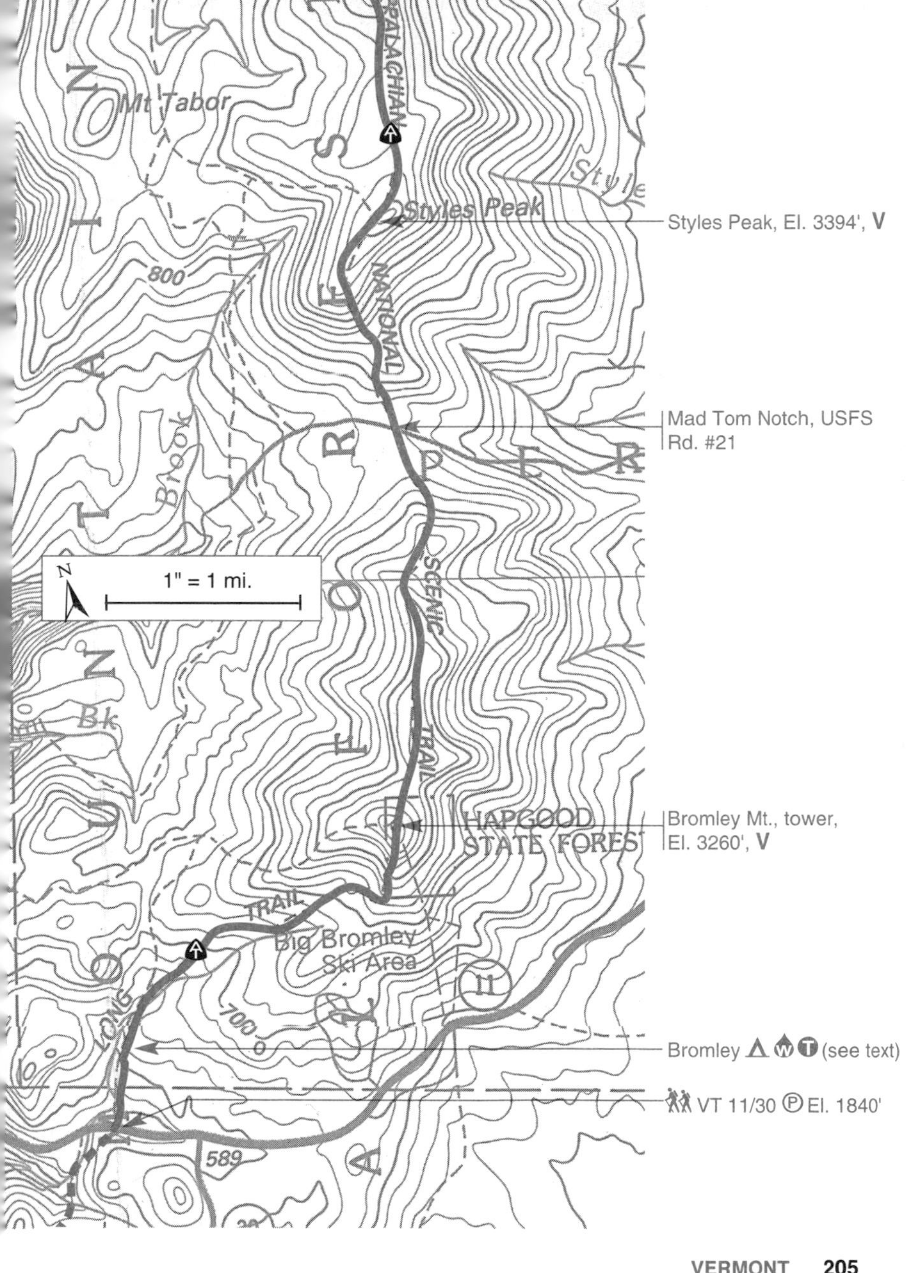

Mt Tabor
Styles Peak
Styles Peak, El. 3394', V
800
Brook
Mad Tom Notch, USFS Rd. #21
1" = 1 mi.
N
APPALACHIAN
NATIONAL
SCENIC
TRAIL
HAPGOOD STATE FOREST
Bromley Mt., tower, El. 3260', V
Big Bromley Ski Area
TRAIL
LONG
700
11
Bromley (see text)
VT 11/30 Ⓟ El. 1840'
589
30
Bk

to the elements as thoroughly as on much higher mountains in New Hampshire and Maine—or at Killington. Follow the blazes on the rocks; there are few trees here. Chew's *Underfoot*, on AT geology, notes: "The upturned grey beds of fine grained rock at Baker Peak contain many parallel thin layers of white-vein quartz. Small folds and faults in the rock show the ancient patterns of movement in the rock. Comparing the bands across the faults shows the Otter Creek sides of the faults have moved north."

Here at the western extremity of the Green Mts., the ledges provide excellent westward views down into Danby (a marble quarry is visible across the Otter Creek / US 7 valley, on the eastern slope of the Taconic Range). To the south, you'll see Stratton (Hike #21) and Peru Peak. Northwest, a really good day reveals the Adirondacks in New York, while almost due north, and right on the AT/LT, are Killington and Pico Peak (hard to pinpoint because of trees in the foreground). Bring maps and a compass to enjoy spotting the individual mountain peaks on the far-off horizon.

Baker Peak, only 4.8 mi. from USFS Rd. #10, is a favorite day-hike destination, like Griffith Lake. In bad weather, use the Baker bypass trail (right/east side of the AT/LT) to avoid the summit. High wind or wet weather can make Baker an inhospitable place. If thunderstorms threaten, be sure to bypass the top.

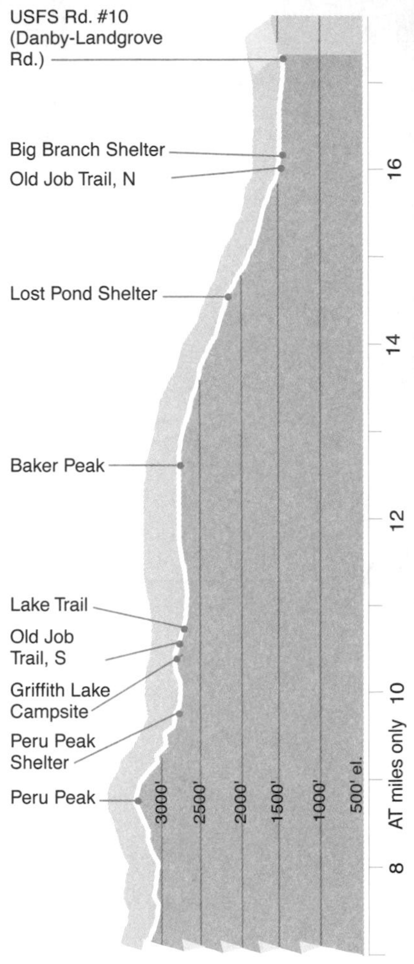

Through large stands of white birch, the descent begins, a bit steeply at first, then leveling off as the trail ambles northward, using woods roads for short sections between long stretches of woodland walking. At 14.5 mi. the Lost Pond Shelter is

USFS Rd. #10 Ⓟ
Big Branch
El. 1470'
Lost Pond El. 2150'
Baker Peak El. 2850', V
Baker Peak Trail
Lake Trail
Old Job Trail
Peru Peak
Griffith Lake
Peru Peak, spur trail,
El. 3429', V
600
800
Old Job
MOUNT
Buckball
Peak
South Buckball
Peak
Baker
Peak
South End
Griffith
Lake
7
1" = 1 mi.
N

Winter '98 Ice Storm Damage

A severe ice storm in early January 1998 damaged countless trees (primarily hardwoods) across northern and central Vermont (as well as in New York, New Hampshire, Maine, and Québec). Some AT/LT officials said the storm's impact was as bad as that of the hurricane of 1938, the worst on record. A major cleanup effort was organizing for the spring of 1998 as this book went to press. Hikers are advised to expect an unusual number of blowdowns in the AT's path from as far south as Spruce Peak and the Lye Brook Wilderness (near Stratton), north to the Killington area and east to the Connecticut River. Volunteers for trail maintenance are especially needed to help cope with this disaster. Contact GMC at 802-244-7037 or at gmc@sover.net.

just off the trail on the right. GMC's *Long Trail Guide* reports that this shelter was built on Cape Cod as a gift of Louis Stare, Jr., then dismantled and trucked to Vermont. Ocean salt air left a tasty residue in the logs, attracting Green Mt. porcupines. Charming story, but be wise and hang your food and pack overnight to avoid the critters. For water at this site, use the brook in the ravine on the far side of the shelter. Tent sites here are flat and close by the shelter.

Another 600 ft. down and 1.5 mi. farther on, over easy trail, the AT/LT passes Big Branch (brook) and the northern junction with Old Job Trail, on the right. Old Job Shelter is 1.1 mi. south on this trail. The AT/LT runs along the broad stream and crosses on a photogenic suspension bridge with pools in the rocks below, inviting midsummer swimmers (16.1 mi.). Here in the Big Branch Wilderness, camping between shelters is permitted—using low-impact methods—and near the stream hereabouts there are appealing level spots. Big Branch Shelter is located at 16.2 mi., with water from the stream and a privy uphill away from the water.

Following the stream, the trail dips and then climbs briefly, reaching USFS Rd. #10 (17.3 mi.) and leaving the Big Branch Wilderness area. The AT/LT uses USFS #10 for 0.3 mi. At the western trailhead is the larger, paved parking lot; at the eastern trailhead (where Hike #22 officially ends) is the smaller, unpaved lot.

HIKE #22 Itinerary

Miles N	NORTH	Elev. (ft./m)	Miles S
17.3	**End: USFS Rd. #10,** overnight parking (paved lot, W trailhead); overflow parking (E trailhead); see information block for safer parking; Danby 3.4 mi. W.	1530/466	0.0
16.2	**Big Branch Shelter,** water, privy.	1470/448	1.1
16.1	**Big Branch,** suspension bridge.	1500/457	1.2
16.0	**Old Job Trail,** N end.	1525/465	1.3
14.5	**Lost Pond Shelter,** water, privy.	2150/655	2.8
12.5	**Baker Peak,** exposed summit, views.	2850/869	4.8
12.4	**Baker Peak Trail.**	2760/841	4.9
10.6	**Lake Trail** heads W, early exit option.	2620/799	6.7
10.5	**Old Job Trail,** S end.	2600/793	6.8
10.3	**Griffith Lake Campsite,** caretaker, water, privy, tent sites.	2600/793	7.0
9.8	**Peru Peak Shelter,** water, privy, tent sites.	2550/777	7.5
8.5	**Peru Peak.**	3429/1045	8.8
6.8	**Styles Peak,** views.	3394/1035	10.5
4.2	**USFS Rd. #21,** Mad Tom Notch, early exit option.	2446/746	13.1
2.7	**Bromley Mt.,** tower.	3260/994	14.6
2.0	Brook; trail turns L (N).		15.3
0.0	**Start: VT 11/30,** 5.8 mi. E of Manchester, overnight parking.	1800/549	17.3

SOUTH

HIKE: #23

Little Rock Pond and White Rocks

Maps: ATC N.H. & Vt. #6; GMC LT #7 & #8

Route: USFS Rd. #10 (Danby-Landgrove Rd.), Danby, to VT 140 (Wallingford Gulf Rd.), Wallingford

Recommended direction: S to N

Distance: 9.0 mi.

Elevation +/-: 1500 to 2560 to 1300 ft.

Effort: Easy to moderate

Day hike: Yes

Overnight backpacking hike: Optional

Duration: 5 to 5½ hr.

Early exit option: None

Natural history features: Little Rock Pond; White Rocks Cliffs

Trailhead access: *Start:* USFS Rd. #10 (closed in winter), overnight parking. Western approach (easier): From US 7, Danby, take USFS Rd. #10 (also called Mt. Tabor Rd.) E 3.4 mi. to USFS AT/LT parking. Eastern approach (more difficult): From Londonderry, take VT 11 / 30 W briefly to Reilly Rd. and turn R, continuing to North Landgrove; follow Weston Rd. to Little Michigan Rd. (also called USFS #10) and turn L; go about 10.5 mi. to AT/LT parking. *End:* VT 140 (Wallingford Gulf Rd.), 2.6 mi. W of East Wallingford, 3.4 mi. E of US 7, Wallingford. (*Note:* Trail relocation expected in 1999, moving crossing about 0.5 mi. W on VT 140. Parking lot to be constructed.)

Camping: Lula Tye Shelter; Little Rock Pond Campsite; Little Rock Pond Shelter; Greenwall Shelter

The rewards of this hike come so early and so often that it may seem like a stock guaranteed to grow, requiring no attention once you've started the investment. However, you will want to pay attention here, not because the walking is difficult (it isn't) but because the woods and the geology are so interesting and beautiful. The only caveat is that Little Rock Pond (toward the south end) and White Rocks Cliff (near the north end) are among the most popular sites on the Vermont AT. If it's solitude you're seeking, seek elsewhere —or seek it here midweek.

The relatively gentle terrain makes for long strides and quick walking. The 9.0 mi. can be covered in 5 hr. or less, but the pond and the cliffs (and perhaps other sweet sites as well) will make you linger. In fact, many hikers make a full day of it, starting early, swimming or fishing, circling the pond or climbing Green Mt. above it, then carrying on to the north on the AT/LT or returning to USFS #10. Equally popular as a shorter day hike is the climb to White Rocks Cliffs from the north end of the hike, at VT 140.

For campers, the Little Rock Pond

area offers several options, all of them appealing because of their proximity to the water. However, to protect the fragile shoreline, none of the tent sites or shelters are on the lake proper.

Given the heavy use of these attractive places, it can't be stressed enough that every hiker has to act responsibly, leaving no trace that he or she has passed through and honoring other hikers' desire for quiet and privacy.

It's a wide, well-worn, and level path that gets you started northward from USFS Rd. #10 (Danby–Landgrove Rd.), twice crossing Little Black Branch. About 30 min. or 1.7 mi. up the trail, after several puncheons, the short side trail to Lula Tye Shelter appears. The lean-to is the standard affair, set on a hillside. Water is 0.3 mi. north on the AT/LT, at a spring just past the caretaker's tent site, a bit inconvenient. A privy is nearby. This shelter took a walk in the woods itself one day. Built in 1962 on the shore of Little Rock Pond, its popularity was its downfall: too many people trampling the pondside plants. A GMC crew took the shelter apart, hefted it up here, and hammered it back together, an admirable trick. The shelter sits in a pleasant clearing, but there is no water view. Given the slope, there are only a few viable tent sites. The caretaker will collect a small fee here and at the other shelters and campsites near the pond.

More puncheons carry the trail alongside the glacial pond itself. Stop for a chat with the caretaker, a GMC employee, usually a young person with a love for the woods and a

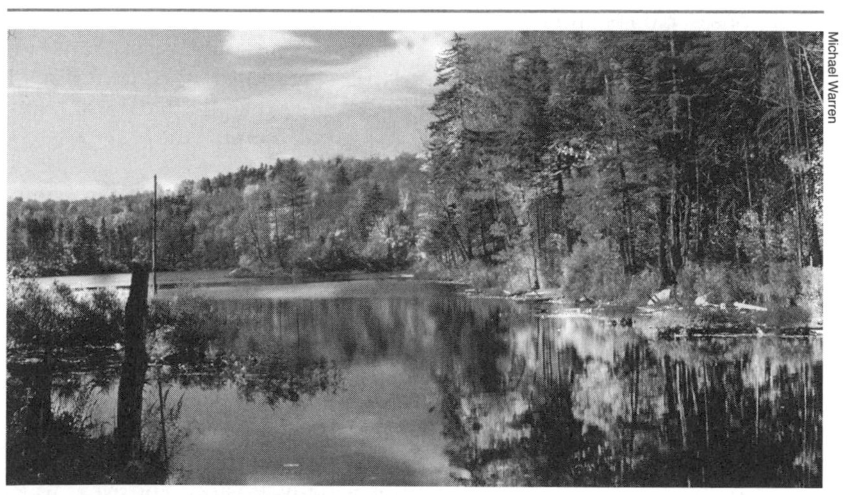

Michael Warren

Little Rock Pond, Green Mt. National Forest

knack for handling people. Sage advice about the network of local side trails can be had for the asking. Among the options is the Little Rock Pond Loop Trail (contiguous here with the AT/LT until it splits off to the left at the north end of the pond to wend its way around the water). Some of the best swimming and sunbathing sites are on the far (west) side of the pond, where there is a small island. The west shore especially has boulders marked by the scraping and buffing of the glacier. A short wooden bridge provides access to the island.

With a proper Vermont license, trout fishing is allowed, and can be quite successful. The steep wall of Green Mt. rises up on the pond's western shore as a sounding board for the evening calls of owls, Canada geese, and the occasional loon. Stunning reflections of clouds, mountainside, and trees change the face of the pond as the hours pass slowly each day. It's a lovely place for quiet meditation. If you want to see the pond from on high, climb the Green Mt. Trail from the pond's north end, quickly affording about a 600-ft. lift skyward. This trail also makes a good loop back to USFS #10, in 6.4 mi. (AT plus Green Mt. Trail)—though the blazing over the heights of Green Mt. is somewhat hard to follow. You will need to explore a bit to find the best overlook above the pond, keeping track of where you left the main trail so as to find your way back to it.

At 2.0 mi., the Little Rock Pond Campsite, set back 100 ft. from the eastern shore, provides tent platforms, privy, fire rings, and spring water. The sites to the north are more open to the sun. At 2.3 mi., at the north end of the pond where Green Mt. Trail departs, Homer Stone Brook Trail heads downhill 2.5 mi. west to South Wallingford and US 7. This trail skirts the north end of Green Mt. (no climbing) but follows a somewhat rugged ravine much of the way down.

At 2.4 mi., just north of the pond, Little Rock Pond Shelter is tucked in the woods off the right side of the trail. Same vintage as Lula Tye, same amenities, and same walk in the woods. This shelter was moved from the island to its present site in 1972. A spring is 0.4 mi. south on the AT/LT.

A long, flat section of trail ensues north of Little Rock Pond. The land falls off sharply to the left, and below, Homer Stone Brook makes a pleasantly rushing sound over rapids and falls. A clearing, in the vicinity of 3.1 mi., is the site of the old Aldrich Job, a logging camp (the camps were called "jobs").

Most of the slopes of the gentle Green Mts. hereabouts were heavily cut for timber by the original settlers. Burning the abundant trees yielded valuable potash, used in making glass and soap. Eventually, sodium (mined) supplanted potash and the demand for burnable timber declined. However, lumber for building (not just for Vermont towns, but for Albany, Boston, and New York) remained in high demand. Pine,

Hiking with a Hand Lens

Some of the best views on the AT require no blue sky: the hairy underside of a lousewort leaf, the downy silencer of a discarded owl feather, the bloodsucking gear of a mosquito.

I always carry a 10X hand lens in my pack. It weighs less than my compass and has a string so that I can hang it around my neck. Most nature centers and college bookstores sell hand lenses.

Make sure you get one that magnifies at least ten times. Plastic 3X or 5X lenses don't help much, though they are easier for small children to use. A glass lens that slides into a protective case will last the longest. You can also buy 16X lenses that require more light and a bit of practice, or compact field microscopes with about 30X magnification and their own light source.

To use a 10X hand lens, place the lens close to your eye, almost touching your eyebrow, and bring, say, the owl feather closer and closer until it's in focus — usually within a few inches. If you want to look at flowers or mosses, get down to their level; don't pick them just to get a good look at them.

Look at everything. For example, whether a flower is new to you or you're reacquainting yourself with a familiar one, look at its stamens and pistil. Look at each plant part to find out why botanists need so many words for "hairy."

Hand lenses are cheaper and lighter than binoculars, and you will get views you never knew were there.

—Doris Gove

David Emblidge

Thistle, going to seed

spruce, oak, and hemlock all had their uses. The hemlock also yielded tannin. An infamous blight took the chestnut trees, and herds of hungry sheep took much of the ground cover, provoking erosion. These were the conditions in the 1840s and on toward the end of the 19th century. Almost all of Green Mt. National Forest is second-growth trees, except for the steepest slopes where timber harvesting was too difficult to be profitable. The labyrinth of abandoned stone walls and woods roads in the forest is a telltale sign of the aggressive agriculture and industry in earlier times. Given another century of regrowth, the Green Mt. forest may begin to recover some of its primeval characteristics.

A bridge crosses Homer Stone Brook at 3.3 mi. at a pleasant rest stop. There has been only a 370-ft. gain in elevation from the start of Hike #23 to this point, but now some uphill work begins. Over the next 2 mi. the trail rises to 2560 ft., nearly to the summit of White Rocks Mt., just off to the east. Stone steps lead to the high point. A spring is 100 yd. off the left side of the trail, just north of the highest point of land. The summit area is wooded, offering no views, but trust the trail: great views are not far ahead now. Hereabouts you're in the White Rocks National Recreation Area.

The trail falls away noticeably now, passing through mixed hardwoods (predominantly birch and maple) and evergreens, occasionally in a steep section over rocks, now and

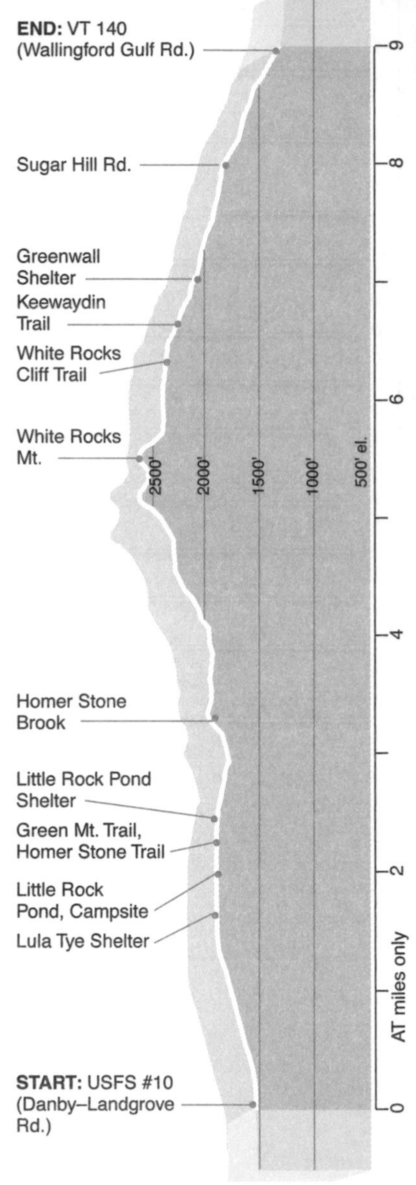

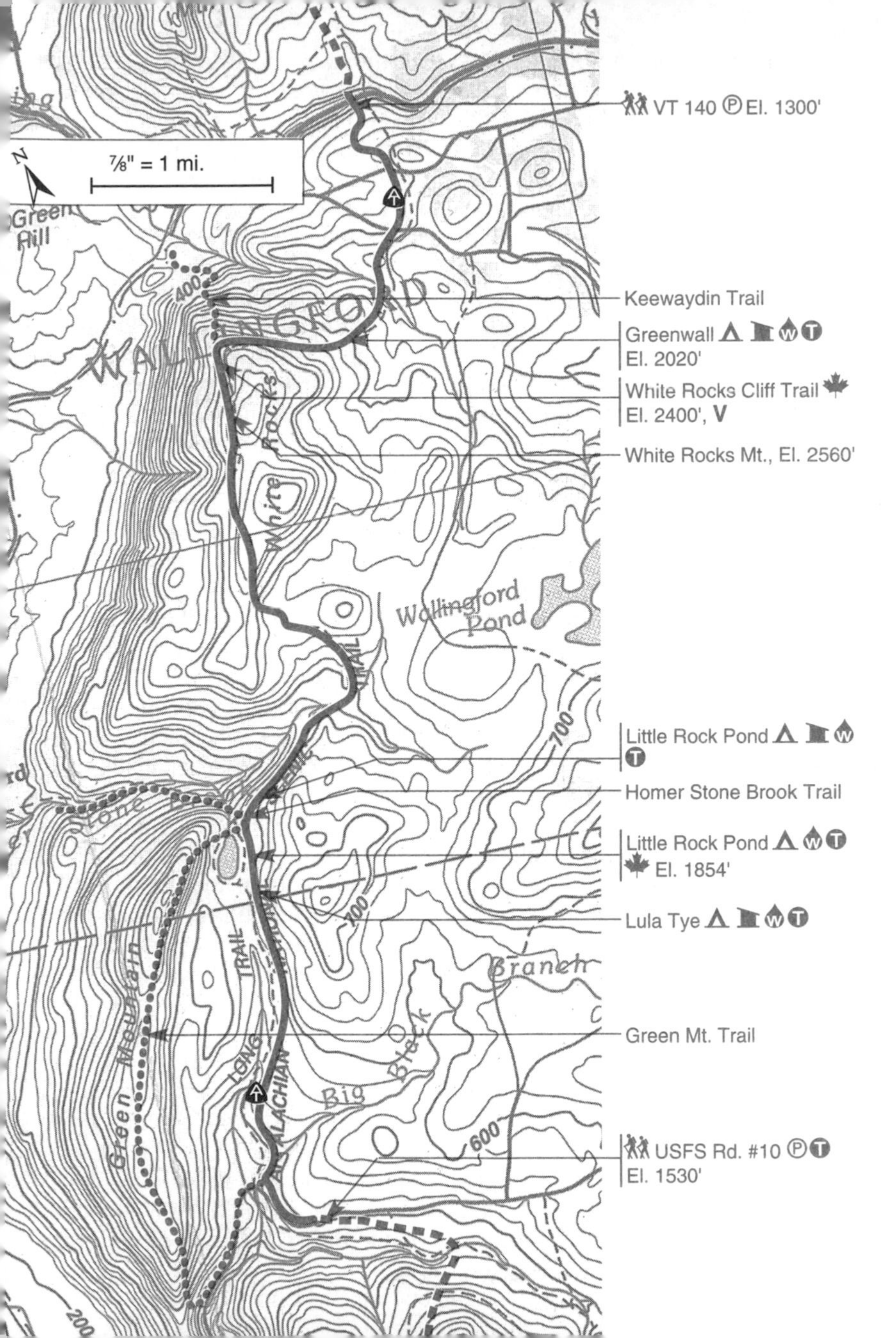

VT 140 Ⓟ El. 1300'
7/8" = 1 mi.
N
Green Hill
WALLINGFORD
White Rocks
Keewaydin Trail
Greenwall
El. 2020'
White Rocks Cliff Trail
El. 2400', V
White Rocks Mt., El. 2560'
Wallingford Pond
TRAIL
Little Rock Pond
Homer Stone Brook Trail
Little Rock Pond
El. 1854'
Lula Tye
Branch
Green Mt. Trail
Green Mountain
LONG TRAIL
APPALACHIAN TRAIL
Big Black
USFS Rd. #10 Ⓟ
El. 1530'

then on a carpet of hemlock needles. In the sag following White Rocks summit, white birch brightens the otherwise cool woods. Large glacial erratics (boulders) litter the forest floor. Surprisingly, highway noise from US 7 in the valley below may filter through the trees. At 6.3 mi. on the left comes the White Rocks Cliff Trail, marked with a cairn and a trail sign. It's not called a cliff trail for nothing: the 0.2-mi. descent to the overlook is rough and steep (and eroding due to heavy use). Stay on the official trail—if you can follow the blue blazes, which seem to peter out as the trail reaches the cliffside. Keep right at the cliff, finding your way to a broad, open, rocky area about 50 ft. square. As you step out of the woods, the world unfolds before you.

South Wallingford is directly below on US 7, with Danby farther south along the same route. The Danby marble quarry is visible across the valley. On the far northwestern horizon are the Adirondacks.

Over the cliffside and below, a broad talus slope spills away from the mountain. The surrounding red spruce forest, with its deep green needles and reddish trunks, highlights the whiteness of the rocks, which are generally quartzite. With binoculars or even the naked eye, you have a good chance here of seeing common ravens and turkey vultures, and an improving chance of spotting a peregrine falcon (a victim of the deadly pesticide DDT, the species nearly disappeared but is now bred in captivity and released to the wild—see "Vermont Raptor Center" in Hike #28).

At 15 to 20 in., the peregrine falcon is about the size of a crow, recognizable at close range by the black sideburns on its cheeks. Gray to black on its sharply pointed wings, the falcon is a mottled brown and white on the belly. It prefers the cliffs for roosting. The common raven, shiny jet black, is a bigger bird, 21 to 27 in., with a wedge-shaped tail and individual feathers spreading widely at the wing tips. Its call is a guttural croak (not the squawk of the crow), and while rising on thermal updrafts, the raven likes to engage in showy acrobatics. Red-tailed and red-shouldered hawks can be seen here as well.

But before you sit down to watch for birds, check around the rocks, especially on a warm, sunny day, for the handsome timber rattlesnake, which can range from 2 to 5 ft. long but is generally on the smaller side. Colors vary—yellow, brown, gray, black—but always in blotches, and always with a black tail. Beware of the coiled rattler, apparently asleep. This is a camouflage and hunting technique, as the snake waits for prey (small rodents and birds) to come within range of a strike. If you see a rattler, admire from afar and choose another rock for a seat.

After climbing back up to the AT/LT, turn left and continue northward. Shortly, at 6.6 mi., the Keewaydin Trail exits left, descending quickly over 1.2 mi. to the USFS White Rocks picnic area. The descent continues on the AT/LT, soon leaving the White Rocks Recreation Area (but still in the national forest), arriving at Greenwall Shelter at 7.1 mi. A large clearing in the forest gives this woodland shelter a spacious feeling. Floor space only here, no bunks. Good tent sites are up and behind the shelter, as is the spring. Just north of Greenwall there's a footbridge over a small brook.

Another 5 min. of walking brings the trail out of the woods, onto gravel Butterworth Rd., proceeding then to Sugar Hill Rd. (8.0 mi.), which is drivable to East Wallingford (3.0 mi.). No parking here. After crossing Sugar Hill Rd., it's back into the woods (some sections here need reblazing), and over the final mile of this hike, the AT/LT rambles through forest and fields, rising and falling over a small hill. After several hours in the woods, the openness of the fields, with their colorful wildflowers, birds, and butterflies, is welcome. Roaring Brook soon appears, across the path of the trail, and just beyond is VT 140 (Wallingford Gulf Rd.), hike's end.

Parking note: Overnight parking is discouraged by GMC at Wallingford Gulf Rd. because of vandalism and crowding. There are a few roadside day-parking spaces. Trail-friendly neighbors across the road may offer a spot in their driveway if you inquire.

HIKE #23 Itinerary

Miles N	NORTH	Elev. (ft./m)	Miles S
9.0	**End: VT 140** (Wallingford Gulf Rd.), across from Bear Mt. Rd.; limited overnight parking; 3.4 mi. W to US 7, Wallingford; 2.6 mi. E to VT 103, East Wallingford. (*Note:* Trail relocation expected in 1999, moving crossing about 0.5 mi. W on VT 140.)	1300/396	0.0
8.0	**Sugar Hill Rd,** no parking.	1680/512	1.0
7.1	**Greenwall Shelter,** water, privy, tent sites.	2020/616	1.9
6.6	**Keewaydin Trail,** 1.2 mi. to picnic area.	2300/701	2.4
6.3	**White Rocks Cliff Trail,** 0.2 mi. to overlook, views.	2400/732	2.7
5.5	**White Rocks Mt.**	2560/780	3.5
3.3	**Homer Stone Brook,** bridge. Trail begins uphill climb.	1900/579	5.7
2.4	**Little Rock Pond Shelter,** water, privy.	1820/555	6.6
2.3	**Green Mt. Trail,** S; **Homer Stone Brook Trail,** W.	1854/565	6.7
2.0	Side trail, E, to **Little Rock Pond Campsite,** water, privy, caretaker, fee; **Little Rock Pond Loop Trail**.	1854/565	7.0
1.7	Side trail, E, to **Lula Tye Shelter,** water, privy.	1865/569	7.3
0.0	**Start: USFS Rd. #10,** Danby, overnight parking at LT/AT Big Branch lot.	1530/446	9.0

SOUTH

HIKE: #24

Clarendon Gorge and Cold River

Maps: ATC N.H. & Vt. #6; GMC LT #8

Route: VT 140 (Wallingford Gulf Rd.), Wallingford, to Clarendon Gorge, across VT 103, to Lower Cold River Rd., North Shrewsbury

Recommended direction: S to N (described here) or N to S

Distance: 9.2 mi.

Elevation +/-: 1300 to 2010 to 800 to 1400 ft.

Effort: Easy to moderate, with one steep ravine

Day hike: Yes

Overnight backpacking hike: Optional

Duration: 5½ hr.

Early exit option: VT 103 (Rutland–Bellows Falls Hwy.), at 5.2 mi.

Natural history features: Clarendon Gorge

Trailhead access: *Start:* VT 140 (Wallingford Gulf Rd. at junction with Bear Mt. Rd.), overnight parking (discouraged); 3.4 mi. E of US 7, Wallingford; 2.6 mi. W of VT 103, East Wallingford. (*Note:* Trail relocation expected in 1999, moving crossing about 0.5 mi. W on VT 140. Parking lot to be constructed.) *End:* Lower Cold River Rd., overnight parking; 2.4 mi. W of North Shrewsbury, 7.3 mi. E of US 7, Rutland. (*Note:* Parking lot planned for 1998.)

Camping: Minerva Hinchey Shelter (discouraged); Clarendon Shelter

Here's a hike with a "major" highway in the middle of it, offering a chance to (a) make it a shorter walk, (b) turn it into two short day hikes in either direction, or (c) hop over the highway and do the entire 9.2 mi. as a day hike or an overnighter. The terrain is easy to moderately rolling countryside, with one steep pitch for about 30 min. of tough climbing (heading north). Just south of the highway, there is a handsome gorge that is crossed by a walkers' suspension bridge, a pretty spot and a definite photo opportunity.

This is a good hike for those who want a variety of landscapes without major climbing, negotiating rough trail, or coping with wild weather at high elevations. Bring along a tree or flower identification book, a camera, or a sketch pad. You will be into the woods and out of it (into grassy areas and on roads) several times today. Plant and bird life will vary considerably.

For a south-to-north walk, begin at VT 140 (Wallingford Gulf Rd.), at its junction with Bear Mt. Rd. See the end of Hike #23 for parking information. (*Note:* Trail relocation expected in 1999; see information block, above.)

The AT/LT heads somewhat steeply uphill on Bear Mt. Rd. (unpaved).

Although you could drive up this part of the trail for 0.5 mi., there is no parking farther on, as indicated by several signs no doubt reflecting private property owners' frustration with hikers or snowmobilers who ignore the rules. Soon the trail enters an old woods road and forks. A steel gate bars the left fork; the AT/LT goes right. The road diminishes to a gently rising grassy path, with morning sun flickering through a thin line of trees to the right. Then a left turn into the deeper woods.

Hundreds of pin oaks grow hereabouts, and it can be a noisy agri-industrial site when squirrels and chipmunks are busy accumulating a winter hoard of acorns. On a fall day, with some wind, the nearly round acorns shower the ground like hailstones. Don't be surprised if you take a hit on the head. Pin oaks like poorly drained, moist areas and uplands. Their 3- to 5-in. shiny green leaves (often twice the size of a sugar maple leaf) have deep lobes; the leaves linger late into the fall, turning red and brown. The "pins" are the little side twigs and spurs on the branches.

The top of Button Hill, this hike's highest point, comes at 1.6 mi. after about 700 ft. of climbing. Only the last few minutes before the top require much effort (during a few switchbacks). An overgrown summit with no view, Button Hill is nonetheless a pleasant spot for a breather. Scout for a big log to use as a seat, and do a little bird-watching into the treetops.

Down now, steadily, passing several woods roads (pay attention to white blazes), until the trail emerges from the woods, if only briefly, at a powerline crossing (2.4 mi.) with no memorable views. Remember that although the AT/LT runs generally north–south, twists and turns can at a given moment have you walking east or west (or even, in the odd case, southward on a northbound hike). Always carry a map or compass.

A giant oak tree comes up just after the power line, and soon the trail reaches a grassy area and a woods road. Minerva Hinchey Shelter is now 200 ft. off to the right, along the road. This shelter will do in a pinch, but it has drawbacks. Set right on the road (evidently easily accessible to off-road vehicles and snowmobiles), it has been trashed by overuse. There is no privacy here and no view. There is one big raised "bunk." A spring is 150 ft. south, and there is a privy. Tent sites seem dubious. We recommend Clarendon Shelter, later in the hike, for north-bounders.

Nearby Spring Lake is private.

After rising modestly uphill behind the shelter, the AT/LT passes through a few minutes of woods and, at 3.2 mi., comes out to a broad meadow, Spring Lake Clearing. Find a good perch in the middle of the meadow and linger a while here, amidst milkweed and Queen Anne's lace, butterflies and bees. Bird-watchers will enjoy the overhead traffic, with large and small birds using both meadow and woods. Among others, juncos and a large gray heron passed by when we rested here. The views are pleasant: the Taconics (west) and Coolidge Range (northeast). You might search the east side of the meadow for possible glimpses of Spring Lake, below. Controlled burning here (by the Forest Service) helps to keep the meadow from growing over, thus preserving a settled wildlife habitat. The Rutland airport is not far off, and there is some noise overhead here, a bit disconcerting.

In fact, Airport Lookout is the next waypoint (4.5 mi.), after an easy descent from the meadow. The overlook is on the left, at a rock outcropping, a popular day-hiker's destination for those coming up from VT 103. The US 7 valley lies below you now, with the city of Rutland due north. With compass in hand, find 310 degrees (NNW), and on a clear day you will have a glimpse of the distant Adirondacks in New York, through a notch in the Taconic Range along Vermont's western border.

Make sure your boots are snugly tied—the descent from Airport Lookout is steep. When it's over, Mill River and the Clarendon Gorge appear (5.2 mi.). If you can't get to Niagara Falls, this gorge will do nicely, though it's quiet and small by comparison. *Underfoot*, V. Collins Chew's guide to AT geology, describes Clarendon as "a sharp defile eroded through light-grey crystalline rock. Near the Robert Brugmann [suspension foot] Bridge, pebbles swirling in eddies have cut potholes in the rock." A "defile" is a narrow passage or gorge.

Terry Karkas

Building an AT shelter

The area just south of the bridge is overused, tired from too much foot traffic. Don't plan on picnicking or camping here. Be careful if you swim below the bridge—a 1973 flood took young hiker Brugmann's life here. The larger pools are fine swimming holes, however. A moment north of the bridge is VT 103, with a large unpaved parking lot. While overnight parking is permitted, it is discouraged by GMC due to vandal-

Free Lunch

If you know where to look, nature's bounty can feed you all along the trail. Distinguishing between safe/tasty plants and poisonous/unpleasantly flavored ones takes some study and experimentation. Basic rules apply: If you're not *sure* it's safe, don't eat it. Carrying a book with drawings or photos of wild plants is your best bet. *Edible Wild Plants,* in the Peterson's Guides series, is excellent. Another rule: Always leave some for the next hikers who will pass this way. We hold these pleasures in common.

This last rule is hard to follow in berry season (mid- to late summer). In sunny, highland New England spots, if the birds and bears haven't dined there first, you can enjoy wild blueberries (low to the ground, smaller berries than the cultivated variety), red and black raspberries (taller bushes), and even wild raisins (another berry). All excellent snacks. Pick only plump ones, though; let the rest ripen. A still-green berry is usually bitter.

At bogside and in cold running water you may find wild watercress, tangy and refreshing, fine for a salad if well cleaned.

David St. James, of the Massachusetts Department of Fisheries and Wildlife, Pittsfield office, waxes enthusiastic about exotic, more ambitious foraging, appropriate to the season. The pod of the milkweed plant, if boiled twice to remove the milky latex substance, is a sweet, tasty vegetable "not really comparable to anything in the stores." The 4- to 6-in. inner shoot of the cattail (a 2- to 3-ft.-tall weed found in wetlands) is tender and delicious, raw or steamed; other parts of the plant are useful too—in salad, as an asparagus substitute, as flour, as a potato—at different times of the year.

Bunchberries, says St. James, whose diminutive flower reveals their family connection to the dogwood tree, are mild in flavor but highly nutritious and are most common at higher elevations. Wild leeks, "our best wild onion," according to Peterson, flower in June, but you'll need the guidebook's drawing to find them: they don't look anything like the leeks in your garden. The edible part is a 1½-in. bulb. Indian cucumber root is a misnomer; it's actually a tuber and thus has no seeds, but it tastes like the domestic cuke.

The list goes on and includes wild plants that are good for sauces, for flavoring a drink (sassafras for sun tea, or wild mint for iced tea), for topping your cereal (walnuts), or for seasoning a cooked dish (wild thyme). For a sharp-eyed hiker, the woods and mountains are Mother Nature's farm market. And you can't beat the prices.

ism. VT 103 north will take you to US 7B (north), which leads to Clarendon (4.2 mi.) and a choice of provisioners. US 7 is 2.4 mi. west, at a point 5.0 mi. south of Rutland. Clarendon General Store is 1.0 mi. west of this trail crossing.

Proceed carefully across the busy highway, crossing railroad tracks on the north side. After stiles over fences, the AT/LT enters a steep ravine, and 30 min. of muscular climbing follow, on rock steps and over boulders, as the trail mounts the hillside, curves right, and arrives at Clarendon Lookout (5.7 mi.). Resting here on the rocky overlook, you may well see hawks against the southern skies as they ride the thermal updrafts. The day's hardest work is now done, and the trail cruises onward without much noticeable change in elevation. After descending a ridge and using a woods road (Crown Point Military Rd., dating back to the French and Indian War in the 1750s), the AT/LT comes to the spur trail, right, for Clarendon Shelter (6.3 mi.). Larger than most shelters, it provides bunk space for twelve hikers. There are tent sites too, in the cleared woods of this level area. A stream is a few steps away.

Another energetic climb follows, easier than the ravine north of VT 103, up to Beacon Hill, the second highest point on Hike #24 at 1740 ft. (6.8 mi.). The beacon serves the nearby airport. Undramatic but pretty views here, of the pastoral lowlands. Indeed, this is farming country, and soon after more woods, the trail passes through wonderful sugar maples, offering brilliant colors in autumn, as it negotiates pastures, including stiles and gates. Be careful to close farm gates to keep the cows where they belong. Be careful too about cow flops underfoot. They may look dry on top, convenient stepping-stones through damp areas, but beneath that crust is a slippery mess waiting to clog the lugs of your boots. If the cattle—usually docile and uninterested in you—are in the path, give them a wide berth.

To distinguish between the sugar maple and, say, the red or silver maple, also common in New England, look at the shape of the leaves. The sugar maple leaf has rounded, U-shaped lobes, while the other maples' lobes are cut more sharply, almost in Vs. A device to remember this: "sugar" has a "u" in it, and "silver" a "v."

Lottery Rd. (gravel) is the next waypoint, at 7.2 mi. Shrewsbury village is east of here, but a long walk. The undependable Hermit Spring (7.6 mi.) precedes a ridge that is followed by more pasture before another gravel road (Keiffer Rd.). The forest between these farmlands is gorgeously dappled with sunlight on a good day. At the Keiffer Rd. crossing an inspiring view lies dead ahead on the northern horizon: the Coolidge Range and Killington Peak (4241 ft., the highest point on the AT in Vermont), the destination of Hike

#25. Yes, it's a long way up, but worth every step.

At 9.2 mi., hike's end, parking at Lower Cold River Rd. (paved) is limited to a few roadside places. Beware of dogs at neighboring houses. The closest town is North Shrewsbury, 2.4 mi. east (see Hike #25).

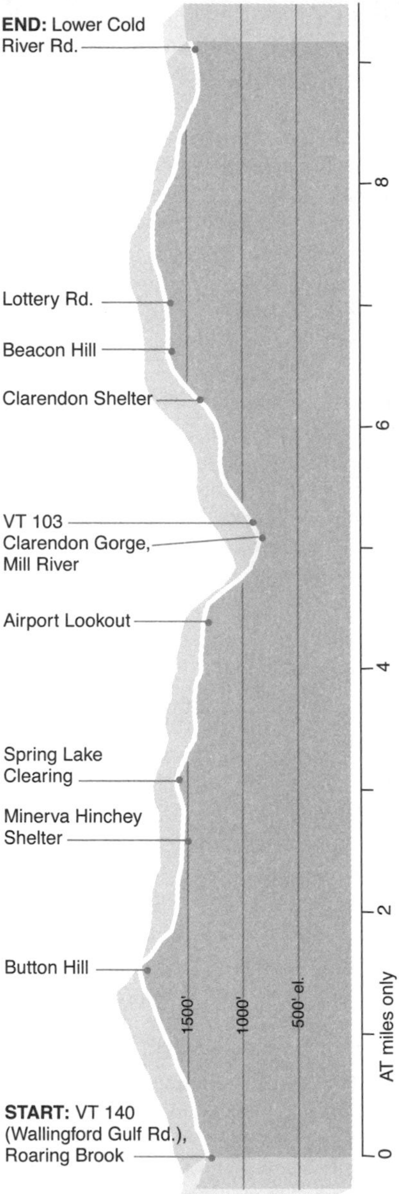

END: Lower Cold River Rd.
Lottery Rd.
Beacon Hill
Clarendon Shelter
VT 103
Clarendon Gorge, Mill River
Airport Lookout
Spring Lake Clearing
Minerva Hinchey Shelter
Button Hill
START: VT 140 (Wallingford Gulf Rd.), Roaring Brook
1500'
1000'
500' el.
0
2
4
6
8
AT miles only

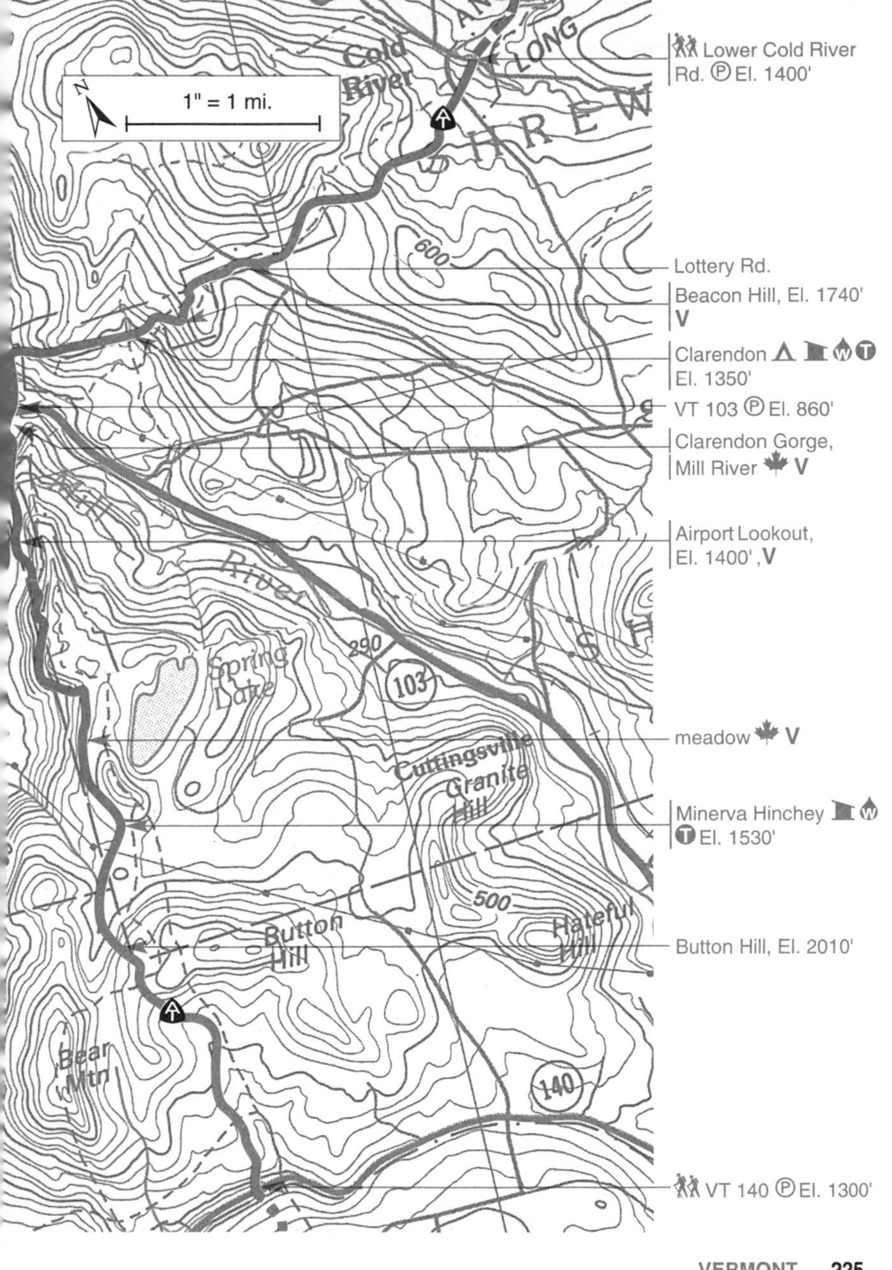
1" = 1 mi.
Cold River
LONG
600
290
103
River
Spring Lake
Cuttingsville Granite Hill
500
Hateful Hill
Button Hill
Bear Mtn
140
Lower Cold River Rd. Ⓟ El. 1400'
Lottery Rd.
Beacon Hill, El. 1740' V
Clarendon El. 1350'
VT 103 Ⓟ El. 860'
Clarendon Gorge, Mill River V
Airport Lookout, El. 1400', V
meadow V
Minerva Hinchey El. 1530'
Button Hill, El. 2010'
VT 140 Ⓟ El. 1300'

HIKE #24 Itinerary

Miles N	NORTH	Elev. (ft./m)	Miles S
9.2	**End: Lower Cold River Rd.,** limited overnight parking, 2.4 mi. W of N. Shrewsbury. (*Note:* Parking lot planned for 1998.)	1400/427	0.0
7.2	**Lottery Rd.**	1700/518	2.0
6.8	**Beacon Hill,** view.	1740/530	2.4
6.3	Side trail to **Clarendon Shelter,** water, privy, tent sites.	1350/412	2.9
5.7	**Clarendon Lookout.**		3.5
5.3	**VT 103** (Rutland–Bellows Falls Hwy.), overnight parking; (2.4 mi. W to US 7). Steep climb follows.	860/262	3.9
5.2	**Clarendon Gorge,** Mill River, bridge, swimming holes.	800/244	4.0
4.5	View at **Airport Lookout.** Steep descent follows.	1400/247	4.7
3.2	**Spring Lake Clearing,** views.	1600/488	6.0
2.6	Side trail to **Minerva Hinchey Shelter,** water, privy; Spring Lake 0.5 mi. N (private).	1530/466	6.6
1.6	**Button Hill.**	2010/613	7.6
0.0	**Start: VT 140** (Wallingford Gulf Rd.), overnight parking; 3.4 mi. E of US 7, Wallingford; 2.6 mi. W of VT 103, East Wallingford. (*Note:* Trail relocation expected in 1999, moving crossing about 0.5 mi. W on VT 140. Parking lot to be constructed.) Head uphill on Bear Mt. Rd.	1300/396	9.2

SOUTH

HIKE: #25

Killington Peak—South

Maps: ATC N.H. & Vt. #6; GMC LT #8 & #9
Route: From Lower Cold River Rd., North Shrewsbury, to Killington Peak, Sherburne; optional descent via gondola or ski trail
Recommended direction: S to N
Distance: 7.0 mi., 7.3 mi to Killington Peak
Acess trail name & length: Killington Spur and link to gondola, 0.3 mi.
Elevation +/-: 1400 to 3870 ft. (4241 ft. at peak)
Effort: Strenuous
Day hike: Yes
Overnight backpacking hike: Optional
Duration: 5 to 5½ hr.
Early exit option: Upper Cold River Rd., at 1.5 mi.
Natural history features: Boreal zone; "above" treeline at Killington Peak
Other features: Merrell Hiking Center
Trailhead access: *Start:* Lower Cold River Rd., limited overnight parking, 2.4 mi. W of North Shrewsbury, 7.3 mi. E of US 7, Rutland. *End:* Cooper Lodge on AT, Killington Mt.; or Killington ski area base lodge via gondola from Killington Peak; hiker parking.
Camping: Governor Clement Shelter (discouraged); Cooper Lodge and tent sites

Pray for good weather. Killington Peak, second highest in Vermont, can offer either the most magnificent views on the AT in southern New England or the most challenging elements on a windswept treeless mountaintop. Either way, it's great fun — unless you arrive at the summit truly in a storm, in which case you'll want to scurry for cover in the woods or for the gondola's summit lodge as fast as possible. Sooner or later, though, every hiker in southern New England will want to "do Killington." It's a big but manageable mountain for those who are willing to work for their pleasure.

Hike #25 approaches the peak from the south. Hike #26 comes at it from the north. Combining the two makes for a grand overnight mountain adventure. Either hike can end with a ride down the Killington gondola, or with a descent via ski trails and ski area maintenance roads. And there are connecting trails around Killington mountain. It's no surprise that the Merrell Boot Co., based in Vermont, chose Killington as the first site for what has become over a dozen hiking centers, offering guided hikes led by well-informed naturalists. More on this later.

Whatever route you choose, be prepared for wild and rapidly changing weather near the mountain's top. True weather buffs know that NOAA broadcasts special reports on weather for

David Emblidge

Killington Peak from Cold River Rd., Shutesbury

elevations above 3000 ft. (often quite different from weather in the valleys). Even on a midsummer day hike, bring clothing to cope with a cold rain and high wind. If you're hiking here in autumn foliage season, be prepared for surprise snow squalls on top, or at least for a chilling rain.

One more warning: Although the AT/LT en route to the top of Killington provides several hours of fine isolation in deep woods (especially this route from the south), as you approach the summit, prepare yourself for a rude awakening. The gondola brings many people to the top, folks who want to enjoy the same views you came for but who can't or don't want to pay the price of the hiking. We found ourselves atop Killington one beautiful fall day, sharing the wildest, most exposed promontory with a man in a tuxedo and a woman in a party dress, high heels and all, both of them with filled champagne glasses in hand: a photo shoot for a catering company that boasted it would serve you dinner anywhere. Cute, but you get the point. It's a bit of a circus some days at the top. If you're lucky, you will be able to climb Killington midweek to avoid any crowds.

These caveats aside, Killington is a marvelous hiking experience. Let's go up.

The AT/LT leaves the north side of Lower Cold River Rd. on a woods road and shortly begins to climb to a ridge (giving one brief view of the Coolidge Range to the north). Within half a mile the trail begins to border a lovely stream on the left. At 0.8 mi., ford Gould Brook. This crossing can be dicey in high water during spring runoff. Find a walking stick for balance, and trust your waterproof boots or tough it out barefoot (beware the slippery rocks underwater). In this section the trail is periodically graced with burbling streams on both sides: stereo water music from Gould and Sargent brooks. No camping permitted here, despite the temptation. A snack or lunch streamside is a fine idea, however.

While you walk the short distance to Upper Cold River Rd. (at 1.5 mi.), take a good look at the forest. In this area, at about 1500 ft., it's mixed deciduous and evergreen (abundant hemlocks here) — the transition forest described in Hike #5. As the land rises over the next several miles on the mountain, you will see significant changes in the woods, until at the top, you see no trees at all! At Upper Cold River Rd. (gravel), it's 2.4 mi. east to North Shrewsbury, an early exit option if needed.

As the trail follows and crosses Sargent Brook (on a bridge) and uses various woods roads now, there are zigs and zags, but still only a modest rise. All along here was once farmland, cleared for crops or for pasture. There's a mix of woods and grassy areas, and in the latter wildflowers are plentiful — milkweed and asters, black-eyed Susans and goldenrod, and many more. After crossing Robinson Brook on another bridge, and another woods road, you'll come to a clearing; on the far side is Governor Clement Shelter. If this were a house for sale, it would be billed as a "handyman special." Ease of access has brought many irresponsible people here for several years (the "party and trash" crowd), leaving this site worn out and broken down. GMC, and we, advise backpackers to plan on overnighting elsewhere if possible. Read on for Cooper Lodge.

In a pinch, Clement Shelter can do, however. It's a large stone lean-to, dating from 1929, with a newish roof. There are bunks and a fireplace inside, though fire in the ring outside is advised. We found the privy in poor shape too. Water can be taken from the stream about 70 yd. east.

GMC and ATC may relocate this shelter, and the trail itself, beginning not far north of here and continuing almost to the summit, in 1998 or soon thereafter. ATC's current maps already show the likely new path, intended to take the LT/AT away from the expanding Killington ski area. From here the relocated trail will most likely shift west to ascend and pass over Little Killington, avoiding the Juggernaut ski trail, then continue to Cooper Lodge (see below). The ruggedness of the present trail, noted below, may diminish somewhat on the newly constructed, relocated trail. You may find this a plus or a minus, depending on how much work you like to do while hiking.

Presently (1997) the AT/LT leaves Clement Shelter on a rising woods road and soon exits left into the forest, climbing.

The forest begins its evolution now, with spruces starting to predominate, a sign of higher elevation — not that you will need any signs. Your muscles will tell you. Over the next 2.5 mi., there is a gain of almost 1700 ft. as the trail becomes steeper and rougher underfoot. On typical days here, temperatures will be noticeably cooler than in the valley where you began. At rest stops, take care not to get a chill as your perspiration evaporates. And keep drinking water, even on cold days. Dehydration is the primary cause of hiker fatigue.

You're working your way up and along the side of Little Killington Mt. now, but on the trail there is no peak

Killington's Boreal Summit

A talk with David Laing, staff naturalist at the Merrell Hiking Center at Killington, opened our eyes to a number of interesting facts about this highest of southern New England mountains. Weather is the key. Killington gets 250 inches of snow, on average, plus plenty of rain and fog, in a year-round flow of short-term storms. There are many sunny days in between for good hiking. Storms arrive here on the eastward-racing polar jet stream. As moisture-laden air cools on its way up the western slopes of Killington and Pico peaks, precipitation ensues. Hikers therefore must be prepared for serious summer thunderstorms.

The treeless rocky summit of Killington might seem to be above treeline, but in fact it's not. At this latitude, 4241 feet isn't high enough to achieve that status. Camel's Hump, farther north in Vermont, is lower but colder and thus does reach above treeline. In 1915 a fire (probably a human accident at the summit house) swept the Killington summit clear of trees. Enjoy it while you can: the balsam fir are coming back. There are no alpine wildflowers here, but you may spot the Bicknell's thrush, Blackpole warbler, or dark-eyed junco in the krummholz, birds typical of above-treeline areas. In truly isolated areas of the krummholz summit, bobcats may sometimes be spotted, hunting for smaller mammals.

Soil is thin or gone altogether at the top. Indeed, at higher elevations soil doesn't form. The organisms needed to break down leaf or needle mold aren't functional here. With few or no deciduous trees up top, the leaf mold that turns to soil in the lower forest is missing. Moreover, whereas deciduous trees take CO_2 from the atmosphere and put it into roots and soil, augmenting the breakdown of rocks into soil by carbonic acid, the conifers that live up top do not.

The rocks you will scramble over and sit on atop Killington are very hard, weather-resistant quartzite. In the lowlands, the underlying gneiss is more erodable. With thin soil and

per se to confirm the top. In the spruce forest are many much larger trees than seen below; the terrain is too rugged to have allowed much logging. This section will show you why Hike #25 is not for small children or people who are badly out of shape. After a good deal of difficult hiking over roots, large rocks, and some wet, boggy spots (in a sometimes eroded trail bed), the trail reaches Consultation Point (5.5 mi.). There's only one problem: no point. Indeed you may find yourself "consulting" the maps and your partners about its location. Perhaps it's a reflection of the mapmakers' own uncertainty that the GMC guides say the elevation is 3520 ft. while the ATC guide says 3760 ft. One way to iden-

hard rock underneath, it's a wonder anything grows here, but the young balsams manage to take a foothold. Gnarled and stunted, they look like krummholz, though botanical purists would say not so. You would have to go higher, say to Mt. Washington in New Hampshire, to see the real thing. The Killington balsams are young and growing slowly (from 1915 and after) in the harsh cold and wind. The colder the air, the less moisture it can hold. Thus, cold mountaintop winds, even in this snowy area, can dry out a conifer and kill it — unless the tree is lucky enough to be buried all winter by the snow. Oddly, the evergreens common to high New England elevations (balsam fir, red spruce) have some traits in common with desert plants: Like desert succulents, they have waxy needles, capable of conserving water in those dry winter winds; also, like a cactus, they have a single, tall, straight trunk, anchored in the wintertime frozen soil; yet their branches are highly flexible, springing up to resume life when the snow melts away. A sugar maple, by contrast, the common tree of the lower transitional forest, is a brittle wood with twisted branches, unsuited to survival at the top.

Overall, says David Laing, the health of the Killington forest is good, with little impact from acid rain. But human development of the mountain has brought other changes. Blowdowns are more common along the ski trails, where gusty winds buffet trees that otherwise would have protection in the forest. The ski trails, many of which are hikable, offer abundant wildflower displays, but many of these flowers are aliens that grow only in the open, sunny areas, not in the dark, cooler forest. Taller red, blue, and purple flowers on the ski trails attract alien European bees for pollination. Compare these to low-lying whiter flowers in the forest, like the common wood sorrel, which is pollinated by flies and moths. The taller flowers on ski trails also use the windier conditions to help seed dispersal.

With David Laing or any of the Merrell Hiking Center guides, rich conversation about the natural history of Killington can go on entertainingly for hours.

tify the spot is to call it the sharp left turn onto the eastern slope of Little Killington—a turn that precedes (by a few minutes) the beginning of a brief descent. Consultation Point is thus a non-event. Press on another 10 min. to the crossing of a ski trail, where you can enjoy the sun during a well-deserved rest and snack.

Shortly after the AT/LT re-enters the woods, at 5.9 mi., Shrewsbury Peak Trail branches off to the right (the AT/LT has now reached 3670 ft.). This well-traveled trail leads to a reliable spring in about 300 ft. (refill here before ascending Killington) and continues 2.0 mi. to the peak (3720 ft., impressive vistas to south and east) and another 1.8 mi. down to CCC Rd. in the valley at a point 3.0 mi. east of

North Shrewsbury. The traverse of Shrewsbury Peak is rugged; it is not an easy early exit option for AT/LT hikers. Shrewsbury Peak Trail makes a fine alternative hike, however, for those who want to climb Killington from east to west, for on the west side the Bucklin Trail heads down the mountain from Cooper Lodge on the AT/LT, just below the summit of Killington. See also Hike #26.

Surprisingly, the trail now levels out, ascending gently across the southwest side of Killington proper. To the left are hints of the views to come up top. Through a thick coniferous forest, patches of light from the valley far below reveal distant horizons, but only for a moment before the trees close in again. Such darkness in the forest precludes much plant life in the understory. You will have noticed waving grasses and wildflowers out on the ski trails, but little grows underfoot here in the high-elevation forest. Deep snows linger far into springtime here, and the cooler temperatures make it an inhospitable territory for the delicate plants we're used to seeing lower down. The very sound of your footsteps tells another part of the geological story. Spruce needles may soften the path somewhat, but there's only a thin layer of topsoil above bedrock (which shows through in many places). Many steps will have a dull thud as the sound reverberates from the underlying rock. After a mile of this interesting traverse, the AT/LT arrives at the Killington Spur (7.0 mi., 3870 ft.) and a decision point.

Weather permitting, you will want to go up the spur trail to the summit. In bad or threatening weather, the climb is not advised. Let's consider the lodging and camping here first, for those who plan to stay overnight or those unlucky few who arrive here and are forced to bivouac.

The AT/LT does not go over the actual summit of Killington. Just downhill (100 ft.) from the spur junction is Cooper Lodge, a good-size stone and wood cabin offering shelter and camaraderie. Inside are twelve bunks and a table, and room enough for packs on a rainy day. Heavily used, Cooper Lodge is a bit the worse for wear (and it's somewhat long in the tooth, built in 1939) but still serviceable. No other shelter on the Long Trail is positioned higher. Two springs provide water (north on AT/LT or west on Bucklin Trail). Expect to pay a small fee if the caretaker is in residence. A few tent sites, with platforms, are located up and behind the lodge, in the spur trail direction. Because camping is not allowed on Killington's summit, Cooper Lodge (or a tent site) is the only choice for those wanting to overnight here. Arrive early to secure your space.

For the final climb to the peak, rev up your engines (chocolate helps) and adjust your pack to move the weight higher on your back. You will soon be scrambling over rocks on a precipitous pitch, and you won't want to tip backward. The spur trail rises quickly, still among spruce, over rock steps and boulders. Quickly too the trees are noticeably shorter, and shorter, until, as you begin to leave the woods altogether, they shrink to krummholz size, miniature trees or giant bonsai.

Take care to supervise kids now. And stay close to anyone who is shaky about climbing rocks in a steep, exposed location. The views are immediately awesome, but they get better, so keep going. Blazes are few on the rocks, but a well-used path, with a few options all tending in the same direction, draws you upward. In fog, clouds, or high wind (all common at this elevation), watch the path carefully. As the trail nears the very summit, small cairns help somewhat, but on the rounded mountaintop, the blazes seem to disappear altogether. You will know you're there when there is no more "up" (elevation: 4241 ft.) and when the quiver of radio, TV, and telephone antennae are dead ahead and a few feet down.

If your prayers for good weather have been answered, you'll have the finest views the AT can offer in Vermont: Green Mts. running south to north, including the one you're standing on; the Connecticut River valley to the east, with the White Mts. in New Hampshire beyond; the Taconic Range on the New York border, west, with the Lake Champlain valley north of that, and the Adirondacks beyond. Stay as long as you can. There are excellent views from the summit ski lodge, minutes away, but not as excellent as these. For notes about the boreal forest and the "above treeline" environment of Killington Peak, see "Killington's Boreal Summit."

To continue north on the AT/LT, retrace your steps down the spur trail to Cooper Lodge. The AT/LT going north is being relocated (1998) slightly to the west (for about a mile) to avoid the ski trails between here and Ram's Head. See Hike #26 for more details.

To reach the Killington gondola, or the ski trails to walk down, descend the summit rocks, skirting the left side of the antennae house, and join a well-marked trail that wends its way over boulders and past nature trail stations. Within minutes the sounds of the gondola and lodge rise up through the thin woods, and after a short drop onto a ski area maintenance road, look left and you will see the lodge.

Inside the spacious building are toilets, a snack bar, tables, phones ... and people. Order that cup of hot chocolate you've been contemplating as a reward for reaching the peak, and pass through the big dining room out onto the deck for another dose of world-class mountain views. If you plan to use the gondola for a ride down, be sure to arrive at the summit lodge by 3:30 p.m. to buy a ticket (about $10) and to enjoy the summit before hopping aboard. The most popular (easiest) hiking route down to the base lodge — as suggested by the Merrell Hiking

Center—is Warbler Trail, 1.5 mi., mostly on an unpaved road (used also by mountain bikers: caution). Pick up a free Merrell Hiking Center map at the summit lodge, the base lodge, or by request at 802-422-6708. The walk down Warbler takes 1 to 1½ hr.; there are numerous other descent options, several of them far more challenging and well off the roads and ski trails. But the ski trails offer the best views. You can hike down for free. The gondola ride is an unusual treat, on the other hand, and it's a whole lot kinder on the knees.

At the base lodge you will find similar services plus hiking gear (to rent or buy) at the Merrell store. Perhaps even more valuable than the gear is the advice and instruction Merrell's guides can offer on short walks and long ones, on a large network of trails of varying degrees of difficulty. Let them know what you need; it's an accommodating service. A free summit circle nature hike is offered daily, weather permitting. The Merrell guides know their rocks, plants, and animals inside and out.

Hikers may park at the base lodge with permission from the Merrell Hiking Center. It is 2 mi. from the base lodge, down Killington Access Rd., to US 4 (east–west) and VT 100 (north–south). Some of the many restaurants and shops in the extensive ski village along the access road are open in summer and fall.

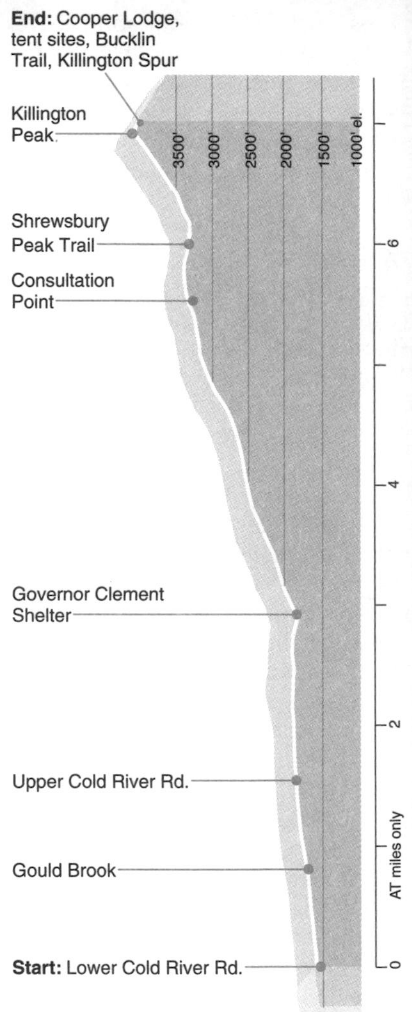

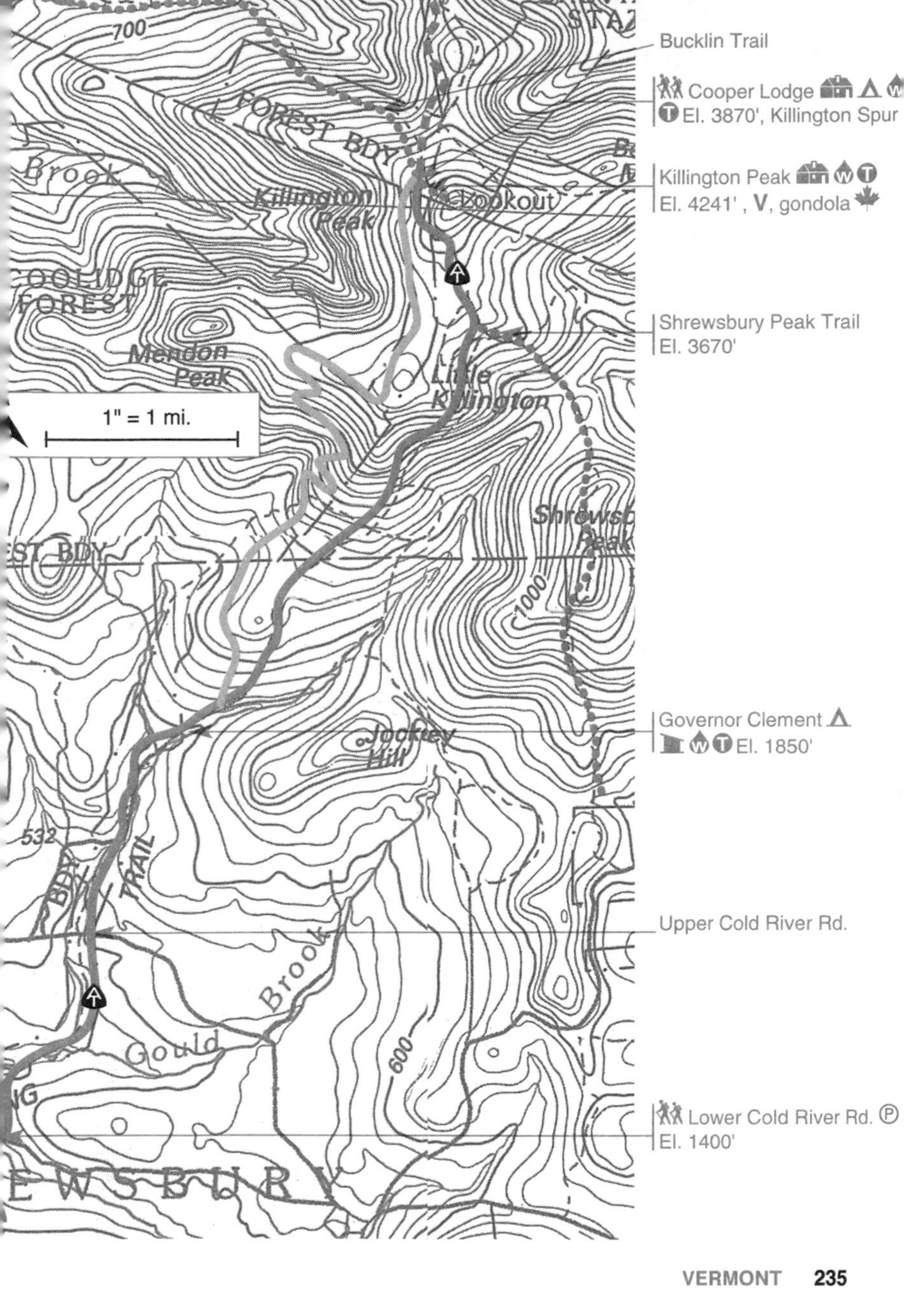

Bucklin Trail
Cooper Lodge
El. 3870', Killington Spur
Killington Peak
El. 4241' , V, gondola
Shrewsbury Peak Trail
El. 3670'
Governor Clement
El. 1850'
Upper Cold River Rd.
Lower Cold River Rd.
El. 1400'
700
FOREST BDY
Brook
Killington Peak
Lookout
COOLIDGE FOREST
Mendon Peak
Little Killington
1" = 1 mi.
1000
Jockey Hill
532
TRAIL
Brook
Gould
600

HIKE #25 Itinerary

Miles N	NORTH	Elev. (ft./m)	Miles S
Total: 7.3 mi. with spur trail to peak and gondola			
7.0	**End: Killington Spur,** at **Cooper Lodge** and tent sites, water, privy; side trail 0.2 mi. up to Killington Peak (4241 ft.), view; about 0.1 mi. farther to gondola (ride to base lodge, hiker parking).	3870/1180	0.0
5.9	**Shrewsbury Peak Trail,** 2.0 mi. to Shrewsbury peak (3720 ft.), 1.8 mi. farther to CCC Rd. to North Shrewsbury.	3670/1119	1.1
5.5	**Consultation Point,** no view.	3520/1073	1.5
2.9	**Governor Clement Shelter** and campsite, water, privy; use discouraged.	1850/564	4.1
1.5	**Upper Cold River Rd.** (gravel), 2.4 mi. E to North Shrewsbury; early exit option.	1630/497	5.5
0.8	**Gould Brook,** ford.	1480/451	6.2
0.0	**Start: Lower Cold River Rd.,** 2.4 mi. W of North Shrewsbury, overnight parking .	1400/427	7.0

SOUTH

HIKE: #26

Killington Peak—North

Maps: ATC N.H. & Vt. #6; GMC LT #8 & #9

Route: From Sherburne Pass to Pico Peak to Killington Peak; optional descent via gondola or ski trail. (*Note:* AT/LT trail relocation planned for 1998–99.)

Recommended direction: N to S

Distance: 5.4 mi., 5.7 mi to Killington Peak

Access trail name & length: Killington Spur and link to gondola, 0.3 mi.

Elevation +/-: 2150 to 3870 ft. (4241 ft. at peak)

Effort: Moderate to strenuous

Day hike: Yes

Overnight backpacking hike: Optional

Duration: 4 to 4½ hr.

Early exit option: None

Natural history features: Boreal zone; "above" treeline at Killington Peak

Other features: Pico alpine slide; Merrell Hiking Center (see Hike #25)

Trailhead access: *Start:* US 4, Sherburne Pass, across from Long Trail Inn, overnight parking; 9.3 mi. W of US 7, Rutland, 1.4 mi. E of VT 100. *End:* Cooper Lodge on AT, Killington Mt.; or Killington ski area base lodge via gondola from Killington Peak; hiker parking.

Camping: Pico Camp; Cooper Lodge and tent sites

Before taking Hike #26, up or down Killington Mt.'s north side, we suggest you read Hike #25 about the southern ascent of Killington. Included there is a good deal of information about the natural history of the mountain and its wild weather. You will need to be well aware of that information to prepare yourself prudently. For while Hike #26—if taken as described here, a north–south excursion—starts out in benign and gently rolling woods, by the time it reaches the gloriously exposed top of Killington, there is nothing between you and the weather but the clothes on your back and the boots on your feet. The best views in southern New England await you at the top, but don't be surprised if you also find the strongest winds and thickest fog.

Hike #26 works well too as a south-to-north affair, either as a continuation of a full traverse of Killington or as a day hike begun with an exhilarating ride up in the Killington gondola from the base lodge. Ambitious hikers may want to ascend and descend in the same day, walking up the AT/LT and down one of the many hiking trails that weave among the ski trails at Killington. See Hike #25 for information about the Merrell Hiking Center at the Killington base lodge (free mountain trail maps).

The Bucklin Trail (see below) offers another way down from Killington summit, without passing through the busy ski center at the top. And a trail relocation on this north side of Killington will add still more options (see "Trail Relocation").

At the US 4 crossing (Sherburne Pass), the AT/LT skirts the hiker/skier parking lot at Long Trail Inn (north side of highway). For over 50 years this modest hostelry has accommodated thru-hikers and other AT aficionados with basic motel rooms, a restaurant, and a cheerful Irish pub. Stop in and try a glass of the locally brewed Long Trail Ale, an amber delight for thirsty foot travelers. If you park here, cross to the south side of US 4, using extreme caution. A larger AT/LT parking lot is on the south side at the trailhead.

The walk to the top of Killington on this northern side is measurably easier than on the southern flank of the mountain. For one thing, the trail begins at 2150 ft. elevation, more than halfway up the mountain. And it's a shorter, less rugged route as well—only 5.7 mi. over the peak to the Killington gondola. Still, you will know you have done some work by the time the trail reaches Killington Peak, and as described in Hike #25, the last bit of scrambling over exposed rocks at the summit is enough to give any hiker a reason to applaud.

David Emblidge

Black bear, foraging

Heading south, the AT/LT leaves the parking lot, enters mixed deciduous hardwood forest, soon crosses an old road, and passes on the left the remains of the original Long Trail Lodge. Just under a mile ahead, after easy climbing on a relatively smooth path, a side trail goes right 0.1 mi. to the Pico alpine slide. Small kids who are not yet long-distance hikers might enjoy a walk to this point followed by a fast slide down the mountain; call Killington at 802-422-3333 to confirm that it's operating.

Shortly after the side trail there is a stream crossing at Sink Hole Brook (1.1 mi.). Another chance for water resupply comes along at 2.1 mi. at a spring to the right of the footpath, just before the trail arrives at Pico Junction—where the AT/LT uses a ski trail to gain a few hundred feet in a hurry before scooting back into the forest. But not for long: at 2.5 mi., in an opening with very good views, stands Pico Camp, a fine rest stop.

Clinging to the shoulder of Pico

Trail Relocation

For many years the AT/LT has passed over the shoulder of Killington Mt., heading north, and then has aimed for the shoulder of Pico ("pie-ko") Peak, a neighboring ski mountain. There was a decade-long period of sometimes rancorous debate about how to keep the trail in a wilderness area while still giving hikers access to the heavily developed summits. Skiers of course would favor carving exciting ski trails out of the forested peak areas. Hikers would prefer to leave them alone. In the mid-1990s the rapidly expanding American Ski Co. became owners of both Killington and Pico ski areas. Other players were the city of Rutland, the U.S. Park Service, and the Appalachian Trail Conference. They all struck a deal providing for an interesting compromise on the land use issue at Killington and Pico peaks.

Seven miles of the official AT/LT will be relocated in a 3000-acre wilderness area (frequented by black bear) to the west of the original trail, and the original trail (renamed Pico Trail) will remain open (though probably with less trail maintenance). The ski company will construct new lifts and trails connecting Killington and Pico. The northbound AT/LT will branch off from the established route at a point about 0.5 mi south of Pico Camp and head west of Pico for a crossing of US 4 about 1.0 mi. west of Sherburne Pass and the Long Trail Inn, where the historical AT/LT has always crossed the highway. The new trail is to be open in 1998 or 1999. A new shelter or campsite is under consideration for the trail section between Ram's Head and Pico Peak. Overnight parking will be available at the new US 4 crossing.

With both the old and new trail sections open, hikers will have a day-hike loop option, beginning and ending at the old and new trailheads on US 4, and reaching into the mountains either to Pico Peak or all the way to Killington Peak. Exact mileages and elevations will be provided in the next edition of this book and in the ATC and GMC guides.

Peak, the camp is actually a cabin with space for twelve, a welcome respite from the wind on cold days. A spring is just seconds back (north) on the AT/LT. Relaxing on the rocky lawn in front of the cabin, hikers get a preview of the day's target, Killington Peak (to the south), and, farther away, Mt. Ascutney (to the southeast). Killington is the high point in the Coolidge Range, which includes Pico to the north and Shrewsbury to the south. Why "Coolidge"? Because Silent Cal, the thirtieth president of the United States, grew up in nearby Plymouth Notch. Jim Chase's *Backpacker Magazine's Guide to the Appalachian Trail* wryly quotes Theodore Roosevelt's "acerbic" daughter, Alice Longworth, who "once described [Coolidge] as looking like he'd been 'weaned on a pickle'; informed of his death, she quipped, 'How can you tell?'"

In heavy traffic periods, expect to find a caretaker at Pico Camp. He or she can tell you about the efforts of the hiking clubs to manage the fragile natural environment at these high Green Mt. elevations (3400 ft. here). Overnighters at Pico Camp should expect to pay a small fee.

If your hike started early in the day, and if weather and ambition are working for you, the 0.4-mi. side trail, Pico Link, from the cabin up to the top of Pico Peak (3957 ft.), is worth the effort —and it is an effort because it gains its 557 ft. rapidly. The payoff is another set of terrific views, and if you're a peak bagger, one more mountain to add to the "been there, done that" list. Bear in mind, though, that Pico is a developed ski mountain. The top is crowned (or blemished) by a gondola. Without the gondola, however, there would be no cleared area for that great view.

Carrying on from Pico Camp, the AT/LT follows the broad shoulder and ridge between Pico and Killington. For what seems like a long time the trail neither rises nor falls noticeably, wandering through red spruce and hemlock and pine, their needles making for a soft walk underfoot. The woods here are dense, and except in late fall or early spring there will be few glimpses of the distant horizon. Under these circumstances it's best to look for interesting things close at hand. Break out the bird book, the wildflower book, the camera, or the hand lens. Once, passing through here, we were startled by the thumping of a ruffed grouse and its explosive liftoff from the forest floor, just a few feet away. Wild turkey are plentiful here as well. Keep an eye peeled for scat on the trail: deer, bear, moose, or other small mammals. If animal footprints in muddy sections are still sharply defined or still hold water from a recent rain, you may be able to spot the animal grazing nearby.

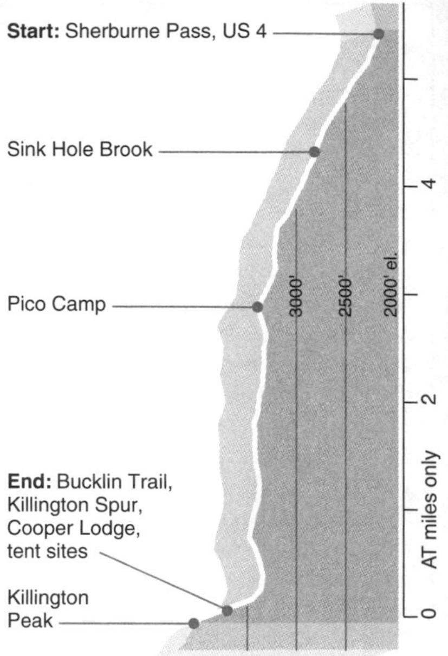

The trail climbs easily, passing fairly close to the top of Ram's Head and its ski lift (you may not see it), and very close to the top of Snowden Peak and its lift (a better chance of noticing this

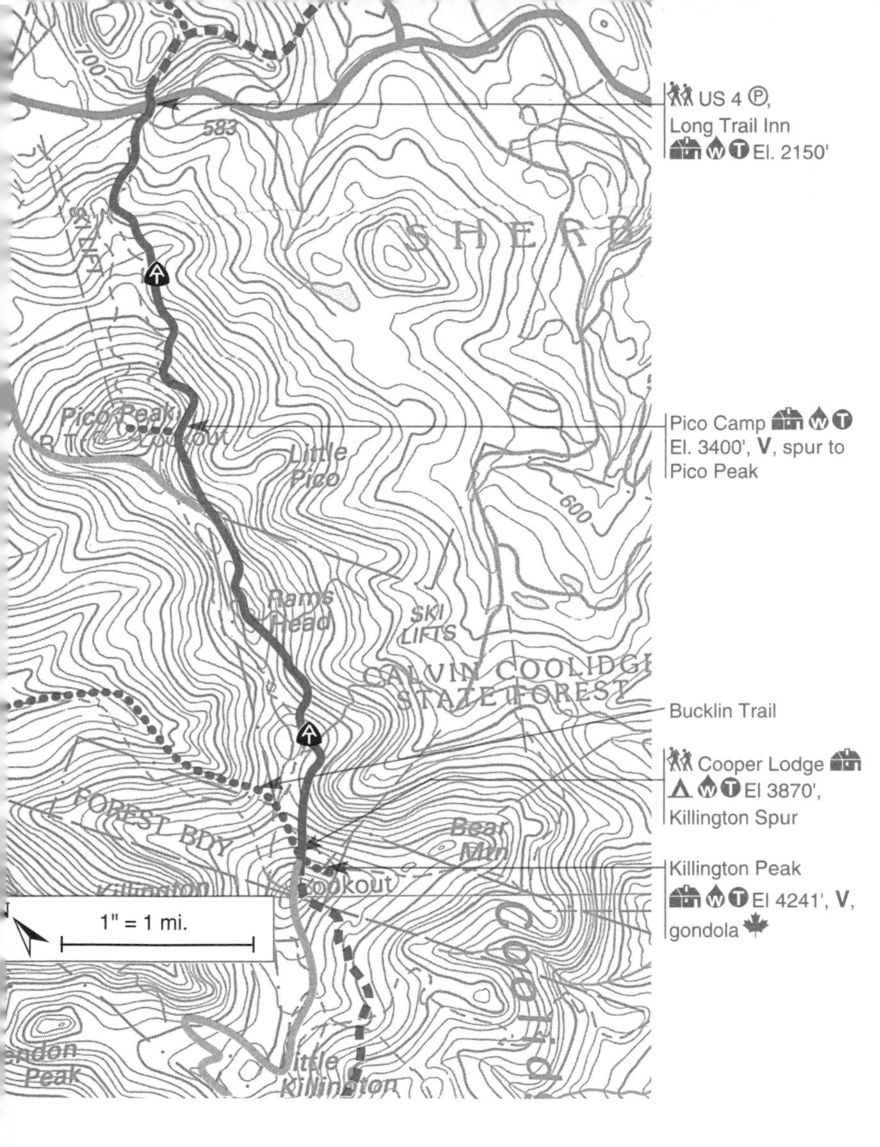
US 4 Ⓟ,
Long Trail Inn
El. 2150'
Pico Camp
El. 3400', V, spur to
Pico Peak
Bucklin Trail
Cooper Lodge
El 3870',
Killington Spur
Killington Peak
El 4241', V,
gondola
583
Pico Peak
Little Pico
600
Rams Head
SKI LIFTS
Bear Mtn
FOREST BDY
1" = 1 mi.

one). Drop down briefly and then reascend, from here on with increasing steepness, on the actual cone of Killington Mt.

At 5.4 mi., after a short period of huffing and puffing, you will reach Bucklin Trail, entering on the right. This trail runs 3.4 mi. back down the mountain to Wheelerville Rd. (parking at a distinct turn called Brewers Corners). It offers an alternative return to the highway, attractive to those who would like a loop hike with a two-car setup.

At the Bucklin Trail junction, the AT/LT passes hard by Cooper Lodge, left, a surprisingly large stone and log structure, somewhat the worse for wear, with space for twelve. Further details on the lodge and its nearby tent sites are given in Hike #25.

From Cooper Lodge, the ascent to the top of Killington follows the same path (Killington Spur) as described in Hike #25. Various options for descending via gondola or ski trails are also described there.

The next few minutes of steep climbing up the Killington Spur—out of the diminishing woods, into the krummholz, and beyond even that to the fully exposed rocky peak—will challenge most hikers and thrill many. It's well worth the effort and the touch of sublime terror that may come with it. The same fair warning as offered in Hike #25 applies: If bad weather has overtaken the mountain, especially thunderstorms or icy conditions, stay off the summit. Either wait out the storm at Cooper Lodge or resign yourself to a walk back down. In good weather, go for it. The top of Killington, at 4241 ft., though not officially on the AT/LT, is the highest point reached by any hike in this book.

HIKE #26 Itinerary

Miles N	NORTH	Elev. (ft./m)	Miles S
Total: 5.7 mi. with spur trail to peak and gondola			
5.4	**Start: US 4,** Sherburne Pass, across from Long Trail Inn, overnight parking; 9.3 mi. W of US 7, Rutland, 1.4 mi. E of VT 100. (*Note:* AT/LT trail relocation planned for 1998–99.)	2150/655	0.0
4.3	**Sink Hole Brook.**	2880/878	1.1
3.3	Spring.		2.1
2.9	**Pico Camp,** cabin, water, privy, view; side trail, **Pico Link,** 0.4 mi. W to Pico Peak, view, 3957 ft.	3400/1037	2.5
0.0	**Bucklin Trail,** W, 3.4 mi. to Wheelerville Rd. (then N to US 4).		5.4
0.0	**End: Killington Spur,** at **Cooper Lodge** and tent sites, water, privy; side trail, 0.2 mi. up to Killington Peak (4241 ft.), view; about 0.1 farther to gondola (ride to base lodge, hiker parking).	3870/1180	5.4

SOUTH

HIKE: #27

Killington to Woodstock

Maps: ATC N.H. & Vt. #5; GMC LT #9

Route: Sherburne Pass / US 4 to Maine Junction, to Gifford Woods State Park, to Kent Pond, to Stony Brook Shelter, to Lakota Lake Lookout, to Winturri Shelter, to VT 12 (Barnard Gulf Rd.), Woodstock

Recommended direction: S to N (described here) or N to S

Distance: 21.6 mi.

Elevation +/-: 2150 to 1214 to 2550 to 1360 to 2640 to 882 ft.

Effort: Moderate to strenuous

Day hike: Optional shorter loops

Overnight backpacking hike: Yes

Duration: 12 to 12½ hr.

Early exit option: Gifford Woods State Park, VT 100, at 1.5 mi.; Thundering Brook Rd., at 2.6 mi.; River Rd., at 4.0 mi.; Stony Brook Rd., at 8.9 mi.

Natural history features: Old-growth forest at Gifford Woods State Park; Kent Pond; Chateaugay Wilderness

Other features: Winter hiking and skiing from Mountain Meadows Inn

Trailhead access: *Start:* US 4, Sherburne Pass, across from Long Trail Inn, overnight parking; 9.3 mi. W of US 7, Rutland, 1.4 mi. E of VT 100. (*Note:* AT/LT trail relocation planned for 1998–99.) *End:* VT 12 (Barnard Gulf Rd.), overnight parking (W side); 4.2 mi. N of Woodstock.

Camping: Tucker Johnson Shelter; Gifford Woods State Park (car camping); Stony Brook Shelter; Winturri Shelter

Lodging: Mountain Meadows Inn

Don't be put off by the 21.6-mi. length of Hike #27. Although the AT passes through a sustained wilderness between Killington and Woodstock, there are good day hikes at the south and north ends of this overnight backpacking trip. In fact, with car-camping possibilities at Gifford Woods State Park and lodging right on the trail at both the Long Trail Inn and Mountain Meadows Inn, this section is particularly appealing to day hikers.

All hikers must bear in mind that shortly after the start of the hike, the Appalachian Trail and Long Trail part company, the LT heading north to Canada (165 mi.), the AT turning east toward New Hampshire. By the compass, the AT then runs west-to-east until it crosses the Connecticut River into New Hampshire. However, even when the compass direction is actually *easterly,* AT lingo says that the trail is going *north* because the overall direction is north, toward Maine and the terminus at Mt. Katahdin.

Day hikes from south end: US 4 to

Maine Junction, to Gifford Woods State Park (old-growth trees), to Thundering Brook Rd. (at Mountain Meadows Inn), 2.6 mi.; or continue to River Rd., 4.0 mi. total (distances are one-way). Additional day hikes can combine AT miles and short trips northward on the Long Trail.

Day hikes from north end: Round-trip of 12.2 mi. from VT 12 to The Lookout and back. Or a two-car loop from VT 12 to the Lookout, then back on AT to Lookout Farm Rd., and down this road to unofficial roadside parking and a short drive to the AT trailhead on US 4.

A backpacking trip through these 21.6 mi. can be a 2- or 3-day affair. Take note of the shelters described below.

Heading from south to north, the trail plunges into the mixed forest off US 4 at Sherburne Pass. The busy highway's noise will be with you for the first hour or so of the trip, but try to put mind over matter: concentrate on what you can see, and use your ears later on in the hike. Modest climbing begins immediately on the well-worn path. Deer Leap Trail splits off to the left 150 ft. up the trail (to join the Long Trail 1.3 mi. farther north, after passing over Deer Leap Cliffs 0.5 mi. from here—worth the detour for those with plenty of time).

Just 0.5 mi. up the AT/LT, a large rock and an equally impressive trail sign mark Maine Junction, the famous spot where the northbound Long Trail finally departs from the Appalachian Trail. Following the Long Trail will lead you to Tucker Johnson Shelter (1.3 mi. ahead) and eventually to Canada; following the AT will take you to New Hampshire and on to Maine.

Doris Gove

Painted trillium

Continuing on the AT, after a short climb and descent, look on the right for a side trail to Ben's Balcony, from which you can catch glimpses of Pico and Killington peaks through the leafy trees. The trail wends its way downhill now, sharply in spots, to Gifford Woods State Park. First the trail passes the upper car-camping area, then a picnic area; just beyond, water and toilets are available. CCC architecture buffs may want to seek out the park's administration building, in stone and timber. After ambling downhill through the camping area, the AT meets VT 100 (1.7 mi).

Excitement lies just ahead: a natural-history rarity, a 12-acre stand of old-growth trees. Cross VT 100, walk about 300 ft. south on the road, and pass through a good day or overnight parking area. Continue on the AT

Autumn Color: Magic and Chemistry

*October is the month for painted leaves. Their rich glow now flashes 'round the world. As fruits and leaves and day itself acquire a bright tint just before they fall, so the year near its setting. October is its sunset sky; November the later twilight.**

What makes the leaves change to such dramatic colors come fall? Anything this good must have a secret formula behind it. Nature writer Edward Abbey explains that the key variable is chlorophyll, "performing the vital synthesizing of sunlight and earth that underlies all life on this planet." In autumn, anticipating winter freezes, a tree, like a savvy householder closing the summer cottage, shuts down its water lines. The sap ceases to flow and the chlorophyll stops functioning. "As the green wastes away from each leaf, the other pigments, red, gold, orange, which had been present all the time but covered by the green, are now revealed, and in their infinitely variable combinations with remaining chlorophyll and other pigments such as the brown of tannin (most noticeable in oaks), the drying leaves produce the spectacle of . . . autumn. The leaves die, but the tree survives."

*Henry David Thoreau

toward Kent Pond (the park extends to this area). A small bridge takes the trail over a Kent Pond feeder stream. In the section just ahead, look about for hemlock, ash, basswood, beech, maple, and birch. Many of these trees are more than 100 ft. tall; some are 300 years old. There is an eastern hemlock over 400 years old, but you may need the park ranger's help to identify it—the office is near the park gate. Not surprisingly, this small but extraordinary forest is a favorite home and migratory stopover for a wide variety of birds. Waterfowl especially like it here, with the old forest and Kent Pond for feeding and safety.

In just moments, after passing a lovely cascade, left, the trail reaches the edge of the pond, which looks natural but isn't (a dam, built in 1965, holds back a stream on the far side). The AT follows the edge of the pond (stocked for fishing), and many places along the shore would make good picnic sites.

As the trail reaches the end of the pond and emerges from the woods onto a mowed lawn, look right to see a large red barn and a white clapboard farmhouse, converted some years ago into Mountain Meadows Inn. If you're lucky (or smart), you're staying here. While the rooms are not fancy, the meals are fine, the hosts unusually accommodating, and the other facilities (outdoor pool and Jacuzzi, sauna, canoes, kids' game room) are top-notch. When Mountain Meadows is not full to capacity, the innkeepers provide bunk space to four long-distance hikers per night at reduced rates.

The trail continues across the lawn, through immature trees to unpaved Thundering Brook Rd. (2.6 mi.), where limited day parking is feasible, roadside. The road is the access to Mountain Meadows Inn. US 4 is a mere 0.4 mi. south (right). This spot makes another good end point for a short day hike. But first enjoy one more treat: Walk north on Thundering Brook Rd., along the pond, and look back (southward) toward Pico and Killington peaks. The view is especially impressive early and late in hiking season, when both are likely to be snowcapped.

Leaving Thundering Brook Rd., the AT meanders through an easy section now, in sun-dappled woods where the understory is thin, giving birders good views through the trees. White-tailed deer are common here. The trail crosses several small streams, rises to a rocky knob, and begins a steady descent, coming out again onto Thundering Brook Rd. Then it turns right, following the road and a switchback to cross the Ottauquechee River. At 4.0 mi., it crosses unpaved River Rd., where limited day parking is possible. About 0.3 mi. to the right are Sherburne town hall (water and toilets) and the village swimming pool, open to the public ($2.50 per day). Better day-hiker parking here (get permission).

The real work begins now. The AT rises steeply from River Rd., using several switchbacks. Climb for half an hour, watching for a well-made set of rock steps and a leftward curve. Rest here, and if the leaves are partially down or gone, enjoy views of Killington Peak, other mountains in the Coolidge Range, and the Ottauquechee River valley. Climb again for another half mile to the wooded top of an unnamed hill, and carry on, following a ridge where the walking is easy and thermals on either side are likely to bring a welcome breeze. At a powerline clearing (5.9 mi.), go to the north side and look back again toward Killington for a good view of the entire ski basin. From this distance, you can easily identify the half-round shape of the glacial cirque that forms the larger part of Killington's ski area.

The easy ridge walk continues, a fine section for enthusiastic birders who want to be looking up, not down at a difficult trail. Second- and third-growth trees here are only modestly tall, and the understory is once again thin. Birding suggestions from David Laing, staff naturalist at the Merrell Hiking Center in Killington: At this elevation (about 2500 ft.), in a northern hardwood forest of sugar maple, beech, and yellow birch, you might look for the American redstart, which likes younger trees, or the black-throated blue warbler, which prefers older-growth trees. The wood thrush is common here. When you see dark, deep holes in decaying trees, look, or better yet listen, for the pileated woodpecker, whose drilling sound is like a drummer's stick on a wooden block. Beech trees yield beechnuts, a favorite food for bears: check the bark for claw marks or look around for scat. (See "Berkshire Bruins" in Hike #16 for more on black bears.)

The trail soon crosses a woods road, after which there's a fine stand of white birch and another briefly arduous climb on switchbacks. The roller-coaster ride continues, first over another unnamed hill, then down and up again, this time on the side of Quimby Mt., then down through a sag, and up to yet another unnamed hill at 2550 ft. and 7.3 mi. (no view), the divide between the watersheds of Ottauquechee River and Stony Brook. In our hike through here we found the trail poorly blazed, with many unremoved blowdowns.

From the high point (which is hard to identify on the trail, though a second stand of white birch is a possible marker), it's quickly downhill to a cascade (a pretty, sharply cut V in the rocks) on the left, a trickle in autumn but likely to be very lively in spring with runoff from melting snow.

Fatigue may have set in by now. Backpackers may want to use Stony Brook Shelter as their overnight accommodation. It was relocated to this area in 1997, and it makes a good overnight stop, roughly in the middle of this hike.

Beyond the shelter another vista appears, just before a log ladder takes the trail down off a rocky outcrop. And the drop-off continues into the valley of Stony Brook at 8.9 mi.

For a hike that never goes above 2700 ft., there is a lot of "up" here, with repeated short climbs and the even more tiring descents. The mountains east of Killington are composed of a different breed of rock. Chew's *Underfoot* notes that the waterfall back at the Kent Pond inlet is slate, "rock formed from mud, that breaks into thin, flat, angular sheets. The mud was laid down in a sea to the east perhaps 500 million years ago and then was heated, altering it to slate." This same slate can be found frequently along the AT between Killington and Woodstock. Chew's description: "steely grey . . . , shiny with mica flakes. The slate lies in flat, upturned sheets, crinkled in places and well exposed in stream valleys and road cuts."

An AT sign at Stony Brook Rd. announces trail mileages north and south. Limited parking is permitted here. Heading left, the road (unpaved) passes Notown, whose odd name, reports Preston Bristow of the Vermont Land Trust, is the result of a colonial-era "lotting" mistake. When the King of England was parceling out land, this 600-acre tract was missed, and *no town* claimed it. It became a popular place to live because there was no municipality to levy taxes. Logging was the primary industry. Tax nirvana disappeared in 1884 when Notown was conveyed to the township of Stockbridge. Most residents left (no surprise), and today Notown is indeed no town, just a remnant logging camp. It does offer a better parking area, however. In roughly 6.0 mi. Stony Brook Rd. reaches VT 107 west of Gaysville and east of Stockbridge (on VT 100). Thus, with two cars or a shuttle ride, a day hike could end here. To the right, the road soon deteriorates and may be impassable. Also to the right is a large cleared space for a current logging operation. If you park hereabouts, keep well off the road to avoid logging trucks.

Stony Brook itself is substantial and quite pretty. It marks the beginning of the Newell Wildlife Management Area. The trail crosses the brook on a bridge and 0.1 mi. farther crosses Mink Brook.

The trail climbs again, somewhat steeply, using switchbacks. Halfway up, a large log, left, hosts a colorful colony of fungi. Here as elsewhere in the southern New England woods, the interdependent plant families—fungi and lichen—can be seen on rock after rock, usually close to the ground. Stone walls are a good place to look as well. Lichens grow at an infinitesimal pace, 0.1 to 10 mm per year. Fortunately they are patient, with one to two *centuries* as an average life span. An alga and a fungus must work together to produce a lichen. Minerals are absorbed by the fungus from moisture and the rocks; the fungus provides shelter too. By photosynthesis, the alga turns sunlight into food for the lichen. Common lichens in the mixed hardwood forest are pixie cups (gray-green), worm lichen (thin, vertical), and British soldiers (red-capped).

Again the AT reaches and follows a ridge, narrow at first, then widening out on a smooth path for easy walking. You will hardly notice a height of land (2260 ft.) known locally as the "Continental Divide" (between two watersheds), around 10.7 mi. Here and there are brief westerly views. The trail rises and falls several times now. On one of the last descents, look for beautiful stands of striped maple, a tree whose green bark has vertical white stripes when young but turns all green when mature.

In due time the AT heads down to unpaved Chateaugay Rd. at 12.7 mi. "Chateaugay" is a sonorous name reflecting the 17th- and 18th-century French presence in Vermont— but, alas, anglicized, it's "shat-a-gee."

With due respect to the ATC's fine hiking guide for Vermont, we disagree that Chateaugay Rd. is practical as an access road for the AT. From either the south (US 4, Bridgewater Corners, via Center Rd.) or the north (VT 12, Morgan Corners, near Barnard), the connecting roads to Chateaugay are generally unmarked, the landmarks hard to find, and Chateaugay Rd. itself inappropriate for conventional cars. For the intrepid or those with four-wheel drive, there is limited parking at the Chateaugay Rd. trail crossing. We once saw a bear-hunting party's pickup truck here (and heard their several hounds as well).

Beyond the road, cross Locust Creek, climb a short hill, and come to another brook, where water may be more dependable. And then back to work: Another set of switchbacks carries the trail up through a handsome stand of evergreens, their needles softening the path. Near the top of the hill, the forest changes back to mixed hardwoods and passes through an extraordinary section of white birch. There are good southwest views at a few points here, and a more dramatic view at 13.8 mi., where the trail reaches Lakota Lake Lookout, the high point on this hike, at 2640 ft. On a good day, New Hampshire's White Mts. are visible to the east.

Another longish (1.7 mi.) ridge walk ensues, rolling gently up and down with the occasional steep spot, through handsome hardwood forest. Cross a woods road and carry on to Lookout Spur on the left at 15.5 mi. The spur is a wide path or woods road, leading onto private property. Hikers are welcome but must respect the cabin (locked) that sits atop the hill just ahead. If conditions are right (no thunderstorms brewing, no ice) and if vertigo is not your bête noir, scale the ladder on the side of the house to the lookout platform on the roof. From here a stunning panorama of eastern Vermont, the approaching Connecticut River valley, and the distant White Mts. is yours. On an autumn day here we spotted snow-capped Mt. Mansfield through the binoculars (northwest).

Return to the AT and follow a woods road sharply downhill—though it's easy walking—to the junction with Lookout Farm Rd. at 16.3 mi. This old dirt road (going left, down steeply) can be used as an

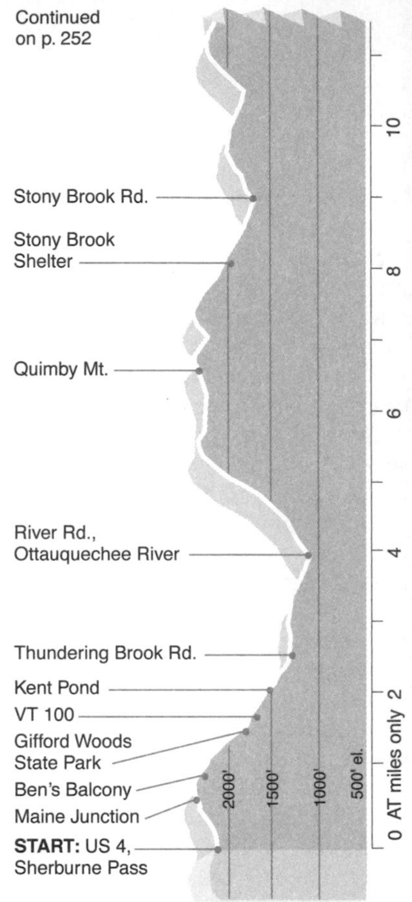

early exit (about 2.5 mi. to VT 12) or as a route to a second car for a day hike from the north end of Hike #27. To make this loop, descend about 0.5 mi. to meet the upper end of the developed road, where unofficial roadside parking is generally feasible (in a wet season you may need to hike 0.5 to 1 mi. farther to good road

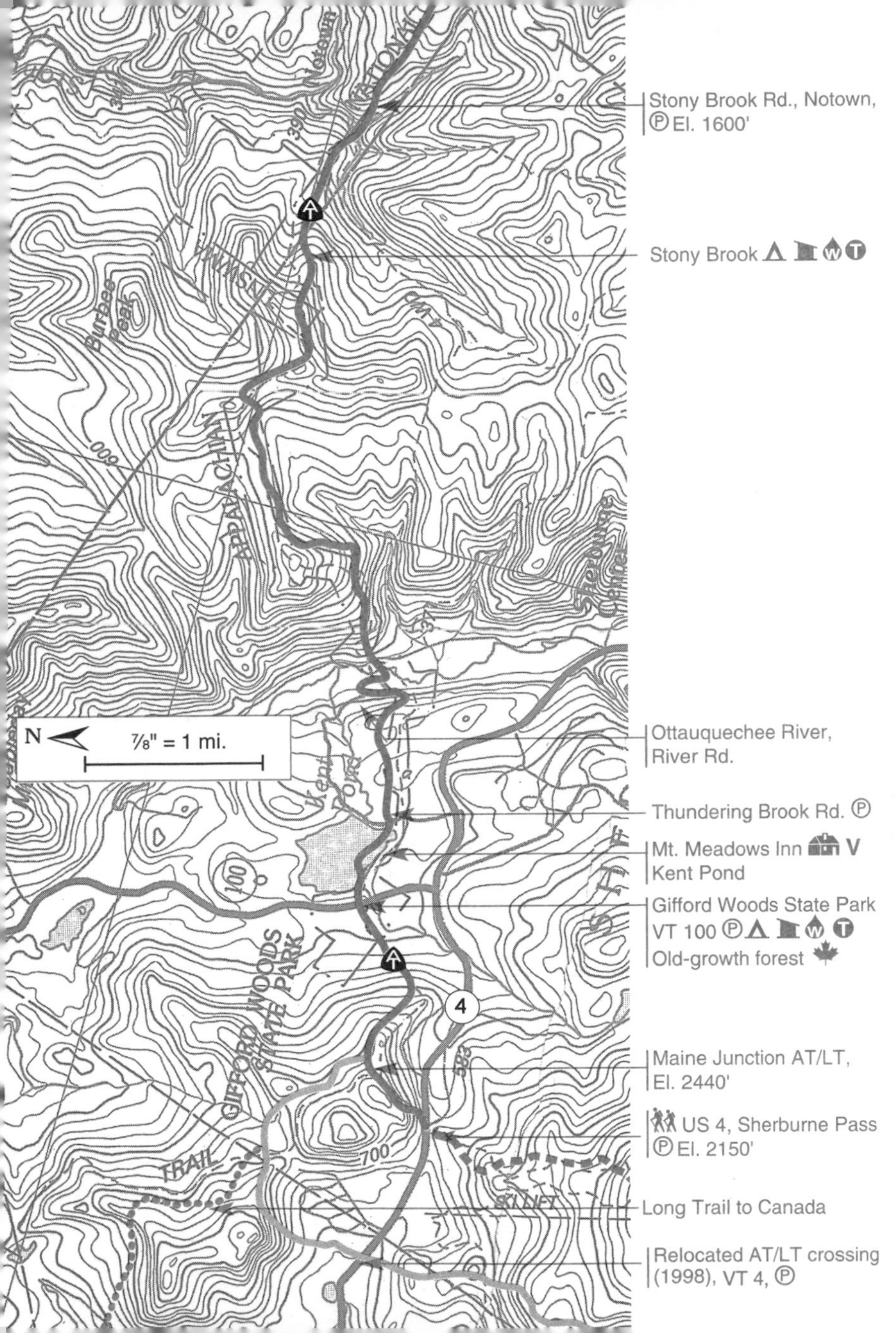

Stony Brook Rd., Notown,
Ⓟ El. 1600'
Stony Brook
Ottauquechee River,
River Rd.
Thundering Brook Rd. Ⓟ
Mt. Meadows Inn V
Kent Pond
Gifford Woods State Park
VT 100 Ⓟ
Old-growth forest
Maine Junction AT/LT,
El. 2440'
US 4, Sherburne Pass
Ⓟ El. 2150'
Long Trail to Canada
Relocated AT/LT crossing
(1998), VT 4, Ⓟ
N
7/8" = 1 mi.
APPALACHIAN
GIFFORD WOODS STATE PARK
TRAIL
Kent Pond
100
4
700

conditions). Follow Lookout Farm Rd. about 2 mi. to VT 12, turn right, and proceed another 2+ mi. to the AT trailhead parking (right).

Continuing on the AT, shortly beyond the junction, the trail goes right onto King Cottage Rd., and in 0.2 mi. veers left into the woods. The trail is climbing again now, here on the southern side of The Pinnacle. A nice view back to the southwest provides a rest spot on the way up.

Crossing over the hill (called Sawyer), the trail works its way easily down the other side and arrives at the side trail (left) to Wintturi Shelter at 17.9 mi. The spur goes downhill about 0.2 mi. to find the new shelter, well situated in an airy grove. There are no bunks, just floor space and a few scattered tent spaces. A hill blocks the chilling wind, and afternoon sun warms the area in front.

The final 3.7 mi. of Hike #27 offer an easy ride over rolling hills with several open views from clearings and the occasional grassy field. The trail is rocky at some points, a bit tiring to the knees, but never very steep. At 18.2 mi. a woods road (used by off-road vehicles) meets the trail. At a woods road crossing at 19.0 mi., look left for an old chimney and cellar hole. This area was no doubt cleared of trees 100 years ago. Ten minutes ahead there is a section of abundant mosses, and soon thereafter a huge fallen maple on the right—33 paces long in the trunk (imagine the lofty crown atop these 99 ft.). At 19.8 and 20.0 mi. fine views, including Mt. Ascutney, appear.

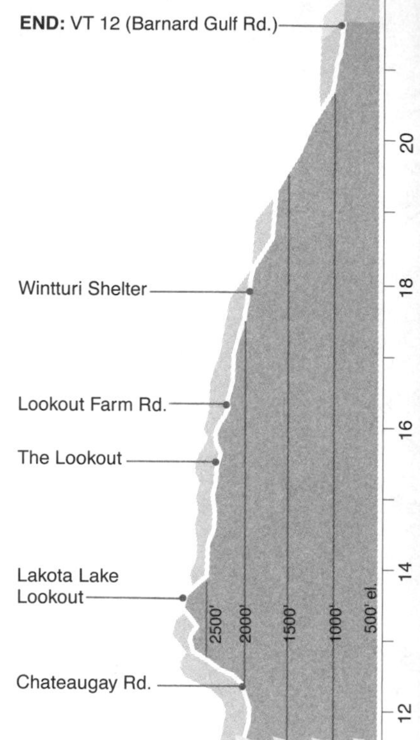

Either of these spots would make a good lunch rest for day hikers coming up from VT 12.

Traffic noise from the valley below is evident now. Broad open fields provide an easy path for the AT's descent. White-tailed deer leapt through shrubs here during our hike, a last sign of wilderness before civilization appeared at the highway and the AT parking lot. Woodstock is 4.2 mi. to the right (south) on VT 12 / Barnard Gulf Rd.; for the town's many attractions, see Hike #28.

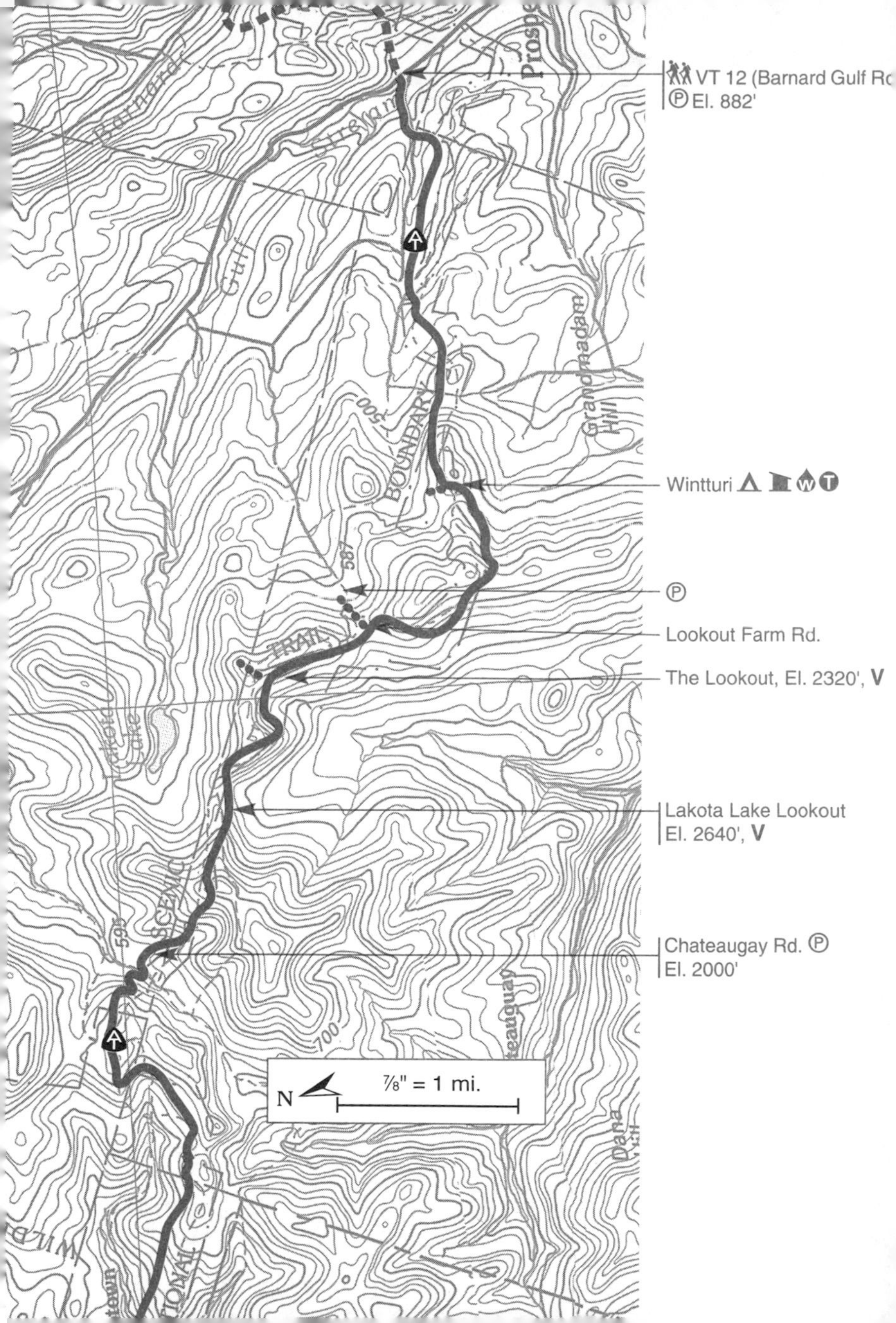

VT 12 (Barnard Gulf Rd
Ⓟ El. 882'
Wintturi
Ⓟ
Lookout Farm Rd.
The Lookout, El. 2320', V
Lakota Lake Lookout
El. 2640', V
Chateaugay Rd. Ⓟ
El. 2000'
N
⅞" = 1 mi.
Barnard
Gulf
Stream
Prospect
BOUNDARY
TRAIL
SCENIC
Grandmadam Hill
Dana Hill
Lakota Lake

HIKE #27 Itinerary

NORTH

Miles N		Elev. (ft./m)	Miles S
21.6	**End: VT 12** (Barnard Gulf Rd.), overnight parking.	882/269	0.0
17.9	Side trail, 0.2 mi. N to **Wintturi Shelter** and campsite, water, privy.	1900/579	3.7
16.3	**Lookout Farm Rd.** (dirt), parking about 5 mi. down road.	2200/671	5.3
15.5	Side trail, N, to **The Lookout,** view.	2320/707	6.1
13.8	**Lakota Lake Lookout,** view.	2640/805	7.8
12.7	**Chateaugay Rd.,** poor access, limited parking.	2000/610	8.9
10.7	High point on unnamed ridge.	2260/689	10.9
8.9	**Stony Brook** and Stony Brook Rd.; limited parking.	1600/488	12.7
7.8	**Stony Brook Shelter** and campsite, water, privy; relocated here 1997; mileage approx.		13.8
7.3	After steep climb, ridge walk to high point.	2550/777	14.3
4.0	**River Rd.** (gravel), limited day parking; 0.3 mi. S to Sherburne Ctr., US 4 & VT 100.	1214/370	17.6
2.6	**Mountain Meadows Inn;** then **Thundering Brook Rd.** (gravel), limited day parking; 0.4 mi. S to US 4 & VT 100.		19.0
2.1	**Kent Pond,** view, old-growth trees.	1540/469	19.5
1.5	**Gifford Woods State Park,** shelters, tent sites, water, toilets, fee. Cross **VT 100,** parking.	1660/506	20.1
0.8	**Ben's Balcony,** view.	2220/677	20.8
0.5	**Maine Junction.** Long Trail goes N to **Tucker Johnson Shelter** (1.3 mi.) and Canada; AT turns E toward NH.	2440/744	21.1
0.0	**Start: US 4,** Sherburne Pass, at Long Trail Inn, overnight parking.	2150/655	21.6

SOUTH

HIKE: #28

Woodstock to West Hartford

Maps: ATC N.H. & Vt. #5

Route: From VT 12 (Barnard Gulf Rd.) to Woodstock (Barnard) Stage Rd., to Pomfret–South Pomfret Rd., to Thistle Shelter, to Joe Ranger Rd., to Quechee–West Hartford Rd. and VT 14.

Recommended direction: S to N

Distance: 13.6 mi.

Elevation +/-: 882 to 1530 to 820 to 1480 to 390 ft.

Effort: Easy

Day hike: Yes

Overnight backpacking hike: Optional

Duration: 7 hr.

Early exit option: Woodstock (Barnard) Stage Rd., at 1.5 mi.; Pomfret–South Pomfret (County) Rd., at 3.7 mi.; Joe Ranger Rd., at 9.3 mi.

Natural history features: Vermont Raptor Center, Woodstock

Social history features: Federal architecture, Woodstock; Billings Farm and Museum, Woodstock

Trailhead access: *Start:* VT 12 (Barnard Gulf Rd.), overnight parking; 4.2 mi. N of Woodstock. *End:* Quechee–West Hartford Rd. (no parking) or VT 14 (day and overnight parking).

Camping: Thistle Hill Shelter

Hikers in the Woodstock area may have trouble tearing themselves away from the pleasures of this beautiful and stimulating town, famous for its Federal architecture and nowadays chock-full of restaurants and boutiques. Suggestions about in-town activities are included at the end of this description. Hike #28 is either an ambitious day hike of 13.6 mi. (the last mile is on a town road, leading to official day or overnight parking in West Hartford). The hike involves little serious up or down. It can also be an easy overnight backpacking trip, with the shelter located about 1 mi. beyond the halfway point. Or you could create a set of shorter, improvised day hikes. The overall hike is a delicious mix of hardwood forest and open fields, some with fine views and many with myriad wildflowers. At least three road crossings work as early exits, further augmenting the short day-hike options.

We begin the south-to-north walk (in AT lingo; by the compass it's more west-to-east) at the AT trailhead 4.2 mi. north of Woodstock on VT 12. Park on the west side of the road in a lot just downhill off the highway.

Long-distance walkers and thru-hikers may want to inquire about camping or bunking in the barn at Appalachian Trail House, the white clapboard farmhouse and red barn just north of the VT 12 crossing. Daniel T. Quinn is a hiker-friendly host who will exchange lodging for a few

David Emblidge

Trout lily

hours' help on the farm. Perhaps the main attraction here—other than the "price"—is a hot outdoor shower.

Follow VT 12 a few hundred feet south before entering the field and approaching the wooded hillside, heading east. It's a steep ascent from VT 12, through many white birch, but soon the grade moderates to an easy walk arriving at Dana Hill (1.2 mi.), an old farm meadow and a wildflower bonanza. There are pastoral views to the south from here. If you have time, stroll around the entire field. The northeast side displays an excellent stand of beech (look for beechnuts on the ground), while the southwest side has plentiful oaks (with acorns beneath). In springtime the old apple and pear trees show off a riot of blossoms. Watch for white-tailed deer and wild turkey, who like to feed here. The occasional bluebird and many swallows and thrushes can be seen in the meadow, particularly early and late in the day. In midsummer we found the field full of bluish light hovering above stands of viper's bugloss (a.k.a. blueweed). Hiding out (in the shade) just up the AT was a perfect yellow lady's-slipper.

The brief descent from Dana Hill is through light-filled hardwood forest, typical of Vermont elevations of around 2000 ft. Watch for the ruins of a farmhouse fireplace, left. In spring Dutchman's-breeches can be spotted along the trail. A red-headed woodpecker was busily banging away when we passed through. The trail runs gently along until the last few moments before it drops down to Woodstock (Barnard) Stage Rd. at 1.5 mi. The drop-off is on the north slope, where different conditions of light and moisture lead to different vegetation, all pine and no hardwoods. A very short day hike could end (or begin, going north–south) right here, although parking is improvised at roadside.

Climbing again, the AT soon reaches open views to the west, including the Suicide Six ski area. Re-entering the woods, the trail hops over a beautiful stone wall. *Underfoot,* by V. Collins Chew, notes that the rocks in this section of the AT are "coarser-grained, a rustier color, more varied, and younger . . . than the rock of the Green Mountains." Layers are more contorted but there are fewer outcrops; quartz is prominent, and mica crystals make extremely thin and shiny sheets, adds Chew. The trail now passes through a lovely pine grove. After a brook there is another field with even better views of the ski area. Descending from the field may be mucky: watch your step.

Cross a small gravel road (town hwy. #38), and rise and descend over another modest hill before reaching the gravel Bartlett Brook Rd. at 3.0 mi., with a small brook just beyond. The cock-a-doodle-doo of roosters from the farm next door may entertain you as the trail passes through this otherwise quiet, hidden valley. No parking here.

Back in the woods, the AT follows a fence and stone walls, left, as it traverses more farm fields, offering more sweet though not too distant views. At 3.7 mi. it reaches the next noteworthy road crossing, Pomfret–South Pomfret (County) Rd. No parking is allowed here. For thru-hikers seeking resupply, Teago's General Store and P.O. are 1.3 mi. south. A handsome brook at the road crossing provides a good place for a refreshing splash of cold water on a sweaty brow.

Rising again on another modest hill, the AT passes under towering pines. In this shady place the midsummer trail is graced by the delicate white blooms of common wood sorrel, with its shamrock-shaped leaves. Soon another meadow opens up with the best views yet of Suicide Six ski area and the western mountains beyond. Under the shade of young maples and sumac and amidst wild strawberries here, enjoy a rest or a snack, but save lunch for a better hill not far ahead.

Leaving the field, the trail briefly follows the old Kings Hwy., with an impressive stone wall on the right. Imagine the sounds of 18th- and 19th-century stagecoaches rumbling through here. After a brief ascent taking the trail out of the forest again, the bald-topped Dupuis Hill (at about 5.0 mi.) spreads out in all directions, its center marked by a cairn. For a relatively lowland section of the AT, the views from Dupuis are superb. Break out the compass and check these readings: Killington Peak at about 265° and Pico Peak at 275°. The views extend east into New Hampshire and far to the northwest. On a perfectly clear day, map aficionados may be able to pinpoint Mt. Mansfield, in the NW direction. Dupuis Hill is also another wildflower paradise, and thus it's home to butterflies, bees, and birds. One could easily spend the afternoon right here.

Down off the hill now for about half a mile through a beautiful glen and then mildly uphill again, bringing the AT at 5.5 mi. to unpaved Cloudland Rd., with a small red house on the right and a tiny brook. The old Cloudland Shelter was closed in 1997. Backpackers should carry on to its replacement, Thistle Hill Shelter, reached after a longish slog through relatively undistinguished woods, with a few minor ups and downs, at 7.5 mi., on the east side of Thistle Hill.

The 1995 ATC Trail Guide and 1996 Long Trail Guide call the new shelter "Cloudland," but on the trail itself it is signed as "Thistle Hill Shelter." Whatever its name, the new shelter is spa-

Vermont Raptor Center

At Woodstock's Vermont Institute of Natural Science (VINS), hikers with an interest in birds of prey will thoroughly enjoy a self-guided walk through the Vermont Raptor Center. Situated on Church Hill Rd., which branches off from the village green, VINS is an 80-acre nature preserve with marked trails, a research center, a bookstore, and an eager, friendly staff. Hawks, owls, eagles, peregrine falcons, and about twenty other species of raptors live here in spacious cages, most of them recovering from injury; some are protected here because they can no longer survive in the wild. Workshops, lectures, and field trips for kids and adults fill out an ambitious program at VINS. The Gordon Welchman Nature Trail is described in a nifty pamphlet, "Interrelationships," a fine introduction to the many fascinating ways that plants and animals depend on one another for survival. Call 802-457-2779 for details.

cious (but there are no bunks). Tenting should be easy here, given the flat terrain. There's no view, but the setting is a sun-dappled clearing in the woods. Farm machinery noise filters through the forest, a hint about the narrowness of the AT corridor. Water may be somewhat unreliable at this site. The stream (in two branches) is downhill about 300 yd. on a blue-blazed trail; go to the second branch at a little waterfall. In a dry season, bring water for overnighting here.

From Thistle Hill the AT proceeds easily downhill over the next several miles, generally in the forest, with welcome breaks in the meadows, where you are likely to see flocks of red-winged blackbirds. At Arms Hill especially, the pastoral views are excellent. Through tall summer grass in a second, giant field with a sharp drop-off, immediately to the right, the AT leads to switchbacks taking the trail down into the ravine traversed by Joe Ranger Rd. at 9.3 mi. Just left across the road is an old stone dam (and a pond above it). Limited parking is available about 0.1 mi. north at the intersection with Bunker Hill Rd.

Quickly the trail rises back up into woods, requiring a bit of work. The next hilltop, this one wooded, is Bunker Hill (Massachusetts residents may resent Vermont's appropriation of this famous Revolutionary War battlefield name). Out again into more fields, the AT provides views now of the white rock outcrops of New Hampshire mountains beckoning on the eastern horizon. The last of the big views (11.8 mi.), from yet another field, looks down into the I-89 and White River valley, toward West Hartford. The hike races toward its conclusion, steadily downhill through a mixed hardwood forest, passing a spur on the left marked "Half Penny

Inn B&B 0.3 mi.," known as another AT-friendly lodging.

The woodland miles of Hike #28 end at paved Quechee–West Hartford Rd. (12.6 mi.), where the AT turns left, heading past suburban houses to the bridge over the White River and the village center beyond. Day and overnight hiker parking is available at the Old West Hartford Village Store at VT 14, after the AT crosses the iron bridge over the White River (13.6 mi.).

West Hartford has seen better days. The village offers few services, and a general store that served thru-hikers has closed. Thru-hikers will need to carry on through the village streets, pass under I-89, and walk up into the woods east of town (an area frequented by off-road vehicles that has little appeal for the casual day hiker) to reach a new shelter, Happy Hill, between West Hartford and Norwich. This book skips the miles between Quechee–West Hartford Rd. and Happy Hill Shelter. Hike #29 is a day-hike circuit from Norwich about halfway back toward West Hartford and then returning to Norwich.

About Woodstock: Woodstock is not your average Vermont town, past or present. U.S. Senator Jacob Collamer, a village resident in the 19th century, said, "The good people of Woodstock have less incentive than others to yearn for heaven," presumably because they recognized they were already almost there. Year-round the village is busy with visitors. Parking near the oval green may be impossible, but a walk from a more distant street has its own rewards. Chosen as shire town (county seat) in the early 1790s, the village was already prosperous due to sawmills, gristmills, and a dam on the Ottauquechee River. A stunning covered bridge, just off the green, affords a lovely river view. In the early 1800s, the town drew professionals in law and business, and prominent citizens outdid themselves building handsome mansions in and around the village, primarily in the Federal architectural style. America's skiing industry was born in Woodstock in the 1930s, and it still brings scads of people to town every winter. A sprawling hotel, the Woodstock Inn, handsomely dominates the center of town, facing the green. The Dana House (1807) is now the home of the Woodstock Historical Society. The public library is a gem, great for rainy days.

Billings Farm and Museum, just north of town on VT 12, re-creates late 19th-century American farm life, with a working dairy, draft horses, Southdown sheep, and other animals. Daily and seasonal events offer visitors a chance to participate in farm life. A research library and 16,000 artifacts testify to the seriousness of purpose here. The farmhouse was home to George Perkins Marsh, one of the fathers of the modern ecology movement; his 1864 book *Man and Nature* belongs beside Thoreau and Muir.

For a short uphill walk in town, ask for a map at the tourist information booth on the green, and follow village streets to the park, where you will find easy switchbacks leading upward to Mt. Tom, from which postcard-perfect pastoral views are the immediate reward. *Window on Woodstock,* free from Woodstock Area Chamber of Commerce (802-457-1042, June–Oct.), is a superior pamphlet describing the town's attractions and history.

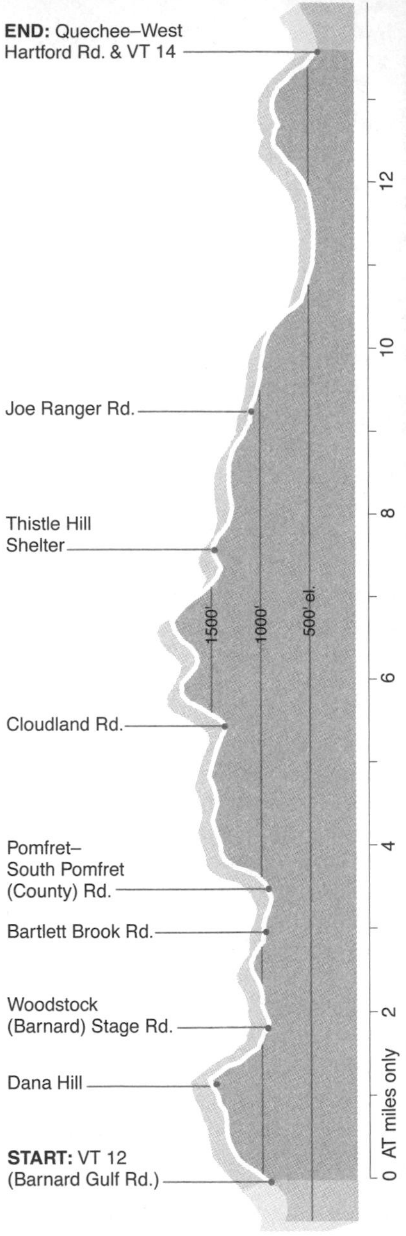

END: Quechee–West Hartford Rd. & VT 14

Joe Ranger Rd.

Thistle Hill Shelter

Cloudland Rd.

Pomfret–South Pomfret (County) Rd.

Bartlett Brook Rd.

Woodstock (Barnard) Stage Rd.

Dana Hill

START: VT 12 (Barnard Gulf Rd.)

1500'

1000'

500' el.

0 AT miles only

2

4

6

8

10

12

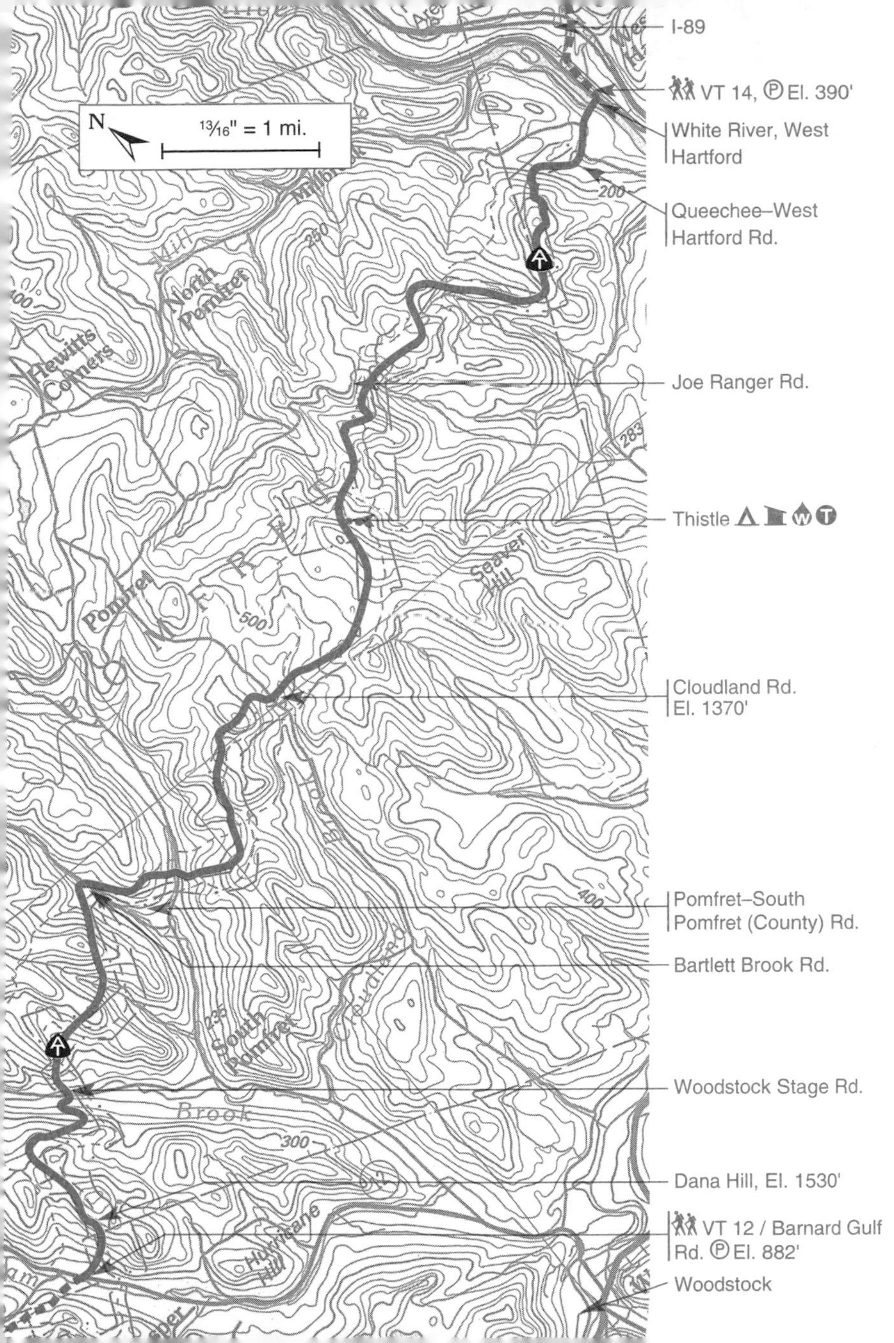
N
13/16" = 1 mi.
I-89
VT 14, Ⓟ El. 390'
White River, West Hartford
Queechee–West Hartford Rd.
Joe Ranger Rd.
Thistle
Cloudland Rd. El. 1370'
Pomfret–South Pomfret (County) Rd.
Bartlett Brook Rd.
Woodstock Stage Rd.
Dana Hill, El. 1530'
VT 12 / Barnard Gulf Rd. Ⓟ El. 882'
Woodstock
North Pomfret
Hewitts Corners
Pomfret
Seaver Hill
South Pomfret
Hurricane Hill
Brook
500
400
300
200

HIKE #28 Itinerary

Miles N	NORTH	Elev. (ft./m)	Miles S
13.6	**End: VT 14,** West Hartford; parking. AT continues through village and under I-89.	390/119	0.0
12.6	**Quechee–West Hartford Rd;** turn L to village, cross White River.		1.0
9.3	**Joe Ranger Rd.** (gravel), limited parking.		3.3
7.9	Side trail to **Thistle Hill Shelter** and campsite, water, privy.	1480/451	5.1
5.5	**Cloudland Rd.** (gravel).	1370/418	7.1
5.0	**Dupuis Hill,** views.		7.6
3.7	**Pomfret–South Pomfret (County) Rd.,** brook, no parking.	980/299	8.9
3.0	**Bartlett Brook Rd.** (gravel).	980/299	9.6
1.5	**Woodstock (Barnard) Stage Rd.,** parking.	820/250	11.1
1.2	**Dana Hill,** views.	1530/466	11.4
0.0	**Start: VT 12** (Barnard Gulf Rd.), overnight parking; 4.2 mi. N of Woodstock.	882/269	13.6

SOUTH

HIKE: #29

Norwich

Maps: ATC N.H. & Vt. #5

Route: Circuit hike from Elm St., Norwich, to Mosley Hill, to Griggs Mt. and back via Tucker Trail to AT trailhead in Norwich

Recommended direction: N to S

Distance: 7.4 mi. (round-trip); 7.8 mi. with side trails

Elevation +/-: 750 ft. to 1570 ft. to 750 ft.

Effort: Easy

Day hike: Yes

Overnight backpacking hike: Optional

Duration: 4 to 4½ hr.

Early exit option: William Tucker Trail, at 2.9 mi.

Natural history features: Montshire Science Museum

Trailhead access: *Start and End:* From village green, Norwich, follow Elm St. 1.0 mi. to AT trailhead, left; roadside parking

Camping: Happy Hill Shelter

The previous hike ends at West Hartford, a short distance from the White River and VT 14. Although the river is a handsome sight from the old iron bridge, the minuscule town has seen better days and offers few amenities. I-89 floods the White River valley with road noise, perhaps necessary but definitely unappealing. See Hike #28 for further notes.

Given the dispiriting section of trail just east of West Hartford, this book skips those miles, turning instead to lovely Norwich—the last Vermont town on the AT for northbound hikers—for a pleasant set of day-hike options. There is a new shelter (Happy Hill, 1998) to replace the old Happy Hill Cabin, offering backpackers an overnight option between Norwich and West Hartford.

Norwich is a beautiful town with stately old homes. It is hiker-friendly and boasts not only a satisfying network of trails that link up with the AT but also a new science museum and immediate access to Hanover, New Hampshire, a great university town, just over the Connecticut River—plus a not-to-be-missed general store, Dan & Whits, on Main St., with every-

Dale Gelfand

Eastern newt

Montshire Museum

On the banks of the Connecticut River at Norwich (Montshire Rd., just above the AT's crossing of the Connecticut River on Ledyard Bridge) is the Montshire Museum of Science, designed for kids and grown-ups. It's a handsome, hands-on, spanking-new museum on a pretty 100-acre site with its own trails to wetlands, the river's banks, and a wooded section. Many exhibits in the museum are interactive in this eye-pleasing, colorful, and fun-filled place. Even the playground for little kids gets a science twist, teaching basic physics with slides and swings. Montshire's facilities are used for lectures, concerts, and special events—such as igloo building in February and "The Nature of Fall Day" in October. Call 802-649-2200 for details.

thing from Phillips screwdrivers to radicchio. Day hikers will want to pick up a free local trail map from the Norwich town hall offices, in the basement of the red brick building facing the village green. Public toilets here too.

When you've finished exploring Norwich, park at the upper Elm St. AT trailhead, 1.0 mi. from the village green. There are a few spaces, roadside; keep well off the street. More spaces are available back down Elm at Hickory Ridge Rd. Leaving Elm St., walk south on the AT. In the first half hour, there are extensive patches of graceful ferns, always lovely, brilliantly green on a rainy day. Many of them are cinnamon fern (brown fuzz at the bottom of the frond stalk), but other varieties can be spotted too. The trail moves gently uphill on a broad, easy path.

At 0.7 mi. a power-line opening gives an even more glorious display of ferns. Detour 50 ft. south here for a look at Wilder Dam (producing 32.4 megawatts, built in 1950) and the Connecticut River. The AT is now crossing Mosley Hill. Long stretches of fairly level trail ensue, soft underfoot, mostly from abundant hemlock needles, though this is predominantly a lowland mixed hardwood forest.

A dirt road, Newton Lane, comes up at about 1.7 mi., and 15 min. later at a stand of white birch there is a good view on the left of distant hills and fields—one of the few openings in the forest on these AT miles.

Although there is some road noise here, the mosses make an inviting cushion for a brief rest. Make sure they're dry, though, for moss retains moisture longer than you might think. Jean Langenheim's *Mountain Flowers of New England* (sadly, out of print) tells us that mosses "play a significant role in moisture conservation. In some types of vegetation, such as sedge meadows, mosses provide seed beds as well as a subsequent favorable habitat for herbaceous and shrubby plants. They themselves seem quite independent of variation in climate. In damp weather they grow with amazing rapidity, and in dry or frozen periods they suspend growth." Look about here during your rest to see where mosses are behaving according to form, with little shrubby plants taking root in their nutrient-rich material, right on top of exposed bedrock.

Ten minutes beyond the opening, look right for a giant multitrunked maple. The trail continues as a flat, easy footpath, pine-needle-cushioned hereabouts. (Hike #29 works well for small kids or for those who are a bit unsteady on their feet.)

Tucker Trail (an old woods road) branches right at 2.9 mi. The road is obvious but its status as a trail is not well marked, except for remnants of Dartmouth Outing Club orange-and-black signs on some trees. The AT joins the road, heading left. From here it's an easy climb on the road to a spur, left, at 3.3 mi., that steps gently downhill to the new Happy Hill Shelter (opening 1998). The shelter is tucked away in the woods with no

The Connecticut River

Although the hikes described in this volume end on Elm St. in Norwich, the AT of course continues northward on VT 10, making its way across the Connecticut River, and the Vermont–New Hampshire state line, on Ledyard Bridge. Across the river is Hanover, home of Dartmouth College, a beautiful village some have called the most sophisticated town on the Appalachian Trail.

The river itself is critically important to New England and is worth a look. Rising in a series of lakes and ponds far to the north, near Québec, the Connecticut River is about 200 miles long, dropping 850 feet en route to Long Island Sound and the ocean. On its Vermont side, it drains no less than 41% of the state's territory. The Connecticut has been used for many industrial purposes, the earliest of which was log traffic in the timber business, from the 1700s onward. Paper plants, dependant on both the trees and the abundant water, have lined its banks for two centuries as well. More recently engineers have harnessed the river's power in six hydroelectric plants on Vermont's river miles (more to the south, in Massachusetts and Connecticut). There is one (needless to say, controversial) nuclear power plant on the Vermont–New Hampshire portion of the river.

Boating of many kinds is popular, and locally the most exciting form to watch is the intercollegiate crew races at Dartmouth. The Dartmouth boathouse, minutes north of Ledyard Bridge on the Hanover side, off a town street, is a good place for a brief river view. Remember, however, that this is private college property.

view, but it makes a good spot for lunch (water and composting privy nearby). The old Happy Hill Cabin, dating from 1918, was demolished in 1997 after years of abuse.

To extend the outward reach of Hike #29 just a bit more, carry on to a high point on the side of Griggs Mt. (no view, 1570 ft., 3.7 mi.). From here it's 3.8 mi. south to West Hartford (VT 14); see Hike #28.

Hike #29 now does an about-face. Backtrack to the Tucker Trail junction, where you can make a choice between following the AT back to Elm St. or varying the return by taking Tucker Trail to the left. There are several options: A second car can be positioned at the Tucker Trail trailhead, minutes away. Or walkers can use Tucker Trail to reach village streets in Norwich, walking back into town. Or, as described here, a circuit hike can be made by following Tucker Trail, a selection of scenic village streets, and then the Heyl Trail back to the AT trailhead on Elm St.

To make the circuit hike, go left down Tucker Trail, a broad woods road, passing ponds on the left, where we saw herons roosting. The area is maintained by the U.S. Forest Service. Underfoot you may notice sheets of the gray slate common to this Connecticut River valley area. The slate often has veins of quartz. Pass a steel gate (5.3 mi.) at the Tucker Trail trailhead, with parking just beyond the gate (do not block gate or hayfield entrance). This is now Happy Hill Rd. (a.k.a. locally as

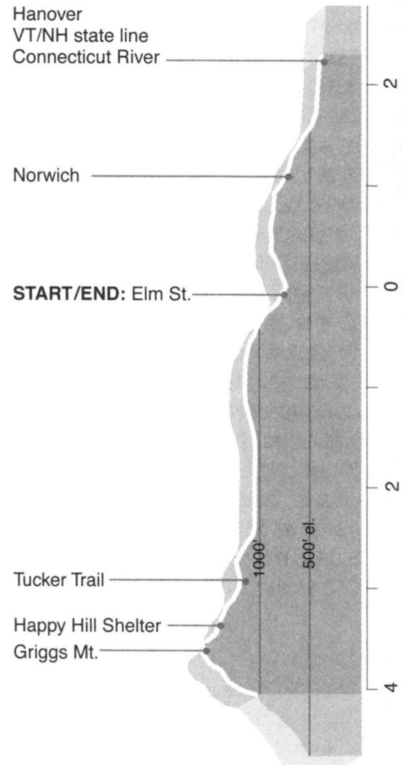

Tucker Trail). There are a few houses on the right and farm fields, barely visible through the woods, on the left. Continue 15 min. to a junction with Bragg Hill Rd. (6.8 mi.). Parking, roadside, on the right is feasible here as well. A right turn takes you toward the village (another 1.2 mi.).

To continue the circuit hike, go left on Bragg Hill Rd., heading away

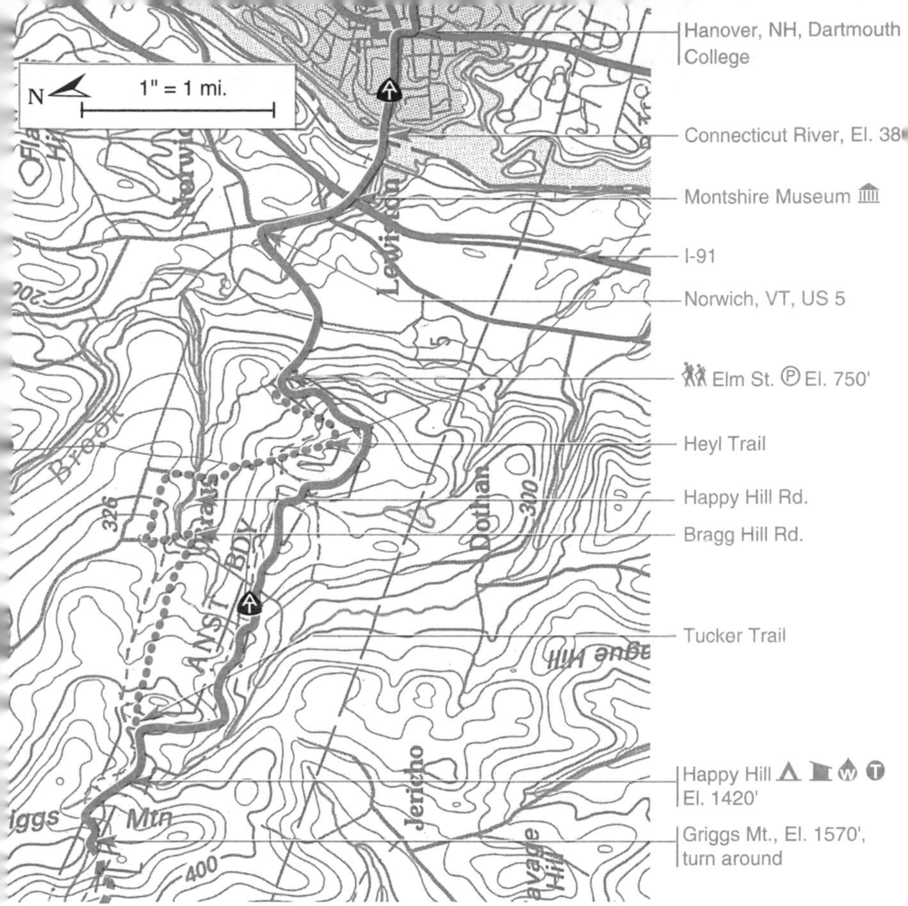

N 1" = 1 mi.

Hanover, NH, Dartmouth College
Connecticut River, El. 38
Montshire Museum
I-91
Norwich, VT, US 5
Elm St. Ⓟ El. 750'
Heyl Trail
Happy Hill Rd.
Bragg Hill Rd.
Tucker Trail
Happy Hill El. 1420'
Griggs Mt., El. 1570', turn around

from town toward gorgeous pastoral views; then soon (in 0.3 mi.) turn right on Dutton Rd., then right (after 0.4 mi.) on Goddard St., and quickly (after 0.3 mi.) rejoin Bragg Hill Rd. These village roads and streets pass lovely homes and gardens. At Bragg Hill Rd., angle left, crossing the road, and veer right onto the Heyl Trail (to the right of a power line). Heyl Trail (blue-and-white signs) wends its way through the woods, turning sharply left at about 0.6 mi. from Bragg Hill Rd., and then makes its way on a course parallel to the AT, ending at Elm St., just above the AT trailhead.

HIKE #29 Itinerary

Miles N	CIRCUIT HIKE	Elev. (ft./m)	Miles S
	Start: Elm St. AT trailhead, limited parking. Go south.	750/229	0.0
	Power-line opening; detour to view of Wilder Dam.		0.7
	Newton Lane.		1.7
	Tucker Trail (woods road), R.	1320/402	2.9
	Side trail, L, to **Happy Hill Shelter** (opening 1998), water, privy.	1420/433	3.3
	Griggs Mt., no view.	1570/479	3.7
	REVERSE DIRECTION. Go north. Read from bottom up.		
7.8	**End: Elm St.,** just above AT trailhead.	750/229	
7.4	Sharp L turn in Heyl Trail, which then parallels AT.		
6.8	Rejoin **Bragg Hill Rd.,** turn L, and shortly turn R into **Heyl Trail** to R of power line.		
6.5	**Goddard Rd.,** turn R.		
6.1	**Dutton Hill Rd.,** turn R; pass Abigail Rd. on L.		
5.8	**Bragg Hill Rd.,** day parking; turn L.		
5.3	**Happy Hill Rd.,** gate, parking.		
4.5	**Tucker Trail** (woods road), L.	1320/402	
4.1	Side trail, R, to **Happy Hill Shelter,** water, privy.	1420/433	

CIRCUIT HIKE

Useful Information

LIST OF MAPS

US Geological Survey Topographic Maps

Note: USGS maps used in this series are scaled at 1:100,000 (1 cm = 1 km), but in this book we have converted the scale generally to 1 in. = 1 mi. or a close fraction thereof. The maps listed below, which cover all the AT miles in this volume, are quadrangles covering the area surrounding the named town (approximately 50 mi. E-W and 35 mi. N-S). The contour interval is 20 meters on these maps.

Rutland, VT
Claremont, VT
Glens Falls, NY
Albany, NY
Pittsfield, MA
Waterbury, CT
Bridgeport, CT

To order USGS maps, see "Web Sites" and the Bibliography.

Appalachian Trail Conference Maps

ATC sells its own 4-color topo hiking maps and some maps published by regional hiking clubs. Together these maps cover the entire AT. Generally ATC maps are scaled at 1:62,500 (1 in. = 1 mi.). Maps referred to in this volume are listed here.

ATC New Hampshire & Vermont, Map 5
(Connecticut River/Norwich to Sherburne Pass/US 4)

ATC New Hampshire & Vermont, Map 6
(Sherburne Pass/US 4 to Danby–Landgrove Road)

ATC New Hampshire & Vermont, Map 7
(Danby–Landgrove Road to Arlington–West Wardsboro Road)

ATC New Hampshire & Vermont, Map 8
(Arlington–West Wardsboro Road to Massachusetts 2 / North Adams)

ATC Massachusetts & Connecticut, Map 1
(Vermont line to Dalton, Mass.)

ATC Massachusetts & Connecticut, Map 2
(Dalton to Upper Goose Pond)

ATC Massachusetts & Connecticut, Map 3
(Upper Goose Pond to Jug End)

ATC Massachusetts & Connecticut, Map 4
(Jug End to Cornwall Bridge, Conn.)

ATC Massachusetts & Connecticut, Map 5
(Cornwall Bridge, Conn., to Pawling, N.Y.)

Many ATC maps are double maps on one sheet (a map on each side); for example, ATC Massachusetts & Connecticut Maps 3 & 4 appear on one sheet.

To order ATC maps, see "Addresses / Phone Numbers" and "Web Sites."

Definitions

Easy: gentle ups and downs, fairly smooth path, few obstacles.

Moderate: elevation gain or loss of up to 1000 ft.; narrower, rocky path; some obstacles (for example, brook crossings with no bridge).

Strenuous: elevation gain or loss of more than 1000 ft.; steep ups and downs; difficult, challenging path; numerous obstacles; possibly unsuitable for young children or the infirm.

Hikes

Easy

#1, Ten Mile River to Bull's Bridge
#4, Housatonic River Walk
#6, Pine Swamp and Sharon Mt.
#7, Falls Village to Salisbury
#10, Sheffield to Jug End, South Egremont
#13, Tyringham to Goose Pond to Becket
#14, Finerty Pond and October Mt. State Forest
#15, Washington to Dalton
#28, Woodstock to West Hartford
#29, Norwich

Easy to Moderate

#5, Silver Hill and Pine Knob Loop Trail
#11, Sheffield to Monterey
#16, Dalton to Cheshire
#23, Little Rock Pond and White Rocks
#24, Clarendon Gorge and Cold River

Moderate

#2, Bull's Bridge to Kent
#3, Kent to St. Johns Ledges
#8, Salisbury to Bear Mt.
#12, Beartown State Forest to Tyringham Cobble

Moderate to Strenuous

#26, Killington Peak—North
#27, Killington to Woodstock

Strenuous

#9, Sages Ravine to Mt. Everett to Jug End
#17, Cheshire to Mt. Greylock
#18, Mt. Greylock to North Adams
#19, North Adams (Eph's Lookout) to Harmon Hill and Bennington
#20, Glastenbury Mt.
#21, Stratton Mt. and Stratton Pond
#22, Bromley Mt.
#25, Killington Peak—South

SHELTERS AND CAMPSITES

SEE PAGE 14 for general notes about shelters and campsites on or close to the AT. We list here the shelters (a.k.a. lean-tos) and named campsites (a.k.a. tent sites) described in this book. When shelters have officially designated tent sites, we indicate "campsite" below. Consult the narrative of each hike for information on unofficial tent sites at some shelters and on shelters that are farther off the AT.

Hike #	Shelter	Campsite	Lodge/Cabin	Name
1	x	x		Ten Mile River
2	x			Schaghticoke Mt.
		x	x	Mt. Algo
4	x	x		Stewart Hollow Brook
		x		Stony Brook
5		x		Silver Hill (tent sites, pavilion)
		x		Housatonic Meadows State Park (car camping)
6		x		Caesar Rd.
	x			Pine Swamp Brook
		x		Sharon Mt.
		x		Housatonic Meadows State Park (car camping)
7	x	x		Limestone Spring
8		x		Plateau
	x	x		Riga
		x		Ball Brook
	x	x		Brassie Brook
		x		Paradise Lane
9		x		Sages Ravine
		x		Bear Rock Stream
		x		Race Brook Falls
	x	x		Glen Brook
11	x	x		Tom Leonard
12		x		Beartown State Forest (Benedict Pond, car camping)
	x			Mt. Wilcox South and North
		x		Shaker
13		x	x	Upper Goose Pond

Continued on next page

Hike #	Shelter	Campsite	Lodge/Cabin	Name
14	x			October Mt.
15	x	x		Kay Wood
16		x		Crystal Mt.
17	x	x		Mark Noepel
	x	x		Sperry Rd. Campground (car camping, off AT)
			x	Bascom Lodge
18	x	x		Wilbur Clearing
19		x		Sherman Brook
	x	x		Seth Warner
	x	x		Condon
20	x	x		Melville Nauheim
	x	x		Goddard (Glastenbury Mt.)
	x			Kid Gore
	x			Caughnawaga
	x	x		Story Spring
21		x		Stratton Pond
	x			Bigelow and Vondell
	x			Douglas
	x			Spruce Peak
22		x		Bromley
	x	x		Peru Peak
		x		Griffith Lake
	x	x		Lost Pond
	x	x		Big Branch
23	x			Lula Tye
	x			Little Rock Pond
		x		Little Rock Pond Tenting
	x	x		Greenwall
24	x			Minerva Hinchey
	x	x		Clarendon
25	x			Governor Clement
		x	x	Cooper Lodge
26			x	Pico Camp
		x	x	Cooper Lodge
27	x			Tucker-Johnson
	x	x		Gifford Woods State Park
	x	x		Stony Brook
	x	x		Wintturi
28	x	x		Thistle Hill
29	x			Happy Hill

THERE ARE SCORES of trails connecting to the southern New England AT, many of them offering vistas and facilities similar to those found on the AT itself. Many short connecting side trails are noted in the hike narratives in this book. Avid hikers and those wanting to avoid crowded conditions on popular sections of the AT may enjoy exploring some of these more extended trail systems.

Connecticut

The Connecticut Forest and Park Association and local hiking clubs maintain the Blue Trail System (mostly blue-blazed) in northwestern Connecticut and elsewhere in the state. Of particular note is Connecticut's Mohawk Trail (not to be confused with another Mohawk Trail in northwestern Massachusetts). The Mohawk Trail in Connecticut (24 mi.) follows several miles of the original AT where it went up the east side of the Housatonic River valley. It loops back to the AT, offering an extended weekend backpacking trip doable with only one car.

For information, call or write Connecticut Forest and Park Assoc., 16 Meriden Rd., Middlefield, CT 06481; 860-346-TREE.

Massachusetts

Starting in extreme southwestern Massachusetts and spilling over the state lines to New York and Connecticut, the South Taconic Trail System (STT) provides a satisfying alternative to the AT, in many places running closely parallel to the AT and almost as high. Hikers can follow the STT for 15.7 mi. as far north as MA/NY 23 (west of South Egremont, MA, near the New York state line). STT crosses Alander Mt., a popular viewpoint looking west toward the Catskills, and descends to the spectacular Bash Bish Falls (200 ft. high) in Bash Bish Falls State Park (adjacent to Mt. Washington State Forest), on the Massachusetts–New York border. See Ryan, *Guide to the Taconic Trail System*. The New York– New Jersey Trail Conference published a good set of maps for the STT, but as of this writing the maps are out of print.

In northwestern Massachusetts, the Taconic Crest Trail begins at Berry Pond in Pittsfield State Forest, meanders into and out of New York around Petersburg Pass (MA/NY 2), comes back into Massachusetts in Taconic Trail State Park and Williams College's Hopkins State Forest, and continues northward into southwestern Vermont, terminating in North Pownal. This high-elevation route is little used and takes hikers to some remote areas in Vermont, including the Dome (fine views) and the Snow Hole (where ice may linger well into summer). For information, use Ryan, *Guide to the Taconic Trail System;* Ryan, *AMC Massachusetts and Rhode Island Trail Guide;* and Stevens, *Hikes & Walks in the Berkshire Hills.*

Also in northwestern Massachusetts, the Mohawk Trail is coming back to life. An ancient Native American and colonial route, from the Connecticut River valley to the Hudson River valley, the trail started as a footpath, evolved over centuries into a highway, and is now being restored as a footpath near the highway. Also called the Mahican-Mohawk Trail, the first 25 mi. were opened in 1997 (from Deerfield to Mohawk Trail State Forest). Contact Historic Deerfield Visitor Information, 413-774-5581.

Vermont

In Vermont there are no other trail *systems* per se close to the AT, but the AT itself, from the Massachusetts line to VT 4 at Sherburne Pass (Killington), rides on the back of a pre-existing trail system, the famous Long Trail, maintained by the Green Mountain Club. Their *Long Trail Guide* provides detailed descriptions of many connecting side trails near the AT.

Not so much a trail system as a trail bonanza is the network of trails on Killington Peak looked after by the Merrell Hiking Center (see Hike #25). Hikers here can spend a day or several days on the mountain, never walking the same path twice. Request a map at the ski area's summit lodge, the base lodge, or by telephone at 802-422-6708.

Much of the AT in Vermont goes through Green Mt. National Forest, and there are many rugged backcountry trails (and some easier trails) in the forest (500 mi.). Certain officially designated wilderness areas within the national forest have trails that are minimally maintained. Contact Green Mt. National Forest at USDA Forest Service, Manchester Ranger District, RR 1, Box 1940, Manchester Center, VT 05255; 802-362-2307. Or at GMNF, P.O. Box 519, 231 North Main St., Rutland, VT 05701; 802-747-6700.

ADDRESS/PHONE NUMBER

General Hiking Clubs

American Hiking Society, 1422 Fenwick La., Silver Spring, MD 20910; 301-565-6704

Appalachian Mountain Club, 5 Joy St., Boston, MA 02108; 617-523-0636. For their hiking guides: Box 298, Gorham, NH 03581; 800-262-4455.

Appalachian Trail Conference, P.O. Box 807, Harpers Ferry, WV 25425-0807; 304-535-633; fax 304-535-2667

Southern New England Regional Hiking Clubs

AMC—Connecticut Chapter, 472 Burlington Ave., Bristol, CT 06010

AMC—Berkshire Chapter, P.O. Box 1800, Lanesboro, MA 01237; 413-443-0011

AMC—Southeastern Massachusetts Chapter, c/o Anne Silva, 140 Summerfield St., Fall River, MA 02720

Green Mountain Club, R.R. 1, Box 650, Route 100, Waterbury Center, VT 05677; 802-244-7037

Dartmouth Outing Club, Robinson Hall, Box 9, Hanover, NH 03755; 603-646-2428

WEB SITES

Note: Almost all Web site addresses begin with http:// preceding www. Most Web sites are updated periodically. Some listed here were still in development when we visited them.

Major Organizations

American Hiking Society www.orca.org/ahs/

Dedicated to promoting hiking and to protecting and maintaining America's trails, AHS offers programs, publications (newsletter), legislative updates, volunteer vacations, and links to many clubs and resources.

Appalachian Long Distance Hikers Association www.connix.com/~aldha/

Aimed primarily at thru-hikers. Savvy advice, networking, forums, volunteering opportunities.

Appalachian Mountain Club www.outdoors.org/

Granddaddy of the eastern hiking clubs, AMC covers not only the northeastern AT but activities and trail reports on many other trails. AMC Books, *AMC Outdoors* (magazine), adult and kids' activities (trips and workshops year-round), conservation initiatives, hiking trip planning, AMC hut reservations, and much more.

Appalachian Trail Conference www.atconf.org/

This site is comprehensive, with many lists of and links to regional trail clubs. ATC's "Ultimate Trail Store" has arguably the biggest selection of AT books and maps anywhere (member discounts). Updated trail conditions, permit regulations, and other helpful subjects.

AT Regional Trail Maintaining Clubs

Many regional hiking clubs have their own Web sites, and most of them can be found easily by way of links from the Appalachian Trail Conference Web site listed above. Here are some Web sites concerned with the AT in the states covered by this book.

AMC—Connecticut Chapter sardon.cs.yale.edu/ATCT/

AMC—Berkshire Chapter www-unix.oit.umass.edu/~berkamc/

Green Mountain Club www.greenmountainclub.org/

GMC is the great-grandaddy of northeastern hiking clubs. Detailed information about segments of the Long Trail (contiguous with AT from Massachusetts –Vermont line to VT 4 (Killington). Links to Web sites of GMC chapters—Bennington, etc. Newsletter, bookstore, hiker supplies, conservation and volunteer activities.

Dartmouth Outing Club www.dartmouth.edu/student/doc/

DOC maintains 70 mi. of the AT in eastern Vermont and western New Hampshire. It is the oldest collegiate outing club in America.

Other AT Web Sites

Appalachian Trail Place www.trailplace.com

Center for Appalachian Trail Studies. Hosted by Dan "Wingfoot" Bruce, a thru-hiker who maintains a hostel by the trail in Virginia. A spin-off from Wingfoot's *Thru-Hiker's Handbook*. Dozens of searchable databases on AT subjects, many especially helpful to long-distance hikers or those with natural history interests. "Mailing lists" of former and would-be thru-hikers, women hikers, teenage hikers, others. Chat rooms. Bibliography. One of the better sites.

The Appalachian Trail Home Page www.fred.net/kathy/at.html

The official-sounding name belies the fact that this is a personal home page built by a thru-hiker, Kathy Bilton. Nonetheless, it's one of the better general sites for miscellaneous information about the AT and for connecting with AT people. Links to AT maintaining clubs (also to the AT organizations and to other National Scenic Trails), forums for AT issues discussions, advice from thru-hikers, and more.

Foot www.yale.edu/yonet/foot/appalachian.html

The AT section of a Yale University outdoor recreation Web site. Nothing very fresh here. Trail descriptions seem derivative (from ATC guides). Language is cute (Sages Ravine is "very purty"). Covers NW Connecticut.

AMC—Southeastern Massachusetts Chapter www.cris.com/~Ndrma/

The basics: club activities, a few savvy essays, links to the AMC home page and other clubs. Oriented more toward the White Mts. than to western New England's AT.

America's Roof—Mt. Greylock www.inch.com/%7Edipper/ma.html

Click on the state map and up comes a home page for the state's highest mountain. This site covers Massachusetts' Mt. Greylock, on the AT. The highest points in Connecticut (Mt. Frissel) and Vermont (Mt. Mansfield) are not on the AT. Mountain information is not extensive here, however.

Commercial and Government Web Sites

General

GORP www.gorp.com

Great Outdoor Recreation Pages. From various purveyors of travel and outdoor adventure information, services, and supplies. The AT is one small part of this huge, diverse site. Rewarding for those with time to kill.

Magazines

Backpacker www.bpbasecamp.com

Extensive, well-researched information about hiking worldwide. Many articles on either the AT specifically or on hiking skills and equipment useful to AT trekkers. "Trail Talk Forums" bring hikers together on-line. An "Encyclopedia" includes a section on "Backcountry Jargon." "Gearfinder" is a searchable database of hiking/camping products. The site is fueled by links to *Backpacker*'s advertisers, a convenience or a distraction depending on your disposition.

Outside outside.starwave.com

Most of the magazine, on-line. Hiking per se and the AT specifically are only occasionally featured in *Outside* (whose travel beat is worldwide), but the treatment is usually in-depth and colorful. Generally aimed at the under-forty crowd. Good articles on fitness and training. Excellent book reviews.

Bookstores

Adventurous Traveler Bookstore www.adventuroustraveler.com

If you are anywhere near Burlington, Vermont, go to this store. Short of that, visit on-line. Over 4000 travel-related titles await you. Extensive AT and other North American hiking book inventory. Maps too. Paper catalogue available.

Globe Corner Travel Bookstore www.globecorner.com

The best travel bookstore in metro Boston, one of the best in the Northeast. Extensive New England selection and a world of maps. On-line catalogue.

Amazon www.amazon.com

The leader in on-line bookstores. Search the database on the words "Appalachian Trail" for a long list of titles.

Barnes & Noble www.barnesandnoble.com

They're everywhere and they carry almost everything. If the local store doesn't have it, search on-line under the subject "Appalachian Trail."

Borders Books & Music www.borders.com

Not quite as widespread as Barnes & Noble, but by spring 1998, Borders expected to have an extensive Web site, offering their entire inventory on-line.

Maps

Delorme Map Co. www.delorme.com

Detailed atlases for the following AT states: North Carolina, Tennessee, Virginia, Maryland, Pennsylvania, New York, Vermont, New Hampshire, Maine.

United States Geologic Survey (USGS)
www.usgs.gov/pubprod/products.html

A giant site for both the general public and scientists. This address is for ordering maps. A database facilitates finding the correct map, at the desired scale, for the area you're hiking.

Perry-Castaneda Library Map Collection
www.lib.utexas.edu/Libs/PCL/Map_collection/Map_collection.html

An extensive collection of links to on-line map resources around the world. Including not only topographic maps but also historical and weather maps.

Weather

The Weather Underground   www.wunderground.com

Up-to-the-hour weather reports and forecasts for many cities in the U.S., including numerous smaller cities near the Appalachian Trail.

National Oceanic & Atmospheric Administration
www.nws.noaa.gov/weather

NOAA offers continuously updated weather reports and forecasts all across the country on dedicated radio channels (a lightweight weather-only radio is worth carrying on extended backpacking trips). Or access NOAA's weather report Web site at the address above (expected to be fully functional in spring 1998).

Bibliography

Hiking Guides

Chase, Jim. *Backpacker Magazine's Guide to the Appalachian Trail.* Stackpole Books, 1989.

Connecticut Forest and Park Association. *Connecticut Walk Book.* Connecticut Forest and Park Association, 1997.

Fitzgerald, Brian T., and Robert P. Lindemann., eds. *Day Hiker's Guide to Vermont.* Green Mountain Club, 1997.

Green Mountain Club. *Long Trail Guide.* Green Mountain Club, 1997.

Hook, David, ed. *Appalachian Trail Guide to New Hampshire–Vermont.* Appalachian Trail Conference, 1998.

Logue, Victoria and Frank. *The Best of the Appalachian Trail Overnight Hikes.* Menasha Ridge Press and Appalachian Trail Conference, 1994.

Norton, Russell. *Long Trail End-to-Ender's Guide.* Green Mountain Club, 1997.

Pletcher, Larry. *Hiking Vermont.* Falcon Press, 1996.

Ryan, Christopher J. *AMC Massachusetts and Rhode Island Trail Guide.* Appalachian Mountain Club Books, 1989.

Ryan, Christopher J. *Guide to the Taconic Trail System.* New England Cartographics, 1989.

Sills, Norman, and Robert Hatton, eds., *Appalachian Trail Guide to Massachusetts–Connecticut.* Appalachian Trail Conference, 1996.

Smith, Charles W.G. *Nature Walks in the Berkshire Hills.* Appalachian Mountain Club Books, 1997.

Stevens, Lauren R. *Hikes & Walks in the Berkshire Hills.* Berkshire House, 1994.

Maps & Atlases

Appalachian Mountain Club. *Shaded Relief Map of Mt. Greylock State Reservation.* Appalachian Mountain Club, 1995.

Connecticut Forest and Park Association. *Connecticut's Blue-Blazed Hiking Trails.* Connecticut Forest and Park Association, 1995.

DeLorme. *Vermont Atlas & Gazetteer.* DeLorme, 1996.

Hagstrom Map Company. *Hagstrom Map of Litchfield County, Connecticut.* Hagstrom Map Company, 1995.

JIMAPCO. *JIMAPCO Road Map of Bennington/Rutland Vermont.* JIMAPCO, 1989.

JIMAPCO. *JIMAPCO Road Map of Berkshire County, Massachusetts.* JIMAPCO, 1991.

New York–New Jersey Trail Conference. *South Taconic Trails.* New York–New Jersey Trail Conference, 1988. [Detailed contour map]

Trails Illustrated. Maps of national parks, which include sections of the AT. Write to P.O. Box 4357, Evergreen, CO 80437; or call 800-962-1643.

U.S. Geological Survey, Topographic maps available in printed versions and on CD-ROM. Call 800-HELP-

MAP; write to USGS, Map Distribution, Box 25286, Denver, CO 80225; or access their Web site (p. 278).

Field Guides

Alden, Peter. *Peterson First Guide to Mammals of North America.* Houghton Mifflin, 1987.

Brown, Cindy Kilgore. *Vermont Wildlife Viewing Guide.* Falcon Press, 1994.

Chew, V. Collins. *Underfoot: A Geologic Guide to the Appalachian Trail.* Appalachian Trail Conference, 1993.

Freeman, Stan, and Mike Nasuti. *The Natural History and Resources of Western Massachusetts.* Hampshire House, 1994.

Hendricks, Bartlett. *Birds of Berkshire County.* Berkshire Museum, 1995.

Jorgensen, Neil. *A Sierra Club Naturalist's Guide to Southern New England.* Sierra Club Books, 1978.

Kirby, Ed. *Exploring the Berkshire Hills.* Valley GEOlogy PUBlications, 1995.

Laing, David. *The Nature of Killington.* Killington Ltd. (Merrell Hiking Center), 1996.

Laubach, René. *A Guide to Natural Places in the Berkshire Hills.* Berkshire House, 1992.

Lawrence, Eleanor, and Cecilia Fitzsimons. *An Instant Guide to Trees.* Longmeadow Press, 1991.

Newcomb, Lawrence. *Newcomb's Wildflower Guide.* Little, Brown, 1977.

Peterson, Lee Allen. *A Field Guide to Edible Wild Plants of Eastern and Central North America.* Houghton Mifflin, 1977.

Peterson, Roger Tory. *Peterson First Guide to Birds of North America.* Houghton Mifflin, 1986.

Peterson, Roger Tory. *Peterson First Guide to Wildflowers of Northeastern and North-central North America.* Houghton Mifflin, 1986.

Slack, Nancy G., and Allison W. Bell. *AMC Field Guide to the New England Alpine Summits.* Appalachian Mountain Club Books, 1995.

Strauch, Joseph G., Jr. *Wildflowers of the Berkshire & Taconic Hills.* Berkshire House, 1995.

Sutton, Ann, and Myron Sutton. *Eastern Forests* (Audubon Field Guide). Alfred A. Knopf, 1993.

Watts, May Theilgaard. *Tree Finder.* Nature Study Guild, 1986.

General Books: Appalachian Trail

Appalachian Trail Conference. *Walking the Appalachian Trail Step by Step.* Appalachian Trail Conference, 1993.

Bruce, Dan "Wingfoot." *The Thru-Hiker's Handbook.* Center for Appalachian Trail Studies, 1997. (Updated annually)

Chazin, Daniel D. *Appalachian Trail Data Book 1996.* Appalachian Trail Conference, 1997. (Updated annually)

Emblidge, David, ed. *The Appalachian Trail Reader.* Oxford University Press, 1997.

Fisher, Ronald M. *The Appalachian Trail.* National Geographic Society, 1972.

O'Brien, Bill, ed. *Appalachian Trail Thru-Hikers' Companion.* Appalachian Trail Conference, 1997. (Updated annually)

Whalen, Christopher. *The Appalachian Trail Workbook for Planning Thru-Hikes,* Appalachian Trail Conference, 1995.

Practical Advice: Hiking & Camping

Berger, Karen. *Hiking & Backpacking: A Complete Guide.* W. W. Norton, 1995.

Cary, Alice. *Parents' Guide to Hiking & Camping.* W. W. Norton, 1997.

Fletcher, Colin. *The Complete Walker.* Alfred A. Knopf, 1984.

Hampton, Bruce, and David Cole. *Soft Paths: How to Enjoy the Wilderness Without Harming It.* Stackpole, 1995.

McManners, Hugh. *The Backpacker's Handbook.* Dorling Kindersley, 1995.

Meyer, Kathleen. *How to Shit in the Woods: An Environmentally Sound Approach to a Lost Art.* Ten Speed Press, 1994.

Viehman, John, ed. *Trailside's Hints & Tips for Outdoor Adventures.* Rodale Press, 1993.

Wood, Robert S. *The 2 Oz. Backpacker.* Ten Speed Press, 1982.

Background Reading

Allport, Susan. *Sermons in Stone: The Stone Walls of New England and New York.* W. W. Norton, 1994.

Bell, Michael. *The Face of Connecticut: People, Geology, and the Land.* Connecticut Geological and Natural History Survey, 1988.

Burns, Deborah E., and Lauren R. Stevens. *Most Excellent Majesty: A History of Mt. Greylock.* Berkshire Natural Resources Council, 1988.

Burns, Ken. *The Shakers* (PBS video). Florentine Films, 1989.

Frazier, Patrick. *The Mohicans of Stockbridge.* University of Nebraska Press, 1994.

Hadsel, Christine. *Vermont Museums, Galleries, and Historic Places.* Vermont Life, 1995.

Huden, John. *Indian Place Names of New England.* Museum of the American Indian, 1962.

Meeks, Harold A. *Vermont's Land and Resources.* New England Press, 1986.

Meyers, Eloise. *Tyringham: A Hinterland Settlement.* Self-published, 1989.

Nunley, Richard, ed. *The Berkshire Reader: Writings from New England's Secluded Paradise.* Berkshire House, 1995.

Radcliffe, Barbara, and Stillman Rogers. *Natural Wonders of Vermont.* Country Roads Press, 1996.

Ritchie, David and Deborah. *Connecticut: Off the Beaten Path.* Globe Pequot, 1995.

Schlesinger, Arthur M., Jr., ed. *The Almanac of American History.* Perigee Books, 1983.

Sternfield, Jonathan. *The Berkshire Book: A Complete Guide.* Berkshire House, 1997.

Stier, Maggie, and Ron McAdow. *Into the Mountains: Stories of New England's Most Celebrated Peaks.* Appalachian Mountain Club Books, 1995.

Stout, Marilyn. *Vermont Walks: Village and Countryside.* Vermont Life, 1995.

Tree, Christina, and Peter Jennison. *Vermont, an Explorer's Guide.* Countryman Press, 1988.

Waterman, Guy and Laura. *Forest and Crag: A History of Hiking, Trail Blazing, and Adventure in the Northeast Mountains.* Appalachian Mountain Club, 1989.

Wessels, Tom. *Reading the Forested Landscape: A Natural History of New England.* Countryman Press, 1997.

Wiencek, Henry, et al. *The Smithsonian Guide to Historic America: Southern New England.* Stewart, Tabori, & Chang, 1989.

Index

Page numbers in *italic* refer to topographic maps and itineraries.